I0888685

Money Laundering and Terrorism Financing in Global Financial Systems

Abdul Rafay
University of Management and Technology, Pakistan

A volume in the Advances in Finance, Accounting, and Economics (AFAE) Book Series

IGI Global
PUBLISHER of TIMELY KNOWLEDGE

Published in the United States of America by
IGI Global
Business Science Reference (an imprint of IGI Global)
701 E. Chocolate Avenue
Hershey PA, USA 17033
Tel: 717-533-8845
Fax: 717-533-8661
E-mail: cust@igi-global.com
Web site: http://www.igi-global.com

Library of Congress Cataloging-in-Publication Data

Names: Rafay, Abdul, 1973- editor.
Title: Money laundering and terrorism financing in global financial systems / Abdul Rafay, editor.
Description: Hershey : Business Science Reference, 2021. | Includes bibliographical references and index. | Summary: "This book is meant to deepen the discourse about the money laundering, terrorism financing and risk management in a modern day environment by providing an invaluable guide for understanding the theory, practice and cases of these topics"-- Provided by publisher.
Identifiers: LCCN 2021008490 (print) | LCCN 2021008491 (ebook) | ISBN 9781799887584 (hardcover) | ISBN 9781799887591 (paperback) | ISBN 9781799887607 (ebook)
Subjects: LCSH: Money laundering--Prevention. | Terrorism--Finance--Prevention. | Organized crime. | Banks and banking--Risk management. | Financial risk management.
Classification: LCC HV6768 .M626 2021 (print) | LCC HV6768 (ebook) | DDC 364.16/8--dc23
LC record available at https://lccn.loc.gov/2021008490
LC ebook record available at https://lccn.loc.gov/2021008491

This book is published in the IGI Global book series Advances in Finance, Accounting, and Economics (AFAE) (ISSN: 2327-5677; eISSN: 2327-5685)

British Cataloguing in Publication Data
A Cataloguing in Publication record for this book is available from the British Library.

All work contributed to this book is new, previously-unpublished material.
The views expressed in this book are those of the authors, but not necessarily of the publisher.

For electronic access to this publication, please contact: eresources@igi-global.com.

Advances in Finance, Accounting, and Economics (AFAE) Book Series

ISSN:2327-5677
EISSN:2327-5685

Editor-in-Chief: Ahmed Driouchi, Al Akhawayn University, Morocco

MISSION

In our changing economic and business environment, it is important to consider the financial changes occurring internationally as well as within individual organizations and business environments. Understanding these changes as well as the factors that influence them is crucial in preparing for our financial future and ensuring economic sustainability and growth.

The **Advances in Finance, Accounting, and Economics (AFAE)** book series aims to publish comprehensive and informative titles in all areas of economics and economic theory, finance, and accounting to assist in advancing the available knowledge and providing for further research development in these dynamic fields.

COVERAGE

- Entrepreneurship in Accounting and Finance
- Field Research
- Auditing
- Economic Downturn
- Borrowing and Lending
- Evidence-Based Studies
- Comparative Accounting Systems
- Internet Banking
- Corporate Finance
- Microfinance

IGI Global is currently accepting manuscripts for publication within this series. To submit a proposal for a volume in this series, please contact our Acquisition Editors at Acquisitions@igi-global.com or visit: http://www.igi-global.com/publish/.

The Advances in Finance, Accounting, and Economics (AFAE) Book Series (ISSN 2327-5677) is published by IGI Global, 701 E. Chocolate Avenue, Hershey, PA 17033-1240, USA, www.igi-global.com. This series is composed of titles available for purchase individually; each title is edited to be contextually exclusive from any other title within the series. For pricing and ordering information please visit http://www.igi-global.com/book-series/advances-finance-accounting-economics/73685. Postmaster: Send all address changes to above address.

Titles in this Series

For a list of additional titles in this series, please visit:
http://www.igi-global.com/book-series/advances-finance-accounting-economics/73685

Comparative Research on Earnings Management, Corporate Governance, and Economic Value
Elisabete S. Vieira (University of Aveiro, Portugal) Mara Madaleno (University of Aveiro, Portugal) and Graça Azevedo (University of Aveiro, Portugal)
Business Science Reference • © 2021 • 433pp • H/C (ISBN: 9781799875963) • US $215.00

Examining the Intersection of Circular Economy, Forestry, and International Trade
Badri Narayanan Gopalakrishnan (University of Washington, USA) Taranjeet Duggal (Amity University, India) and Tavishi Tewary (Amity University, India)
Business Science Reference • © 2021 • 315pp • H/C (ISBN: 9781799849902) • US $195.00

Influence of FinTech on Management Transformation
Amira Sghari (Faculty of Economics and Management, University of Sfax, Tunisia) and Karim Mezghani (Al Imam Mohammad Ibn Saud Islamic University, Saudi Arabia & University of Sfax, Tunisia)
Business Science Reference • © 2021 • 273pp • H/C (ISBN: 9781799871101) • US $215.00

Handbook of Research on Institutional, Economic, and Social Impacts of Globalization and Liberalization
Yilmaz Bayar (Bandirma Onyedi Eylul University, Turkey)
Information Science Reference • © 2021 • 699pp • H/C (ISBN: 9781799844594) • US $445.00

Bridging Microeconomics and Macroeconomics and the Effects on Economic Development and Growth
Pantelis C. Kostis (National and Kapodistrian University of Athens, Greece)
Business Science Reference • © 2021 • 340pp • H/C (ISBN: 9781799849339) • US $195.00

For an entire list of titles in this series, please visit:
http://www.igi-global.com/book-series/advances-finance-accounting-economics/73685

IGI Global
PUBLISHER of TIMELY KNOWLEDGE

701 East Chocolate Avenue, Hershey, PA 17033, USA
Tel: 717-533-8845 x100 • Fax: 717-533-8661
E-Mail: cust@igi-global.com • www.igi-global.com

This book is dedicated to **Shahid Hafeez Kardar**, *a person of impeccable integrity and a visionary practitioner of economics & finance in Pakistan. His scholarly and practical contribution in the respective fields made him a person of great depth and integrity.*

He attended University of Oxford and is a member of the Institute of Chartered Accountants in England & Wales (ICAEW). He served as the Governor of State Bank of Pakistan (2010-2011) and a Minister (1999-2001) of the province of Punjab in Pakistan. He had also held several other key positions including Chairman of the Punjab Education Foundation (2006-2008), Member of the National Commission for Government Reforms (2006-2008) and Member of the Banking Laws Review Commission (2004-2007). Currently, he is the Vice-Chancellor of Beaconhouse National University in Pakistan.

He is also a regular guest speaker at seminars organized around the globe by academic institutions, multilateral and bilateral financial institutions and NGOs. He has authored three books namely "Reflections on Pakistan's Economy", "The Political Economy of Pakistan" and "Polarization in the Regions: The Roots of Discontent," besides writing several research papers covering economic and social issues of the country.

Editorial Advisory Board

Table of Contents

Detailed Table of Contents

This chapter intends to discuss in detail the complex phenomena of money laundering. This chapter presents the definition, the three stages, characteristics, the negative consequences, and recent trends in money laundering. This chapter demonstrates that money laundering is an international issue by discussing the occurrence of money laundering cases around the globe. This chapter further identifies global efforts to prevent money laundering. This chapter is of value to the layman, government, policymakers, and law enforcement agencies to understand the concept of money laundering. While the chapter presents the basic understanding of the concept of money laundering, the overall finding proves that money laundering is an organized crime. Wherever cash-intensive business exists, there exists the opportunity for money laundering through financial arrangements. Therefore, collaborative domestic and international efforts are needed to combat this crime.

Nigeria is a country in the center of financial crimes and money laundering in Africa right from her pre-independence, independence, and post-independence eras. The aim of this study was to analyze the religio-spiritual effects of financial corruption

under favorable conditions. However, if money launderers manage to infiltrate these institutions with bribery and corruption, then it becomes incredibly difficult to stop the planned crimes like money laundering.

The insurance sector mainly consists of insurance companies, insurance agencies, brokers, and reinsurers. For many years, false damages, without being linked to money, have undoubtedly been the most attractive aspect of the insurance industry. However, for quite some time, the insurance sector is also used by money launders to launder crime revenues due to the increasing volume of money transactions day by day. In order to mitigate the risk of money laundering, the insurance sector in Turkey is implementing the compliance program of Turkish Law No: 5549 on "prevention of laundering proceeds of crime." The main components of this compliance program are the identification of the customers and reporting of suspicious transactions. It is concluded that the risk of money laundering should also be considered during damages and compensation payments, especially in life and pension companies. Policy and contract cancellations should be periodically reviewed, and the reasons for cancellations should be documented well.

Money laundering is a global issue that must be effectively mitigated across the nation. Despite various initiatives, investigation outcome either in the form of prosecution, conviction, or confiscation remains low. Therefore, this study aims to investigate the factors influencing money laundering investigating outcome, based on rational choice theory. The study conducted focus group interviews with 15 investigating officers to have an in-depth understanding of factors and challenges faced by investigating officers in conducting money laundering investigation which influences their investigation outcome. The findings demonstrate that money laundering investigation outcome is influenced by three factors, which are cost-benefit analysis, individual belief, and organizational context. The findings of the study provide significant contributions in confirming the theoretical foundations underpinning this research and suggest recommendations for the relevant regulators in improving money laundering investigation and prosecution decision making.

Terrorism is a global security concern that dominates the theatre of intellectual discourse in the contemporary world. This chapter is taking the case of one of the deadliest insurgents and a terrorist group in the history of Nigeria and also examined various sources of finances of this group in detail. From radical preaching, this group transformed into a terrorist group attacking security, innocent citizens, and all and sundry. As a qualitative study, the social conflict model is adopted in explaining the framework of the existing literature. The data obtained was analyzed critically using content analysis. The study discovered that insurgents sourced their finances through internal and external sources, legal and illegal engagements. The study recommends among several others that the Nigerian Government and security operatives should intensify the process of identifying, tracing, and blockage of the sources of finances for terrorism.

Investment is a part and parcel of life. There are various avenues to invest and one of those is the stock market. But the decision of the investor depends on various factors and one of these factors is terrorism. The chapter focuses on the long and short-run association (LSA) and the influence of terrorism on major global stock indices and gold. The Paris attacks of 2015 are taken as a base, and the ARDL model is used to study the long and short-run impact on the selected stock indices. An attempt is also made to study the impact of terrorism on the stock returns using the Miller and Modigliani model. The study reveals a short-run impact of terrorism on the five selected global indices, but there is no long-run impact.

defaulters are more technical and complex in nature. To tackle these crimes, banks need to improve their working system and technologies. In this chapter, cases of recent banking scams in India have been analyzed to find out the operational loopholes present in the system which led to such a crisis. Further, the measures taken by the Government of India to detect and prevent such scams have been discussed. On the basis of an in-depth study of the cases, researchers suggested certain feasible solutions to overcome such crises in the future. These recommendations shall prove useful to strengthen the banking sector, which is believed to be having considerable socio-economic significance to bring back confidence among the stakeholders and to safeguard the money of the masses.

Preface

The editing of a handbook of research on Money Laundering (ML) and Terrorism Financing (TF) is more exciting and challenging than ever before. The past few decades have been eventful one for these issues. These terminologies have become a buzzword from G20 to World Economic Forum to global and national economic agendas. Today tackling the ML and TF is being considered as a key issue in developed and developing countries alike.

MONEY LAUNDERING AND TERRORISM FINANCING: THE CONCEPT

Money Laundering is any action taken to conceal, arrange, use or possess the proceeds of any criminal conduct (National Crime Agency, UK)

The conversion or transfer of property, knowing that such property is the proceeds of crime, for the purpose of concealing or disguising the illicit origin of the property or of helping any person who is involved in the commission of the predicate offence to evade the legal consequences of his or her action; or the concealment or disguise of the true nature, source, location, disposition, movement or ownership of or rights with respect to property, knowing that such property is the proceeds of crime. (Article 6, UN Convention against Transnational Organized Crime)

Terrorist financing is the financing of terrorist acts, and of terrorists and terrorist organizations. Terrorist financing offence refer not only to the primary offence or offences, but also to ancillary offences (Financial Action Task Force – FATF)

Eradication of money laundering and terrorism financing through a holistic approach of awareness, prevention and enforcement is the need of the hour. It has enabled the birth of new regulatory regime based on strict compliance, robust processes and technology.

FATF, REGIONAL BODIES, AND REGULATIONS

In 1970, the first legislation regarding money laundering was enacted in the US through Bank Secrecy Act (Powis, 1992). In modern times, Financial Action Task Force (FATF), an inter-governmental body, is acting as a global watchdog for ML and TF. For collective global response FATF has recommended guidelines to handle money laundering, terrorist financing, proliferation financing and illegal money through drugs, human trafficking and similar crimes. There is a global network of similar bodies referred to as Financial Action Task Force-Style Regional Bodies (FSRBs) (Table 1). The aim of FSRBs is to implement the international standards against money laundering, terrorist financing and proliferation financing related to weapons of mass destruction.

In order to take cognizance of all these offences, every country has established various apex anti-fraud bodies and implemented specific legislations (Table 2). For effective money laundering investigations Financial Action Task Force (FATF, 2013) recommended that it is important to have; (i) clear aim of investigation, (ii) investigation capability, (iii) asset recovery mechanism, (iv) financial intelligence capability, and (v) domestic and international collaboration (Cheng, 2012). According to a survey (Deloitte, 2020), 81% of AML programs are compliant (in terms of regulatory requirements) and 87% of AML risk management program have been adopted the enterprise wide approach.

WHAT THE GURUS SAID?

Robert E. Powis was the Deputy Assistant Secretary of the US Treasury for Enforcement (1981-1984). He played a key role in overseeing the dismantling of major laundering organizations. He conducted hundreds of interviews with those involved in the laundering operations, as well as the law enforcement personnel, judges and lawyers.

Money laundering has always been used to dispose of the proceeds of a variety of criminal offenses that involve payments for contraband goods or illegal services. However, the explosion of drug use dating back to the late 1970s has made money laundering a familiar topic (p. vii). Money laundering is a vital and infamous component of international narcotics trafficking (p. 67). (Powis, 1992)

Enrique Pena Nieto was the President (2012-2018) of the United Mexican States. He is a lawyer cum politician. In 2015, he was awarded the Collar of the Royal and Distinguished Spanish Order of Carlos III.

Table 1. Financial Action Task Force-style regional bodies (FSRBs)

Year	FSRB	Base Country	Member Countries
1995	Asia/Pacific Group on Money Laundering (APG)	Australia	Afghanistan, Australia, Bangladesh, Bhutan, Kingdom of Brunei Darussalam, Cambodia, Canada, China, Chinese Taipei, Cook Islands, Fiji, Hong Kong, India, Indonesia, Japan, Korea, Republic of Korea (South Korea), Lao, Macao, Malaysia, Maldives, Marshall Islands, Mongolia, Myanmar, Nauru, Nepal, New Zealand, Niue, Pakistan, Palau, Papua New Guinea, Philippines, Samoa, Singapore, Solomon Islands, Sri Lanka, Thailand, Timor-Leste, Tonga, United States of America, Vanuatu
1996	Caribbean Financial Action Task Force (CFATF)	Port of Spain, Trinidad and Tobago	Anguilla, Antigua & Barbuda, Aruba, Bahamas, Barbados, Belize, Bermuda, British Virgin Islands, Cayman Islands, Curaçao, Dominica, El Salvador, Grenada, Guyana, Haiti, Jamaica, Montserrat, St. Kitts & Nevis, St. Lucia, St. Maarten, St. Vincent & the Grenadines, Suriname, Trinidad & Tobago, Turks & Caicos Islands, Venezuela
1997	Council of Europe Anti-Money Laundering Group (MONEYVAL)	France	Albania, Andorra, Armenia, Azerbaijan, Bosnia and Herzegovina, Bulgaria, Croatia, Cyprus, Czech Republic, Estonia, Georgia, Hungary, The Holy See (including the Vatican City State), Israel, Latvia, Liechtenstein, Lithuania, Malta, Moldova, Monaco, Montenegro, Poland, Romania, Russian Federation, San Marino, Serbia, Slovak Republic, Slovenia, Macedonia, The UK Crown Dependencies of Guernsey, The UK Crown Dependencies of Jersey, The UK Crown Dependencies of the Isle of Man, The British Overseas Territory of Gibraltar, Ukraine
1999	West Africa Money Laundering Group (GIABA)	Senegal	Benin, Burkina Faso, Cape Verde, Comoros, Côte d'Ivoire, Gambia, Ghana, Guinea Bissau, Guinea Conakry, Liberia, Mali, Niger, Nigeria, Senegal, Sierra Leone, Togo
1999	Eastern & Southern Africa Anti-Money Laundering Group (ESAAMLG)	Tanzania	Angola, Botswana, Ethiopia, Eswatini, Kenya, Lesotho, Madagascar, Malawi, Mauritius, Mozambique, Namibia, Rwanda, South Africa, Seychelles, Tanzania, Uganda, Zambia, Zimbabwe
2000	Latin America Anti-Money Laundering Group (GAFILAT)	Argentina	Argentina, Bolivia, Brazil, Chile, Colombia, Costa Rica, Cuba, Ecuador, Guatemala, Honduras, Mexico, Nicaragua, Panama, Paraguay, Peru, Uruguay
2000	Central Africa Anti-Money Laundering Group (GABAC)	Gabon	Cameroon, Central African Republic, Chad Republic of the Congo, Democratic Republic of the Congo (DRC), Equatorial Guinea, Gabon
2004	Middle East and North Africa Financial Action Task Force (MENAFATF)	Bahrain	Algeria, Bahrain, Djibouti, Egypt, Mauritania, Jordan, Kuwait, Lebanon, Libya, Morocco, Oman, Palestinian Authority, Qatar, Iraq, Saudi Arabia, Somalia, Sudan, Syria, Tunisia, United Arab Emirates, Yemen
2004	Eurasian Group (EAG)	Russia	Belarus, China, India, Kazakhstan, Kyrgyzstan, Russian Federation, Tajikistan, Turkmenistan, Uzbekistan

Source: Author's Compilation

Table 2. AML-related authorities and regulations in G20 countries

Country	Authority Responsible for AML/CTF Issues	Relevant Regulations
Argentina	Argentine Central Bank (BCRA)	Anti-Money Laundering law (25.246), 2000 The counter – terrorist Law (26,268) 2001
Australia	The Australian Transaction Reports and Analysis Centre (AUSTRAC)	Anti-Money Laundering and Counter-Terrorism Financing Act 2006
Brazil	Council for Financial Activities Control (COAF)	Law No 683/12, 2012 Circular 3,978/20, 2020
Canada	Financial Transactions and Reports Analysis Centre (FINTRAC)	Proceeds of Crime (Money Laundering) and Terrorist Financing Act, 2001
China	China Banking and Insurance Regulatory Commission (CBIRC)	The Anti-Money Laundering Law of the People's Republic of China, 2007
EU	European Banking Authority (EBA)	6th Money Laundering Directive, 2020
France	Intelligence Processing and Action against Clandestine Financial Circuits (TRACFIN)	The Monetary & Financial Code, AML Obligations for financial institutions and Other Businesses (Title VI of Book V)
Germany	The Federal Financial Supervisory Authority (BaFin)	Federal Anti-Money laundering Act, 2017
India	The Financial Intelligence Unit (FIU)	Prevention of Money Laundering Act, 2002
Indonesia	Otoritas Jasa Keuangan (OJK)	OJK Regulation No.12/POJK.01/2017
Italy	Financial Information Unit for Italy (UIF)	• Legislative Decree No. 109/2007 • Law 197/31 • Legislative Decree no. 231/2007
Japan	The Financial Services Agency (FSA)	Act on Punishment of Organized Crimes and by other Related Acts, 1999.
Mexico	*Unidad de Inteligencia Financiera Mexico* (Mexican Financial Intelligence Unit - FIU)	Mexican AML Regulations and Mexican Law
Russia	Federal Financial Monitoring Service (FFMS)	Federal Law No. 115 – FZ as of 1 August 2001 On Countering the Legalization of Proceeds of a Crime (Money Laundering)
Saudi Arabia	Saudi Arabian Financial Intelligence Unit (FIU)	Anti-Money Laundering Statute, 2003
South Africa	South African Financial Intelligence Center (FIC)	• The Proceeds of Crime Act, 1996 • Prevention of Organized Crime Act, 1998 • The Money Laundering and Terrorist Financing Control Regulations, 2002.
South Korea	Korea Financial Intelligence Unit (KoFIU)	• Proceeds of Crime Act (POCA), 2001 • Financial Transaction Reports Act (FTRA), 2001 • Act on Prohibition Against the Financing of Terrorism and Proliferation of Weapons of Mass Destruction (PFOPIA), 2007
Turkey	The Financial Crimes Investigation Board (MASAK)	• Prevention of Laundering the Proceeds of Crime (No. 5549), 2006 • Prevention of the Financing of Terrorism (No. 6415), 2013
UK	Financial Conduct Authority (FCA)	• The Money Laundering and Terrorist Financing (Amendment) Regulations, 2019. • Proceeds of Crime Act 2002.
USA	• Financial Crimes Enforcement Network (FinCEN) • Money Laundering and Asset Recovery Section of USDoJ	• 18 U.S. Code § 1956 and 1957

Source: Author's Compilation

I think money laundering is given oxygen to organized crime (Enrique Pena Nieto)

Janet Reno (1938-2016) was the first woman to serve as Attorney General of the United States (1993-2001). She attended Cornell and Harvard Law School before starting her career as a lawyer. In 2000, she was inducted into the American National Women's Hall of Fame and was awarded the Justice Award by the American Judicature Society in recognition of her services in justice administration within the US.

Money laundering is a very sophisticated crime and we must be equally sophisticated. (Janet Reno)

AWARENESS CAMPAIGN

The World Customs Organization (WCO) established its Anti-Money Laundering/ Counter-Terrorism Financing Programme in 2018. It has a comprehensive set of recommendations to develop and strengthen the role of customs administrations in tackling money laundering and recovering the proceeds of crime (WCO, 2021). Similarly, The United Nations Office on Drugs and Crime (UNODC) has been working with the Governments to strengthen frameworks and capacities of state and regulatory institutions that are performing key roles in fight against money laundering and terrorist financing. In line with its country programmes, the UNODC has planned a series of outreach sessions in collaboration with the respective governments to build awareness on the risks and controls against financial crimes especially money laundering and terrorist financing. In the planning and delivery of these outreach sessions, UNODC has worked closely with key governmental institutions that are central to the framework of Anti–Money Laundering (AML)/Combating the Financing for Terrorism (CFT)/Counter-Terrorism Financing (CTF) of the country (UNODC, 2021). The outreach sessions are aimed at providing expert information of the legal framework, institutional activities and international standards on AML/CFT/CTF with special emphasis on counter measures for Targeted Financial Sanctions (TFS), Proliferation Financing (PF) and Beneficial Ownership (BO) among other topics. These sessions help in building understanding and enhancing capacity of private sector AML/CFT reporting firms, with respect to their role in the counter measures against money laundering and terrorist financing (ICAP, 2021).

INVESTMENT IN TECHNOLOGY

In the words of Powis (1992) "*The ability of a financial institution to recognize, evaluate, and refer suspicious activity is critical to the maintenance of its good name (p. 326)*". For this purpose, investment in new technologies is inevitable including machine learning, Artificial Intelligence (AI) and behavioral biometrics. These steps will prove effective for customer due diligence, transaction monitoring, sanction screening, data accuracy, data sufficiency, data structure issues, workflow management, control effectiveness, false positives, risk assessment, integration with core financial system, multi-jurisdictional requirements, trade based money laundering and inadequate fuzzy logic capabilities (Deloitte, 2020). Robust processes and technology have proved effective for the prevention of AML/CFT/CTF, although it may be expensive to introduce, create, and retain these prevention controls (PwC, 2020). The benefits are high enough to warrant these preventive control expenses (Hicks, 2019) as the regulatory fines are running in billions of dollars for non-compliance of AML/CFT/CTF regulations (Andersen & Dilley, 2014).

.... both HSBC and Standard Chartered rarely troubled the headlines in the tumultuous years of the credit crunch, in 2012, just as the furore of the financial crisis was starting to fade from view, they both found themselves directly in the line of fire. After lengthy and painstaking investigations, US regulators decided to fine the two institutions $2.6 billion. Unlike their rivals they were not found guilty of manipulating Libor, rigging the foreign-exchange market, issuing dodgy products, or indulging in questionable off-balance- sheet enterprises. Instead both were found guilty of offences that seem on the surface a thousand miles away from normal international commercial banking operations: money laundering and sanctions busting (p. 183).(Brummer, 2014)

CONTEXT AND ORGANIZATION OF THIS VOLUME

Regardless of whether you are a beginner or a seasoned researcher, this handbook of research will deepen the discourse about the money laundering, terrorism financing and risk management in a modern day environment. I am hopeful that this handbook of research is a fascinating and invaluable guide for understanding the theory, practice and cases of these topics.

This handbook of research is organized into two sections that consist of thirteen chapters by writers from eight countries. Twenty-Eight authors contributed from disparate parts of the world; Canada, UAE, Turkey, India, Pakistan, Sri Lanka, UAE and Nigeria.

Section 1 addresses "Money Laundering and Terrorism Financing" with a set of eight chapters authored by writers from Canada, Malaysia, Turkey, Nigeria, India, and Pakistan. Section 2 addresses "Financial Governance and Risk Management" with a set of five chapters contributed by authors from India, Sri Lanka, Malaysia and UAE.

In Section 1, the first chapter, "Money Laundering: A Thought-Provoking Crime," by Sadia Saeed, Fauzia Mubarik and Sehar Zulfiqar of National University of Modern Languages, Pakistan, demonstrates that money laundering is an international issue and identifies global efforts to prevent money laundering. While the chapter presents the basic understanding of the concept of money laundering, the overall finding proves that money laundering is an organized crime. The second chapter, "Religio-Spiritual Implications of Corruption and Money Laundering: The Case of Nigeria," by Adebayo Rafiu Ibrahim of University of Ilorin, Nigeria, observed that religion was dubiously used for money laundering activities, while some manipulated religion to exploit others. It is concluded that religion has to be properly regulated to avoid its manipulation by some individuals while there is a need to review some anti-money laundering policies that reduced religion to mere worship in the four corners of places of worship and do not allow it to feature in humanitarian volunteerism. The third chapter, "Money Laundering in Real Estate (RE): The Case of Canada," by Mark Lokanan and Gaurav Chopra of Royal Roads University, Canada, illuminates a broad range of problems around the investigations of unlawful investments and recommends pragmatic solutions to the illicit flow of money in real estate sector of Canada. Using data from the Cullen Commission about Money Laundering in Canada, this chapter is an effort to examine the nuances that law enforcement encounters while investigating illegal investment operations. The fourth chapter, "Money Laundering and Institutional Quality: The Case of Developing Countries," by Maryam Muhammad Amjad (University of Management and Technology, Pakistan), Noman Arshed (University of Management and Technology, Pakistan), and Muhammad Awais Anwar (University of Education, Pakistan), investigates the relationship between money laundering and institutional quality by considering several variables such as government stability, corruption, bureaucracy quality, law and order, and democratic accountability. The fifth chapter, "Anti-Money Laundering in Insurance Sector: The Turkish Case," by Ismail Yildirim (Hitit University, Turkey) and Abdul Rafay (University of Management & Technology, Pakistan), highlights that insurance sector is also used by money launders to launder crime revenues due to the increasing volume of money transactions day by day. The chapter focuses on the compliance program of Turkish Law No: 5549 on "Prevention of laundering proceeds of crime" which is vital to mitigate the risk of money laundering in Turkey. The sixth chapter, "Factors Influencing the Outcome of Money Laundering Investigations," by Salwa Zolkaflil, Sharifah Nazatul Faiza Syed Mustapha Nazri, and Normah Omar of Universiti Teknologi MARA, Malaysia, highlights that despite various initiatives, investigation outcome either in the forms of prosecution, conviction or confiscation remains low. The findings of the study provide significant contributions in confirming the theoretical foundations underpinning this research and offer contributions for the relevant regulators in improving money laundering investigation and prosecution decision making. The seventh chapter, "Financing as a Livewire for Terrorism: The Case of North-Eastern Nigeria," by Usman Sambo (Yobe State University, Nigeria) and Babayo Sule (Federal University of Kashere, Nigeria), examines various sources of finances to one of the deadliest insurgents and a terrorist group in the history of Nigeria. As a qualitative study, the Social Conflict Model is adopted in explaining the framework of the existing literature. The chapter recommends among several others that the Nigerian Government and security operatives should intensify the process of identifying, tracing and blockage of the sources of finances for terrorism. The eighth chapter, "Effect of Terrorism Financing on Selected Global Indices: The Case of 2015 Paris Attacks," by Laila Amir Memdani (IFHE University, Hyderabad, India), Tasiu Tijjani Kademi (Rabiu Musa Kwankwaso College of Advance and Remedial Studies, Nigeria), and Abdul Rafay (University of Management & Technology, Pakistan), focuses on the Long and Short-run Association (LSA) and the influence of terrorism on major global stock indices and Gold. The Paris attacks of 2015 are taken as a base and the ARDL model is used to study the long and short-run impact on the selected stock indices. The study reveals a short-run impact of terrorism on the five selected global indices but there is no long-run impact.

In Section 2, the ninth chapter, "Risk-Based AML/CFT Regulations for Effective Supervision," by S. G. Sisira Dharmasri Jayasekara of Central Bank of Sri Lanka, discusses the implementation of a sound risk-based AML/CFT supervision of financial institutions as well as designated non-finance business and professions. The chapter suggested that a sound regime of AML/CFT supervision is essential to support global initiatives in this regard. The tenth chapter, "Compliance Monitoring and Testing Seismometer to Detect Compliquake," by Sachin Shah, an independent researcher from India, discusses that the compliance function is a key component of Financial Institutions' (FIs) lines of defence in terms of managing and mitigating the risks. Compliance monitoring and testing by the compliance departments can act as an effective "Seismometer" in detecting the "Compliquakes" in the FIs if implemented effectively. The eleventh chapter, "Shariah Governance Systems of Islamic Banks in Bangladesh: A Comparison With Global Governance Practices," by Md. Kausar Alam (Universiti Putra Malaysia), Mosab I. Tabash (AL Ain University, UAE), Md. Farjin Hassan, (Universiti Putra Malaysia), Nihad Hossain (Universiti Putra Malaysia), and Akib Javed (Universiti Putra Malaysia), highlights that Islamic banks are not practicing true Islamic banking because of the predetermined profit rate and violation of the Shariah principles. But the central bank has accepted it due to social demand and people's expectations. The chapter also explores the Shariah Governance (SG) mechanism of Islamic banks in Bangladesh as compared to global SG practices. The twelfth chapter, "Fraud Risk Management in Banks: An Overview of Failures and Best Practices," by Abhishek Sinha of Vignana Jyothi Institute of

Management, India, pinpoints the best practices in developing fraud prevention frameworks and emphasizes the importance of corporate governance in preventing such frauds. Best practices and future trends are also identified that are important to prevent and detect banking frauds. The thirteenth chapter, "Banking Scams in India: A Case-Based Analysis," by Rohan Prasad Gupta and Bappaditya Biswas of University of Calcutta, India, discusses cases of recent banking scams in India to find out the operational loopholes. Researchers suggested certain feasible solutions to overcome such crises in the future. These recommendations shall prove useful to strengthen the banking sector, which is believed to be having considerable socio-economic significance to bring back stakeholders' confidence.

I thank the contributors and also the external reviewers who have patiently critiqued these chapters to meet the minimum acceptable standard. While the publisher and the Editor (myself) have used their best efforts in preparing this book, they make no representations and warranties with respect to the accuracy or completeness of the contents of this book and specifically disclaim any implied warranties of merchantability or fitness for a particular purpose. The strategies or suggestions or whatsoever contained in this book may not be suitable for any specific situation for which anyone should consult with a professional, where appropriate. Neither the publisher nor the editor shall be liable for any loss of profit or any other commercial damages, including but not limited to special, incidental, consequential, or other damages.

Abdul Rafay
University of Management and Technology, Pakistan
March 2021

REFERENCES

Andersen, J., & Dilley, B. (2014). *Global Anti-Money Laundering Survey*. KPMG.

Brummer, A. (2014). The Perils of Global Banking: Money Laundering. In *Bad banks: greed, incompetence and the next global crisis*. Random House Business Books.

Cheng, N. Y. (2012). *The Effectiveness of Money Laundering Investigations in Fighting Transnational Crime: A Comparison of the United States and Hong Kong*. Retrieved from https://www.brookings.edu/research/the-effectiveness-of-money-laundering-investigations-in-fighting-transnational-crime-a-comparison-of-the-united-states-and-hong-kong/

Deloitte. (2020). Key Observations. In *Anti Money Laundering Preparedness Survey Report*. Deloitte.

FATF. (2013). *Methodology for Assessing Technical Compliance with the FATF Recommendations and the Effectiveness of AML/CFT Systems.* Financial Action Task Force. Retrieved from https://www.fatf-gafi.org/

Hicks, D. (2019). *Global Banking Fraud Survey*. KPMG.

ICAP. (2021). *Money Laundering*. Karachi: The Institute of Chartered Accountants of Pakistan. Retrieved from https://www.icap.org.pk

Powis, R. E. (1992). *The money launderers: lessons from the drug wars, how billions of illegal dollars are washed through banks & businesses*. Probus Publishing Co.

PwC. (2020). *Fighting Fraud: A never ending battle. PwC's Global Economic Crime and Fraud Survey*. London: PwC.

UNODC. (2021). *Money Laundering*. United Nations Office on Drug and Crime. Retrieved from https://www.unodc.org/westandcentralafrica/en/newrosenwebsite/anti-corruption/money -laundering.html

WTO. (2021). *Money Laundering and Terrorist Financing*. World Customs Organization. Retrieved from http://www.wcoomd.org/en/topics/enforcement-and-compliance/activities-and-programmes/money-laundering-and-terrorist-financing.aspx

Section 1
Money Laundering and Terrorism Financing

Chapter 1
Money Laundering:
A Thought-Provoking Crime

Sadia Saeed
National University of Modern Languages, Pakistan

Fauzia Mubarik
National University of Modern Languages, Pakistan

Sehar Zulfiqar
National University of Modern Languages, Pakistan

ABSTRACT

This chapter intends to discuss in detail the complex phenomena of money laundering. This chapter presents the definition, the three stages, characteristics, the negative consequences, and recent trends in money laundering. This chapter demonstrates that money laundering is an international issue by discussing the occurrence of money laundering cases around the globe. This chapter further identifies global efforts to prevent money laundering. This chapter is of value to the layman, government, policymakers, and law enforcement agencies to understand the concept of money laundering. While the chapter presents the basic understanding of the concept of money laundering, the overall finding proves that money laundering is an organized crime. Wherever cash-intensive business exists, there exists the opportunity for money laundering through financial arrangements. Therefore, collaborative domestic and international efforts are needed to combat this crime.

DOI: 10.4018/978-1-7998-8758-4.ch001

INTRODUCTION

The word money laundering refers to show that illegal money is legal. In money laundering officers do corruption and disguise technically the source of illicit income. These illicit monetary assets are converted into legitimate assets. Levi & Soudijn (2020) refers to money laundering as a thought crime because money launderers intentionally transform the monetary proceeds derived from criminal activities into funds with an apparently legal source.

Money laundering involves two crimes. The first crime in money laundering is to hide the source of profited money and the second one is to exploit the financial institutions by making these proceeds legitimate. Grujić & Šikman (2020) discuss various forms of money laundering. It is done through smurfing; a large amount of dirty money is converted into checks of smaller amounts that are not suspicious to banks. Trade-based laundering and casino laundering are also common ways of money laundering. Invoices or business documents are altered to disguise the illegal profits. Dirty money is invested in purchasing chips in casino and can claim total cash generated by turning back the total chips as gambling winnings.

Money laundering is also common in banks and real estate fields. Money launderers usually own the bank and legally transfer the money from one bank to another bank. It is very difficult to detect money laundering when it is done through banks. Similarly, the quick selling of property on huge profits helps in cleaning the dirty money. Cash-based laundering is also common in the economy. A large amount of cash is transferred to banks for heavy cash businesses. It is very difficult for the bank to know that the profit has been earned through legal sources or not. Money laundering exists everywhere in the world that's why it is a global financial issue and poses a great threat to security at the national and international levels. Therefore, the primary objective of this chapter is to address the complex topic of money laundering. This chapter intends to provide an overview of this complex phenomenon. Further, this chapter highlights the issues and challenges related to money laundering and its prevention.

BACKGROUND

Money Laundering Process

Teichmann (2019) identified money laundering as a three-tier process. It includes:

Placement

Putting the money earned through crimes into circulation. At the first stage of money laundering money is transferred from its source to different places. Money is moved from the home source to other countries where financial control is weak. Money is converted into smaller amounts and deposited into various bank accounts and invested in foreign exchanges. Placement is the best means to blend the dirty money with clean money and makes it less suspicious for law enforcement.

Money laundering is a cash-intensive business generating money from criminal actions including tax crimes, frauds, embezzlement, drugs, theft, bribery and corruption. Money launderers usually shift illegal money from a place of acquisition into the financial system, retail economy and smuggle it out of the country. The main objective of the first phase of money laundering is to transform illicit money into different forms of assets.

Layering

The second way to make illegal money less suspicious is layering. Once the placement is successful and funds are transferred to various places from the home source. Then, this dirty money is utilized for purchasing monetary instruments, for buying and selling financial securities and for selling the products of companies locally or abroad to show that all the money is legal and make it untraceable for law companies to detect the illegal source.

Layering is composed of a series of complex transactions planned to place the distance between the source of illegal proceeds and their current status to confuse the criminal investigation. The primary objective of layering is to disguise the audit trail and source of ownership of funds. The layering of funds is done through electronic funds transfer by transferring the illicit money in and out of offshore bank accounts. The disclosure of information on a single wire transfer is not enough to recognize the dirty money. Therefore, it is an excellent technique to transfer illicit money. Moreover, illicit money is invested in stocks, commodities and futures in financial markets. As anonymity is available to a high degree in financial markets, therefore, the chance to trace the transactions is insignificant.

Integration

Integration is the shifting of funds back to the home economy through legitimate sources. Investment is done in business ventures and luxury assets are purchased with this laundered money. The criminals lend to front companies that are running with strict secrecy laws of the corporation. The proceeds are given to these companies by doing a business transaction that seems to be legitimate but, it is not. The most common way of integration in economies is the use of false receipts of imports and exports. The overvaluation of entry documents is done to justify the funds deposited in domestic banks while exporting goods.

Thus, at the third stage of money laundering, money launderers inject money into the home economy making it appear to have been legally earned. It is in fact very difficult to differentiate legal wealth from illegal wealth by this stage. In the integration stage, money launderers can receive money from their original illicit source in the form of the new business such as car wash, departmental store, restaurant, jewelry and laundry business. These businesses follow all rules and regulations required in home country to avoid detection. Employees are regularly paid, and tax returns are filed timely in order to avoid the attention of law-enforcing agencies.

All money laundering transactions do not pass through these three stages. However, these three stages may transpire individually or simultaneously. Since the technique used to wash dirty money involves more than one country at one time. It is therefore a global issue of financial crime.

Figure 1. Process of Money laundering
(one top brokers, 2020)

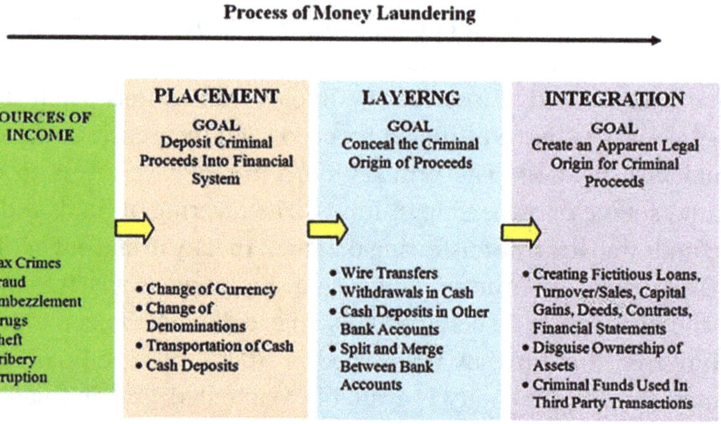

SALIENT FEATURES OF MONEY LAUNDERING

Money laundering is an ideology based on evil thought. Sohraby, *et al.* (2016) discuss the following criminological aspects of money laundering

Money Laundering: An Organized Crime

Money laundering does not occur at the individual level. It is done by an organized criminal group comprising three or more than three persons. This group is formed for a specific period and it is run by an organization. The first member of the group conceals the origin of illegal proceeds and its true ownership. The second member of the group achieves full control over the proceeds and the third member changes the forms of the proceeds so that they appear to be legitimate. Money laundering is a team effort and evil minds accomplish it technically. So, it is very difficult for law enforcement agencies to detect it.

Money Laundering: A Transnational Crime

The effects of money laundering are not limited to one country and that makes it a transnational crime (Albanese, 2012). There are four cases of money laundering in the context of the place of money laundering and predicate offenses. If an offense and criminal act belong to one country, it is interstate money laundering. The reverse case of the interstate is abroad money laundering that includes committing predicate offense and money laundering crime outside the country. In intrastate money laundering, the predicate offense is home country whereas the criminal impact of money laundering is stanch outside the country. Unlike intrastate money laundering imported money laundering includes committing crime inside the country, but predicate offense is done outside the country. Intra and imported money laundering cases have transnational outcome. In order to combat transnational money laundering global cooperation is needed.

Money Laundering: A Victimless Crime

According to Chandra (2019), money laundering is one of the financial crimes with no real victim cost. Money laundering is an illegal act but does not harm the rights of another person. Therefore, people don't call the police for their help and this situation leads to increase delinquency. The detective rate for chasing money laundering is less in the absence of practical claims. However, the practical cases of money laundering including drug wars in Mexico, prostitution in Romania, human trafficking in Malaysia and dangerous buildings in Kenya. All these examples show that human cost in financial crime is real.

Money Laundering: A Financial Crime

It is a common observation that public officials, political parties and financial institutions do corruption in the event of public procurement contracts and privatization of state assets and enterprises. This illicit or black money is hurriedly and secretly shifted from the place of origin without the knowledge of others. If it is disclosed, the giver and receiver would be sanctioned and the agreement would become void because it is an illicit financial gain (Amara & Khlif, 2018). Moreover, dirty money cannot be exposed publicly because it would raise questions about the credibility of officers and create doubts about transparency of the award of contract to hide this corrupt act the proof which is usually in the form of cash must be transferred outside the country. Once the illegal money has been successfully shifted, it is legally retransferred to the place of origin. The process of disguising the original source of money and reintroducing the money through legitimate means in financial markets shows that money laundering is a financial crime act.

LAUNDERING AGENTS

Rose-Ackerman & Palifka (2018) identifies the laundering agents that are available within the country to facilitate laundering services. The most common laundering agents are employees within the financial institutions. The bank employees can be easily bribed or coerced for non-reporting suspicious activities. The second most prominent agents for laundering money are lawyers. Lawyers can use their names on behalf of clients to procure credit cards, loan contracts and other money laundering tools. Besides, lawyers set up shell corporations, trusts, NGOs and partnerships for facilitating people to do money laundering easily. In the USA, lawyers take huge fees to launder money in setting annuity packages for a client and hide the money laundering. Similarly, lawyers use false means to issue credit cards to clients and charge flat fees for it. The card issuer knows the identity of the lawyer, but he does not know the identity of the client who will use a credit card in the future. Many other professionals including accountant, notaries, stockbrokers, financial advisors, insurance agents and real estate agents are also involved, and they assist money laundering. Stockbrokers assist money laundering by accepting cash receipts from customers and deposit in the customer's relative money market account through financing in financial securities. These dirty funds are withdrawn by checks without revealing the customer's identity. Brokerage firms also expedite money laundering globally. These firms open various accounts including a non-resident account. Thus, dirty money received across countries is invested in listed stocks of public limited companies. The non-resident account is considered as the conduit for transferring the amount received from securities transaction and heavy commission is charged for doing it.

HAWALA -AN ALTERNATIVE REMITTANCE SYSTEM

Another technique that facilitates the transfer of illicit proceeds is *Hawala*. The word *Hawala* has an Arabic origin which means change or transform. In Urdu and Hindi it means trust that is the prime basis of the *Hawala* system. *Hawala* is also known as *Hundi* which means to collect. Both terms *Hawala* and *Hundi* are interchangeably used. *Hawala* is an alternate remittance system that operates outside the formal banking system and other financial channels. *Hawala* system is often called underground banking which is probably not true because this system has existed for centuries with full legitimacy and its history can be traced back to the 11th century in India. *Hawala* is different from the other remittance system because it is based on trust and extensive use of connections for the transfer of money. Unlike the formal banking system that uses formal instruments for the transfer of money in *Hawala* system there is minimum or often no use of such instruments. Transfer of money is based on trust and communication between *Hawala* dealers (members of the *Hawala* system).

There is inherently nothing illegal about *Hawala*. It is an inexpensive and informal remittance system that is mostly used by skilled immigrants to transfer money to their families. *Hawala* is more popular in developing countries where the financial legislations and heavy taxations restrict foreign exchange. Moreover, the banking systems in these countries are connected in the urban areas, whereas most of the immigrants have families in far rural areas that are accessible to *Hawala* dealers. *Hawala* system is purely based on trust and it is difficult for the investigators to trace and investigate because there is no formal written or electronic record of transactions. This operative aspect of the *Hawala* system makes it susceptible to misuses like money laundering and funding of illegal activities such as drug trafficking and even terrorist financing (Nasir, 2020).

ISSUES ASSOCIATED WITH MONEY LAUNDERING

Money Laundering- A Global Phenomena

The promising yet challenging virtual networks have speeded up the illegal flow of money worldwide. According to a report (UNODC, 2019), the amount of dirty money (illicit flow of funds) laundered around the world in a year is about two to five percent of global GDP which is approximately two trillion US dollars. Developing countries especially face a major challenge regarding the illicit financial flows in political, economic and security contexts. The illicit flow of funds varies in various aspects such as the illicit manipulation of natural resources, ordered crime, corruption, tax elusion, international trade deception, money deviation from public priorities and deforestation connected with mineral extraction, fishing and illegal logging.

The developing countries are the prospect avenues for the launderers because of the weak financial systems, less compromise on capital arrangements, corrupt judicial system, lack of independence in the public audit offices, greedy political parties, poor protection of property rights, etc. A report (GFI, 2019) documented the illegal flow of financial funds from across 148 developing countries. Based on the quintiles of 30 countries, the worldwide developing countries are vulnerable to the illicit financial flows either them being the resource-abundant countries, the trade with advanced economic countries and the inflows with unknown origin. Amongst the wider set of governance challenges, illicit flow is also an indication of a complete failure of governance usually where the weak institutions are combined with high corruption levels or where sometimes such outflows are caused by illicit rules.

Empirical research emphasis the evil of money laundering as a basic hurdle in the economic growth of a developing country Aluko & Bagheri (2012). It creates turbulence in the smooth functioning of the state and private institutions and also badly affects the goodwill of the political regimes respectively. According to Uche (1998), most of the literature focuses on the money laundry issue only in developed countries but it is a major issue occurring globally. International policies and opinions on fighting with money laundering are created for developed countries and they are only applicable for developed countries. The author argues that since money laundering is an international phenomenon therefore money launders are always searching for various ways to use their source of wealth and they find their ways easily by getting some of the attractive characteristics of developing countries. It is important to make the economic, environmental, political and social structures of developing countries safe from money laundering.

According to the report published by OECD (2014), the OECD countries have been a prospect avenue for the money launderers because of substantial deficiencies in financial systems. Therefore, the business transactions which are conducted through these financial systems offer considerable threat of money laundering. Another major problem in undertaking the illicit financial flow and financial crime is the weak beneficial ownership requirements. It is easy for criminals to take advantage of weak beneficial owner requirement by misusing corporate vehicles and shell companies to hide ownership. The companies hide themselves to cover up illegal activities or to carry out businesses by using misappropriate funds. The ability to stem illegitimate flows depends upon the will of OECD countries to place a system of prevention, detection, financial crime and sanctions respectively.

Another major venue of money laundering is Sub-Saharan Africa which received nearly 2 trillion dollars in official development assistance and foreign direct investment between 1980 and 2018, out of which 1 trillion dollars were emitted in illicit financial flows. Trade mis-invoicing was the major way of transferring money to another country and it originated the illicit financial flows. Trade mis-invoicing is therefore defined as the misreporting of value and quantity of services and goods made by importers and exporters. The importers and exporters do this in order to avoid paying taxes, laundering money, taking advantage of tax incentives to evade capital controls.

It is evident that the higher illegitimate financial outflows are caused by higher inflation and higher taxes. It is therefore suggested that more stable and fiscal environments should be sought out by firms for their funds. It is reported that in recent years, the major destination of illicit flows from Africa are the Middle East and Asia. The justification of this can be explained by the trade level deficiencies with developed economies while causing a large shift of illicit flows to these countries. The illicit flow of funds takes another sign of power and violence usually enacted by the rebel group of people, terrorism, political government and criminals. For example, oil conflict in Nigeria, conflict of opium, precious stones and timber in Cambodia and Myanmar, and that of diamonds in Liberia. Similarly, the illicit flows have also produced rebel groups such as the National Union for the Total Independence of Angola (UNITA) and the Revolutionary United Front as well as the Paramilitary groups of Northern Ireland who relied on the proceeds of organized crime. Another rebellious group was formed with the proceeds from cocoa in Colombia, Peru and Bolivia, while the opium proceeds created the rebellious groups in Afghanistan, Pakistan, Myanmar and Kosovo. The proceeds of narcotics included the Abu Sayyaf Group in the Philippines, Al Qaeda in Afghanistan and Pakistan, the Kosovo Liberation Army, the Kurdish Workers Party of Turkey, the Liberation Tigers of Tamil Eelam of Sri Lanka, and the Revolutionary Armed Forces of Colombia.

POPULAR CASES OF MONEY LAUNDERING ACROSS THE GLOBE

Some popular cases on money laundering are briefly explained below:

The Bank of Credit and Commercial International founded in 1972 in Luxembourg turned out to face a grave allegation of money laundering worth of $23 billion in 1988. On investigations, it was found that the bank had been involved in falsified transactions and the large deposits were kept unrecorded.

Naura an island of Australia became a hub of money laundering worth $70 billion in the 1990s. It became possible by the implementation of shell banks by the then government who did not bother to inquire about the customers' identity and the money was deposited in the banks; an opportunity that was misused by Russia and Al-Qaeda.

The most recent scandal of money laundering worth of $229 Billion is of Danske Bank of Denmark which acquired the Estonian branch of Sampo Bank. The basic problem arose because of the suspicious large transactions made by the non-residents especially from Russia. The case is still on and the senior executives are already charged for $2million by the Danish authorities. Wachovia bank is another example that was found involved in money laundering worth $380 billion. The money laundering became possible in the bank because of it readily used currency exchange houses service which provided the prospect chance to the Mexican drug cartels to launder their money. The higher management of the bank deliberately ignored this practice until the scandal became public and the bank was fined $160 million respectively.

The Halk Bank of Turkey was accused of laundering hundreds of millions of dollars. The Halk Bank in fact, used a very creative method and produced an oil deed on behalf of Iran through the U.S. financial system in petrodollars and the shipment of gold to Iran.

In April 2016 Sueddeutsche Zeitung a Panamanian firm with the collaboration of investigative journalists exposed politicians and leaders who were enlisted for corruption and money laundering. Secret files from Panamanian law firm leaked the names of well renowned and powerful leaders including, The King of Saudi Arabia, the Prime minister of Iceland and Vladimir Putin from Russia among many others. 2.4 terabyte data had been publically presented and it announced that 214,000 companies and 200 countries were involved in criminal activities including money laundering, corruption and evil acts (Scilla, 2018).

Sigmunder David, the prime minister of Iceland had to resign over the company having co-ownership with her wife. Besides these Panama papers forced the prime minister of UK to reveal the secret holdings in an investment fund generated by his father for investment in offshore companies. The prime minister of Spain resigned from his post after being caught in a series of money laundering cases.

In an Indian money laundering case for domestic violence in northeast Delhi, Tahir Hussain, Aam Aadmi Party (AAP) councilor had been suspended and sentenced to 30 years to prison in 2020. 50 people had lost their lives in this terrorist activity. In Delhi High Court it was proved that Tahir Hussain did money laundering of Rs.1.10 crore and fraudulently transferred money using shell companies to finance this terrorism.

Emirsyah Satar, chief executive officer of Garuda Indonesia, a popular airline had been proved money launderer in 2020 by Indonesia's Corruption Eradication

Commission (KPK). CEO, Satar was involved in excess payments of Rp 20 billion from 2005 to 2014 for the procurement of Roll-Royce Trent 700 engines and Airbus A320 and A330 planes. The corruption courts of Malaysia sentenced him to prison for eight years and fined 1.5 million for this illegal act (Prakasa, 2019).

The 1MBD scandal case of money laundering originated in 2015 when money had been transferred from one Malaysian Development Berhad (1MBD) to a personal account of Najib Razak. The prime suspect of this case was Jho Low, a Malaysian financier. Jho Low strengthened the relationship with Sheikh Saba the son of the royal family of Kuwait and started new channels of money laundering. Investigation agents identified the track of money being laundered from China to Malaysia. $1 billion were transferred to China and then to a Chinese bank in Kuwait. From Kuwait, the funds were transferred to an enterprise in the Cayman Islands that was controlled by a Low Payment of $1 billion done in Malaysia for the financial obligations of 1MBD. On account of this money laundering and other cases including the laundering of billions of dollars in kickbacks provided by state companies in China, Sheikh Saba was sentenced to 35 years to prison in 2020.

The above cases of money laundering have turned attention to the grave crime of money laundering in a global village. Similarly Kirti *et al.*, (2009) belief on Slaughter's theory of global problems need global solutions and Keohane (2001) concept of governance, emphasis on the stringent role played by the International Monetary Fund (IMF) and the Financial Action Task Force (FATF) to battle against money laundry.

NEGATIVE EFFECTS OF MONEY LAUNDERING ON ECONOMY

Money laundering promotes corruption and crime that slows down the efficiency of the real sector in the economy. Moreover, it also affects the financial institutions that play a pivotal role in the economic growth of the country. The controlling mechanism of money laundering is efficient in developed economies as compared to emerging ones therefore developing economies are severely affected by money laundering.

Drug Trafficking and Terrorist Attacks

Developing economies are open to money laundering activities. Drug trafficking and terrorist attacks are the most common negative effects of money laundering (Clarke, 2016). Drug trafficking is the cultivation, distribution and sale of such substances that are against the drug rules and regulation. When people use drugs, they are more violent and commit more crimes. Terrorists also knock down money that makes it difficult for authorities to monitor them therefore their planned attacks cannot

Figure 2. Negative Effects of Money Laundering

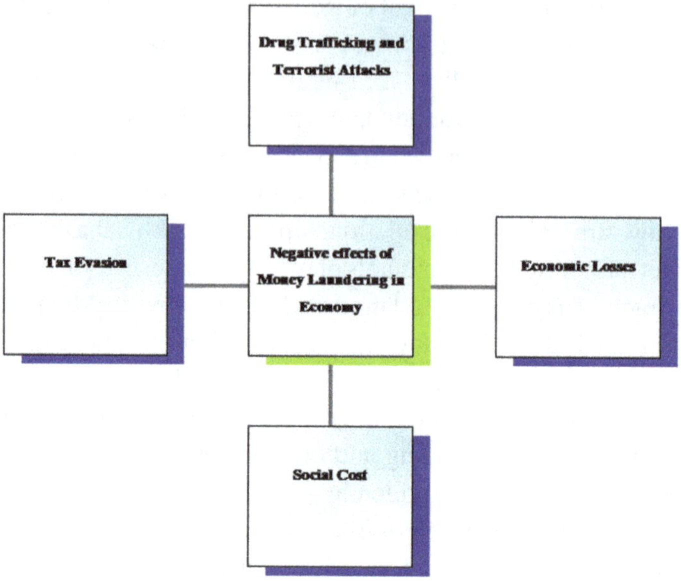

be prevented. In response to drug trafficking and terrorist attacks, unpredictable changes occur in money demand, exchange rates and international flow of capital.

Tax Evasion

The biggest source of government revenue is earned through tax. Due to money laundering tax is not collected on illicit money. As a result, tax revenue decreases and consequently it slows down economic growth. Money launderers make the tax collection difficult for the government as well. The government devises new methods for the transparent collection of taxes. This increases the cost of collecting taxes and taxpayers also have to pay taxes at high rates. The scenario will be entirely different if illegal proceeds are taxed just as tax imposed on legal money (Amoh & Adafula, 2019).

Economic Losses

The main interest of money launderers is to protect the illicit proceeds instead of profitable investment. They usually do low-quality investment that affects the economic growth of the country. In some countries, illicit money has been invested in real estate projects and hotels. These projects are not demanded in these countries instead the purpose of financing is to hide the illegal money. If money launderers lose interest, they abandon the investment that leads to ruin these sectors causing a gigantic loss to the economy (Hetemi *et al.* 2018).

Social Cost

Hendriyetty & Grewal (2017) explain that economies have to bear the social cost of money laundering. The effects of social costs are diverse. Dirty money from criminal activities is merged into legitimate money and these funds are used for the extension of existing criminal activities and the finance of new ones. As a result, the economic power of the country is transferred from the government, citizens and markets to criminals causing a spread of corruption in all elements of society. The increase in criminal activities and corruption compels government to allocate the increased amount for law enforcement agencies and health care facilities.

RECENT TRENDS IN MONEY LAUNDERING

Figure 3. Recent Trends in Money Laundering

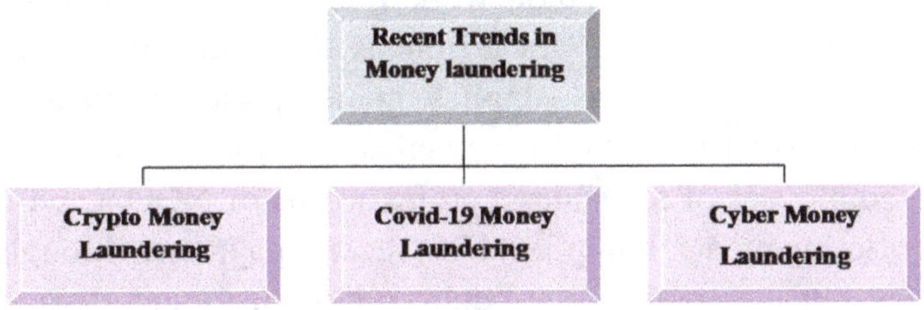

Crypto Money Laundering

Recently in money laundering, new technology has been developed to conceal the illegal proceeds as a virtual currency. Bitcoin, Ether and Ripple are used in laundering money just like ordinary currency (Rafay, 2019). These are used as media of exchange having units of accounts and storing capacity. In contrast to normal currencies, virtual currencies are not legally acceptable. Therefore, taxes are not imposed on virtual currencies and these are not acceptable to creditors for the repayment of debt. Laundering the money using virtual currencies is practically called crypto money laundering (Albrecht *et al.*, 2019).

In crypto money laundering virtual currencies can be purchased through exchanges. Some exchanges are legitimate and follow a code of regulatory conduct including identity, verification and sources of funds. These legitimate exchanges are anti-money laundering (AML) compliant and help to report suspicious business transactions. Other exchanges are not AML and do not allow matching the transaction data with the corresponding customer causing anonymity for each transaction.

Once a virtual currency is purchased through exchanges, money launderers convert one virtual currency into another virtual currency to hide the digital origin of funds. Exchanges use the argument for hiding coins is that they are responsible for protecting the privacy of customers. Now it is very difficult to trace the link between dirty currency and criminal activity (FATF, 2020).

Money launderers can explain the possession of currency easily. The way to legitimize the illicit proceeds is the result of currency appreciation and the formation of an online company. In the capital market, one-coin value changes within a second. Therefore, it is very difficult to disprove currency appreciation. Secondly, the online company is created to clean dirty proceeds of money laundering.

COVID- 19 Money Laundering

To control COVID -19 pandemic governments' efforts all over the world have been observed. The most common government response is social support, travel restriction, tax relief policies, lockdown and remote work by turning to an online system. These measures open new opportunities for criminals to launder illicit money. In this pandemic, the demand for medical supplies including kits, ventilators, masks and medicines has been irresistible. In this pathetic condition, money launderers show themselves as employees of a business, professionals of NGO's and international organizations offering medical supplies. They receive payments through credit cards or shipping fees, but the goods are not delivered to customers. It is very difficult for a law enforcement agency to locate the cyber-crime. Once the money has been received through a criminal activity it is invested in financial institutions, financial markets and local goods thereby hiding the illegitimate source (FATF, 2020).

Another most popular money laundering activity that has been seen in COVID-19 is fake fundraising for victims of the pandemic. Criminals post themselves as NGOs or charity organizations and circulate emails for collecting donations for affecters. A clear direction has been made to do payment through credit cards. In that way, the personal information of customers including the title of account and password can be taken. The proceeds collected are not used for helping the needy instead various topologies have been used to legitimate the unlawful proceeds.

Cyber Money Laundering

Cyber money laundering is a social engineering crime comprising of phishing emails and mobile messages from spam campaigns. Fraudulent websites and malicious attachments in emails have been used to get personal payment information. Malware is inserted on computers and mobile devices. Cybercriminals post themselves as the world health organization and sent emails to individuals. Ignorant individuals click malicious links and open the attachments that reveal enough information regarding individual names and passwords. Another way to do cyber money laundering is posting of SMS by criminals personating themselves as government employees. These SMS are the way to receive personal information of individuals. The proceeds collected through this fraud are tried to make legal by investment in legitimate assets.

Cybercriminals have expertise in engineering network techniques. They exploit the weaknesses of network security in business to secure the information of customer and business transactions. Phishing emails are sent to targeted customers and request payment for legitimate goods and services. In the email, the direction is given to deposit cash in their illicit account. Dirty money from the illicit account is cleaned by turning in to legitimate money (Button & Cross, 2017).

Irwin & Dawson (2019) discuss the installation of ransom ware in computers and mobiles as another way to launder money. In the COVID-19 pandemic, cybercriminals share COVID-19 related information including active cases of the corona, vaccination used in controlling corona in different countries, increasing death rate due to corona in different countries and precautionary measures taken by the government in controlling corona. Hospitals and health care institutions are the victims of this criminal activity. This information is shared through ransom ware to gain and lock access to devices of victims until payment is received. This payment is invested in different sectors to conceal its illicit nature.

ISSUES AND CHALLENGES IN THE PREVENTION OF MONEY LAUNDERING

Money laundering is a serious crime therefore serious efforts are needed to prevent it (Sittlington & Harvey, 2018).

Criminological Theories and Anti- Money Laundering Framework

To develop strategic and tactical preventative activities to combat money laundering; it is instrumental to understand and integrate the various criminological theoretical perspectives (Gilmour, 2016b). Situational crime theory and rational choice theory are widely used criminological theories to understand the prevention process of money laundering.

Situational Crime Theory

Situational crime theory focuses on the crime setting rather than the criminal. It can be applied to define almost all types of crimes accurately. Previously researchers have used this theory to discuss various types of crimes such as prison violence, frauds associated with cheques, and credit card. The methodology behind situational crime theory is to identify and analyze the events of a crime rather than analyzing the chain of crimes. The analysis is intended to identify the spots for intervention so the environment can be altered and the opportunities that lead to crime can be reduced. Situational crime theory takes into consideration human psychology and assumes that criminal behavior is derived from the environment in which it exist. According to the situational crime theory, criminals analyze the cues in the environment around them; therefore, to prevent the crime it is important to alter the environment so that it no longer remains hospitable for committing the crime (Gilmour, 2016a).

Gilmour (2016a) discusses situational crime theory in relation to money laundering and highlights the weaknesses of applying situational crime theory to money laundering by arguing that the preventive measures associated with money laundering are isolated to the particular stages of money laundering giving money launderers enough roam to clean their illegal funds. Money launderers are ambitious and reactive to critics. Though situational crime theory is effective in predicting the crime when enough number of cases have occurred, money laundering is a diverse process and needs little modifications by money launderers to remain successful. Therefore, it can be said that the situational crime theory helps in understanding the crime of money laundering and but is fragile to criminal efficiency. Gilmour (2016a) further argues that the effectiveness of applying situational crime prevention methods is highly dependent on coherent international efforts. To combat money laundering domestic and international cooperation is needed to eliminate all methods through which money laundering takes place. Since money launderers are clever; regional efforts are not enough to stop them because they can invest illegal funds at the alternate location. There are differences in the legislation and implementation of AML measures across borders and this has worked in the favor of money launderers as they move to the less regulated locations with lenient AML policies. Therefore, a holistic international approach characterized by partner identification and intelligence and information sharing is needed to prevent money laundering.

Rational Choice Theory

The rational choice theory supports situational crime prevention by providing theoretical support. In recent literature, the rational choice theory is considered as one of the most comprehensive theoretical criminological frameworks to study and understand the money laundering and its prevention (Gilmour, 2016b). It analyzes the criminal's perception of risk, effort, and accumulated reward. The discussion on rational choice theory revolves around two schools of thought: the neo-classical utility school of thought argues that criminal decision making is based on rational cost and benefit analysis. Criminals are rational decision-makers who choose the outcome that maximizes their personal benefits. The other school of thought highlights the imperfectability of human decision-making owing to the condition of bounded rationality. According to this school of thought the criminals' ability to weigh risk and reward of crime is bounded by the availability of information and the precision of their judgment to evaluate the cost of future outcomes is comparable to the current impact. The criminals compare the future cost in terms of punishment and the current gains associated with the crime and if the punishment outweighs the present benefits of committing the crime than the immediate benefits weigh disproportionately within the criminal benefit formula. In this case, a criminal would most likely to commit resources in the crime where the current benefits outweigh the sum of the current cost of punishment plus the future cost of anxiety (Sittlington & Harvey, 2018).

According to rational choice theory, it can be argued that money launderers are rational decision-makers and choose their actions carefully after weighing the risk and reward. For instance, asset recovery is positively endorsed by the government as deterrence against money laundering but academics using the rational choice perspective are quite skeptical about its success. They argue that the success of asset recovery is very much dependent on the type of criminal being investigated. They believe that the lack of erudition on part of criminals is one cause for the success of asset recovery. Criminals who use sophisticated ways to convert their illicit money don't leave assets for confiscation and they simply devour the proceeds soon after they acquire them. They use a combination of simple and sophisticated ways to justify the origin of their funds. They prefer to rent rather than buying high-value assets or simply gift the expensive assets to third parties. Additionally, academics criticize the way investigative agencies choose to proceed against the criminals they argue that they pick only those money laundering cases that are easy to investigate, prove, and neglect the white-collar crimes that require complex and rigorous investigations (Sittlington & Harvey, 2018). Therefore, to prevent money laundering government should construct a legislative framework to ensure that the cost of offense should exceed the benefits derived from the offense by introducing stiffer sentences against offenders. Further cooperation over competition is needed to prosecute the criminals of money laundering.

GLOBAL EFFORTS TO PREVENT MONEY LAUNDERING

There are international organizations such as International Monetary Fund (IMF), The World Bank, International Accords, and the Financial Action Task Force (FATF) have devised detailed regulatory, operational, and legal frameworks to combat money laundering.

IMF and the World Bank

IMF and The World Bank are very actively working to combat money laundering. They are involved in international efforts to strengthen financial institutions by focusing on supervision and good governance. In this regard, they share resources and provide technical support and facilitate capacity building (Okoye, Akamobi, & Akamobi, 2008). The World Bank's reference guide provides a lawful and institutional structure for anti-money laundering (AML). The World Bank has suggested preventive measures e.g. the financial institutions in a country should put in place the proper customer identification system and due diligence procedure, financial institutions should maintain a record of customer's financial transactions for at least a minimum of five years. Moreover, financial institutions should report suspicious transactions, and to facilitate such reporting countries should make necessary amendments in the privacy laws that may restrict the discloser of such information.

Financial Action Task Force (FATF)

IMF and The World Bank work in close collaboration with FATF to devise a legal mechanism for AML and Counter Terror Financing (CTF) (Okoye *et al.*, 2008). FATF standards are based on many United Nations (UN) resolutions that support international collaboration for combating organized crime, drug dealing, and terror financing. FATF standards are a guide for AML regimes emphasizing the possible actions that can be taken to prevent money laundering within the legal and regulatory framework. It outlines the preventive actions for financial institutions, businesses, and international collaboration for AML and CTF. FATF has forty recommendations for the countries to implement strict policies for money laundering; these include the declaration of money laundering as a crime and allowing authorities to take necessary actions to eliminate it. The main highlight of FATF recommendation is establishing the Financial Intelligence Unit (FIU) that aims to detect and prevent money laundering by reporting suspicious transactions. Countries should establish financial intelligence units in order to deal with money laundering. Besides; countries are expected to cooperate internationally in investigations related to money laundering. Major FATF supervisory recommendations support AML and CTF by facilitating the implementation of rules such as know your customer, reporting of suspicious transactions, and other requirements related to due diligence.

Article 14 of the United Nations Convention Against Corruption

Under article 14 of the UN, numbers of measures are suggested to introduce the comprehensive AML regimes that can identify money laundering and are willing to exchange the information needed by the designated authorities to combat money laundering. Some of these measures are optional while others are obligatory to implement. In line with the recommendations of FATF; Article 14 of the UN also requires the countries' financial institutions to introduce measures such as knowing your customer, record keeping of financial transactions, and reporting of suspicious transactions. Article 14 prescribes countries to take tangible measures to screen the movement of capital across borders. These measures are intended to allow countries to identify and screen any illegal movement of money across its borders without creating any obstacles for a legal movement of cash. In this regard, countries may introduce the disclosure system that requires travelers to declare information about the money if its value exceeds the already prescribed threshold. Another important recommendation of Article 14 is that countries should adopt meaningful measures to encourage their financial institutions to introduce correct and precise information in the forms of the electronic transfer of funds about the originator and this information should be kept all through the payment chain. Increased scrutiny should be applied to the case of fund transfers with incomplete information (Weilert, 2016).

The USA PATRIOT Act

The USA PATRIOT Act is related to discouraging and punishing terrorist acts in the USA and around the globe through increased enforcement of investigation tools required to capture and impede terrorism. The purpose of this act is to strengthen U.S. actions to stop, identify and impeach international money laundering and terrorism financing. It focuses on the inquiry of foreign authority, foreign financial system, and susceptible foreign accounts and transactions. It requires all suitable stakeholders of the financial sector to report the susceptible occurrence of money laundering, take all necessary actions to strengthen the measures to stop utilization of USA financial system for personal benefits by corrupt foreign nationals and assist repatriation of stolen resources to the nations to whom such resources belong.

Figure 4. Effectiveness of AML supervision across countries
(BIG, 2020)

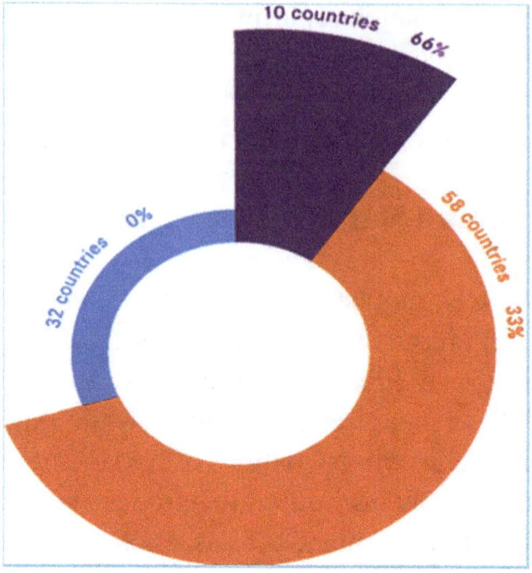

The Basel Committee on Banking Supervision

It sets up the worldwide guidelines for the banks. It is an international forum for setting up the agreed-upon regulations for the conduct of banks. So far, the committee has outlined various guidelines related to capital adequacy, agreement on the management of cross-border banking and the principles for the efficiency of banking supervision. The committee has made several recommendations for the exchange of information and collaboration in terms of authorization connected processes of the banks, continuing supervision, and compliance actions. Recommendations are also made to devise a possible framework for extending collaboration and exchange at the jurisdictional and global level. Figure 4 and 5 shows the effectiveness of AML supervision across the world. Figures show that 32 countries have zero percent, 58 countries have 33% and 10 countries have 66% level of AML supervision.

The Wolfsberg Principles

The Wolfberg group is a non-governmental association of thirteen international private banks (they are the major players of the global industry having a third of global private bank funds). The main objective of The Wolfberg group is to devise guidelines for AML, CTF, and know your customer.

Figure 5. Effectiveness of AML supervision around the world
(BIG, 2020)

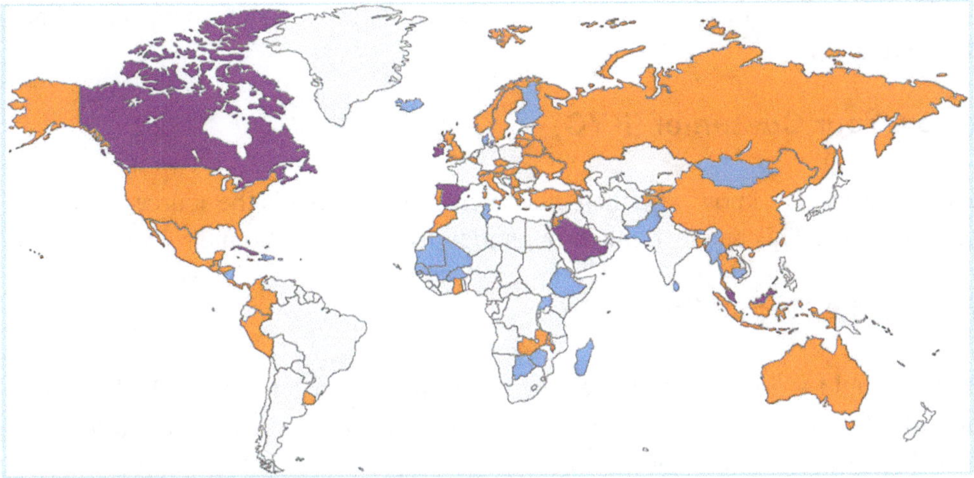

ROLE OF BANKS IN THE PREVENTION OF MONEY LAUNDERING

Legislation requires banks to adopt measures to prevent money laundering. But these measures are not for free and there is a cost associated to adopt preventative measures which sometimes is more than the rewards gained through the implementation of AML measures. It is fair for the state to ask banks to implement AML measures and bear the cost. Banks are part of the financial systems and enjoy various externalities. For banks, it is easy and inexpensive to implement preventive measures against money laundering. Therefore, banks are strictly monitored and guided to exercise strict controls to prevent money laundering as compare to the other financial entities that are still prone to the occurrence of such crimes. Through legislation, AML regimes ask banks to carry out public law functions. As discussed earlier according to the rational choice theory, one way to combat money laundering is to raise its cost so that it no longer remains feasible for the individuals to engage in it. Banking legislations prevent money laundering and its multiple effects because money launderers use liquid assets to invest laundered money in legal or illegal activities. AML measures adopted by banks can considerably reduce the occurrence of such crimes. The main idea behind the AML legislation is to stop the flow of the laundered money in the banking system and measures should be taken to detect when such an instance occurs. One of the problems in implementation of these AML measures can be competition whereby banks may knowingly ignore the occurrence of money laundering to earn more profits. But at the same time, these competitive pressures can motivate banks to improve their reputation to survive by implementing socially desirable AML measures (Ahtik, Pilipovic, & Marelja, 2019).

Gilmore (2004) made several recommendations for the banks to prevent money laundering:

Know Your Customer (KYC)

The banks need to know who their customers are and what is the source and origin of their funds. This can be done through identity cards and biometric verification.

Follow the Regulations

Banks should follow the AML regulations in true letter and spirit. Banks should not offer the services to the clients about whom they have even a fraction of doubt that they are engaged in money laundering. Banks should set up high moral and ethical standards for business and should cooperate with the concerned authorities to prevent money laundering in all suspected cases of money laundering.

Train and Inform Employees

All bank employees should be given training and should be informed about the laws and actions related to money laundering. Key aspects of the training should be the maintenance of customer record for at least five years, retrieving the sequence of transactions, and implementation of decisions related to establishing the lawful identity of the parties.

Suspicious Transaction Reporting (STR)

Financial institutions are required to submit Suspicious Transaction Report (STR) to the Financial Intelligence Unit (FIU), whenever there is any occurrence of a susceptible case of money laundering. These reports are important tools for monitoring any susceptible illegal activity within the financial service industry. The standards of STR vary across countries even institutions and are based on the nature of the illegal activity and the type of financial institutions. STR can be a result of the following susceptible instances: if financial institutions find any employee engaged in insider activity, they must generate STR. It is not only restricted to employees, but financial institutions must monitor the customer transactions and if they notice any prospective case of money laundering the report is immediately generated. If any customer is found running an illegal or unlicensed business, the report is needed. In case any illegal activity is detected the financial institutions are supposed to submit the STR within 30 days. In case if more investigation is needed to identify the suspect then an extension is available but not more than 60 days. Lastly, STR must be kept in record for 5 years from the date of reporting. Financial institutions which fail to comply with these requirements may face legal actions that can result in civil and criminal punishments such as heavy fines, detection, cancelation of business licenses and other legal restrictions.

DISCUSSION

The financial infrastructure is developed into a continuous operating global system with the help of which "megabyte money" can move anywhere with ease and speed. Every year, billions of dollars are estimated to be illegally moving out of the economies of developing countries. This public resource drain, therefore, weakens the countries' effort to mobilize more domestic resources to accomplish internationally agreed Sustainable Development Goals (SDGs). The problem of illicit financial inflow is serious as much as illicit capital outflows. Smuggling of drugs and valuable minerals, arms, tax elusion, criminal networks engaged in human trafficking are the main causes of illegal inflows. Tax, not being paid to governments is the root cause of illicit cash inflow and outflow. Trade-based money laundering is used by sophisticated criminal operations which lead to trade mis-invoicing to move large quantities of illegal money between countries. Launderers can cover the main source of illegal money by exchanging the proceeds of crime with the proceeds of legitimate business. There are widespread economic and social consequences of money laundering. Economic policy is falsely influenced by the creation of wrong demand and disturbance caused by money laundering.

Money laundering is not a phenomenon related to any one country or region of the world; it is perhaps a challenge worldwide for the whole world. Financial crimes initiate from every nook and corner of the world. The illicit funds are transferred worldwide by the money launderers through various channels thereby hiding the origin of the funds. The origin of the funds is hidden by the launderers because the generation of funds is related to some criminal activity and therefore to avoid the out-reach of the law enforcement agencies.

The main problem with combating money laundering is the skill of the money launderers to stay ahead to those who are fighting against this financial crime. The money launderers pave their ways in various domains to clean their dirty money. At one point of time, they may enter into the real estate market, at the other point of time they may enter into the financial market and sometimes they enter into the unregulated markets such as the art and crafts market (which is now becoming the most popular market for money launderers) to clean their money. Foreign exchange, settlement, cashier check, deposit box, acceptance, loan, discounts are the multiple services that are provided by banking institutions and money launderers frequently use these instruments. It is convenient and fast to transfer funds across international borders with the help of integrated financial markets and the global economy. Many countries allow an unspecified fund to transfer due to their inflexible bank secrecy laws. Therefore, the criminals get the advantage to transfer money into other countries thereby provoking evils of the society in the form of drugs, human trafficking, political corruption and financing of terrorism.

There is a very complex connection between money laundering and terrorism. For the survival of a terrorist organization, it plays an important role. To carry out their attacks, terrorists get resources through the raising and processing of funds from terrorism financing. Similarly, there is also a simple relation of narcotics financing and money laundering because drug traffickers have only one goal to bring to more and more drug on the streets.

Many financial institutions consider that compliance with the anti-money laundering programs needs to be solved at the national and business unit level. Regulatory law across markets and geography are a challenge for financial institutions. The need of the hour is to change the anti-money regulations all over the world.

To ensure efficiency in daily business operations, countries are obliged to perform extra activities besides conforming to laws. Financial institutions require extraordinary efforts to keep a check on transactions involving transfer of illicit proceeds. Monitoring payment messages, finding and applying an appropriated risk-based approach, know your customer policy, keep the special agreement department and the appropriate technical solutions to meet compliance requirements are the main efforts that are required by the financial institutions.

CONCLUSION

Money laundering is a technical organized crime of filtering ill-gotten gains into apparently legitimate assets. It is embedded in financial crime rather than an evil crime. A strong mechanism comprising of placement, layering and integration has been designed for this illegal act. The advancement of technology in money laundering techniques has made it possible to be conducted in cross-border territories and reduced its chances of detection to the minimum level.

Money laundering has been extended from conventional to professional means. Conventional sources are sophisticated technologies including virtual currency, phishing emails and fraudulent websites. Professionals including lawyers, financial institutions, political parties and public officials assist in designing a scheme for conducting money laundering.

It is difficult to trace the original cause of money because the money laundering process involves several steps starting with the transfer of the money between the bank accounts, breaking up of the large amounts of money into small units (deposits), or buying the acceptable forms of money respectively. There is an important role of the time of deposit and amount of time money sits in a specific place in money laundering. To avoid facing punishment and being caught, this process is usually intended to be administered slowly and technically.

In response to the progress of money laundering globally, an anti-money laundering regime based upon criminalization and internationalization has developed its standards. FATF focuses on internationalization and has developed a code of regulations from domestic to the international level to combat money laundering. Besides this, FATF supports courts of the country to consider money laundering as a crime and perpetrator to launder money is a criminal. Criminals are sentenced for this illegal act just like other evil crimes.

Researchers in future can identify the circumstances that lead the money launderers to select methods at a time. Similarly, researchers can investigate the smart obstacles in the prevention of money laundering through empirical analysis of the data currently available and suggest the most efficient ways to overcome these obstacles.

RECOMMENDATIONS AND FUTURE DIRECTIONS

Money laundering is an international issue and it is conducted in cross-border territories employing a series of complex techniques. The international standard has been developed to cope with money laundering transactions and events globally. There is a need to implement such international standard to regulate the general acceptance of the behavior of individuals, estates and companies involved in money laundering. A sanction should be imposed on countries that are not compliant with the international standard maintained for anti-money laundering.

Developed countries have developed a long-arm jurisdiction theory that focuses on criminal jurisdiction. Long-arm jurisdiction has been successfully implemented in solving and anticipating the multifaceted nature of money laundering practices. The developing countries should use criminal jurisdiction theory for anti-money laundering practices. More research is required in future to empirically investigate the role of long-arm jurisdiction theory in monitoring the money laundering process in developing countries.

International cooperation is needed to deal with money laundering globally. International cooperation is a blend of extradition, mutual legal assistance and confiscation of the proceeds of the crime. International cooperation is challenging in law enforcement practices therefore many money laundering cases are in courts but not decided yet. The research in the future should be conducted to explore the factors that create hurdles in interstate cooperation for law enforcement.

DISCLAIMER

The contents and views of this chapter are expressed by the authors in their personal capacities. It is not necessary for the Editor and the Publisher to agree with these viewpoints and they are not responsible for any duty of care in this regard.

ACKNOWLEDGMENT

The authors extend sincere gratitude to:

- The Editor-in-Chief and International Editorial Advisory Board (IEAB) of this book who initially desk reviewed, arranged a rigorous double/triple blind review process and conducted a thorough, minute and critical final review before accepting the chapter for publication.
- All anonymous reviewers who provided very constructive feedbacks for thorough revision, improvement, extension and fine-tuning of the chapter.
- All colleagues, assistants and well-wishers who assisted the authors to complete this task.

REFERENCES

Ahtik, M., Pilipovic, O., & Marelja, M. (2019). Economic analysis of money laundering prevention in Croatia and Slovenia. *Journal of Money Laundering Control*, *22*(1), 97–109. doi:10.1108/JMLC-01-2018-0009

Albanese, J. S. (2012). Deciphering the linkages between organized crime and transnational crime. *Journal of International Affairs*, *66*(1), 1–16.

Albrecht, C., Duffin, K. M., Hawkins, S., & Rocha, V. M. M. (2019). The use of cryptocurrencies in the money laundering process. *Journal of Money Laundering Control*, *22*(2), 210–216. doi:10.1108/JMLC-12-2017-0074

Aluko, A., & Bagheri, M. (2012). The impact of money laundering on economic and financial stability and on political development in developing countries. *Journal of Money Laundering Control*, *15*(4), 442–457. doi:10.1108/13685201211266024

Amara, I., & Khlif, H. (2018). Financial crime, corruption and tax evasion: A cross-country investigation. *Journal of Money Laundering Control*, *21*(4), 545–554. doi:10.1108/JMLC-10-2017-0059

Amoh, J. K., & Adafula, B. (2019). An estimation of the underground economy and tax evasion. *Journal of Money Laundering Control*, *22*(4), 626–645. doi:10.1108/JMLC-01-2019-0002

BIG. (2020). *Basel AML index 2020: Ranking money laundering and terrorist financing risks around the world*. Basel Institute on Governance. Retrieved from https://baselgovernance.org/sites/default/files/2020-07/basel_aml_index_2020_web.pdf

Button, M., & Cross, C. (2017). *Cyber frauds, scams and their victims*. Taylor & Francis. doi:10.4324/9781315679877

Chandra, E. M. (2019). Victimless Crime in Indonesia: Should We Punished Them? *Padjadjaran Journal of Law*, *6*(2), 216–232.

Clarke, C. P. (2016). Drugs & thugs: Funding terrorism through narcotics trafficking. *Journal of Strategic Security*, *9*(3), 1–15. doi:10.5038/1944-0472.9.3.1536

FATF. (2020). *COVID-19-related Money Laundering and Terrorist Financing – Risks and Policy Responses*. Financial Action Task Force.

GFI. (2019). *Illicit financial flows to and from 148 developing countries: 2006-2015*. Global Financial Integrity. Retrieved from https://www.gfintegrity.org/wp-content/uploads/2019/01/GFI-2019-IFF-Update-Report-1.29.18.pdf

Gilmore, W. (2004). *Dirty money : the evolution of money laundering counter-measures*. Council of Europe Publishing.

Gilmour, N. (2016a). Preventing money laundering: A test of situational crime prevention theory. *Journal of Money Laundering Control*, *19*(4), 376–396. doi:10.1108/JMLC-10-2015-0045

Gilmour, N. (2016b). Understanding the practices behind money laundering - A rational choice interpretation. *International Journal of Law, Crime and Justice*, *44*, 1–13. doi:10.1016/j.ijlcj.2015.03.002

Grujić, M., & Šikman, M. (2020). Certain Manifestation Forms and Proving Money Laundering In The Emerging Market. *Acta Economica*, *18*(32), 175–201.

Guevara, M. W. (2016, May 9). *ICIJ releases database revealing thousands of secret offshore companies*. International Consortium of Investigative Journalists. Retrieved from https://panamapapers.icij.org/blog/20160509-offshore-database-release.html

Hendriyetty, N., & Grewal, B. S. (2017). Macroeconomics of money laundering: Effects and measurements. *Journal of Financial Crime*, *24*(1), 65–81. doi:10.1108/JFC-01-2016-0004

Hetemi, A., Merovci, S., & Gulhan, O. (2018). Consequences of money laundering on economic growth – The Case of Kosovo and its Trade Partners. *Acta Universitatis Danubius Œconomica*, *14*(3), 113–125.

Irwin, A. S., & Dawson, C. (2019). Following the cyber money trail: Global challenges when investigating ransomware attacks and how regulation can help. *Journal of Money Laundering Control*, *22*(1), 110–131. doi:10.1108/JMLC-08-2017-0041

Keohane, R. O. (2001). Governance in a Partially Globalized World Presidential Address, American Political Science Association 2000. *The American Political Science Review*, *95*(1), 1–13. doi:10.1017/S0003055401000016

Kirti, A., Kumar, P., & Yadav, R. (2011). The face of honour based crimes: Global concerns and solutions. *International Journal of Criminal Justice Sciences*, *6*(1/2), 343.

Levi, M., & Soudijn, M. (2020). Understanding the laundering of organized crime money. *Crime and Justice*, *49*(1), 1–53. doi:10.1086/708047

Nasir, M. A. (2020). The Relevance of Maqasid al Shari'ah to Anti-Money Laundering and Terrorism Financing. In A. Rafay (Ed.), *Handbook of Research on Theory and Practice of Global Islamic Finance* (pp. 179–194). IGI Global. doi:10.4018/978-1-7998-0218-1.ch010

OECD. (2014). *Illicit financial flows from developing countries: Measuring OECD responses*. Organisation for Economic Co-operation and Development. Retrieved from https://www.OECD.org/corruption/Illicit_Financial_Flows_from_Developing_Countries.pdf

Okoye, E. I., Akamobi, N. L., & Akamobi, A. A. (2008). Effectiveness of Nigeria's Financial System for Prevention of Money Laundering. *Journal of Applied Economics and Business*, *1*(1), 93–103.

Prakasa, S. U. W. (2019). Garuda Indonesia-Rolls Royce Corruption, Transnational Crime, and Eradication Measures. *Lentera Hukum*, *6*(3), 409–426. doi:10.19184/ejlh.v6i3.14112

Rafay, A. (2019). *FinTech as a Disruptive Technology for Financial Institutions*. IGI Global. doi:10.4018/978-1-5225-7805-5

Rose-Ackerman, S., & Palifka, B. J. (2018). Corruption, organized crime, and money laundering. In K. Basu & T. Cordella (Eds.), *Institutions, Governance and the Control of Corruption* (pp. 75–111). Palgrave Macmillan. doi:10.1007/978-3-319-65684-7_4

Scilla, A. (2018). *ICIJ releases database revealing thousands of secret offshore companies*. Retrieved from https://www.icij.org/investigations/panama-papers/former-pakistan-pm-sharif-sentenced-to-10-years-over-panama-papers

Sittlington, S., & Harvey, J. (2018). Prevention of money laundering and the role of asset recovery. *Crime, Law, and Social Change*, *70*(4), 421–441. doi:10.100710611-018-9773-z

Sohraby, F., Habibitabur, H., & Masoudzade, M. R. (2016). Money Laundering Crime and Its Situational Prevention in Iranian Law and International Law. *Journal of Politics and Law*, *9*(7), 57–63. doi:10.5539/jpl.v9n7p57

Teichmann, F. M. J. (2019). Money laundering and terrorism financing through consulting companies. *Journal of Money Laundering Control*, *22*(1), 32–37. doi:10.1108/JMLC-10-2017-0056

Uche, U. C. (1998). The adoption of a money-laundering law in Nigeria. *Journal of Money Laundering Control*, *1*(3), 220–228. doi:10.1108/eb027144

UNODC. (2019). *Money laundering and globalization*. United Nations Office of Drug and Crime. Retrieved from https://www.unodc.org/unodc/en/money-laundering/globalization.html

Verhage, A. (2009). Between the hammer and the anvil? the anti-money laundering-complex and its interactions with the compliance industry. *Crime, Law, and Social Change*, *52*(1), 9–32. doi:10.100710611-008-9174-9

Weilert, A. K. (2016). United Nations Convention against Corruption (UNCAC) – After Ten Years of Being in Force. *Max Planck Yearbook of United Nations Law Online*, *19*(1), 216–240. doi:10.1163/18757413-00190008

Chapter 2
Religio-Spiritual Implications of Corruption and Money Laundering:
The Case of Nigeria

Adebayo Rafiu Ibrahim
University of Ilorin, Nigeria

ABSTRACT

Nigeria is a country in the center of financial crimes and money laundering in Africa right from her pre-independence, independence, and post-independence eras. The aim of this study was to analyze the religio-spiritual effects of financial corruption and money laundering in Nigeria. The study answered such questions as what is the role of religious practitioners in aiding and abetting money laundering in Nigeria and how anti-money laundering strategies affect religion. The study observed that religion was dubiously used for money laundering activities, while some manipulated religion to exploit others. Some, for money ritual, also employed evil spirituality. The study concluded that religion has to be properly regulated to avoid its manipulation by some individuals while there is a need to review some anti-money laundering policies that reduced religion to mere worship in the four corners of places of worship and do not allow it to feature in humanitarian volunteerism.

DOI: 10.4018/978-1-7998-8758-4.ch002

INTRODUCTION

Money laundering has become a global pandemic sparing no nation, race, or tribe. It takes various dimensions ranging from such criminal activities as embezzlement, prostitution, and corruption, to all sorts of ill-gotten wealth and criminal incomes. It assumes an international dimension when such notorious dealings are perfected for cross-border movements to finance terrorism (Nasir, 2020). Money laundering is a means of illegal acquisition of wealth to conceal its illegal origins. Money laundering and financial corruption are closely related that attempts to demarcate the two have been fruitless. Financial crimes dovetail to money laundering, as efforts are made to conceal or disguise such criminal acts or disguise the illicit origin of the property to evade the legal consequences of the actions. Corruption is also a category of predicate criminality for money laundering. Such corrupt practices include tax evasion and smuggling among others. According to the 2010 GIABA Report, government revenue loss from tax evasion is as high as 50% of potential revenue and tax evasion can be concealed as business profits and be diverted into the informal economy and real estate sector. The report also traces smuggling to trade-based money laundering, as valuable goods are concealed amongst commodities with low import tariffs to avoid paying full import tax. It also takes the form of smuggling portable and easily concealable commodities like diamonds in a person's belonging when traveling. This corrupt practice aided the smuggling of illicit commodities, such as guns, which are sources of illicit funds, and as well aided some militant groups to have access to arms to carry out their nefarious activities.

Some corrupt practices, which aided trade-based money laundering through smuggling, include over- and under-invoicing of goods and services and falsely describing goods and services as well as multiple invoicing of goods and services. Indeed, the Mafia Ownership of Laundromats in the United States, which was said to have been the origin of money laundering, generated their monies from corrupt means such as extortion, prostitution, gambling, and bootleg liquor (Ogbodo & Mieseigha, 2013). While emphasizing the close link between money laundering and corruption, the 2010 GIABA report has it that:

"Corruption thrives thanks to insufficient and poorly implemented institutional safeguards and a lack of freedom of information; it is also a major predicate offense for money laundering purposes, a significant source of illegal proceeds, and a means by which efforts to prevent money laundering are undermined. Corrupt officials often use their position of power to aid the laundering of the proceeds of corruption, highlighting the need for strong provisions regarding PEPs in AML/CFT regimes. The property and formal banking sector are particularly at risk from funds derived from corruption (p.7)." (GIABA, 2010)

There is no doubt that money laundering has serious negative impacts on any nation's economy and financial system. It also affects both the integrity of domestic economies and global financial systems. In Nigeria, a one-time Chairman of the Economic and Financial Crime Commission, Nuhu Ribadu gave an estimated amount of $100 billion, corruptly exported from Nigeria between the mid-1980s and 1999. He observed that more than $1 trillion illicit funds flowed into the United States annually through the international financial systems; proceeds from drug trafficking and other forms of economic and financial crimes (Ogbodo & Mieseigha, 2013).

Corruption and money laundering are global practices, which have become pandemic that all nations are finding means of checking the menace. As far back as the 1930s, when the United States government declared money laundering a crime, governments at all levels have not relented in fighting corruption and in putting in place anti-money laundering policies and institutions. Several conventions were held globally to address this menace as well. The Vienna Convention of 1988, Wolfsberg Principles in 2000, the Palermo Convention in 2001, and Merida Convention in 2005 are few examples of these conventions. In addition to this, some measures taken to deal with the situation as mentioned by Kingston (2011) include the Money Laundering Regulations 2007 in the United Kingdom; the Financial Services and Markets Act of 2000; the Patriot Act of 2001 and the Bank Secrecy Act of 1970 in the United States, among others. There was also the Organization for Economic Cooperation and Development (OECD) countries, which was instrumental to the establishment of the Financial Action Task Force (FATF) for combating the menace of money laundering.

There is no doubt that financial corruption and money laundering have effected negatively on every sphere of life of citizens of Nigeria. Scholars like Ogbodo and Mieseigha (2013), Okoye and Gbegi (2013), and Enofe, Aliu, and Ombu (2018) among others, have delved into the economic implications of money laundering in Nigeria. Such scholars used various variables and methodologies to look at the impact of money laundering on the Nigerian economy with various findings. As apt as their findings are, a serious lacuna is that the religious and spiritual implications of financial corruption and money laundering have not been given the desired attention looking at the level of religiosity and spirituality of Nigerians generally. This study intends to fill this gap.

RELIGION, SPIRITUALITY AND WEALTH ACQUISITION

There are principles on the ground that guide against illegal acquisition of wealth. In Islam, man is restricted in the way he acquires, invests, and utilizes this wealth. He is to acquire his wealth through legitimate means like legal employment, inheritance, donations, and grants. As such, he should only embark on a business approved by Allah. As the vicegerent of Allah, he should not engage in business that would harm him or others. This explains why transactions in alcohol, pork, obscene material or narcotic, human and drug trafficking, smuggling, bunkering, banditry, burglary, mugging, vandalism, kidnapping, and others such, are strictly forbidden in Islam. Furthermore, the Principle of Unity (PU) encapsulates the nature of business Muslims should embark upon. It sees race, country, and language as mere means of identification, which should not hamper the spirit of unity. As such, unjust dealings, oppression, lie, and other means of misappropriation of one another's property would undoubtedly severe this spirit. Therefore, Islam adds spirituality to commercial and financial transactions using inner consciousness *('Iman)*, vicegerency of Allah *(Istikhlaf)*, and hereafter *(al-akhirah)* for individuals to guide themselves in their material pursuits. A Muslim through this knows that all resources are made available to him to facilitate his duty as Allah's vicegerent on earth and shall be accountable for such in the hereafter.

As a means of discouraging money laundering and other corrupt means of acquiring wealth, the *Qur'an* warns that Muslims should not be lured into such action looking at the lavish lives of those who engage in them. It reads:

So let not their wealth or their children amaze you; in reality, Allah plans to punish them with these things in the life of this world, and that their souls shall depart (die) while they are disbelievers (Q9: 55).

The above verse is emphasizing the importance of spirituality in wealth acquisition, as it gives the impression that anybody who lacks spiritual development has no development at all. So, a nation that gives no preference to spiritual development witnesses pseudo development. As such, spirituality will make him look beyond his terrestrial comfort, and to see his existence in this world as temporal while a more durable enjoyment awaits him in the hereafter if he is not deceived by worldly enjoyment.

One crucial religious and spiritual factor relevant to anti-money laundering is faith popularly referred to as *Iman*. Lack of *iman* is a factor for the rampancy of money laundering activities. A faithless person can go at any length and as well as step on toes to achieve its financial targets. It is expedient to note that the basis of all Islamic rituals is to inculcate *Iman* that leads to *taqwah* (consciousness of Allah). For instance, the *Qur'an* informs that the essence of *salat* is to guard against *fahshah* (abominable acts) and so a major means of remembering Allah. In the same vein, fasting *(sawm)* is instituted for inculcating *taqwah*. A Muslim who is conscious of Allah will not engage in corruption and money laundering; hence, *taqwah* is a great anti-laundering spiritual measure, which strikes his mind and calls him to order whenever he finds himself in a position to carry out any illicit activity. A faithless person uses any opportunity that comes his way to loot and exploit people. The level of knowledge of a person does not count where there is no faith. Indeed, an uncivilized nation with *Iman* is better than a civilized nation with no faith. Mutahheri (1977) posits that knowledge without faith is like a sharp sword in the hand of a drunken brute and a lamp in the hand of a thief to help him pick up the best article at midnight.

One major factor responsible for the persistence of corruption and money laundering is the type of education bequeathed to Nigeria by the colonial masters. The man-made education adopted by Nigeria is secular and does not recognize God as a source of knowledge. It, therefore, produces faithless candidates whose sense of accountability in the hereafter is at zero levels. There is therefore no difference in the conduct of the uneducated man of yesterday and the educated man of today. The illiterate but faithful man of yesterday is preferable to the faithless but educated man of today. Sarwar (1996: 7) aptly describes the system of education adopted by many countries and its consequences on the society when he writes:

Man-made education has led to many forms of social degeneration; misuse of human intellect and creativity to suit political and economic objectives; abuse of drugs, power, authority, and wealth; increased murder and crime; and self-abasement through suicide and euthanasia. The race for the acquisition of nuclear and other weapons, the hoarding and willful destruction of food (whilst millions starve across the world), discrimination based on race, color, sex, and religion, and attempts to legitimize and even celebrate unnatural acts (sodomy, homosexuality, sadomasochism, etc) are further instances of our moral decline. Corruption and greed, poverty and lack of basic amenities, and limitations on freedom of expression, even in Muslim countries, make the situation bleaker.

Contrary to the above, Islam sees truth, values, and ethics as parts of what constitutes knowledge and a means through which man can earn a great reward with Allah. In a hadith cited by Al-Ghazaali (1998:22), the Prophet is quoted to have apportioned every stage of knowledge an act of worship in the following words:

Acquire knowledge, for seeking it for the sake of Allah is piety (Khasyatullah), searching for it is devotional worship ('ibadah); studying it is the glorification of Allah (Tasbih); conducting an inquiry on it is striving in the cause of Allah (jihad); imparting it on those who do not know is the bestowal of alms (sadaqah) and spreading it among its possessors is sacrifice (Qurba).

FINANCIAL CORRUPTION AND MONEY LAUNDERING ACTIVITIES IN NIGERIA

Nigeria is blessed with abundant natural resources is a fact that cannot be denied. The country is so blessed that once upon a time, it was regarded as the giant of Africa. As one of the prominent exporters of oil, the country assumes an enviable position among the comity of nations that the then Head of the state, Gen. Yakubu Gowon was said to have declared in 1973 that money was not the problem of Nigeria but how to spend it[1]. As if the discovery of oil was a curse in disguise to the country, the nation turned back from its initial sources of income and concentrated only on the oil boom leaving other sources unattended. Coupled with this is the high rate of corruption in virtually every fabric of Nigerian society. These two factors work together to spell doom for the nation, as it ranks high among the world's poorest nations despite its resources. According to the 2019 Corruption Perceptions Index reported by Transparency International, Nigeria is the 146 least corrupt nation out of 180 countries[2]. Fig. 1 below expresses this better.

Figure 1. Corruption Perceptions Index
Source: Tradingeconomics.com / transparency international.

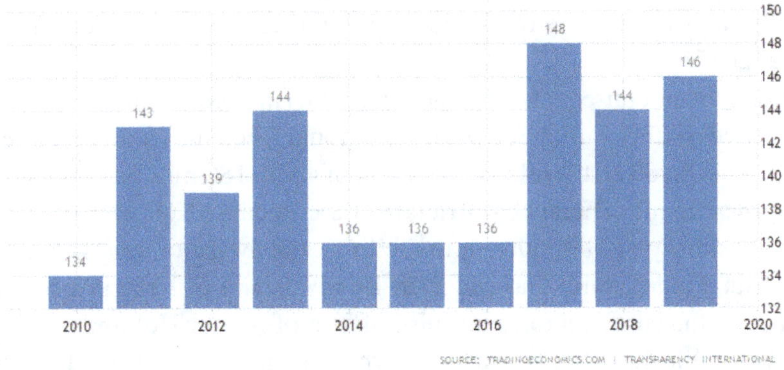

It is also unbelievable that a country with abundant natural and human resources could also sink in external debt that it continues borrowing on annual basis with not much to show for it. The country has consistently been borrowing that its external debt increases from USD8.82 billion as of December 31, 2013, to a whopping USD22.07 billion as of March 31, 2018 (Urama, Ekeocha, and Iloh, 2018). While external borrowing may not be an issue if its purpose is viable and justifiable, and to address expenditure needs on national budgetary deficits, it seems that the nation is borrowing not only for capital projects and human development but also for those who are smart enough to siphon it for their benefits. Not this alone, Urama, Ekeocha, and Iloh, (2018) observed that many of the state governments have exceeded the red line debt accumulation, which is 50% of the state statutory revenue by more than 200% and some by almost 500%. Despite the heavy indebtedness, many of the Nigerian citizens could not afford the necessities of life such as education and medical facilities. In other words, the education sector is bedridden while the health sector is in a state of comatose. Some hitherto thriving manufacturing companies had collapsed; many citizens had become unemployed, while the take-home of those in service could not take them home. Little wonder then those young and virile citizens of the country checked out of the country to the world of uncertainty, looking for means of sustenance. Those who could not check out resorted to establishing places of worship organizing different religious programs to make the ends meet. As religious businesses thrived, the onetime flourishing warehouses of government setup producing goods and services were turned to churches, while spaces that could have been good for the production of goods and services became houses of worship.

Money laundering in Nigeria is not gendered discriminatory, as both male and female public officials siphoned and laundered the country's resources to their accounts. The first Nigeria female Minister of Petroleum Resources between 2010 and 2015, Diezani Alison-Madueke, was implicated in corruption, misappropriation of the country's funds, and money laundering cases in Nigeria, Britain, Italy, and the United States to the tune of US $90 billion allegedly stolen from the country (Chironda, 2017).

The above are the consequences of money laundering and a high level of corruption in public offices of the country. At the international level, the Halliburton scandal is prominent. This involved the alleged payment of about 180 million dollars to certain Nigerian government officials by officials of a company, Kellog Brown and Root (KBR), a subsidiary of Halliburton, to facilitate the award of contracts to them to build the Liquefied Natural Gas plant on Bonny Island in Nigeria's Niger Delta. There was also the case of a former senior officer of Armor Holdings Incorporated of Jacksonville, Florida, Richard Bistrong who was said to have bribed an official of the Independent National Electoral Commission (INEC) for the award of contracts for the supply of fingerprint ink pads. Scholars like Obiora Chinedu Okafor and Benson Chinedu Olugbuo (2011) had discussed similar examples like these.

In recent time, the Interim Management Committee (IMC) of the Niger Delta Development Commission (NDDC) was asked by the Senate to refund a total sum of N4.9 billion, which was paid to staff of the Commission in the beach of procurement process and approval. The Commission was said to have spent N1.9 billion for Lassa fever kits; N1.1 billion for 'public communication' and N1.5 billion for COVID-19 relief, in addition to spending N85.7 million for overseas travels to the United Kingdom and N164.2 million for union members trip to Italy among others.

Also, the Commission was said to have spent over N40 billion without recourse to established processes of funds disbursement[3]. The EFCC, the anti-graft agency itself, is not free of corruption and money laundering, as some of the top officials of the Commission were recently suspended from office, while the top boss was equally alleged of diverting recovered funds and seized assets to his accounts.

Nigeria itself was proactive in taking legislative measures with the inauguration of the National Drug Law Enforcement Agency (NDLEA) Act in 1989 and the Money Laundering Decree 164 of 1995, which were predicated on money laundering from drugs. This was expanded to other crimes or illegal acts in the amended Act of 2002. The signing into law of the Anti-Corruption Bill and the consequent establishment of the Independent Corrupt Practices and other Related Offences Commission (ICPC) is a major step taken to address the endemic corrupt practices in Nigeria. In the same vein, in December 2002, the country enacted the Economic and Financial Crime Commission (EFCC) (Establishment) Act which was commissioned in April 2003 with the responsibility of investigating money laundering cases from predicate offenses other than drug trafficking and to enforce the money laundering legislation.

The establishment of the EFCC was a response to the hues and cries of Nigerian citizens on the high rate of looting of the public treasury by public officers. It was as well a response to the reactions from the international front and agencies such as the Financial Action Task Force (FAFT), which blacklisted the country by including it on her list of non-cooperative countries in the task of fighting corruption in 2001. The EFCC is responsible for coordinating the various institutions involved in the fight against money laundering and enforcement of all laws dealing with economic and financial crimes (Sec 2 of the EFCC Act). Despite all these efforts and organizations on the ground, money laundering in Nigeria persists at national and international levels.

RELIGION AND MONEY LAUNDERING IN NIGERIA

There is evidence to support the fact that Nigerians are highly religious. The whole nation hosts many religious centers located within a few hundred yards of each other with widespread spiritual revival activities championed by pastors who attribute to themselves the power to heal, prophesize, and perform miracles. Most of these churches are moneymaking ventures. According to Agazue (2016), the rate at which the residents of southern Nigeria patronize pastors is alarming as almost every street in the urban regions of southern Nigeria has a church, while there are widespread spiritual revivals, religio-commercial services offered by the pastors of prophetic and miracle-working churches grow stronger daily. He, therefore, sees Pentecostalism as *"the fastest growing industry in Nigeria and the second most popular export (after crude oil)*." In the same vein, mosques spring up on daily basis with numerous Muslim prayer groups organizing *asalatu* and *tahajjud* programs.[4] It is interesting to note that Muslim clerics are now joining their Christian counterparts in organizing prayer sessions on mountains and beside rivers all in the name of finding a spiritual solution to the challenges facing their clients. Apart from airing different religious programs on radio and television, social media also serve as means of disseminating religious programs, while public places are littered with posters of different religious connotations.

The geometric proliferation of places of worship and spiritual centers in Nigeria could have been considered a good omen for the country if not for the fact that the more the worship centers are emerging, the farther the worshippers are moving away from God. As much as people are flocking places of worship, the impact of religion is not felt much in their conduct. The ever-increasing rate of criminality, insecurity, and lack of peace being witnessed in the country makes one conclude that religion has been rendered to a means of exploiting others to acquire wealth in Nigeria. The competition for establishing places of worship with millions of people attending crusades, revivals, vigils, mountains, miracle centers, *Asalatu* programs become suspicious, as they hardly have positive impacts on the congregations.

The high rate of financial corruption in public offices led to a serious economic crisis in the mid-1980s in Nigeria and this forced the country to resort to the adoption of World Band/IMF-designed Structural Adjustment, which had serious and unpalatable consequences on Nigerians. This development led to the retrenchment of workers, high graduate unemployment, and economic meltdown, which culminated in people looking for a spiritual solution to their social, material, and financial predicaments. New Religious Movement, therefore, became thriving among adherents of Islam and Christianity. According to Agazue (2016), religious participation and activities are higher in societies experiencing economic hardship and political tension. They, therefore, rush to places of worship to find succor. Some so-called men of God grasp this opportunity to exploit their clients. Adebayo (2018: 39) captured the situation succinctly when he writes:

Many places of worship spring up daily, while 'Ministers of God' advertise their products every day – miracles, prosperity, and protection against evils. Rather than taking advantage of their natural resources with which they are blessed, Nigerians go for proclaiming and eulogizing the name of the Provider, forgetting that they need prayers only when they please the Provider. The love of prayers has blindfolded them that they cannot strike a balance between prayer and work. When other nations are working tirelessly to invest in technology, agriculture, industrialization, education, and massive infrastructural development, Nigerians are busy praying and putting up gigantic places of worship.

It is pertinent to mention that there is nothing wrong in seeking spiritual assistance through prayers; but more importantly, Nigerians seek this assistance through miracles, as they want instant answers to their spiritual requests. Owoyemi (2016), saw this as a new development in religion occasioned by "*the economic meltdown and the problem of ineffective governance which facilitated the institutionalization of corruption*." Religion, therefore, becomes an alternative means of wealth acquisition where they could not have access to public funds. Many pastors and few Muslim clerics are therefore riding exotic cars in convoys and flying from one country to another in private and chartered jets, while the congregations through which they got the money are languishing in abject poverty. It is disheartening to mention that most of the schools and institutions established through the finances of some religious bodies are not accessible to children of poor members of such bodies because of the high rate of school fees charged, as only the affluent members could afford that.

It should be noticed that religion is dragged into the mess of money laundering at every phase of the act. This is espoused in the three phases of money laundering, namely: placement, layering, and integration. At the placement phase, the launderer deposits whatever he acquired illegitimately into a financial institution breaking such into smaller amounts to avoid being suspected, or rather, he transfers it to other forms of assets. He then moves to the second phase, which is layering in form of buying and selling assets at local and international levels so that the source of the money becomes untraceable. The final stage is where he integrates the illicit money into the economy through investment in real estate or business ventures. Figure 2 illustrates this further.

Figure 2. Phases of Money Laundering

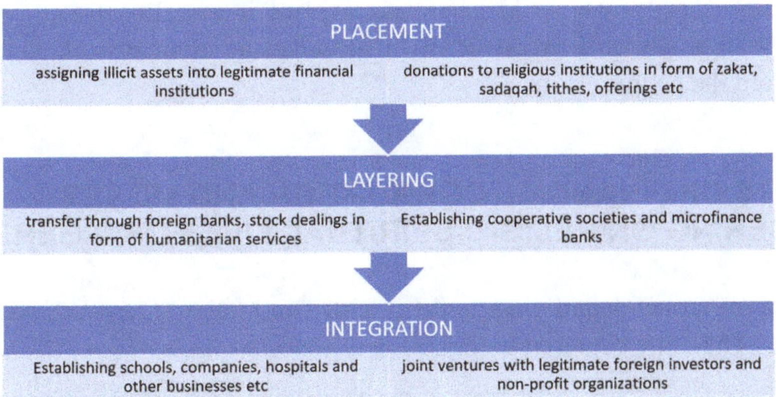

Figure 2 above demonstrates the relevance of religion to the three phases of money laundering. Religion becomes relevant in the three phases, as the launderer who is a member of a religious body advances the course of money laundering by contributing to the programs of the religion. He may decide to pay *zakat* or *sadaqah* if he is a Muslim; or give tithes, offerings, or seed sowing with the illegally acquired funds if a Christian. Such funds become the mosque or church's money and they are deposited into the bank account of the mosque or church. At the layering stage, the illegally acquired money is separated from its source by layers of financial transaction and so its source is concealed. The integration phase is where the money donated for religious purposes is used on what appears to be normal business transactions, as the wealth re-enters into the economy to create the perception of legitimacy.

In a study, Kingston (2011), submitted "*the establishment of multiple branches of the same church enabling each branch to operate a separate bank account in various banks facilitates the splitting of huge criminal assets into small units for easier concealment by the churches and private educational institutions*." Kingston (2011) further exposed different methods adopted by churches to involve themselves in money laundering activities. Such include churches appointing several individuals as pastors and splitting large sizes of their illicit assets to smaller units by encouraging breaking away to establish new independent churches to conceal the assets in banks and other financial institutions. He further submitted that some church officials were actively involved in such criminal activities as rape, extortion, false miracle, sodomy, drug trafficking, and large-scale fraud. He did not however disclose instances of these acts in this study. In the same vein, Essien (2018) identified various schemes of exploitation introduced by some prosperity gospel pastors to retrieve money from their clients. Such include charging counseling fees and selling different items to build the faith of the people unto materialism. This is also the submission of Abioje (2017) that many 'prophets' had been accused of immorality, fraud, and ritual murder, while many of them advertised themselves as miracle workers to exhort money from the people.

EFFECTS OF FINANCIAL CORRUPTION AND MONEY LAUNDERING ON RELIGIO-SPIRITUAL LIVES OF NIGERIANS

The effects of money laundering on the spiritual and religious lives of Nigeria are enormous. These are captured in the following sub-headings:

Commercialization of Religion

One of the implications of money laundering and financial corruption is that it leads to the commercialization of religion. Religion, which is supposed to guide the thoughts of men, now becomes a means through which one can become rich quickly. People flock to places of worship not because they love God but to seek spiritual assistance for prosperity. In a study carried out by Muhammed *et al.* (2018), the majority of the respondents confessed that the reason for their attendance of places of worship especially Prayer Mountain was the quest for materialism. Apart from this, those who are rich look towards places of worship to cleanse their wealth by donating generously to the worship centers thinking such can make their ill-gotten wealth clean.

Religious leaders too use the opportunity to enrich themselves through different means. The case is no better than the papal age when the church became extremely powerful both in spiritual and political matters that it became wealthy and also corrupt to the point of selling indulgences indiscriminately. The sale of indulgences multiplied to the extent that those who committed grave sins were asked to do penance and were thereafter assured of the forgiveness of the sins committed. In case the sinner could not do the penance, he monetized it instead of penance by paying the church a certain amount and this became a new source of generating funds for the church. It got to a point when the Pope intended to build St. Peter's church in Rome, he had to send to all Christian countries to sell indulgences to raise money for the proposed church project (Adetoro, 1980: 135). The consequence of commercialization of religion is aptly given by Apenda (2006: 132) when he writes:

The proliferating, commercial church parade fake prophets, fake healers, left-over spiritualists, façade harlot pastors, and all sorts of beamlike evangelists who are mushrooming on the country's religious landscape. They sell candles, oils, soaps, and sponges to their helpless clients at inflated prices after 'blessing' them. These pseudo spiritualists, hollow religionists, and pseudo churches have transformed religion into a multi-millionaire business.

Furthermore, many of the money launderers have influenced the so-called men of God that they could not tell them the truth so as not to lose them. Such launderers donate generously, give out cars as a donation to the men of God and so the nation's looters, robbers, thieves, and corrupt public officials become partners in the work of God participating in form of donating their ill-gotten wealth to numerous projects going on in churches and mosques.

Insincerity of Some Religious Agents

Despite the teaching of Islam on trust *(Amanah)*, the spirit of materialism via corruption has undermined this all-important virtue to the extent that there are cases of financial mismanagement in places of worship and religious organizations. Some individuals who served as agents of some international charitable bodies and were charged with the responsibility of executing some projects have been found guilty of financial mismanagement. The submission of Adebayo (2016) that some Muslim leaders get financial assistance from charity organizations is relevant here. Such leaders used the opportunity to enrich themselves by not rendering the expected charitable assignment given to them. According to him, the spirit of materialism had driven such people to sacrifice their spiritual conscience and to forget their accountability to man and to God their creator, to collect from a sponsor without executing any project. He gave instances where money sent for constructing mosques was diverted, and those in charge only sent fake pictures of already completed mosques elsewhere to the sponsors abroad, giving a false impression that they had carried out the assignment.

Syncretic and Magical Use of the Scripture for Money Rituals

To find a spiritual solution to their financial problems, some Muslim clerics engage in manipulating the *Qur'an* to achieve their magical practices for money rituals. Adetona and Raji (2016), while analyzing how Muslim clerics misuse the *Qur'an* for spiritual moneymaking purposes, write with particular reference to Surat Yasin wrote:

For accumulation of wealth, Sūratu Yāsīn is written ninety-nine (99) times, ground bone of a dead person among other items are mixed with the written portion, and then mixed with black soap for bathing. It is also written three (3) times on a black wooden slate and washed with water. The liquid content with other ingredients added is used to seek sustenance (ar-Rizq). Similarly, the whole of the Sūrah is written nine (9) times and washed with schnapps in addition to other ingredients to amass wealth.

The precious time that could have been used to engage in meaningful commercial transactions and other profitable ventures is used to write a long chapter of the *Qur'an* severally. One wonders the number of hours it would take to write *Suratu Yasin* ninety-nine times and the number of the person that would be engaged to write the same to save time. In the same vein, the ingredients popularly called *Gaari tira*[5] in Yorubaland to be ground and mixed with the written liquid is another amazing thing for a Muslim who believes in the sacredness of human life and body whether living or dead. One also doubts the state of *Iman* of the person who uses the concoction if efficacious. Will he believe that it is the work of Allah that he becomes rich or the work of the cleric who did it for him? What becomes of the verses of the *Qur'an* written and washed with liquors like schnapps all in the name of amassing wealth?

Rise of Fake Clerics/ Prophets Specialized in Money Rituals

Because people are so desperate to become rich, they resort to rituals of all kinds to make ends meet. There are instances where even human beings were said to have been buried in places of worship to attract more congregation. Some so-called men of God engage in illicit affairs just to get money. The spirit of materialism has driven some into desperation resulting in unimaginable acts like murdering human beings for money rituals, rape, and all sorts of evil acts. Some instances can be cited to illustrate this. There is the case of a 42-year-old self-acclaimed pastor, Segun Philip, who was arrested by the Ogun State Police Command for allegedly killing a final year Sociology student at the Lagos State University, Favour Daley-Oladele, for money ritual. The woman was said to have left her home to visit her boyfriend named Adeeko Owolabi, not knowing that she was going to a land of no return. Her boyfriend lured her to Ikoyi-Ile, a town in Osun State where he had perfected plans with the self-acclaimed pastor to kill her for a moneymaking ritual (Kayode-Adedeji, 2019). In an exclusive interview with *Punch Metro*, the self-acclaimed pastor of the Cherubim and Seraphim Church claimed to have collected a sum of N210,000 (not up to US$550); removed her breasts, heart, and other vital organs from her body, to prepare a concoction for his clients[6].

There was also the confession of a suspect, Ikechukwu Friday that a pastor asked him to kill a young girl and get her feces with the promise of paying him N100,000 for the assignment[7]. Another pastor and his wife, Benjamin and Patience Ojobu were also arrested in Benin City for allegedly using human heads to prepare prosperity rituals for church members[8].

There was also the case of one 65-year-old pastor, Festus Adebayo, who conspired with a 24-year-old boy, Gbemisola Olufusi to collect the menstrual pad of his girlfriend to use it for rituals (Afolabi, 2020). Also, there was a Pastor, Sunday Egbo, the founder of the Christ Mercy Ministry, Ajuona Obukpa in Nsukka Local Government Area of Enugu State, who on November 9, 2019, invited a female member of his church to a crusade, and asked her to bring the picture of her sick brother for deliverance prayers. On arrival, he locked her up and forcefully raped her. He also seized her pants, brassiere, and attempted to insert a small bottle in her private parts before the girl managed to escape naked to the door and shouted. The neighbors came to her rescue and got the pastor arrested by the police. He later confessed to the police that in his quest to become a millionaire, he contacted a native doctor who gave him a small coffin and other items and some other instructions. However, luck ran against him, as he could not successfully carry out the instruction to the letter (Ede, 2019).

Another example is that of two Muslim clerics (alfa) - Owolabi Salaudeen and Usman Saliu, who were arrested with a fresh human skull on 23 July 2014. Another instance is that of one *alfa* Alaba Isiaka who was at large when his name was mentioned with one Gabriel Josaya aka Eli- Wakuku, the prophet and founder of St. Moses Orimolade Cherubim and Seraphim Church, Osere area, Ilorin. He was caught selling human skulls in Kwara State (Ogbeche, 2016). It is alien that Muslims should make use of the human part for healing purposes. However, the involvement of Muslims in the preparation of medicinal concoction, amulets, and charms, make some of them become acquainted with such practice.

Furthermore, the case of one Alfa Gani in Laduba community, Ilorin was reported who was allegedly caught with the placenta of a baby as well as some human parts. Another Islamic cleric, Babatunde Suleiman of Oloje area, Ilorin was also arrested in August 2017 for allegedly having a human head, two legs, and two hands. He was said to have exhumed the corpse of his friend for money ritual purposes (Young, 2017).

As if the above is not enough, another Muslim cleric, Abdulfatai Kayode was arrested by the Lagos State Police Command for having female private parts, a kidney, intestines, a heart, lap, and other human parts. The man was said to have confessed that he collected the human parts from an herbalist named Sadiq to use for money rituals for a client (Bakare, 2018). To crown this, the Nigerian Police in Ilorin Kwara State paraded on October 17, 2018, some suspects involved in kidnapping, murder, ritual killings, exhuming of dead bodies, and removing their vital body parts for money ritual and spiritual powers. The suspects confessed that they had sold thirty-one human heads to some personalities in Ilorin and other towns in the State. Most of these suspects bore Muslim names[9].

MONEY LAUNDERING AND TERRORISM FINANCING: IMPLICATION FOR ISLAM IN NIGERIA

The September 11, 2001, terrorist attack on the United States of America re-awakened money laundering and terrorism financing among the committee of nations, hence numerous anti-money laundering laws are put in place to address the situation and these have serious consequences on Islam and Muslims generally. The incident halted the activities of some foreign Islamic organizations in Nigeria as many of them were suspected and labeled as sponsors of terror. The International Islamic Relief Organization (IIRO) suffered a lot in this aspect because Steven Emerson at the National Commission of Terrorist Attacks upon the United States listed it amongst the major Islamic organizations fueling Islamic militancy around the world.

One Abdul Al-Hamid Sulaiman Al-Mujil was accused of being a member of *al-Qaeda* and a local terrorist group, the *Jemaah Islamiyah*. Many of its employees were thereafter imprisoned, while the United States forced some branches of the IIRO to close down.

The Haramain Islamic Foundation was also forced by the United States to fold up, as it impounded and froze the Foundation's assets in February 2004 for an unsubstantiated allegation of sponsoring terrorism. In Nigeria, the Haramain was listed as one of the Islamic organizations harboring terrorists and this made the Oyo State Government order its immediate closure. Although the organization was exonerated at the court of law, the image of the organization had been dented beyond repair to sustain its continuity in Nigeria. The International Institute of Islamic Thought (IIIT)'s headquarters in the United States, which was also attacked soon after the September 11 attack on the US, affected the Nigeria office of the Institute. The annual subvention from the headquarters of the organization was stopped and so it experienced serious setbacks in her programs, which are mainly educational.

From all indications, the US determines who terrorist groups are. It declares a group a terrorist by its yardstick. The Hezbollah and to a lesser extent to Amal were declared terrorist organizations in the US and several other countries. As such, financing the activities of these groups would therefore tantamount to sponsoring criminality and terrorism under the garb of legitimate charitable donations. The involvement of the Côte d'Ivoire branch of Hezbollah in the diamond trade and cocoa industry and other legitimate transactions linked to the group were blocked by the US for fear that profits from the trade could be used to finance terrorism. Besides, charitable donations to this body were blocked for fear that the body may use such donations made by members of this community for anything else.

Apart from the above, the United States of America under the pretext of curbing financing terrorism through money laundering blacklisted the Islamic banking and financial institutions of harboring money launderers to finance terrorism. The US State Department advanced three reasons why many of the Islamic banks are suspicious of harboring and sponsoring terrorism. Firstly, a wide range of anti-money laundering regulations and controls normally imposed on secular commercial banks do not apply to the Islamic banks; and secondly, the Islamic banks do not undergo the regulatory or supervisory scrutiny by bank regulators through periodic bank examinations or inspections as applicable to the secular banks. Lastly, there is no control mechanism to assure compliance or the implementation of updated anti-money laundering policies.

The above reasons have been considered weak, unfounded, and mere blanket allegations with no concrete evidence to support them. Nasir (2018), debunked these allegations citing Malaysia as a country where Islamic banking and institutions thrive, and it is generally acknowledged to have a robust policy framework for

Anti-Money Laundering Law (AML) and have a strong political commitment and well-functioning coordination structures for Anti-Money Laundering Laws and Combating Financing Terrorism (AML/CFT). He also considered the astronomical rate at which Islamic banking institutions are spreading to more than 50 countries of the world with estimated assets of more than US$1.4 trillion globally as of 2018 as another point to debunk the allegation. Nasir further considered the participatory nature of the Islamic banking system as a quick means of knowing how funds were utilized to display the transparent nature of the system to guard against money laundering. To him, deficiencies in the strategic AML/CFT are more common in countries like Ecuador, Ethiopia, Kenya, Myanmar, Vietnam, Tanzania, Indonesia, Pakistan, Syria, and many others, than in countries like Malaysia, Brunei, and the United Kingdom, and other countries that embraced Islamic banking system. He substantiated this by emphasizing that none of the Islamic banks or other Islamic financial institutions had been sanctioned for non-compliance with AML related issues in the UK unlike other conventional institutions there.

In addition to the above, Adebayo and Hassan (2013) has a list of some regulating bodies set up to see the activities and ethical values of Islamic banking and financial institutions. Popular among them is the Accounting and Auditing Organization for Islamic Financial Institutions (AAOIFI) which was set up in 1990 to standardize the governance of every Islamic business product and service. It is a body working tirelessly to enhance the transparency of financial statements through the constant publication of accounting, auditing, and governance standards for Islamic financial institutions (Rafay, Sadiq & Ajmal, 2017). There is also the Islamic Financial Services Board, which is an international standard-setting organization established in Kuala Lumpur, Malaysia in 2002 to promote and enhance the soundness and stability of the Islamic financial services industry. The International Islamic Financial Market (IIFM) is another non-profit global market standard-setting body of the Islamic Financial Services Industry (IFSI) established by the collective efforts of the Central banks of Bahrain, Indonesia, Sudan, Labuan Offshore Financial Services Authority (Malaysia), Islamic Development Bank, and Ministry of Finance Brunei Darussalam. All these agencies are put in place to ensure full compliance of Islamic banks and financial institutions with the teachings of Islam and the *maqasid ash-shari'ah* (Rafay & Farid, 2017) and so could not harbor terrorists.

The above notwithstanding, there is every likelihood that the assumption that Islamic financial institutions harbor terrorism has its toll on private charities embarked upon by organizations and individual donors, as they were denied the opportunity to extend their hands of generosity to the less-privileged ones in their communities and beyond. Even, the institution of *zakat*, which is meant to take care of the less privileged ones in the society, becomes restricted. This is because those who used to send out excesses of their *zakat* to other countries for distribution could no longer do so (Adebayo, 2020). The spirit of unity and goodwill inherent in the institutions of *zakat, sadaqah*, and *waqf* could no longer be demonstrated consequent upon different policies put in place by the US and its allies all in the name of curbing money laundering.

It suffices to mention the activities of some of these organizations in Nigeria, which had been ended consequent upon the September 11 attack on the US. The International Islamic Relief Organisation (IIRO), which is an affiliate of the Muslim World League (MWL), established a clinic in Jalingo, Taraba State in Nigeria; mosques in Ifon and Ibadan; and Arabic schools in Ibadan, Ilorin, and Kaduna. It also sunk wells in some places in Lagos, Ibadan, and Ilorin, to ease the challenges of shortage of drinkable water in the areas. In the same vein, Al-Haramain Islamic Foundation (HIF), a charitable body with its headquarters in Riyadh, Saudi Arabia with Nigeria office in Ibadan established mosques in towns and villages in Ibadan, Oyo, Iwo, Ogbomoso. It made donations to orphanage and rehabilitation centers; paid hospital bills for patients who could not afford payment; and established a vocational center in Ibadan where women particularly orphans and widows learned tailoring, weaving, soap-making, and other vocations. All these projects were abruptly suspended when the organization became moribund consequent upon its stigmatization and anti-laundering policies (Adebayo, 2016).

CONCLUSION

This chapter has delved into the influence of financial corruption and money laundering activities on the religious and spiritual lives of Nigerians. It submitted that money laundering has nothing to do with religion, as religion moderates the economic and financial activities of its adherents. Meanwhile, the wide gap between the rich and the poor has tempted some people to manipulate religion for unlawful acquisition of money and use of evil spirituality to become rich through magic or other evil means not minding the stand of their religion on such acts. As such, some stakeholders in religions have involved themselves in the nefarious acts of ritual killings and money laundering, consciously, or unconsciously. This made us conclude that there is a close relationship between religion and spirituality and that religion is a component of spirituality, but in some senses, spirituality may not be religiosity.

Some anti-money laundering policies are harmful to religion, particularly Islam. This is because such policies deny the well-to-do to carry out their humanitarian services to the less-privileged ones; some religious organizations were tagged sponsors of terrorists and so were discouraged from assisting others.

There is no doubt that money laundering is a global problem that demands global solutions. Non-consideration of some stakeholders in this could therefore be considered as being sentimental. To have a wholesome solution to the problem of financial corruption and money laundering, therefore, the bull has to be taken by the horn in form of going to the drawing board to address the nature of education adopted by Nigeria. For Nigeria to have a positive response to corruption and money laundering therefore, we recommend a thorough overhauling of the education system, which does not recognize God in its policies and contents. Men of God should as well desist from materialism and preach the real words of God for salvation in this world and the hereafter. Those in authority should declare their assets, and as well account for the sources of their wealth and properties. The wide gap between the leaders and the led should be bridged so that those who are not in the corridor of power would not be tempted to adopt evil spirituality to get quick money. Lastly, clerics of different religions should take note of their sayings and deeds so that they do not soil their religion in their attempt to satisfy their worldly desires.

DISCLAIMER

The contents and views of this chapter are expressed by the author in his personal capacity. It is not necessary for the Editor and the Publisher to agree with these viewpoints and they are not responsible for any duty of care in this regard.

ACKNOWLEDGMENT

The author extends sincere gratitude to:

- The Editor-in-Chief and International Editorial Advisory Board (IEAB) of this book who initially desk reviewed, arranged a rigorous double/triple blind review process and conducted a thorough, minute and critical final review before accepting the chapter for publication.
- All anonymous reviewers who provided very constructive feedbacks for thorough revision, improvement, extension and finetuning of the chapter.
- All colleagues, assistants and well-wishers who assisted the author to complete this task.

REFERENCES

Abioje, P. O. (2017). Christian prophets and other prophets in Nigeria. The 167th Inaugural Lecture, University of Ilorin.

Adebayo, R. I. (2016). Dividends of international Islamic organisations in Nigeria. In Y. A. Quadri, R. W. Omotoye, & R. I. Adebayo (Eds.), *Religion in Contemporary Nigeria* (pp. 241–267). Adonis & Abbey Publishers Ltd.

Adebayo, R. I. (2017). *Qur'an*otherapy and the Quest for Islamisation of Yorubaland, Nigeria. In S. D. Mills (Ed.), *Religion: past, present and future perspectives* (pp. 27–61). Nova Science Publishers.

Adebayo, R. I. (2018). Muslim involvement in *Ori-Oke* prayers in Nigeria. In S. N. Yaovi, P. U. Nwosu, A. G. Alamu, L. E. Odeh, & A. Y. Mohammed (Eds.), *Ori-Oke spirituality and social change in Africa: Contemporary perspectives* (pp. 21–44). Langaa Research & Publishing Common Initiative Group. doi:10.2307/j.ctvh9vtpk.6

Adebayo, R. I. (2020). Zakat Distribution in the Context of Shari'ah Corporate Governance: Evidence from South-Western Nigeria. In A. Rafay (Ed.), *Handbook of Research on Theory and Practice of Global Islamic Finance* (pp. 161–178). IGI Global.

Adebayo, R. I., & Hassan, M. K. (2013). Ethical principles of Islamic financial institutions. *Journal of Economic Cooperation & Development, 34*(2), 63–90.

Adetona, L. M., & Raji, M. O. (2016). A study of the misuse of Sūratu Yāsīn among Yoruba Muslims. *Ilorin Journal of Religious Studies, 6*(1), 1–15.

Adetoro, J. E. (1980). *History of West Africa, Bk 2*. African University Press.

Afolabi, A. (2020, August 14). Boyfriend, pastor nabbed for allegedly using apostle's daughter for ritual in Ondo. *The Guardian*. Retrieved from https://guardian.ng/news/boyfriend-pastor-nabbed-for-allegedly-using-apostles-daughter-for-ritual-in-ondo/

Agazue, C. (2016). He told me that my waist and private parts have been ravaged by demons:" sexual exploitation of female church members by "prophets" in Nigeria. *Dignity: A Journal on Sexual Exploitation and Violence, 1*(1). Retrieved from https://digitalcommons.uri.edu/dignity/vol1/iss1/10

Al Agha, S. (2007). Money laundering from Islamic perspective. *Journal of Money Laundering Control, 10*(4), 406–411. doi:10.1108/13685200710830899

Al-Ghazaali, M. (1998). Al-Mankhul min ta'liqat al-'Usul (a book on usul al-fiqh). Dar al-Fikr.

Apenda, A. Z. (2006). Spirituality or materialism: The dilemma of contemporary church in Nigeria. In M.T. Yahya, A.P. Dopamu, R.A. Raji, E.A. Odumuyiwa, D. Shishima, S.A. Owoeye & P.O. Abioje (Eds.), Issues in the Practice of Religion in Nigeria (pp. 125-139). Nigeria Association for the Study of Religions (NASR).

Bakare, Y. (2018). Police arrest Muslim cleric with human parts in Lagos. *Vanguard*. Retrieved from https://www.vanguardngr.com/2018/01/breaking-police-arrest-muslim-cleric-human-parts/

Chironda, M. (2017, September 29). Nigeria: How Much Did Former Oil Minister 'Steal'? *allAfrica Blog*. Retrieved from https://allafrica.com/stories/201709290489.html

Dopamu, A.P. (2009). *In the Service of Humanity*. A Farewell Lecture, University of Ilorin, Ilorin.

Ede, R. E. (2019, November 20). Police parade Enugu pastor for rape, money ritual. *Punch*. Retrieved from https://punchng.com/police-parade-enugu-pastor-for-rape-money-rituals/

Enofe, A. O., Aliu, A. K., & Ombu, A. (2018). Money laundering and the Nigerian Economy. *International Journal of Advanced Academic Research*, *4*(4), 185–210.

Essien, D. E. (2018). Ethical audit of prosperity gospel: Psychological manipulation or social ministry. *International Journal of Knowledge-Based Organizations*, *8*(2), 53–64. doi:10.4018/IJKBO.2018040105

GIABA. (2010). *Threat Assessment of Money Laundering and Terrorist Financing in West Africa*. Inter-Governmental action group against money laundering in West Africa. Retrieved from www.GIABA.org

Kayode-Adedeji, D. (2019, December 29). Man takes girlfriend to 'pastor' for money ritual where she's beheaded – Police. *Premium Times*. Retrieved from https://www.premiumtimesng.com/news/more-news/370259-man-takes-girlfriend-to-pastor-for-money-ritual-where-shes-beheaded-police.html

Kingston, K. G. (2011). Churches and private educational institutions as facilitator of money laundering in Nigeria. *African Journal of Education and Technology*, *1*(1), 30–38.

Muhammed, A. Y., Sulaiman, L. A., Raji, A., & Oluyemi, J. (2018). Materialism or Paradise: A Psycho-Spiritual Inquiry into Why People go to Prayer Mountains in South-West Nigeria. In S. N. Yaovi, P. U. Nwosu, A. G. Alamu, L. E. Odeh, & A. Y. Mohammed (Eds.), *Ori-Oke spirituality and social change in Africa: Contemporary perspectives* (pp. 45–60). Langaa Research & Publishing Common Initiative Group. doi:10.2307/j.ctvh9vtpk.7

Mutahheri, A. M. (1977). *Islam, man and universe*. The Islamic Seminary.

Nasir, M. A. (2018). Compatibility of Islamic finance and anti-money laundering laws: A myth or reality? *IIUM Law Journal*, *26*(1), 55–78. doi:10.31436/iiumlj.v26i1.344

Nasir, M. A. (2020). The Relevance of Maqasid al Shari'ah to Anti-Money Laundering and Terrorism Financing. In A. Rafay (Ed.), *Handbook of Research on Theory and Practice of Global Islamic Finance* (pp. 179–194). IGI Global. doi:10.4018/978-1-7998-0218-1.ch010

Obiora, C. O., & Olugbuo, B. C. (2011). The economic and financial crimes commission and the accountability of corrupt foreign actors in Nigeria. *The Law and Development Review*, *4*(3), 2–26.

Ogbeche, D. (2016, March 18). Kwara takes over prosecution of prophet alfa who visit cemetery for human heads. *Daily Post*. Retrieved from https://dailypost.ng/2016/03/18/kwara-takes-over-prosecution-of-prophet-alfa-who-visit-cementary-for-human-heads/

Ogbodo, U. K., & Mieseigha, E. G. (2013). The economic implications of money laundering in Nigeria. *International Journal of Academic Research in Accounting. Finance and Management Sciences*, *3*(4), 170–184.

Okoye, E. I., & Gbegi, D. O. (2013). Forensic accounting: A tool for fraud detection and prevention in the public sector. (A study of selected ministries in Kogi State). *International Journal of Academic Research in Business & Social Sciences*, *3*(3), 1–19.

Owoyemi, M. Y. (2016). The obsession of Nigerians with miracles in the Islamic and Christian religions. In Y. A. Quadri, R. W. Omotoye, & R. I. Adebayo (Eds.), *Religion in contemporary Nigeria* (pp. 297–322). Adonis & Abbey Publishers.

Rafay, A., & Farid, S. (2017). Maqasid-al-Shari'ah vs. Contemporary Islamic Banking and Finance: The Case of Pakistan. *Journal of Islamic Thought and Civilization*, *7*(2), 41–51. doi:10.29145/2017/jitc/72/070203

Rafay, A., Sadiq, R., & Ajmal, M. M. (2017). Uniform Framework for Sukuk-Al-Ijara – A proposed model for all madhahib. *Journal of Islamic Accounting and Business Research*, *8*(4), 420–454. doi:10.1108/JIABR-09-2015-0042

Sarwar, G. (1996). Islamic Education: its meaning, problems and prospects. In Issues in Islamic education. The Muslim Education Trust.

Urama, N. E., Ekeocha, Q., & Iloh, E. C. (2018). *Nigeria's debt burden: implications for human development* (AfriHeritage Policy Brief No 20). Enugu: African Heritage Institution. Retrieved from https://media.africaportal.org/documents/Nigerias_debt_burden.pdf

Young. (2017, August 18). Islamic Cleric Caught With Human Parts in Ilorin. *Information Nigeria*. Retrieved from https://www.informationng.com/2017/08/islamic-cleric-caught-human-parts-ilorin.html

ENDNOTES

1 https://www.nairaland.com/979808/money-not-problem-how-spend

2 https://tradingeconomics.com/nigeria/corruption-rank

3 https://www.premiumtimesng.com/news/headlines/404652

4 *Asalatu* groups are common among the Muslim youth in the southwestern part of Nigeria. They are organized prayer groups who meet every Sunday to offer special supplications and prayer sessions for members. They also organize occasional *tahajjud* (night vigil) in Ramadan.

5 *Gaari tira* are those additional items added to the verses or chapters of the *Qur'an* written on black slate, washed, and given to the client to either drink or bathe. It can be in form of the root of a particular tree, a ground part of an animal, or other items.

6 https://punchng.com

7 https://www.nairaland.com/1585926/pastor-sign-fireman-arrested-ritual

8 https://allafrica.com/stories/200806020944

9 https://www.vanguardngr.com/2018/10/

Chapter 3
Money Laundering in Real Estate (RE):
The Case of Canada

Mark Lokanan
Royal Roads University, Canada

Gaurav Chopra
Royal Roads University, Canada

ABSTRACT

Money laundering is a defiance of law and order within the real estate (RE) sector in Canada. Laundering of illicit funds impacts the stability, reliability, and integrity of the government, financial institutions, and the economic sectors. Due to its mysterious nature, there are more unknowns about the quantum of snow washing in the property market or its effects on price inflation. Using data from the Cullen Commission about money laundering in Canada, this chapter is an effort to examine the nuances that law enforcement encounters while investigating illegal investment operations. This chapter illuminates a broad range of problems around the investigations of unlawful investments and recommends pragmatic solutions to the illicit flow of money in RE sector of Canada.

1. INTRODUCTION

Canadian Real Estate (RE) has been grasped by the spreading roots of Money Laundering, a peril to the safety and security of Canadian society. Money Laundering is a systematic practice by criminals that helps them obscures the source of unlawful

DOI: 10.4018/978-1-7998-8758-4.ch003

proceeds, to brand them as earnings created through a legitimate source (Schneider, 2020a, 2020b; Wakefield, 2019). Such actions aim at amassing coffers from illegitimate sources and enshrouding their purpose to support unlawful activities in the society like terrorist funding, causing destruction and loss of life (Department of Finance Canada, 2018). Money Laundering objectives may differ from the objectives of terrorist financing; however, they exploit similar flaws in the system to wash illegitimate money through the property business (OAS-CICTE, 2015).

Crooks aggressively look for resources in the property market that allows them to uphold their inconspicuousness; often via lax government regulations that pave the way for such criminality (CBC, 2018; Cuellar, 2003). A bubble is fashioned in the property market in such a way that asset rates get inflated, leaving a throbbing dent on the rest of the economy (Schneider, 2004a). The RE luxury segment is a prevalent zone to excavate hoarded investments, especially in several metropolises in Canada that have been a witness to the distortion of property prices because of the incursion of laundered money (Hudak, 2017).

High asset rates in this industry are top priority of criminals buying RE assets and has a bearing effect on the broader RE sector, due to which widespread inflation of property has an unsound level of indebtedness on the property industry (Eurostat, 2017). Extravagant housing prices wear away affordable housing for the masses which is caused by Money Laundering (Lochead & Dhanraj, 2019). Such a scenario will potentially upset the overall economy if the unlawfully obtained money continues to circulate in the market (McDowell & Novis, 2001).

This chapter approaches and evaluates the recognized problem through primary and secondary research that includes interviews, journals, scholarly articles and non-academic literature sources. The research findings form the basis for an analysis of the problem and suggested recommendations for the issues identified. Finally, an implementation plan, is suggested to aid the accomplishment of the recommendations.

2. LITERATURE REVIEW

2.1 Attention Towards Money Laundering

Money Laundering has illegal economic effects and chips into abetting and perpetuating criminal activities. The laundered money subdues quality of life and oppresses the steadiness of an economy by corroding its various industries like the property sector (Maloney *et al.*, 2019). It typically gets transformed to merchandise or assets in RE, laundered through dummy companies, moved overseas, or placed in the name of a relative (Miralis, 2018). The never-ending permutations involved makes it troublesome to understand Money Laundering and allows the criminals to obscure their origins and clean the criminal stain off them (Hernandez, 2019).

Money Laundering has had consequentially long-lasting effects on all stakeholders and will repeatedly leave an appalling impression on the lives of Canadians (Eurostat, 2017). IMF has pointed out that actions against Money Laundering proceedings not just addresses the economic need but is a moral imperative (IMF, 2016). Money launderers take undue advantage of the intricacies immanent in the financial systems and authorities with weak governance are more likely to attract such criminals (IMF, 2016). Money Laundering is proving to be a serious challenge to preserve law and order within nations, as markets get distorted due to the influx of kleptocratic proceeds in Canada (D'Antuono, 2018).

The strategies to combat Money Laundering across borders remain back in the Stone Age even while dirty money gets washed across national boundaries at lights speed (WSJ, 1997). Driven by the event of globalization and monetary liberalization, whole world experiences the threat of dishonest money being piled more than ever before (Expert Panel on Emerging Crime, 2005). Sophisticated financial technology (FinTech) is also playing a role in it (Rafay, 2019) Introducing and acquainting compelling regimes to overcome these threats is vital to protect the financial system, the integrity of industries like RE and the broader society itself as Anti-Money Laundering (AML) policies would act as a deterrent to financial crimes.

While this problem has received attention in British Columbia (BC), a westernmost province in Canada, between the Pacific Ocean and the Rocky Mountains. However, Money Laundering is a national concern and necessitates criminal justice and regulatory retort from all jurisdictions (Hernandez, 2019). The high-risk sectors identified by regulatory bodies like FATF should receive more attention from authorities in Canada (Comply Advantage, 2020). Therefore, dirty money appears be clear threat to industries in Canada and presents several good reasons to attract immediate attention towards the criminals who are laundering money (Verver, 2017).

2.2 Tempting Factors for Criminals

Property market is an appealing segment to criminals. It is susceptible to Money Laundering exercises due to its sheer size as there are approximately 20,784 RE agents, developers and other intermediaries that offer products and services consisting of monetary dealings that can be susceptible to unlawful activities (Department of Finance, 2015). This industry has been growing exponentially in Canada over the years and is a significant contributor to the GDP (Mordor, 2021). Other snow washing attracting factors are lack of ownership transparency as information about beneficial owners are not kept by Canadian land title offices, dearth in AML compliance from RE professionals and sloppy enforcement of AML laws on caught criminals (Ross, 2017).

RE is vulnerable to criminals due to internal and external factors of the industry which makes it a pulling force for launderers. In a report by Organization for Economic Co-operation and Development (OECD) in 2007 on fraud vulnerabilities concerning the RE sector, the most attractive factors for launderers are:

- RE investments are considered safe investments, with rising property prices;
- Problems in identifying the real beneficial owners of complex company structures;
- Fronting through the use of nominees and acquisitions across international borders;
- High revenues involved in RE and series of rapid transactions;
- Use of large cash amounts and banking information inaccessibility for administration;
- Abuse of notaries and mortgages frauds;
- The role of intermediaries like RE agents and others as potential key enablers;

The property sector in Canada also frequently witnesses mounting prices and the anti-corruption group has highlighted that these highly priced RE properties are used by criminals to launder money (Lee-Shanok, 2019).

Criminals can easily misuse the appealing diversity within the Canadian RE industry. Within the high number of diversely scale transactions in property market, the genuine commercial and residential transactions can easily camouflage the Money Laundering transactions, which creates the opportunity for offenders to exercise their criminal abilities due to the potential to combine both genuine and ill-conceived funds in this line (FATF, 2007). Also, the factors like obsolete laws and guidelines regarding RE along with lack of enforcement of the rules makes it convenient for money launderers to anonymously finance dirty money in property deals (Scrinko, 2018). The literature review revealed many attracting factors and it became vital to understand the basic methods and techniques that money launderers employ to further their infamous interests in RE.

2.3 Nitty-Gritty of Money Laundering

Snow washing in RE is carried out in multiple phases. According to MREA (2014), there are essentially three recognized steps in the process of Money Laundering and all of them can be applied to RE transactions. The stages entailing the Money Laundering process are placement, layering, integration and extraction or repatriation (Cullen Commission, 2020a; Chen & Anderson, 2020; ABC Solutions, 2021)

Firstly, placement phase for the launderers consists of inducing dirty money into a financial system or other legit institution through movement of funds unswervingly connected with a crime (European Parliament, 2019). Money launderers give the dirty money to an agent in a RE institution to buy a property so as to place the illegitimately obtained money into the construction of RE. This phase is also regarded as susceptible stage for criminals because currency bills are substantially heavy, and it becomes tough to obscure and transfer large amounts (ABC Solutions, 2021). After placement is accomplished, the next phase of snow washing is layering which involves steering a chain of financial dealings quickly through different bank accounts to hide the origins of the ill-gotten funds via its breakup into smaller transactions (Cullen Commission, 2020g). The most commonly used medium of layering is wire transferring the funds from other jurisdictions or institutions, investments into genuine businesses and other RE, transferring cash to traveller checks or other monetary instruments (Akyay, 2001; Cullen Commission, 2020h; ACAMS, 2007). For layering phase in RE, the launderers could introduce the involvement of shell companies, straw buyers or nominees to falsely illustrate change of beneficial ownership or even try a technique like borrowing a loan in one jurisdiction and repaying it in another (Maloney *et al.*, 2019). For assistance with RE foreign schemes, intermediaries, inclusive of lawyers, knowingly or not, may be used as channels to succeed (German, 2018).

The third step is integration, which is specifically central to the idea of snow washing in RE sector. Integration stage comes into play when, in order to cement the authenticity of the criminal funds, transactions are merged into the legitimate economy so that they literally embed themselves with the legitimate economy (Cullen Commission, 2020a). During this stage, the ill-gotten funds turn back into the economy as authentic payment is received from RE property sold to a bona fide buyer through an intermediary (Start KYC Limited, 2019). Therefore, the illicit funds become indistinguishable with all the other properties in the industry by merging with the legitimate economic and financial system (Arnone & Borlini, 2010).

There is another step of extraction or repatriation of funds, also a part of integration phase. Principally, this stage of Money Laundering takes place when criminal gets the money back in his hands to enjoy it (Cullen Commission, 2020a). The role of shell companies again comes into picture as criminals show the claim of proceeds from a legitimate source, allowing the criminals to satisfy the objectives through a common technique (Cullen Commission, 2020a). All these stages may also transpire simultaneously or more likely, may take place at the same time, whereas in other situations the basic steps are often clearly distinct (Arnone & Borlini, 2010). Further, recent reports by experts and media have shed light on the extent of Money Laundering taking place in Canadian RE because of which the economy has to bear ripple effects.

2.4 Instances and Effects on Real Estate

The bearings of Money Laundering are observed today in various forms, eroding trust in one's economy and institutions, affecting business competitiveness, facilitating criminal activities and driving up the cost of commodities in every corner of the world as well as in Canada (McDowell & Novis, 2001). In September 2016, Financial Action Task Force (FATF), the global AML governing body, publicized an appraisal of Canadian execution of AML practices, which brought to light that Canada's RE industry is alarmingly susceptible to Money Laundering (FATF, 2016). The government of Canada arrived at a similar conclusion based on a risk valuation steered in 2015 (Department of Finance Canada, 2015). Also, the exposition of FATF specifically points towards instances of Chinese officers laundering the criminal proceeds via the Canadian property market, particularly in Vancouver (FATF, 2016). Some estimate numbers that give an idea of the situation are given in the following section.

2.4.1 Money Laundering Instances

Felonious buyers and dirty money are widespread in the housing markets of Canada. In 2018, an estimated 7.4 billion dollars were illegally washed in BC and experts found that RE was the recipient of a significant chunk of these investments, projected to the tune of up to 5.3 billion dollars, forming five percent of the entire volume of RE transactions carried out in the province (Cullen Commission, 2020b; Denis & Ball, 2019). Occurrence of Money Laundering in the western province's RE is dated back to 1990's. A Royal Canadian Mounted Police (RCMP) case studied by Schneider (2004b) highlights that in 1996, a property purchased in British Columbia by a nominee was transferred to Alvie Singer who transacted through 450,000 dollars of laundered money. Funds from illegal sources used to purchase properties is a growing concern to the property market in cities across Canada as interests surge swiftly.

Hoffman mentioned that many properties worth 22 million dollars were confiscated in Greater Montreal and Toronto areas on multiple charges including Money Laundering in RE in 17 individual cases (Cullen Commission, 2020b). Reports suggest that in this decade 20 billion dollars entered the property market without oversight on beneficial owners in the steeply rising RE of Greater Toronto area where 1.4 million property transactions were examined (TI Canada, 2019). According to Cohen (2020), many West African nationals who were politically exposed along with government authorities with endemic corruption bought properties to the tune of 30 million dollars in the RE of Montreal (Cullen Commission, 2020c).

The dirty funds in the Canadian RE makes the local hard-working people suffer due to unaffordability of unjust-fully high property prices (Planner, 2019). According to Eby, one of the costliest households in Vancouver was sold significantly above its estimated value by a government fundraiser to a student for 31 million dollars (Olivier, 2016). Money Laundering in RE inflates property prices in B.C. to the tune of 3.7 to 7.5 percent (Cullen Commission, 2020b). It is worth noting the effects that Money Laundering has on the housing affordability in Canada.

2.4.2 Effects on Housing Affordability

Galloway (2019) states that both the liberals and the conservative's in Canada have recognized the role played by shady dealings to have inflated RE prices in cities like Vancouver and Toronto. Recent reports have implied that this problem was enormous in the RE markets of the Prairies region along with Ontario and British Columbia (Galloway, 2019). Large amounts of illegal investments originating from foreign shores zigzagging across the world have the potential to inflate prices in the Canadian housing market and aids the foreign criminals to land on luxury properties in Canada (Reynolds, 2019). Bullough also supports that RE prices get artificially inflated by activities of money launderers, who specifically target major cities in the Western liberal democracies where large amount of dirty money is coming from all around the world because of weak AML laws (Cullen Commission, 2020d). As a result of over the sealing prices of RE in locations across the country, housing affordability for a lot of people has taken a hit.

Substantially varying prices in the property sector are observed across localities in Canada due to extensive Money Laundering practices taking place. The statistics of average housing cost in Canada as 562,000 dollars was reported in housing affordability report of Royal Bank of Canada (RBC), which also highlighted Toronto's average household cost to be 850,000 dollars (Lochead & Dhanraj, 2019). On the other hand, as per the data shared by RPS (2020), average cost of houses in Vancouver, Victoria, Hamilton, Calgary and Montreal is 1,038,300, 798,600, 587,300, 491,200 and 459,200 dollars, respectively. A noteworthy proportion of the skyrocketing in housing prices is linked to dirty money being dumped in the property sector. The Anti-Corruption Digest (2019) mentioned that, "*according to Geordie Dent, existence of more Money Laundering practices in RE has a domino effect on housing prices*". A RE expert panel in BC points towards almost five percent increase in housing costs inflicted as a direct result of more than 7 billion dollars of snow washing in the province itself (BCGN, 2019a; Denis & Ball, 2019).

2.5 Steps Taken to Prevent Money Laundering

Setting the record straight on the responsibilities between federal and provincial governments in Canada, keeping in mind the historical and institutional differences will be key to construct an AML regime (Reuter & Truman, 2004). According to India Wentworth (2018), Rules and regulations have been introduced in the form of Proceeds of Crime Act 2002, Terrorism Act 2000, Criminal Finance Act 2017, Anti-Money Laundering Act 2018, Money Laundering-Terrorist Financing and Transfer of Funds Regulations 2017. As per Financial Transactions and Reports Analysis Centre of Canada (FINTRAC) was formed and head officed in Ottawa as a regulatory body in the year 2000 (Duhaime, 2021). FINTRAC plays a crucial role to combat Money Laundering in Canada by assessing penalties for violations of Acts introduced to prevent Money Laundering and disclosure of suspicious transactions to Canada Revenue Agency (CRA), Canada Border Services Agency (CBSA) and other police forces (Duhaime, 2021). FINTRAC along with another self-regulated agency, the Investment Industry Regulatory Organization of Canada (IIROC), have formed a pact to improve protection against snow washing in the country (IIROC, 2019).

The FATF and the IMF have published many reports over the years, bringing the RE to everyone is notice for being a key medium used to launder the illegally obtained money by criminal organisations and individuals (ESAAMLG, 2013). The governments at all levels in Canada have launched probe into Money Laundering in Canadian RE and formulate policies to overcome this problematic situation. In 2002, Proceeds of Crime and Terrorist Financing Act was introduced, mandating agents to intimate FINTRAC about cash transactions involving a sum of 10,000 dollars or above (FINTRAC, 2019b).

BC is formulating and implementing a long-term regional AML and is the front runner in Canada when it comes to taking decisions to combat Money Laundering in property industry (BCGN, 2019c). In order to tackle housing affordability in British Columbia, the provincial government will be making an investment of seven billion dollars over a period of 10 years along with implementing a 30-point plan to overcome the problem (BCGN, 2019b). This plot by the government revolves around stabilizing the housing market, cracking down on tax fraud and closing loopholes, building more properties, security for renters and supporting partnering associations to build and preserve affordable housing (BC Budget, 2018). According to BCGN (2019a), addressing tax fraud and vulnerabilities, the British Columbian government has followed a housing plan with the following activities to combat illicit capital investments in RE sector:

- Elimination of hidden ownership through public registry of beneficial owners.

- Online register for pre-sale condo sales for crackdown on largescale dealings.
- Amended property transfer tax return has been updated, revealing beneficial owners.
- Established a link for federal-provincial workings on Money Laundering and tax fraud.

Hughes mentions that Land-Owner Transparency Registry, the formation of the Financial Services Authority and bringing the Mortgage Brokers Act under reviewing stage for its replacement are some of the recent steps taken by BC (Cullen Commission, 2020b). Also, establishment of Finance, Real Estate and Data Analytics (FREDA) unit is another step by the government to combat the increasingly vulnerable state of RE sector (Cullen Commission, 2020f). Hughes highlighted that Business Corporations Act was modified in 2019, necessitating private companies in British Columbia to maintain transparency registers from updated with information about true shareholders with accuracy from first May 2020 (Cullen Commission, 2020b). The federal government is looking to make the company beneficial ownership record as a public registry (Cohen, 2020). Also, safeguarding efforts against the misuse of RE, corporations, legal professionals and money service businesses by criminals have been recognized by the authorities and the governments at the federal, provincial and territorial level are working together in this battle against the Money Laundering (Department of Finance Canada, 2019).

3. RESEARCH METHODOLOGY

The word frequencies from the secondary research resources were characterized into themes that indicate key issues related to Money Laundering in property industry. The arising themes from the research, as illustrated in the figure below, were abridged into headers to shed light on the unpredictable aspects of RE Money Laundering. Investigating around these themes formed base for an in-depth understanding of Money Laundering spread within the property sector. The literature review shaped this research journey and helped to design the structure of primary research to explore what the RE stakeholders think about the topic, what is missing from the currently established framework, what needs to be done now and what the future holds for vulnerabilities of Canadian RE.

The selection of research methodology for this chapter was formed based on available information to identify the effects on Canadian RE owing to Money Laundering practices, the causes of Money Laundering in RE and measures taken at different levels in the government to combat dirty money in the property market. The research methodology for this project involved a comprehensive literature

Figure 1. Arising themes
Source: *Author*

review as part of secondary research, and primary research encompassing expert interviews. The literature review was drawn from both academic and non-academic sources which offered critical context and needed to analyze the research problem.

3.1 Secondary Research

3.1.1 Data Sources

The leading source of data for the secondary research of this chapter were the transcripts from the commission of inquiry into the Money Laundering in British Columbia. Headed by commissioner Austin Cullen, the commission was announced by the British Columbia premier John Horgan on 15th May,2019 to examine the scope of snow washing in the province, including the spread in RE sector (Cullen Commission, 2020i). The mandate of the ongoing inquiry was to reveal the methods used in evolution of Money Laundering, the AML effectiveness and problems faced while combatting the situation in British Columbia. A total of 35 participants are involved in the inquiry, representing the institutions associated with this matter like the BC RE Association, Government of Canada, Ministry of Finance etc. There are 13 testimonies, with many more lined up for the ongoing hearings on the topic (Cullen Commission, 2019). Some of the excerpts of the texts analyzed from the transcripts, academic and non-academic sources which provided the themes for this chapter are:

3.2 Primary Research

3.2.1 Sampling

Expert interviews formed another source for this chapter. Interviewees were selected on the basis of sampling method, with individuals who are experts of this

Table 1. Main Themes

Frequent Themes	Criterion	Available Information and Analysis
Importance of Snow washing	Secretive Nature	Not much has been identified about quantum of real estate money laundering due to it secretive nature (Maloney et al, 2019, p. 1). The situation requires imminent attention to convert unknowns into knows.
	Lack of Political Will	The investigations and prosecution on the basis of Fintrac rules is not happening which suggests towards unwillingness to act (Brown, 2018, paras. 6-7). Importance to available information should be given through necessary actions.
Laundering Estimations	Average of Range	Gravity model for money laundering estimations formulated in 1994 suggests two to five percent figure of GDP (Unger & Walker, 2009). An average of this range is considered to estimate realistic money laundering numbers over the years, ditching the low end estimates of range due to magnitude of laundering.
Housing Impact	Average of Range of price Inflation	Prices up by 3.7 percentage to 7.5 percentage due to money laundering (Maloney et al, 2019, p. 57). For estimating an accurate figure of price inflation due to money laundering an average of the given range is considered.
	Involvement of another factor	Demand and supply are key to deciding housing prices (Hall, 2020). The role of demand and supply is deemed important while analysing inflation of property rates.
Reforms	Breakthrough Opportunities	The rule of Ownership registry has been applied by the government of British Columbia from first May 2020 (Cullen Commission, 2020b, p. 23, para. 2). Other breakthrough measures analyzed are Mortgage Brokers Act, introduction of FREDA and Financial Services Authority.
Shell Company	Frequent Method	Purchase of properties without any brokerage through companies is three times more likely than individuals (Cullen Commission, 2020b, p. 33, para. 6). Figure 4 illustrates money laundering steps via Shell companies
Anticipating Surge	Student Ownership	Reports have suggested that illicit funds have been flowing in from Chinese officials (FATF, 2016, p. 16). The case of Chinese student without a job owning multiple million dollar property has been mentioned (Olivier, 2016). This implies towards an Asian link with Canadian real estate money laundering.

Source: Authors' Own Creation.

topic representing the population of all the experts in the industry. The insights shared by the experts in an industry are considered to be at saturation in qualitative research, which has received extensive acceptance and collection of additional data is not necessary (Saunders *et al.*, 2017). The information shared by the experts is considered to be credible and vastly recognized due to their extensive knowledge about the industry.

The number of years of experience of the experts formed a crucial criterion behind the selection of such specialists. Interviews with expert of the RE Money Laundering subject matter having more than 15 years of experience provided essential research data to complete the in-depth investigation required for this chapter More importantly, negotiations were held to successfully obtain necessary consent of the participants and thereby, names and entities of the participants will not be disclosed due to confidentiality and anonymity concerns. Appendix C offers a detailed insight into the questions that formed the basis of the interviews with experts. Table 2 provides the description of the interviewees based on the number of years of experience in the industry.

Table 2. Interview Participants

Career/Industry	Total Number of Years in Industry	Number
Legal Services	21	N1
Financial Services	16	N2
Total	37	

4. PRIMARY RESEARCH FINDINGS

Primary research was based on knowledge obtained from experts of the subject matter. In order to understand the problems being faced while administering Money Laundering problems in Canadian RE, it was important to obtain the perspective of experts in the industry. Figure 2 below depicts the key themes arising from the primary research. The research on mentioned topics was also helpful because it widely believed that there is much more unknown information than it is known, when it comes to RE Money Laundering (Moranis, 2019).

4.1 The Case of Conservative Estimates?

The insights into estimations related to Money Laundering numbers and its impacts emerged through the responses received from the expert interviews. When discussing the possibility of estimations for dirty money washed in RE industry during the recent years being a result of conservative approach, there were no shared perceptions:

I think that the 5.3 billion dollars estimate for RE snow washing in British Columbia seems to be rational, when taking into consideration the FATF's evaluation of 42.7 billion dollars to 106.8 billion dollars of Money Laundering for entire Canada, which is based on Money Laundering as two to five percentage of the country's GDP. For example, if we bear in mind that there are many other industries in Canada that

Figure 2. Themes from Expert Interview
Source: Authors' Own Creation

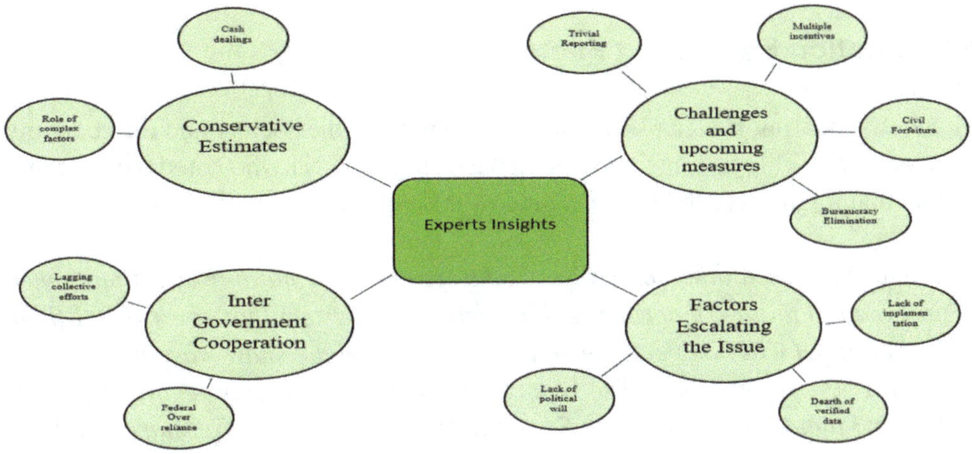

are falling prey to Money Laundering in Canada, these estimates for the property industry in a specific region seem to be defensible. (N1)

The other expert contextualized their accounts in terms of involvement of several intricate factors and lack of measured data in the RE Money Laundering:

When considering the complexity of factors involved within the RE industry, the estimates seem to be on a lower side. The criminals find such factors extremely attractive to invest illegally obtained funds because the involvement of so many secretive aspects abetting Money Laundering in property market makes it exceedingly difficult to track such fraudulent dealings. The absence of adequate data related to this problem creates a lot of hindrance while estimations are determined and if we look especially at the involvement of huge amounts of hard cash in RE dealings, the task of assessing the magnitude of illegal capitals involved gets even more daunting, which makes the current estimates actually seem like a result of conservative approach. (N2)

In terms of use of cash that makes estimating a difficult job, Chen & Anderson (2020) conferred that, criminals break hefty amounts of cash into many deposits spreading over multiple accounts. The use of large amounts of cash is evident as Stephen Schneider also pointed that, "*even some of the more sophisticated money launderers still have to deal with transferring cash and still like just to pack cash into suitcases and transport that way*" (Cullen Commission, 2020a). The total amount of money circulating through the laundry cycle is hard to estimate due to the clandestine nature of snow washing (UNODC, 2010; Maloney *et al.*, 2019).

4.2 Situation Escalating Factors

Money Laundering is a crime that has been a peril to the society and the economy for a long time. This feeling is evident in the response of N1 who noted the alarming factors that might have led to worsening of this situation:

It has only been escalating to new levels and spreading in multiple directions, much to the credit of failure of certain features within the system that governs it. I think lack of political will has been the chief contributor to the snow washing situation escalating to current levels. The reports by some of the highly regarded experts of Money Laundering matter like Steven Schneider and Peter German have been highlighting the magnitude of snow washing for a long time now. Their reports over the years since late 1990's have been identical, mentioning dirty money being invested in RE industry, luxury car market, casinos and other industries. Although, the same issues are emphasized by experts over and over again, the matter has still received miniscule reactions from the authorities. This simply indicates towards lack of political will to act since the laundering issues have been known all along and there has been basically no interest in tackling the problem, which has now escalated. (N1)

Such perspective on lack of willingness to act gets echoed, as Hennig (2017) highlighted Rampone's comments that lack of political will is the first and foremost reason behind Money Laundering in Casino's. According to N1, rest of the economic sectors including the RE industry are no different in this regard.

The systems in place to combat situations like Money Laundering in Canadian RE can only be as good as the information it has and the extent to which the system is able to take actions basis the available information. The response to the quality on obtainable data and importance of follow-up actions to handle the situation were:

Records maintained with respect to guidelines set by agencies like FINTRAC have data with minimal verification. The problem will persist unless the profits being generated for criminals through property purchases are tracked, which requires accurately verified information. Otherwise, lack of verified data with the agencies tracking snow washing, will lead to further intensification of Money Laundering in RE. Another failure on the part of systems has been lack of implementation and virtually, there has been next to no enforcement, which would have ideally deterred the money launderers to invest illicit funds. However, even when criminals are caught and charged, it is unlikely that one will be prosecuted. And if by any chance one gets prosecuted, its less likely they will face jail time. On top of that, it is even less likely that the illegal money will be recovered. (N2)

On the backdrop of such insights, it is apparent that understanding the impact of Money Laundering needs incessant efforts as the actual numbers could be unknown and hard to measure due to factors like lack of consistent and measured data (Cullen Commission, 2020c). In terms of enforcement, Bruce McMeekin's remarks that, "*We have in Canada a lacklustre record when it comes to the investigation and prosecution of financial crimes including Money Laundering*" (Brown, 2018). Non-existence of enforcement by the system causes no deterrence for RE money launderers. Due to this, within the new strategies focussing on various objectives to counter Money Laundering in Canada, the emphasis to strengthen law enforcement has increased (Auditor General of Canada, 2003).

4.3 Cooperation Among Different Government Levels

The suggestions by experts in the industry to clamp down on Money Laundering in RE markets across Canada have been met by differing reactions at the different government levels. The following is the context of the experts with regards to governments response to measures like the call for publicly accessible database that requires people who are trying to be anonymous, with the help of companies making property purchases for such people, to identify themselves:

Although, this proposal has been widely accepted to be the foremost step to combat the given circumstances, little action has been taken the governments on a collective basis. (N2)

There has been an understanding by only some provinces that the decision to implement ownership registry should be taken by the provincial jurisdictions on an individual basis, whereas many other provinces rely on the federal government to apply beneficial ownership nationwide, despite having autonomy to take the necessary actions. Therefore, due to this over reliance, confusion still remains about the level of government at which this decision should be made. To be able to benefit from the suggestions by experts to upstage the criminals, a cohesive approach and cooperation is necessary among the Federal and Provincial governments in order to fast track the implementation of AML policies proposed by industry experts. (N1)

Over the last year, Canada has been bolstering AML across the board with stronger rules targeting riskier sectors like virtual currencies, cracking open beneficial ownership bastions and boosting budgets for investigators (Monroe 2020). In terms of cooperation among Federal and Provincial governments, no support from federal official had been received for the BC Money Laundering case report (Meissner, 2019a). Among the jurisdiction, government of British Columbia is the only one to have taken a stern decision to go ahead with the beneficial ownership transparency proposal and from May 2020 onwards, the province has made it compulsory for the companies in British Columbia to maintain beneficial ownership records (Cullen Commission, 2020b).

4.4 Current Challenges Faced and the Way Forward

One of the discouraging conditions being encountered is the reporting of the RE transactions for potential fraud. Response to reporting and other challenges being faced to avert Money Laundering, along with need for upcoming steps were:

There are more than 30,000 reporting entities in the country, however, the required number of cases are just not being reported. These reporting entities collectively conduct 300 transaction examinations a year which is extremely low in the current scenario of heightened snow washing in the industry. It is particularly important to manage such incentives offered in the property industry as they pose a serious challenge to Money Laundering deterrence in the industry. In order to steer the RE economy out of Money Laundering ambit, mistakes from the past must be learned and measures should be taken accordingly. Going forward, making better use of civil forfeiture will be important to deter launderers to carry out criminal activities in this industry. And also, there should be a multi-jurisdictional effort to combat illicit investments in the property market and lead should be taken by Provincial governments, rather than awaiting Federal mandate. (N1)

Only so much can be achieved by looking at only one percent of the data set of RE transactions, making the current rate of surveillance and reporting on the matter as categorically insufficient, thus, making it a huge challenge faced by authorities while preventing Money Laundering in property sector. On the contrary, this serves as another incentive for committing the crime for money launderers, as they are aware that most likely their dealings will not be scrutinized. This is in addition to the multiple other dividends that RE holds to attract offenders for snow washing. Actions against this problem taken by one jurisdiction should be encouraged for wider acceptance and a collective effort on the part of provincial governments is required going forward. A setup for multi-organizational effort should be endorsed by governments, particularly in the areas of tax involvement. There is also a need to put a break to all the ongoing administrative bureaucracy in order to penalize people for silly compliance violations. (N2)

The need to ramp up the enforcement is a key while addressing the issue going forward. Recently, FINTRAC revised its expectations for reporting entities that are unable to meet obligations to report, requiring such entities to self-declare regarding non-compliance and maintaining records of details concerning non-compliance and actions taken to mitigate the risk (Leslie, 2020). According to N1, until there are harsher punishments for offenders, the flow of dirty money into one of the most rewarding sectors for money launderers will continue to surge. Currently, non-applicability of criminal and administrative penalties against same non-compliance case exists (FINTRAC, 2019a). The primary objectives of forfeiting property acquired or used through unlawful dealings is to punish and deter the offenders by depriving them of using such property (USDG, 2019). In terms of administrative bureaucracy, the regulatory fragmentation at the national level leads to complex bureaucracy and inconsistencies which poses a challenge for regulatory bodies like FATF (Lowery & Ramachandran, 2015).

5. ANALYSIS

5.1 Laundering Estimation Criterion for Canada

People across multiple sectors in the country are affected as snow washing in Canada abets crime facilitation, housing affordability and business due diligence to name a few. But still, there have been no certain estimates for Money Laundering in Canada, as reiterated by Maloney (Wakefield, 2019). With the help of researched data, it was imperative to analyze the nationwide Money Laundering estimate model for Canada before getting to the effects that black money has particularly on RE, which is one of the prominent Canadian economic sectors targeted by criminals (Schneider, 2006).

The wet finger estimates also known as the rule of thumb is the most commonly discussed model for estimating Money Laundering in an economy (Maloney *et al*, 2019). The consensus range of estimating Money Laundering at two to five percentage of the global Gross Domestic Product (GDP) was conveyed by IMF's managing director to FATF in 1998, however, the academics working within the IMF or anyone else has not been able to explain the method behind such estimate range (Walker & Unger, 2009). Considering this along with insights from expert interviews about possible underestimation of Money Laundering figures, it was important to distinguish the gap between the conservative estimate and a fairly reasonable estimate. Figure 3 illustrates the difference between the Money Laundering estimates at a more realistic level of three and a half percentage, which is the average of two to five percentage of entire GDP mentioned as the wet finger estimate, from the lower end estimate of two percentage mark.

Figure 3. Money Laundering Estimates
Source: Statistics Canada, 2021

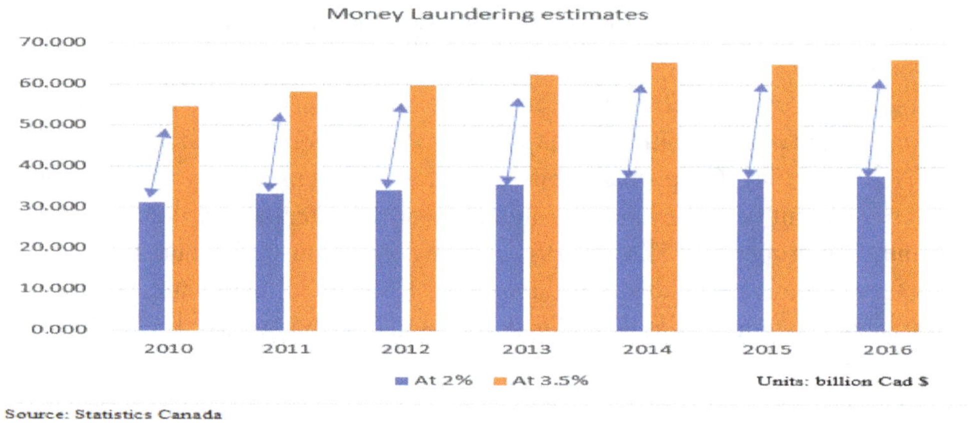

Data available for the GDP of Canada over a seven year period ranging from 2010 to 2016 from has been used for scrutiny (Statistics Canada, 2021). At three and a half percentage level, Money Laundering estimates were observed to be doubling from the conservative approach level. Also, the widespread of cleaning dirty money in Canada is much evident, as a result of which it has received the tag of "*snow washing*" (Cullen Commission, 2020c). Therefore, estimations at an average of the wet finger estimates for calculating Money Laundering in Canada seems to be more practical mainly due to two factors, the huge gap comparison with the conservative approach and the magnitude of current dilemma of illegal investments in the country.

The Walker gravity model projecting Money Laundering in a region to be around two to five percentage of Gross national product was developed in the year 1994 (Walker & Unger, 2009). Although this Money Laundering estimation model is one of its kinds available till date, it has only been minutely modified over the years, with the percentage figures remaining the same. As expert interview highlighted, it is worth noting that the estimation criterion remains unfairly indistinguishable even when the peril of Money Laundering has only amplified over the years, constantly spreading its grasp and severely impacting the nation's economic sectors like Real Estate.

5.2 Estimated Impact on Prices

One of the most sought after zones targeted by criminals to obscure their illicit funds is property investment, as they are able to camouflage the source of black money used for payment and enjoy the assets as well (European Parliament, 2019). Experts in the industry have detailed that dirty money laundered by criminals in the RE is inflating house prices (Shaw & Young, 2019). Since it has been detected that the prices of properties across different regions in Canada have been north bound, it is vital to look at how much of the increase in prices are affected by Money Laundering in the country and get an idea of black money numbers involved in RE.

5.2.1 Illicit Funds Causing Price Inflation

The combination of both literature review and primary research facilitated deeper understanding of snow washing as a part of price change in RE. The dirty money investments in property sector have inflated the housing prices to the tune of 3.7 percentage to 7.5 percentage (Cullen Commission, 2020b). Figure 4 illustrates the role played by Money Laundering in increasing current housing prices in some of the metropolitan cities across Canada and the housing price in the country as a whole.

Figure 4. Money Laundering as a part of housing price inflation
Source: RPS, 2020

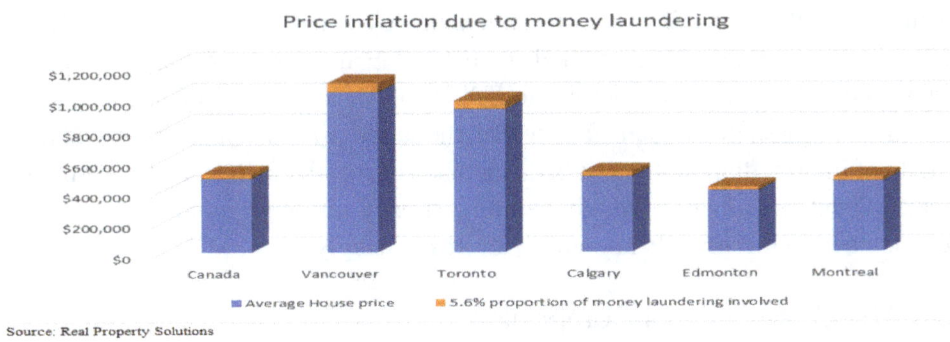

Data available for the current average housing price across metropolitan cities of Canada has been derived from RPS (2020) for scrutiny on the subject. The average of the range of 3.7 percentage to 7.5 percentage proposed by experts, which is 5.6 percentage has been taken, based on aforementioned discussion on realistic average to calculate the proportion of laundered money involved in house prices in different cities. The largest amounts of estimated illicit money reside in the housing prices of Vancouver and Toronto. Money Laundering in the housing market will set a property purchasers purse by 58,144.80 dollars and 52,029.60 dollars, respectively in these cities, whereas people in Edmonton and Montreal will have to shell out an extra 22,164.80 dollars and 25,715.20 dollars on an average, the least among the compared cities. Also, people in Edmonton and Montreal are the only ones among people from the chosen set of metropolitan cities to be paying less of the inflated price than the average Canadian, as on a national basis, people in Canada have to bear an extra 26,921.61 dollars out of their pocket as a result of inflated prices due to Money Laundering in Canadian RE. To some extent, the average price of houses would become less without the involvement of Money Laundering and housing affordability will improve modestly (Maloney *et al.*, 2019).

5.3 Frequently Used Medium for Property Investments

The property investments in the RE sector are considered one of the safest bets by criminals to integrate dirty money back into the legitimate economy (European Parliament, 2019). One of the most commonly used media used are the shell companies, as hidden black money behind these companies is widespread in Canada (Kane, 2020). It was observed that investing in RE through such companies is easier as it mitigates the risk of sharing the identity of the actual person behind the property purchase.

The motives of converting black money into legit funds without even getting traced for the wrongdoing plays a huge role in attracting offenders to take the route of snow washing through companies. The findings listed by experts indicated towards the companies being three times more likely to make a RE investment without a mortgage than the individuals (Cullen Commission, 2020b). A major criterion of investments through a foreign shell company falls within the scope of purchasing properties with the help of intermediary company. This media is one of the favourites for criminals to make illegal investments through their dirty money, although genuinely operating ones too abet such criminals knowingly or unknowingly.

5.3.1 The Case of Shell Companies

Criminals when washing dirty investments into buying a property through a company like to use a foreign shell company, a non-trading entity used for financial manoeuvres and existing only on papers (Marria, 2018). A comprehensive research revealed how exactly such dealings are perfected by the criminals to purchase a property through an overseas company in Canada with their investments. Figure 5 below illustrates the mechanism of snow washing in the RE sector by such offenders through a shell corporation.

Figure 5. Use of a shell company
Source: Authors' Own Creation

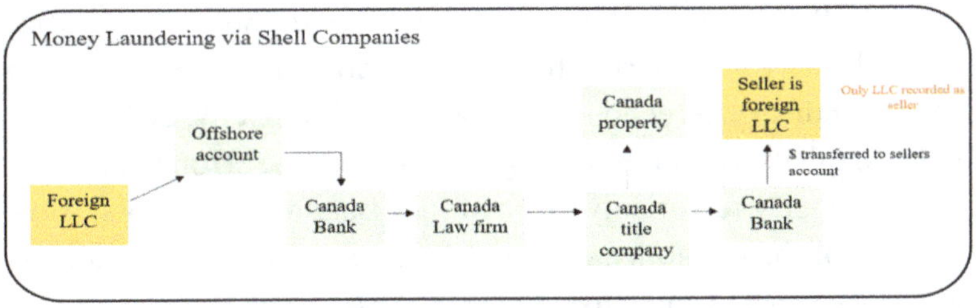

The figure illustrates the process used by criminals from scratch to end in order to purchase a property in Canadian lands from a business outside the borders of the country. At the initial point, overseas or even a local individual might start a foreign-incorporated limited liability company, under the rules and regulations of that country's jurisdiction, which would pose a particular encounter to a law enforcement authority in Canada seeking to interrogate about the purchase in future. Interchangeably, the overseas or the local person could also create a Canadian limited liability company established in a Canadian province with just a registered agent, as corporations are required to have registered agents by certain provinces in Canada (CF, 2021).

The limited liability company could make payment for the property transaction from a foreign bank account via wire transfer. Also, the foreign shell company or the firm positioned in Canada can introduce a Canadian bank account for the transaction of buying the property. However, in this scenario, the beneficial ownership information will not be flagged automatically to the Money Laundering regulator and the enforcement agency will need to obtain the ownership information about the foreign company used to make payment, which is a lot more difficult due to the foreign location of the company and their local connections (D'Antuono, 2019).

The wire transfers or other modes of payments from the involved law firm presents additional hurdle for the law enforcement agency, who will have to go through another barrier to obtain the information. And then, the proceedings are directed to the title company, which undertakes the sale of the property and ultimately dispensing the payment to the seller's account. In this process, the actual people on either ends of the property sales dealings may remain hidden if the selling party conceals their identity through a shell company as well.

5.4 Other Reasons for Property Price Inflation in Canada

There is no doubt that there has been a constant rise in the property prices across the country and Money Laundering has played a considerable role in fashioning a bubble in the RE industry, as echoed by expert panels (BCGN, 2019a). However, it was revealed through the research findings that it would be erroneous to attribute the steep rise in the property sector only to the Money Laundering factors. As prominent in the other areas of the economy, demand and supply plays a key role in deciding price in the property circle and (Investopedia Staff, 2020).

Although, as the magnitude of Money Laundering spreads throughout Canada and engulfs most of its economic sectors in its trail, it is not unnatural to link inflation in RE to snow washing. However, in doing so the role of demand and supply gets undermined. As Canada witness's significant influx of immigrants from all over the world, the demand for RE properties is on a rise (McClelland, 2019). With a constant surge in the demand for housing and other properties, the supply in this area has been pointedly adrift which has sharply increased the national home prices (Royal LePage, 2020).

With the already strained market in terms of supply of properties in RE, coupled with the growing demand and influx of immigrants, the ongoing housing pricing crisis are set to reach new levels if the supply of properties is not met with constantly rising demand. Also, as discussed earlier, the increase in demand in the RE sector can be linked to increase in demands of criminals looking to invest in properties. The federal immigration policies have also led to explosion of the informal economy at various fronts including Money Laundering and other illegal activities and has affected housing prices (Grubel, 2009)

5.5 Possible Upcoming Surge

The rise in the number of Money Laundering cases in the property sector over the years has indicated towards a link with Asia. A FATF report emphasised that high risk clients notably from Asia have been imposing their will on the RE sector in Canada (FATF, 2016). Many Chinese students owning hefty properties in Canada raises many eyebrows. The case of a 31.1 million dollar mansion, overpaid by approximately five million dollars above its market value, stood out as it was listed in the name of a student with no job (Olivier, 2016).

A report by Colliers International which covered RE investments by people from China, suggests that the outpouring into the RE across the world by Chinese nationals has increased from US$2.3 billion in 2010 to US$18 billion in 2015 (O'Brien, 2015). Increase in immigration numbers from China to Canada is one of the highest over the years (Chan, 2019). Therefore, a considerable number of aforementioned investments are parked in the Canadian property market from China, giving rise to Money Laundering in the RE industry here (Evans, 2018). The arrival of growing number of immigrants and other individuals, especially like Chinese students in Canada will increase the chances of money launderers trying to hoard their suspected illegal investments in the property sector through nominees.

The Chinese officials involved in Money Laundering through Canadian RE in Vancouver have been referred to in a report which briefs that in order to recover the proceeds of corruption, the Chinese government wishes to target the Canadian RE (FATF, 2016). Another reason of a possible surge in the snow washing in the RE of Canada is relaxation on foreign investments by China. Recently, China reached a trade agreement with the US wherein, the Chinese government relaxed some restrictions for its citizens regarding investments in the US (MW, 2019). This will encourage outpour of Chinese investments in US, which could also mean that money launderers will be able to obscure larger amounts of funds into the Canadian economy via US. Therefore, a possible upcoming surge in such criminal activities and overall amounts of dirty money can reach the Canadian RE shores, resulting in the need to analyze regulatory measures in this area.

5.6 Regulatory Reforms: Work in Progress

Snow washing disintegrates the set rules and regulations, boosts unlawful activities, and distorts economic sectors, ultimately impacts economic development due to its negative effects (Bartlett, 2002). A comprehensive AML regime across the country will serve the purpose of improving housing affordability, even if they are not utmost significant by magnitude, but will be still very noticeable (N1). The research elaborated that some of the steps to combat Money Laundering in Canada have been taken by the government by introducing rules and regulations like Proceeds of Crime Act 2002, Terrorism Act 2000, Criminal Finance Act 2017, Anti-Money Laundering Act 2018, Money Laundering-Terrorist Financing and Transfer of Funds Regulations 2017 (Wentworth, 2018). These policies have been introduced to scrutinize potential Money Laundering activities in RE as well as Canada in general. The aim to improve financial intelligence flow through AML overhaul in Canada (Chan, 2018).

The information on beneficial ownership is pursued by the government to be more transparent through a public registry, as it looks for opinion of stakeholders including Canadians and industry experts for improvement (Government of Canada, 2020). Recently, the provincial government of British Columbia took some stern steps to combat Money Laundering and tax fraud, as revealed by Finance Minister Carole James (James, 2019). Some of the current substantial steps taken to enhance

AML structure in Canada to recuperate against the extensive Money Laundering practices have been analyzed.

5.6.1 Ownership Registry

The dilemma of concealed ownership structures has permitted launderers to maintain their anonymity for a long time now and has also facilitated a blanket with which they conceal snow washing activities in RE, as revealed in the research findings. A public corporate registry would prove a game changer for snow washing (Wood, 2020). One of the chief reasons that the transparency registry is vital is because it has been recognized at various government levels that information of who owns and manages corporations is necessary for the authorities to know (Cullen Commission, 2020b). Therefore, the governments have considered mandating all the private players operating throughout Canada to maintain accurately updated ownership records. Also, the provincial government in British Columbia passed the land ownership transparency act last year itself as it recognized the need for fast-tracking the first of its kind rule in Canada to combat the mounting situation in the province, as revealed by the findings as well (Burr & Horte, 2019).

Although land ownership transparency act has been predicted to be the single most effective step if applied successfully across all the provinces, however, some experts do not see the act as a full proof solution. It was found through the research that lawyers with expertise in AML practice have voiced their concern that the actual beneficial owners of the property can still conceal themselves, as nothing can prevent the law agents from maintaining secrecy of client identity (Pang, 2018). This has given new directions for the AML regulatory bodies and cover some of the loopholes of the act that money launderers could still get away with. Nonetheless, the deliberations by the experts on disclosure of corporate beneficial ownership emphasizes the importance of ownership transparency to the Money Laundering disruption in RE and the role of governments and legal professionals being vital to make ownership registry a success (LTSA, 2021).

5.6.2 Mortgage Brokers Act and FREDA

The research findings also highlighted that fraudulent mortgages are obtained by money launderers to hide their illegal investments in RE (Finney, 2020). The act of obtaining a mortgage just for the sake of it is undertaken by criminals in order to make the transaction look like a legitimate one. In order to overcome this situation, Mortgage Brokers act was established in way back in 1972, however, it has not been able to keep pace with the evolving issues related to Money Laundering in RE (Cullen Commission, 2020b). As mentioned in the research findings, the authorities have considered replacing the act by a formidable new statute to combat the situation, on recommendation of experts in the industry (Cullen Commission, 2020b). Thereby, the government has already started in the direction of implementing the recommendations and have opened a consultative inquiry seeking feedback on replacing the existing mortgage brokers act from the involved stakeholders.

Another step taken by the government to tackle the rising situation of snow washing in the RE is the setup of the FREDA, as unveiled by the research findings (Cullen Commission, 2020b). The unit oversees the RE legislative framework and maintains data to support the activities of reforming the policies on the basis of evolving Money Laundering situation in the property industry. This unit also covers the Money Laundering initiatives that falls under the scope of the Mortgage brokers act under the umbrella of the Finance ministry (Cullen Commission, 2020f). The decisions recommended by expert panels and enacted by the levels of governments are reflected in the framework of FREDA. Therefore, formation of the analytics unit is a key step in the direction to overcome the situation.

5.6.3 Financial Services Authority

The creation of a single regulator is particularly important to combat the Money Laundering crisis in the RE industry (BCGN, 2019d). The research finds brought to the notice that the government of British Columbia have formed the British Columbia Financial Services Authority (BCFCA) to regulate the RE industry, recognizing the barriers to effective regulations in the previous regulatory structure. Following the recommendations from combatting Money Laundering in real report on RE, the provincial government merged the office of RE council of British Columbia and the office of RE superintendent (Cullen Commission, 2020b). The commission also implied that the previous regulatory body was dissolved by the government and the subsequent formation of BCFCA reflects the commitment of the authorities to bringing reforms to the existing rules and regulations in order to pave the way for a robust AML framework (Cullen Commission, 2020b). Also, compliance and enforcement of the rules and regulations formed will be an as important step for the government to combat Canadian RE Money Laundering.

5.6.4 Need for More Measures

Research revealed that even though essential steps have been taken by the authorities to potentially affect the downfall of Money Laundering situation in the Canadian RE, however, much still needs to be done to stop such investment (Ross, 2020). Experts have raised concerns about that the federal government and RCMP were aware about much worse estimates, but chose not to convey facts to provincial governments, as exclaimed by BC Attorney General David Eby (Meissner, 2019b). Even the current steps being taken are understood to be miniscule and often prove to be inefficient to even control and letting alone thoughts of eliminating Money Laundering in the property market. (N2)

The research discovered that the entities under the ambit of FINTRAC have to flag cash dealings above the set threshold of 10,000 dollars (Cullen Commission, 2020a). However, the research also revealed that although the rules for reporting such transactions are set, however, the reporting is simply not being done. A very few transactions that are reported to the AML agencies and even then, not many actions are taken to prosecute the offenders, which is contradicting in this situation where much needs to be done (N2).

6. CONCLUSION

In this chapter, the Canadian RE has been studied from the angle of illegal investments facilitating environments and situations. The commencement of the chapter was with opportunities that exist to commit unlawful activities when a fitting target is present and proficient regimes are absent. The Canadian property market lends itself suitably to the tangling of unlawful activities, as industry sets level field for dishonest individuals by offering safe investment havens. Property industry is a flourishing business and entices hefty investment sums from both foreign and domestic players. The sector is a fastened economic precinct, dominated by old regulatory guidelines, and favours the opportunities to secrete indiscretions. Regulatory policies and enforcement control appear to be laughable. Thereby, the RE industry in Canada is less transparent and more attractive for criminals.

Instances of alarming arrangements of illicit activities linked to the Canadian RE market highlights the vulnerability of the industry, even though pragmatic numbers are infrequent. Given the severity of the situation, a distinction between the conservative approach and practical average line taken was made to get rational estimate figures. Deceitful undertakings in the property industry seem to be interlinked with other activities like overseas investments, immigration, gambling in casinos. With regards to findings, the utmost conspicuous indicators of corruption are housing price inflation by Money Laundering through shell companies, mortgage frauds, nominees, intermediary's and even financial systems. An overall conclusion is that the property market is the perfect place for legitimate and illegitimate entrepreneurs to meet, co-operate and share expertise and knowledge.

The scope for robust regimes to contest and thwart stern procedures of crime in the property market oscillate from the step of self-regulatory and administrative actions to its implementation on a regular basis. Encompassing a comparative and profound study on the province specific figures and the situation of other countries with identical RE structure will be a challenge of the near future, to uproot snow washing activities in the industry. To accomplish displacement of the vulnerability of illegitimate investment crimes in Canadian RE, a multidisciplinary tactic is required, implying that criminologists need to form robust AML regimes taking notions from past experiences and ongoing academic work on the matter.

DISCLAIMER

The contents and views of this chapter are expressed by the authors in their personal capacities. It is not necessary for the Editor and the Publisher to agree with these viewpoints and they are not responsible for any duty of care in this regard.

ACKNOWLEDGMENT

The authors extend sincere gratitude to

- The Editor-in-Chief and International Editorial Advisory Board (IEAB) of this book who initially desk reviewed, arranged a rigorous double/triple blind review process and conducted a thorough, minute and critical final review before accepting the chapter for publication.
- All anonymous reviewers who provided very constructive feedbacks for thorough revision, improvement, extension and finetuning of the chapter.
- All colleagues, assistants and well-wishers who assisted the authors to complete this task.

REFERENCES

ABC Solutions. (2021). *Money Laundering: A Three – stage Process.* About Business Crime Solutions Incorporation. Retrieved from https://www.moneylaundering.ca/public/law /3_stages_ML.php

ACAMS. (2007). Risks and Methods of Money Laundering and Terrorist Financing. In *Study Guide for the CAMS Certification Examination* (pp. 13-110). Miami: Association of Certified Anti-Money Laundering Specialists. Retrieved from http://files.acams.org/pdfs/English_Study_Guide/Chapter_2.pdf

Akyay, I. (2001). *Problems Encountered in Money Laundering Investigations* (Unpublished Master's Thesis). University of North Texas, Texas. Retrieved from https://digital.library.unt.edu/ark:/67531/metadc2856/

Anti-Corruption Digest. (2019, July 12). Money Laundering and housing affordability in GTA. *Anti-Corruption Digest*. Retrieved from https://anticorruptiondigest.com/2019/07/12/ money-laundering-and-housing-affordability-in-gta/#axzz6TFHLOLK6

Arnone, M., & Borlini, L. (2010). International anti-Money Laundering programs: Empirical assessment and issues in criminal regulation. *Journal of Money Laundering Control*, *13*(3), 226–271. doi:10.1108/13685201011057136

Auditor General of Canada. (2003). *Canada's Strategy to Combat Money Laundering*. Report of the Auditor General of Canada to the House of Commons. Retrieved from https://www.oag-bvg.gc.ca/internet/docs/20030403ce.pdf

Bartlett, B. L. (2002). *The Negative Effects of Money Laundering on Economic Development*. Asian Development Bank. Retrieved from https://waleolusi.files.wordpress.com /2013/05/the-negative-effects-of-money-laundering-on-econom.pdf

BCGN. (2019a, May 9). Billions in Money Laundering increased B.C. housing prices, expert panel finds. *British Columbia Government News*. Retrieved from https://news.gov.bc.ca/releases/2019FIN0051-000914

BCGN. (2019b, May 10). B.C. government addressing housing affordability challenges. *British Columbia Government News*. Retrieved from https://news.gov.bc.ca/factsheets/bc-government-addressing-housing-affordability-challenges

BCGN. (2019c, June 12). B.C.'s efforts front and centre at anti-Money Laundering meeting. *British Columbia Government News*. Retrieved from https://news.gov.bc.ca/releases/2019FIN0061-001233

BCGN. (2019d, November 12). Single real estate regulator protects people, combats Money Laundering. *British Columbia Government News*. Retrieved from https://news.gov.bc.ca/releases/2019FIN0115-002149

Brown, J. (2018, August 20). Enforcement lacking in anti-money-laundering efforts. *Canadian Lawyer*. Retrieved from https://www.canadianlawyermag.com/news/general/enforcement-lacking-in-anti-money-laundering-efforts/275393

Budget, B. C. (2018). *Homes for B.C: A 30-Point Plan for Housing Affordability in British Columbia*. Retrieved from https://www.bcbudget.gov.bc.ca/2018/homesbc/2018 _homes_for_bc.pdf

Burr, R., & Horte, C. (2019, May). British Columbia Landowner Transparency Act becomes law. *Norton Rose Fulbright*. Retrieved from https://www.nortonrosefulbright.com/en /knowledge/publications/deee862a/british-columbia-land-owner-transparency-act-becomes-law#:~:text=In%20its%202018%20budget%2C%20 the,of%20land%20in%20 the%20province.

Canada, T. I. (2019). Opacity: Why Criminals Love Canadian Real Estate (And How to Fix it). *Static1. Transparency International Canada*. Retrieved from https://static1.squarespace.com/static/5c8938b492441bf93fdbc536/t/5c92f6ec104c7b75c315b507/1553135372459/BOT-GTA-Report-English.pdf

CBC. (2018). Weak regulations make Canada a money-launderer's playground, says report. *CBC News*. Retrieved from https://www.cbc.ca/news/politics/money-laundering-howe-meunier-1.4811911

CF. (2021). Company Formations. *Canada Registered Agent Services*. Retrieved from https://companyformations.ca/canada-registered-agent-service/

Chan, A. (2019, May 22). Chinese Canadians. *The Canadian Encyclopedia*. Retrieved from https://www.thecanadianencyclopedia.ca/en/article/chinese-canadians

Chen, J. (2020, July 7). Money Laundering. *Investopedia*. Retrieved from https://www.investopedia.com/terms/m/moneylaundering.asp

Cohen. (2020). Commission of Inquiry into Money Laundering in British Columbia. *Cullen Commission*. Retrieved from https://cullencommission.ca/data/transcripts/2020%2002%2026%%20Transcripts%20-%20Opening%20Statements.pdf

Comply Advantage. (2020). Anti-Money Laundering in Canada 2020. *Comply Advantage*. Retrieved from https://complyadvantage.com/anti-money-laundering-in-canada-2020/

Cuellar, M. (2003). The Tenuous Relationship between the Fight against Money Laundering and the Disruption of Criminal Finance. *The Journal of Criminal Law & Criminology*, *93*(2-3), 311–466.

Cullen Commission. (2019, July 1). *Commission of Inquiry into Money Laundering in British Columbia*. Retrieved from https://cullencommission.ca/comm-statements/

Cullen Commission. (2020a, May 25). *Commission of Inquiry into Money Laundering in British Columbia*. Retrieved from https://cullencommission.ca/data/transcripts/Transcript%20May %2025,%202020.pdf

Cullen Commission. (2020b, Feb 24). *Commission of Inquiry into Money Laundering in British Columbia.* Retrieved from https://cullencommission.ca/data/transcripts/2020%2002%2024%20 Hearing%20Transcripts%20-%20Opening%20Statements.pdf

Cullen Commission. (2020c, Feb 26). *Commission of Inquiry into Money Laundering in British Columbia.* Retrieved from https://cullencommission.ca/data/transcripts/2020%2002%2026%20 Hearing%20Transcripts%20- %20Opening%20Statements.pdf

Cullen Commission. (2020d, Jun 2). *Commission of Inquiry into Money Laundering in British Columbia.* Retrieved from https://cullencommission.ca/data/transcripts/Transcript%20June %202,%202020.pdf

Cullen Commission. (2020e, Jun 3). *Commission of Inquiry into Money Laundering in British Columbia.* Retrieved from https://cullencommission.ca/data/transcripts/Transcript%20June %203,%202020.pdf

Cullen Commission. (2020f, Jun 11). *Commission of Inquiry into Money Laundering in British Columbia.* Retrieved from https://cullencommission.ca/data/transcripts/Transcript%20June %2011,%202020.pdf

Cullen Commission. (2020g, May 28). *Commission of Inquiry into Money Laundering in British Columbia.* Retrieved from https://cullencommission.ca/data/transcripts/Transcript%20May%2028,%202020.pdf

Cullen Commission. (2020h, May 26). *Commission of Inquiry into Money Laundering in British Columbia.* Retrieved from https://cullencommission.ca/data/transripts/Transcript %20May%2026,%202020.pdf

Cullen Commission. (2020i, July 9). *Commission of Inquiry into Money Laundering in British Columbia.* Retrieved from https://cullencommission.ca/media/?open=19

D'Antuono, S. M. (2018, November 29). Combating Money Laundering and Other Forms of Illicit Finance: Regulator and Law Enforcement Perspectives on Reform. *FBI News.* Retrieved from https://www.fbi.gov/news/testimony/combating-money-laundering-and-other-forms-of-illicit-finance

D'Antuono, S. M. (2019, May 21). Combating Illicit Financing by Anonymous Shell Companies. *FBI News.* Retrieved from https://www.fbi.gov/news/testimony/combating-illicit-financing-by-anonymous-shell-companies

Denis, J. S., & Ball, D. P. (2019, May 9). $7.4B Money Laundering scheme spiked B.C. home costs 5 per cent, reports find. *Toronto Star*. Retrieved from https://www.thestar.com/vancouver/2019/05/09/74-billion-in-illegal-cash-drove-up-bc-house-prices-by-5-per-cent-attracted-more-organized-crime-says-report.html

Department of Finance Canada. (2015). Assessment of Inherent Risks of Money Laundering and Terrorist Financing in Canada. *Government of Canada*. Retrieved from https://www.canada.ca/ content/dam/fin/migration/pub/mltf-rpcfat/mltf-rpcfat-eng.pdf

Department of Finance Canada. (2018, February 7). Reviewing Canada's Anti-Money Laundering and Anti-Terrorist Financing Regime. *Government of Canada*. Retrieved from https://www.canada.ca/content/dam/fin/migration/activty/consult/amlatfr-rpcfa-eng.pdf

Department of Finance Canada. (2019, June 14). *Joint Statement – Federal, provincial and territorial governments working together to combat Money Laundering and terrorist financing in Canada*. Retrieved from https://www.canada.ca/en/department-finance/news/2019/06/joint-statement--federal-provincial-and-territorial-governments-working-together-to-combat-money-laundering-and-terrorist-financing-in-canada.html

Duhaime. (2021). Role of FINTRAC. *Duhaime's Anti-Money Laundering Law in Canada*. Retrieved from https://www.antimoneylaunderinglaw.com/aml-law/role-of-regulator

ESAAMLG. (2013). *Typologies Report on Money Laundering through the Real Estate Sector in The ESAAMLG Region*. Tanzania: The Eastern and Southern Africa Anti-Money Laundering Group (ESAAMLG). Retrieved from https://esaamlg.org/reports/TYPOLOGIES-REPORT-ON-MoneyLaundering-THROUGH-THE-REAL-ESTATE-SECTOR.pdf

European Parliament. (2019). *Understanding Money Laundering through real estate transactions*. Retrieved from https://www.europarl.europa.eu/cmsdata/161094/7%20-%2001%20EPRS_Understanding %20money%20laundering%20through%20real%20estate%20transactions.pdf

Eurostat. (2017). *Commercial Property Price Indicators: Sources, methods and issues*. Luxembourg: Eurostat Statistical Reports. Retrieved from https://ec.europa.eu/eurostat/documents/7870049/8545612/KS-FT-16-001-EN-N.pdf/9e4bbc9b-8c6f-44a9-b686-1083a7a8fa0f

Evans, J. (2018, April 30). Court Hears of Unexplained Millions from China and Toronto Real Estate. *Better Dwelling*. Retrieved from https://betterdwelling.com/city/toronto/court-hears-of-unexplained-millions-from-china-and-toronto-real-estate/

Expert Panel on Emerging Crimes. (2005, January 7). *How is crime changing in the 21st Century?* Ottawa: Department of Justice, Canada. Retrieved from https://www.justice.gc.ca/eng/rp-pr/csj-sjc/crime/rr03_20/p1.html

FATF. (2007). *Money Laundering & Terrorist Financing through the Real Estate Sector*. Financial Action Task Force. Retrieved from https://www.fatf-gafi.org/documents/documents/moneylaunderingandterroristfinancingthroughtherealestatesector.html

FATF. (2016, September). *Anti-Money Laundering and counter-terrorist financing measures -Canada*. Paris: Financial Action Task Force. Retrieved from http://www.fatf-gafi.org/media/fatf/documents/reports/mer4/MER-Canada-2016.pdf

Finney, D. (2020, May 10). Mortgage Fraud: Understanding and Avoiding It. *Investopedia*. Retrieved from https://www.investopedia.com/articles/mortgages-real-estate/10/how-mortgage-fraud-affects-markets.asp

FINTRAC. (2019a, June 21). *Penalties for non-compliance*. Financial Transactions and Reports Analysis Center of Canada, Government of Canada. Retrieved from https://www.fintrac-canafe.gc.ca/pen/1-eng

FINTRAC. (2019b, August). *Guideline 7A: Submitting Large Cash Transaction Reports to FINTRAC Electronically*. Financial Transactions and Reports Analysis Center of Canada, Government of Canada. Retrieved from https://www.fintrac-canafe.gc.ca/guidance-directives/transaction-operation/Guide7A/lctr-eng

Galloway, G. (2019, October 17). Election Special: Parties Target Money Laundering Housing Schemes. *Toronto Storeys*. Retrieved from https://torontostoreys.com/federal-election-toronto/

German, P. M. (2018, March 31). *Dirty money*. Retrieved from https://s3.amazonaws.com/tld-documents.llnassets.com/0019000/19257/german_gaming_final_report.pdf

Government of Canada. (2020, February). Strengthening Corporate Beneficial Ownership Transparency in Canada. *Government of Canada*. Retrieved from https://www.ic.gc.ca/eic/site/142.nsf/eng/00001.html

Grubel, H. (Ed.). (2009). *The Effects of Mass Immigration on Canadian Living Standards and Society*. Fraser Institute. Retrieved from https://www.fraserinstitute.org/sites/default/files/ EffectsofMassImmigration.pdf

Hennig, C. (2017, October 2). 'Political will' needed to stop Money Laundering in casinos, former investigator says. *CBC News.* Retrieved from https://www.cbc.ca/news/canada /british-columbia/former-director-of-casino-investigations-political-will-1.4317138

Hernandez, J. (2019). Money Laundering is a national crisis. What now? *CPA Canada.* Retrieved from https://www.cpacanada.ca/en/news/pivot-magazine/2019-07-03-jose-hernandez-money-laundering

Hudak, S. (2017, August 22). FinCEN Targets Shell Companies Purchasing Luxury Properties in Seven Major Metropolitan Areas. *The Financial Crimes Enforcement Network.* Retrieved from https://www.fincen.gov/news/news-releases/fincen-targets-shell-companies-purchasing-luxury-properties-seven-major

IIROC. (2019, May 30). IIROC and FINTRAC enhance cooperation to protect against Money Laundering. *Newswire.* Retrieved from https://www.newswire.ca/news-releases/iiroc-and-fintrac-enhance-cooperation-to-protect-against-money-laundering-840123760.html

IMF. (2016, March 21). The IMF and the Fight against Money Laundering and the Financing of Terrorism. *International Monetary Fund.* Retrieved from https://www.imf.org/en/About/Factsheets/Sheets/2016/08/01/16/31/Fight-Against-Money-Laundering-the-Financing-of-Terrorism

Investopedia Staff. (2020, September 2). How Does Supply and Demand Affect the Housing Market? *Investopedia.* Retrieved from https://www.investopedia.com/ask/answers/040215/how-does-law-supply-and-demand-affect-housing-market.asp

James, C. (2019, May 9). What steps will province take to combat Money Laundering in B.C. *Global News.* Retrieved from https://globalnews.ca/video/5259885/what-steps-will-province-take-to-combat-money-laundering-in-b-c

Kane, L. D. (2020, February 27). Canada must expose hidden company owners to end 'snow washing,' inquiry hears. *CBC News.* Retrieved from https://www.cbc.ca/news/canada/british-columbia/money-laundering-bc-inquiry-snow-washing-1.5477916

Lee-Shanok, P. (2019, March 21). Criminals hiding billions of dollars in GTA real estate, watchdog claims. *CBC News.* Retrieved from https://www.cbc.ca/news/canada/toronto/anti-corruption-group-claims-criminals-laundering-money-through-toronto-real-estate-1.5065777

Leslie, D. (2020, March 31). FINTRAC revises expectations for reporting entities amid pandemic. *Financial services: Regulation tomorrow. Norton Rose Fulbright.* Retrieved from https://www.regulationtomorrow.com/ca/fintrac-revises-expectations-for-reporting-entities-amid-pandemic/

Lochead, D., & Dhanraj, T. (2019, July 11). Empty properties: Money Laundering and housing affordability in GTA. *Global News.* Retrieved from https://globalnews.ca/news/5484606/money-laundering-housing-affordability-in-gta/

Lokanan, M. E. (2019). Data mining for statistical analysis of Money Laundering transactions. *Journal of Money Laundering Control*, *22*(4), 753–763. doi:10.1108/JMLC-03-2019-0024

Lowery, C., & Ramachandran, V. (2015, November 9). Unintended Consequences of Anti–Money Laundering Policies for Poor Countries. *Center for Global Development.* Retrieved from https://www.cgdev.org/publication/unintended-consequences-anti-money-laundering-policies-poor-countries

LTSA. (2021). 8 Key Facts about the Landowner Transparency Registry. *Land and Title and Service Authority*. Retrieved from https://ltsa.ca/

Maloney, M., Somerville, T., & Unger, B. (2019, May 31). Combatting Money Laundering in BC Real Estate. *Cullen Commission*. Retrieved from https://cullencommission.ca/files/Combatting_Money_Laundering_Report.pdf

Marria, V. (2018, November 21). Criminals are Using Your Dream Home to Clean Dirty Money. *Forbes*. Retrieved from https://www.forbes.com/sites/vishalmarria/2018/11/21/criminals-are-filling-your-dream-home-with-dirty-money/?sh=2b8052fd22e3

McClelland, C. (2019, October 16). Immigrant-fuelled demand is helping to power Canada's housing market *Financial Post*. Retrieved from https://financialpost.com/real-estate/immigrant-fuelled-demand-is-helping-to-power-canadas-housing-market

McDowell, J., & Novis, G. (2001). The Consequences of Money Laundering and Financial Crime. *Economic Perspectives*, *6*(2), 6–8. https://www.hsdl.org/?view&did=3549

Meissner, D. (2019a, April 8). B.C. Money Laundering report finds no federal officers dedicated to case. *The London Free Press*. Retrieved from https://lfpress.com/pmn/news-pmn/canada-news-pmn/b-c-money-laundering-report-finds-no-federal-officers-dedicated-to-case/wcm/94c06dc8-f147-4095-8f04-d3447a9d1086/

Meissner, D. (2019b, January 18). Money Laundering in B.C. estimated at $1B a year — but reports were not shared with province, AG says. *CBC News*. Retrieved from https://www.cbc.ca/news/canada/british-columbia/money-laundering-billions-bc-david-eby-1.4983471

Miralis, N. G. (2018, May 14). How is money laundered through real estate? *Lexology*. Retrieved from https://www.lexology.com/library/detail.aspx?g=4242839e-373c-4525-a853-3ad5cc84a17b

Monroe, B. (2020, June 18). *Regional Report Canada: As gun-shy FINTRAC regains penalty powers, government strengthens Anti-Money Laundering, will enforcement rise?* Association of Certified Financial Crime Specialist. Retrieved from https://www.acfcs.org/regional-report-canada-as-gun-shy-fintrac-regains-penalty-powers-government-strengthens-aml-will-enforcement-rise/

Moranis, H. (2019, May 16). When it comes to Money Laundering in real estate, there are more unknowns than knowns. *Financial Post*. Retrieved from https://financialpost.com/real-estate/when-it-comes-to-money-laundering-in-real-estate-there-are-more-unknowns-than-knowns

Mordor. (2021). Canada Real Estate Services Market - Growth, Trends, Covid-19 Impact, And Forecasts (2021 - 2026). *Mordor Intelligence*. Retrieved from https://www.mordorintelligence.com/industry-reports/canada-real-estate-services-market---growth-trends-and-forecast-2020---2025

MREA. (2014). *Money Laundering*. Manitoba Real Estate Association Retrieved from https://realestatemanitoba.com/module3/unit12/unit12new_sess1_money_laundering.htm

MW. (2019, June 30). China relaxes some foreign-investment restrictions. *Market Watch*. Retrieved from https://www.marketwatch.com/story/china-relaxes-some-foreign-investment-restrictions-2019-06-30

O'Brien, F. (2015). Property sales spike sparks money laundering fears. *BIV*. Retrieved from https://biv.com/article/2015/04/property-sales-spike-sparks-money-laundering-fears

OAS-CICTE. (2015). Technical Assessment-Comparative Analysis of Typologies and Patterns of Money Laundering and Terrorism Financing in Three Free Trade Zones in Latin America. *Inter-American Committee against Terrorism*. Retrieved from https://www.oas.org/en/sms/cicte/documents.asp

OECD. (2007). *Report on Tax Fraud and Money Laundering Vulnerabilities Involving the Real Estate Sector.* Center for Tax Policy and Administration, OECD. Retrieved from http://www.oecd.org/ctp/exchange-of-tax-information/42223621.pdf

Olivier, C. (2016, May 12). $31.1-million Point Grey mansion owned by 'student'. *Vancouver Sun.* Retrieved from https://vancouversun.com/business/real-estate/31-1-million-point-grey-mansion-owned-by-student

Pang, G. (2018, April 26). Lawyers Must Keep Client Identity Confidential. *Jackpot Lawyer.* Retrieved from https://www.jackpotlawyer.ca/why-solicitor-client-privilege-matters/#:~:text=A%20lawyer%20cannot%20be%20forced,This%20means%20complete%20confidentiality

Planner, S. J. (2019, May 10). Surprise! Money Laundering DID impact Real Estate Market. *Price Tags.* Retrieved from https://pricetags.ca/2019/05/10/surprise-money-laundering-did-impact-real-estate-market/

Rafay, A. (Ed.). (2019). *FinTech as a Disruptive Technology for Financial Institutions.* IGI Global. doi:10.4018/978-1-5225-7805-5

Reuter, P., & Truman, E. M. (2004). The Anti-Money Laundering Regime. In *Chasing Dirty Money: The Fight against Money Laundering* (pp. 45–103). Peterson Institute for International Economics. Retrieved from https://www.piie.com/publications/chapters_preview/381/4iie3705.pdf

Reynolds, C. (2019, May 10). Why criminals look to Canada to launder their money through real estate. *Financial Post.* Retrieved from https://financialpost.com/pmn/business-pmn/why-criminals-look-to-canada-to-launder-their-money-through-real-estate

Ross, A. (2017, May 9). On Our Doorsteps: Money Laundering in Canadian Real Estate. *The Canadian Bar Association.* Retrieved from https://www.cba.org/Sections/Business-Law/Articles/2017/May/On-our-doorsteps

Royal LePage. (2020, July 9). National home prices rise sharply in second quarter as housing supply struggles to keep up with surge in demand. *Newswire.* Retrieved from https://www.newswire.ca/news-releases/royal-lepage-national-home-prices-rise-sharply-in-second-quarter-as-housing-supply-struggles-to-keep-up-with-surge-in-demand-806605598.html

RPS. (2020, December). RPS House Price Index - Public Release. *Real Property Solutions.* Retrieved from https://www.rpsrealsolutions.com/house-price-index/house-price-index

Saunders, B., Sim, J., Kingstone, T., Baker, S., Waterfield, J., Bartlam, B., Burroughs, H., & Jinks, C. (2018). Saturation in qualitative research: Exploring its conceptualization and operationalization. *Quality & Quantity*, *52*(4), 1893–1907. doi:10.100711135-017-0574-8 PMID:29937585

Schneider, S. (2004a). Organized crime, money laundering, and the real estate market in Canada. *Journal of Property Research*, *21*(2), 99–118. doi:10.1080/09599910420003288O1

Schneider, S. (2004b). Money laundering in Canada: A quantitative analysis of Royal Canadian Mounted Police cases. *Journal of Financial Crime*, *11*(3), 282–291. doi:10.1108/13590790410809220

Schneider, S. (2006). Testing the limits of solicitor-client privilege: Lawyers, money laundering, and suspicious transaction reporting. *Journal of Money Laundering Control*, *9*(1), 27–47. doi:10.1108/13685200610645201

Schneider, S. (2020a, May 25). Commission of Inquiry into Money Laundering in British Columbia. *Cullen Commission.* Retrieved from https://cullencommission.ca/data/transcripts/Transcript%20May%2025,%202020.pdf

Schneider, S. (2020b, May 26). Transcripts. *Commission of Inquiry into Money Laundering in British Columbia.* Retrieved from cullencommission.ca/data/transcripts/Transcript%20May%2026,%202020.pdf

Scrinko, J. (2018, December 26). Money Laundering in Toronto's Real Estate Market: Analysis & Facts. *Precondo.* Retrieved from https://precondo.ca/toronto-real-estate-money-laundering/

Shaw, R., & Young, J. L. (2019, May 9). $5 billion laundered through B.C. real estate, inflating home prices: report. *Vancouver Sun*. Retrieved from https://vancouversun.com/business/real-estate/money-laundering-hikes-b-c-real-estate-prices-report

Start, K. Y. C. Limited. (2019, February 24). Money laundering in real estate. *Start KYC*. Retrieved from https://startkyc.com/en/blog/money-laundering-in-real-estate/

Statistics Canada. (2021). Gross domestic product (GDP) at basic prices, by industry (x 1,000,000). *Statistics Canada*. Retrieved from https://www150.statcan.gc.ca/t1/tbl1/en/tv.action?pid=3610040101

Sun, K. (2015). *Foreign investment in real estate in Canada: Key issues* (Occasional Paper Series Vol. 2, Issue No. 3). China Institute, University of Alberta. Retrieved from https://era.library.ualberta.ca/items/33a5de89-1e3d-4607-a22b-650f0b807875/view/30cef061 -41e7-41e3-92f6-322bbfe1324f/CIOPS_2_2_2015.pdf

UNODC. (2010). *Money-Laundering and Globalization*. Retrieved from https://www.unodc.org

USDG. (2019). *Asset Forfeiture Policy Manual*. U.S. Department of Justice, Criminal Division, Money Laundering and Asset Recovery Section. Retrieved from https://www.justice.gov /criminal-afmls/file/839521/download

Verver, J. (2017, February 24). Why You Really Need to Pay Attention to Money-Laundering Risks. *Corporate Compliance Insights*. Retrieved from https://www.corporatecomplianceinsights.com/why-you-really-need-to-pay-attention-to-money-laundering-risks/

Wakefield, J. (2019, May 21). Is Alberta really Canada's Money Laundering capital? B.C. report met with skepticism, calls for more study. *Edmonton Journal*. Retrieved from https://edmontonjournal.com/news/crime/is-alberta-really-canadas-money-laundering-capital-b-c-report-met-with-skepticism-calls-for-more-study

Walker, J., & Unger, B. (2009). Measuring Global Money Laundering: "The Walker Gravity Model. *Review of Law & Economics*, *5*(2), 821–853. doi:10.2202/1555-5879.1418

Wentworth, I. (2018, September 6). What are the Anti-Money Laundering Laws and Regulations? *Delta Net International*. Retrieved from https://www.delta-net.com/compliance/anti-money-laundering/faqs/what-are-the-anti-money-laundering-laws-and-regulations

Wood, G. (2020, January 21). Public B.C. corporate registry would be 'game changer' for Money Laundering. *Western Investor*. Retrieved from https://www.westerninvestor.com/news/british-columbia/public-b-c-corporate-registry-would-be-game-changer-for-money-laundering-1.24057481

WSJ. (1997, February 21). Money laundering alert. *Wall Street Journal*. Retrieved from https://www.wsj.com/articles/SB856480045800862500

Chapter 4
Money Laundering and Institutional Quality:
The Case of Developing Countries

Maryam Muhammad Amjad
University of Management and Technology, Pakistan

Noman Arshed
https://orcid.org/0000-0002-8940-5391
University of Management and Technology, Pakistan

Muhammad Awais Anwar
University of Education, Pakistan

ABSTRACT

Money laundering is considered an illegitimate global phenomenon that deteriorates any country's economic stability. The main objective of this chapter is to investigate the relationship between money laundering and institutional quality by considering several variables such as government stability, corruption, bureaucracy quality, law and order, and democratic accountability. The study investigates these relationships by using panel quantile regression. The findings suggest a significant relationship between good governance and money laundering and a significant negative relationship between government stability and illicit financial flows. In order to eradicate or control money laundering, governments need to be stable, and institutions should operate under favorable conditions. However, if money launderers manage to infiltrate these institutions with bribery and corruption, then it becomes incredibly difficult to stop the planned crimes like money laundering.

DOI: 10.4018/978-1-7998-8758-4.ch004

1. OVERVIEW

Governance applies to a group of organizations and entities derived not only from the state but also outside the state. Governance is defined as a set of tradition and institutions used to be practiced by the regulatory authority. The authority of the state or the constitution in the conventional sense insists that the state power is not centralized. However, the control exerted by a public or private entity is accepted by the people, it is likely to become a power base. It is the development of protocols and the constant monitoring of their application by the representatives of the ruling body of the organization. It requires the structures that needed to balance the interests of the members (with the related accountability) and their primary responsibility to improve the stability and development of the country (Rodrick & Subramanian, 2003). Good governance needs a long duration of time and continuous efforts. Furthermore, it also requires a sense of commitment to change things and an optimistic approach from the entire nation. The three main pillars of the nation are, the government, the private sector, and the general population. In order to achieve good governance, these three pillars have to unite and work together with harmony. Taking account of broader perspective, governance can be defined as "the institution needs to follow some conditions so that they can perform effectively". The key indicators such as government stability, controlling terrorism & crime, effectiveness of government, prevalence of law & order and quality of regulatory authority which determine the level of governance in any country (Kaufmann *et al.*, 2010; Nasir, 2020). Good governance increases the productivity of human and physical capital which can build better institutions and attracts foreign direct investment (Nofianti *et al.*, 2014; Rodrick, & Subramanian, 2003) further it leads to better standard of living (Hassan, Bukhari & Arshed, 2020; Arshed *et al.* 2020; Abdulqayumov, Arshed, & Bukhari, 2020) and self-employment (Aziz, Grant & Arshed, 2020).

Every initiative comes along with its own set of challenges. Achieving good governance has some complex issues such as corruption & effectiveness of bureaucracy in both public and private sectors that need to be discussed seriously. PERC (2018) shows that Indonesia's corruption rate is skyrocketing between the gaps of two years. Corruption rates of Indonesia were higher among Asia Pacific countries from 2010-2015. One of the reasons for such excessive rates of corruption is linked with the bureaucracy of the country. The formidable condition of the bureaucratic institutions is the result of ineffective accountability. Therefore, the execution of good governance needs improvement.

Many studies such as (Rodrick, & Subramanian, 2003; Vaithilingam & Nair, 2007; Nofianti *et al.*, 2014; Asongu & Kodila-Tedika, 2016) investigates the negative relationship between governance and crime rate in several economies around the globe. Taking account of Malaysia (Rahman, 2015), Increase in governance leads to a decrease in financial crime. However, various governance measures have been used such as regulatory quality, political stability, rule of law and corruption to investigate the relationship between governance and different crimes empirically. Corruption appeared to be an effective variable to decrease transactional crimes in most significant ways in Africa's case (Habibullah *et al.*, 2016; Asongu & Kodila-Tedika, 2016). Moreover, Vaithilingam and Nair (2007) investigates the determinants of money laundering in developing and developed countries. An empirical model was built for 88 countries. The empirical findings reveal that the cooperate governance coupled with efficient legal framework lowered money laundering. The study also further researched that countries with robust institutions, effective legal framework and efficient governance structure lowered money laundering in developing countries. Alemika (2013) estimates the relationship between political instability and crime in case of developing economies. The estimated results show that instability was the main reason for excessive crimes among developing countries. The study includes several crimes such as money laundering, arms manufacturing and arms trafficking, advanced fee fraud, oil bunkering and piracy. They all seem to be positively relates with political instability.

In addition, Montes and Paschoal (2016) elucidate the relationship between corruption and quality of governance. The empirical results reveal that increase in corruption leads to worsening of public and private institutions. However, institutions are more inclined towards achieving their countries development goals. Most of the literature shows a positive and significant relationship between corruption and money laundering. Corruption usually takes place in the form of bribery and fraud from public funds. Politician and administrative personnel commit these crimes in order to gain control and fulfil their private agendas. In order to hide the money from corruption, people carefully launder their money so that illicit funds can flow freely without consequence (FATF, 2011). However, Draghi (2011) shows a negative relationship between corruption and social capital. The study proved that increasing corruption could cause poverty traps and wastage of social capital. Moreover, stronger law & order situation and better legal frameworks lead to an increase in the conviction of criminals. This reduces crime rates in a country due to fear of increasing conviction rate. These results are consistent with the findings of (Becker, 1968; Cohen, 2005).

In addition, Matthew *et al.* (2020) wanted to examine the challenges of accountability and development in Nigeria. The study estimates the impact of corruption on political accountability and governance. Increasing corruption has slowed down economic development in Nigeria. The study recommends that accountability act as a critical component of good governance, which efficiently manages resources and ensures transparency in the usage of funds collected by the government while the lack accountability encourages corruption and other financial crimes. Bajrang *et al.* (2012) investigate the determinants of money laundering in case of developing economies. The estimates results reveal that money can become the root cause of crimes like corruption, smuggling, trafficking, tax evasion and black marketing. However, many people do not hesitate to accept money regardless of its source (black or white). The study also gauges the impact of different socioeconomic variables such as education, business sophistication, and macroeconomic stability on illicit financial funds. The results indicate a negative relationship between all three variables and illegitimate financial flows. The findings indicate that increased education, business sophistication and macroeconomic stability lead to a decrease in the illicit flow of funds among developing economies. In addition, Okunlola (2014) estimates the relationship between institutional quality and money laundering in the case of Nigeria. The study gauged the effects of illicit flow of funds on the institutions, economy, society, political stability, and society structure. The findings reveal that money laundering has disastrous effects on the economic and political stability of Nigeria.

1.1 Money Laundering

Money laundering refers to the transfer of illegally obtained money in order to make it seem to have come from legitimate sources. Money earned through crimes and illicit activity such as trade in insiders, extortion, illicit gambling, drug & human trafficking, tax evasion, fraud, bribery, misuse of public funds and even armed robbery comes under the umbrella of money laundering (Fossen, 2003; Zia, Abbas, & Arshed, 2020). The word laundering was invented in the 1920s when some mafia tried to own Laundromats in the USA and legalized proceeds from illegal activities by using those proceeds to acquire legitimate businesses (Schneider, 2008; Aluko & Bagheri, 2012). Money laundering was first practiced in 1930's in United States after the prohibition on the manufacture of alcoholic beverages by private means and stopped the monopolization of this practice. This phenomenon helps the private manufacturer to gain fat profits. These profits will further utilize for illegitimate activities. Therefore, the name of the money laundering comes from making illegal money legal. However, the government of different economies has taken the necessary steps in the last 15 years to minimize money laundering. The governments of different states restructure the financial transection laws and enforce international conventions (Brown, 2009). The concept of money laundering also discusses the different channels for handling profits of corrupt entities which are originated by means of illegitimate activities such as narcotics revenue, trafficking and theft etc. The laundering of these funds is often carried out through illegal financial transactions, which seems legitimate. The inspiration came from the start of the twentieth century, where perpetrators utilized laundry companies to conceal vast quantities of money in the eyes of the government, because they were made solely out of criminal activity. Moreover, Table 1 shows the increasing trend of money laundering in different regions of the world from 2000-2005.

Table 1. Annual Money Laundering by region, Billion US$ (2000-2005)

Regions	2000	2002	2005
America	313	328	350
Asia-Pacific	246	254	292
Europe	230	234	241
Middle East/ Africa	38	40	44
Total	827	856	927

Source: Anti-Money Laundering: A Brave new world for financial institution (Katkov, 2014)

Figure 1 shows the average percentage of economic crimes in the world from 2000-2018. Percentage of crimes has fluctuated in a given sample. However, the crime has been decreased by 30% in 2009 and increase in 2018 by 49%. However, authorities of each nation give a budget estimate for the number of funds embezzlement in their domestic economy. The IMF (International Monetary Fund) reports that global economy is actively engaged in laundering by 2% to 5% in 1996. FATF (Financial Action Task Force) has been nominated to counter the money laundering around the globe. According to FATF, it is impossible to estimate the correct amount of money laundering each year (Aluko & Bagheri, 2012; Chaikin, 2017). Money laundering not only conducted by traditional financial firms but also banks, capital markets

Figure 1. The reported rate of world economic crimes
Source: Global Economic Crime & Fraud Survey (GECF) 2018

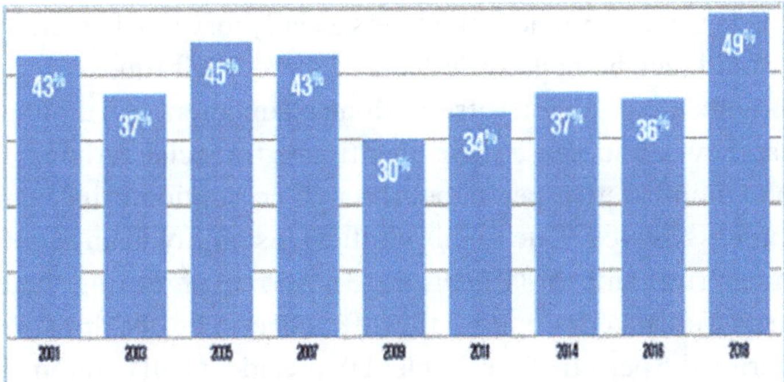

Source: Global Economic Crime & Fraud Survey 2018

and companies, non-banking financial firms, insurance, foreign exchange offices and notaries are also used several tools to clear illegitimate funds domestically and internationally. Moreover, it is predicted that anti-money laundering markets will significantly increase in the coming years.

1.2 The Consequences of Money Laundering

Many economies will experience financial and economic losses due to money laundering. Many people use different techniques to launder money due to which the global economy will deteriorate with the passage of time. However, it is estimated that $27.40 billion has been laundered every year in Australia. Similarly, the per capita loss from crime increased from AU$4.8 billion to AU$6.3 billion approximately. It is difficult to estimate the exact amount of money laundering. From this, we can conclude that the exact amount of money laundering is greater from estimated. Australia's example, more noteworthy cases of money laundering and financial crimes have emerged in the past with significant amounts being laundered and causing further damage to the global economy (ACCR, 2015; Godspower-Akpomiemie & Ojah, 2018). Money launderers will achieve a high level of gain from money laundering due to which they can purchase expensive commodities. This phenomenon will inflate the actual price of a commodity which makes difficult for honest buyers to buy. Money laundering promotes corruption and bribery in the country among financial and non-financial institutions which further deteriorates the other sector of the economy. Money laundering will also increase the terrorist and criminal activity because these people will gain more profits, and these profits will finance terrorist and criminal activity (Rodrick, & Subramanian, 2003).

Money laundering can also damage the prosperity of the country. Funds generated from money laundering will further utilize bribery and corruption, which slow down economic activity. Money laundering can cause extreme poverty, inequality and lower levels of GDP of an economy. However, money laundering can also improve the economic condition as well in some cases. It usually happens, when country becomes a tax haven, where money launderers usually forward there illicit funds. The host country would face no negative effects of these illicit funds since the crime is not being committed in the country itself. Money launderers will try to gain political control, so that they can increase their illegitimate financial activity. They control politicians and administrative personnel through corruption bribery and infiltrate the electoral process as well. Due to this political instability in an economy can rise and terrorism can run rampant (Unger, 2013). Moreover, during the era of 1980, anti-money steps were taken to control the different crimes like drug trafficking and smuggling. During the period of the former US president Bill Clinton, drug dealers' incomes were confiscated in an attempt to discourage them from such practices. The president started a "War on drugs" quoting *"If one could not get to drug dealers, then at least they should be discouraged, with the realization that they could not reap the monetary benefit of the illicit acts"* (Unger, 2013). Due to these anti-drug laws, the US government also established its first law against money laundering in 1986 (MLCA, 1986), making money laundering a federal crime.

Many studies such as (Brown, 2009; Poormazahaeri *et al.*, 2013; Aluko & Bagheri, 2012; Chaikin, 2017) discuss the relationship between money laundering and institutional quality. However, several factors such as political stability, corruption, law & order, and accountability can affect money laundering. Moreover, increasing the level of corruption in any country will increase money laundering because many officials and influenced individuals will corrupt the whole system by inserting money earned from illegitimate activity to economic and political structure. This will corrupt many government officials and economic segments. These corrupt officials want to hide their dirty money, leading to increased illicit financial flows from one country to another. Moreover, the efficiency of bureaucracy is also playing a key role in curtailing the problem of money laundering. Delays and loopholes in investigating procedures regarding financial crime give more time to the corrupt individuals to escape or use political influence to halt investigation (Lewisch, 2018)

In addition, money has been generated by many illegitimate activities such as the sale of firearms, drugs and from terrorist activity. These activities may deteriorate law & order and generate a big amount of illegitimate money that can be laundered from one country to another. This phenomenon will increase the level of money laundering in an economy. Furthermore, money laundering would, short of use of violence infiltrate the political composition within the society. This could be by the penetration of the enforcement agencies or the political parties by means of immense financing of the political process (Aluko & Bagheri, 2012; Bergström *et al.*, 2011).

During the period of 1980, an organization named as Financial Action Task Force (FATF) was built to control money laundering activities around the world. FATF regulate anti-money laundering laws which further implemented in different economies. Initially, seven countries become a member of FATF. The main task of FATF is to make regulations and policies regarding anti-money laundering measures and bring an improvement in the laws and legislation that already exist for money laundering. FATF also controls terrorist financing and funds generated for weapons. Furthermore, FATF also works at a national level in order to gauge the threats against a country's financial system and protect from exploitation. FATF proposed several measures for every economy to control money laundering and terrorist financing (FATF, 2011).

The main involvement of the present study is to evaluate the empirical relationship between governance and money laundering among developing economies. The motivation to examine the relationship between governance and money laundering among developing countries is that individuals belong to developing economies and have funds from illegitimate source usually wants to hide their money outside from their own country to avoid scrutiny and differentiating their portfolio investment. Individuals not only prefer countries having a stable and predictable financial system but also with weak detection laws. According to United Nations (2009), illegitimate proceeds amounted to 3.6% of the world's GDP, with 2.6% is being laundered. However, investors belong to Europe and choose to invest 80% of investment in Central Europe like Switzerland, British Isles or Luxemburg. Investors belonging to North America also prefer close geographical locations. Investors belonging to Latin America also prefer to invest 33% and 20% of their financial investment in Caribbean, Panama and 34% USA. Investors belonging to Asia prefer investments in offshore centers which are located in countries like Hong Kong, Singapore or China (UNODC, 2011). The literature on the impact of governance on money laundering with empirical analysis scarcely exists. The study is set to find whether there is any significant relationship between the two variables. The topic of money laundering and risk assessment has been overlooked in academic literature for years, despite its importance at policies and legislative level. Practitioners in this area have gone well beyond what the researchers made. However, most of the money laundering risk assessment exercises that are available for developed by both governments and agreed agencies which depend on poor theoretical and analytical frameworks and weak empirical proof (Savona & Riccardi, 2019).

2. METHODS AND DATA SOURCES

This section provides the means and methods to find predictable patterns in the empirical incidence of money laundering in the developing economies. This empirical investigation will be focusing on the institutional quality/governance related indicators. The secondary data will be collected for 80 middle income and lower middle income countries spanning across 1985 and 2015. The construction and sources of the data are provided in table 2.

The study has selected regression analysis with an assumption that there is a rhythm in empirical patterns of money laundering and institutional quality. Regression analysis places weights (slopes and intercept) to convert the proportional relationship to equality. It helps estimate how independent variables would have affected the dependent variable assuming other excluded variables are not changing drastically. The functional and stochastic form of the regression model is provided below.

Illicit financial flows = f (government stability, corruption, bureaucracy quality, law and order, democratic accountability).

Table 2. Variables and data sources

Variable Name	Explanation	Source
Illicit financial flows (IFF)	Illegal movements of money or capital from one country to another.	Global financial Integrity
Government stability (GS)	The likelihood of political instability and/or politically motivated violence	The PRS Group
Corruption (COR)	Dishonest or fraudulent conduct by those in power, typically involving bribery	The PRS Group
Bureaucracy Quality (BQ)	Institutional strength and quality of the bureaucracy is a shock absorber that tends to minimize revisions of policy when governments change	The PRS Group
Law & Order (LA)	A situation characterized by respect for and obedience to the rules of a society	The PRS Group
Democratic Accountability (DA)	When a politician makes choices on behalf of the people and the people have the ability to reward or sanction the politician	The PRS Group

$$IFF = \beta_1 (LnGS_1) + \beta_2 (LnCOR_2) + \beta_3 (LnBQ_3) + \beta_4 (LnLO_4) + \beta_5 (LnDA_5) + \varepsilon$$

The variables are transformed into natural log to linearize the relationship (Benoit, 2011) and convert the slope coefficients to elasticities. Also since the data is changing across time and countries, this spatial-temporal data must be handled with appropriate panel data models. Most commonly used models are Fixed effect (FE) – Random effect (RE) model which assumes that the cross sectional differences are deterministic while the time differences are random and the variables are normally distributed. FE and RE model is operationalized by allowing the intercept to vary across cross sections (Gujarati & Porter, 2009).

Further, this study also adds that most of the secondary variables are non-normal. This study will use the robust approach to handle non-normality. This model is known as Panel Quantile Regression (Angrist & Pischke, 2008) which estimates then center using median rather than mean, which is not distribution sensitive. Further, this study will estimate the model for three difference positions in the distribution of money laundering (i.e. 25th Percentile, 50th Percentile, and 75th Percentile) so that the non-linear effects because of non-normal distribution can be assessed.

3. RESULTS AND DISCUSSION

Table 3 represents the descriptive statistics of the variables used in the model. Since all the variables have a mean value greater than the standard deviation, they are under-dispersed. Further, none of the variable have mean value equating median or skewness = 0 and kurtosis = 3, this means that the variables at not normally distributed. The significant probability values of Jarque Bera (JB), Shapiro Wilk (SW) and Shapiro Francia (SF) tests also confirm the non-normality. Thus models using mean as central tendency (OLS models) are not suitable for inference.

Table 3. Descriptive Statistics

Stats	LNIFF	LNGS	LNCOR	LNBQ	LNLO	LNDA
Mean	7.160	1.932	0.844	0.561	1.065	1.098
Standard deviation	1.952	0.369	0.421	0.437	0.437	0.524
Median	7.356	1.998	0.916	0.693	1.098	1.217
Range	13.796	2.484	4.276	3.158	2.659	5.010
Skewness	-0.442	-1.587	-1.124	-0.724	-0.886	-1.303
Kurtosis	3.459	6.887	8.051	4.051	3.508	6.124
Prob. JB Test	0.00	0.00	0.00	0.00	0.00	0.00
Prob. SW Test	0.00	0.00	0.00	0.00	0.00	0.00
Prob. SF Test	0.00	0.00	0.00	0.00	0.00	0.00

Table 4 provides the VIF test for the presence of multicollinearity among the independent variables. Since none of the VIF values are above 2 confirming that variables are not collinear, making regression estimates unbiased.

Table 4. Multicollinearity test

Variable	VIF	1/VIF
lncor	1.30	0.770
lnda	1.24	0.808
lnlo	1.20	0.835
lnbq	1.19	0.839
lngs	1.10	0.905

3.1. Panel Quantile Regression Estimates

Under the condition of non-normal variables, the OLS estimates will not be suitable for inference. Table 5 provides the estimates for the panel quantile regression. The total sample is comprised of 740 observations based on 80 countries.

Table 5. Quantile Regression Statistics

Quantile Regression for Panel Quantile Regression	
Number of obs:	740
Number of groups:	80
Min obs per group:	1
Max obs per group:	10

Here in table 6 we can see the effect of different indicators of institutional quality for three different positions in the data set. It can be seen that government stability can have a money laundering detrimental effect for the case of 25th and 75th Percentile. According to (Aluko, & Bagheri, 2012) money laundering is negatively affected by political stability and development in Nigeria.

Table 6. Quantile Regression Estimates (Dep. Var. LnIFF)

Variables	25th PERCentile	50th PERCentile	75th PERCentile
	Coef. (prob.)	Coef. (prob.)	Coef. (prob.)
LnGS	-0.37 (0.00)***	-0.15 (0.33)	-0.17 (0.07)*
LnCorr	0.01 (0.90)	0.04 (0.81)	-0.12 (0.52)
LnBQ	0.49 (0.00)***	0.65 (0.00)***	1.03 (0.00)***
LnLO	0.51 (0.00)***	0.45 (0.02)**	-0.33 (0.00)***
LnDA	0.21 (0.01)**	0.17 (0.00)***	-0.12 (0.25)

Probability values are provided in parenthesis. *** significant at 1%, ** significant at 5% and * significant at 10%

Here bureaucratic quality has a positive effect on the money laundering, Maulidi (2020) has found evidence of the bureaucracy committing fraud in Indonesia. A study conducted by (Saleemi *et al.*, 2019), showed a significant positive relationship between bureaucracy quality and crime rate. The study further explained this positive relationship could exist due to the ineffectiveness of the bureaucracies in developing countries.

Law and order is only expected to control the high levels of money laundering (75th Percentile and above) while it is increasing at low levels. A strong legal system can effectively curb laundering and illicit flow of funds from a country. This evidence is against most empirical evidences collected by researchers, since the improvement in law should decrease the crime rate. However, an explanation indicated by (Reganati & Oliva, 2018), who also showed significant positive results, explained that law and order become ineffective when it is not able to instil fear of consequences in criminals.

Lastly, we have democratic accountability which is a central piece of good governance. It allows the public to decentralize power, ensures checks and balances so that public control have power over resources. Here the results show a positive and significant relationship between accountability and illicit financial flows. A simple explanation could be politicians and administrative personnel involved in marinating accountability could be involved in corruption and bribery by themselves (AFP, 2012). Money launders can entice people working in institutions by offering large bribes and gifts to allow the illicit flow of funds. Due to this accountability become ineffective and increases money laundering. Saleemi *et al.* (2019) also found that democratic accountability has a significant positive relationship with crime. The reason suggested by the study also indicated the ineffectiveness of the institutions.

4. CONCLUSION AND POLICY RECOMMENDATIONS

Most of the developing and developed countries have various legal, administrative, operational frameworks and financial system design to deter victimless crimes, but their structures differ from one another. Therefore, one cannot opt a single measure to tackle victimless crime like money laundering. This led to the evolution of FATF, which developed case based recommendations to counter money laundering. The advisory team picks the policies and measures that are required for each countries conditions. Following are the (FATF, 2011) generally approved recommendations.

- Identify threats, and establish policies and coordination within the country
- Keep pursuing money laundering, terrorist funding and the financing of proliferation;
- Set competent authority at responsibilities and obligations (e.g. investigators, law enforcement and supervisors) and other actions;
- Improve accountability and provision of beneficial ownership information and regulations for legal persons

- Facilitate cooperation internationally.

This study focuses on the problem of money laundering and how institutional quality / good governance of developing countries can tackle such kind of criminal activities. The research has selected key indicators like government stability, corruption, bureaucratic policies, law & order, & democratic accountability have an impact on money laundering. The study suggested a negative significant relationship with government stability.

Countries should set-in effective legal frameworks and take legislative measure in order to seize and confiscate any property, tangible or non-tangible assets that are somehow linked to money laundering. The legal team set towards catching criminals who launder money should also be competent in their tasks. They should be able to effectively trace individuals who have links with illicitly transferring funds from one place to another. Overall criminal infiltrating legal sectors of the economy and trapping their illegal fund and buying people off with bribes and corruption can disrupt socioeconomic and living conditions of the economy. That is why effective regulations and control and implementation of Anti Money Laundering (AML) measures are necessary in order to combat money laundering.

DISCLAIMER

The contents and views of this chapter are expressed by the authors in their personal capacities. It is not necessary for the Editor and the Publisher to agree with these viewpoints and they are not responsible for any duty of care in this regard.

ACKNOWLEDGMENT

The authors extend sincere gratitude to:

- The Editor-in-Chief and International Editorial Advisory Board (IEAB) of this book who initially desk reviewed, arranged a rigorous double/triple blind review process and conducted a thorough, minute and critical final review before accepting the chapter for publication.
- All anonymous reviewers who provided very constructive feedbacks for thorough revision, improvement, extension and finetuning of the chapter.
- All colleagues, assistants and well-wishers who assisted the authors to complete this task.

REFERENCES

Abdulqayumov, S., Arshed, N., & Bukhari, S. (2020). Economic impact of institutional quality on environmental performance on post-soviet countries. *Transition Studies Review*, *27*(2), 13–24.

ACCR. (2015). *Australian Crime Commission Annual Report*. Australian Criminal Intelligence Commision.

AFP. (2012, December 12). Report Unmasks Tax Evasion Among Pakistan Leaders. *The Express Tribune*. Retrieved from https://tribune.com.pk/story/478812/report-unmasks-tax-evasion-amongpakistan-leaders

Alemika, E. E. (2013). *The impact of organized crime on governance in West Africa*. Friedrich-Ebert-Stiftung.

Aluko, A., & Bagheri, M. (2012). The impact of money laundering on economic and financial stability and on political development in developing countries. *Journal of Money Laundering Control*, *15*(4), 442–457. doi:10.1108/13685201211266024

Arshed, N., Arif, A., Abbas, R. Z., & Hameed, K. (2020). Comparing quality of institutions with happiness of Asian people. *Studies in Applied Economics*, *39*(2).

Asongu, S., & Kodila-Tedika, O. (2016). Fighting African conflicts and crimes: Which governance tools matter? *International Journal of Social Economics*, *43*(5), 466–485. doi:10.1108/IJSE-11-2014-0233

Aziz, O., Grant, K. A., & Arshed, N. (2020). Does entrepreneurial activity assist in alleviation of poverty? *Journal of Applied Business & Economics*, *22*(7), 114–132.

Bajrang, P., Ritika, P., Puneet, & Parashar, N. (2012). Factors Affecting Money Laundering: A Lesson for Developing Countries. *Drishtikon: A Management Journal*, *3*(2), 108-139.

Becker, G. S. (1968). Crime and punishment: An economic approach. In N. G. Fielding, A. Clarke, & R. Witt (Eds.), *The economic dimensions of crime*. Macmillan. doi:10.1007/978-1-349-62853-7_2

Benoit, K. (2011). Linear regression models with logarithmic transformations. *London School of Economics*, *22*(1), 23-36.

Bergström, M., Svedberg Helgesson, K., & Mörth, U. (2011). A new role for for-profit actors? The case of anti-money laundering and risk management. *Journal of Common Market Studies*, *49*(5), 1043–1064. doi:10.1111/j.1468-5965.2010.02167.x

Brown, A. N. (2009). *Brown Money Laundering*. Green.

Chaikin, D. (2017). Money laundering and tax evasion–the assisting of the banking sector. In M. S. Aßländer & S. Hudson (Eds.), *The Handbook of Business and Corruption*. Emerald. doi:10.1108/978-1-78635-445-720161012

Cohen, M. A. (2005). *The costs of crime and justice*. Routledge. doi:10.4324/9780203313145

Draghi, M. (2011). *Le mafie a Milano e nel Nord: aspetti sociali ed economici.* Retrieved from https://www.bancaditalia.it/pubblicazioni/interventigovernatore/integov2011/Draghi-110311.pdf

FATF. (2011). Laundering the Proceeds of corruption in FATF Report. *Financial Action Task Force.* Retrieved from http://www.FATF-gafi.org

Fossen, A. (2003). Money Laundering, Global Financial Instability, and Tax Havens in the Pacific Islands. *The Contemporary Pacific, 15*(2), 237–275. doi:10.1353/cp.2003.0058

GECF. (2018). Global Economic Crime and Fraud Survey. *German Prevention Congress.*

Godspower-Akpomiemie, E., & Ojah, K. (2018). *Money laundering, Tax havens, Transparency and Board of Directors of Banks* (MPRA Paper No. 89550). Wits Business School, University of the Witwatersrand. Retrieved from https://mpra.ub.unimuenchen.de/89550/https://www.acic.gov.au/sites/g/files/net1491/f/2017/08/oca_2017_230817_1830.pdf

Gujarati, D. N., & Porter, D. (2009). *Basic Econometrics*. McGraw-Hill.

Habibullah, M. S., & Din, B., & Abdul Hamid, B. (2016). Good governance and crime rates in Malaysia. *International Journal of Social Economics, 43*(3), 308–320. doi:10.1108/IJSE-05-2014-0096

Hassan, M. S., Bukhari, S., & Arshed, N. (2020). Competitiveness, governance and globalization: What matters for poverty alleviation? *Environment, Development and Sustainability, 22*(4), 3491–3518. doi:10.100710668-019-00355-y

Katkov, N. (2014). *Anti-Money Laundering: A Brave New World for Financial Institutions*. CELENT.

Kaufmann, D., Kraay, A., & Mastruzzi, M. (2010). *The Worldwide Governance Indicators: Methodology and Analytical Issues* (Draft Policy Research Working Paper). The World Bank.

Lewisch, P. (2018). Corporate criminal liability for foreign bribery: Perspectives from civil law jurisdictions within the European Union. *Law and Financial Markets Review*, *12*(1), 31–38. doi:10.1080/17521440.2018.1435457

Matthew, O. A., Babajide, A. A., Osabohien, R., Adeniji, A., Ewetan, O. O., Adu, O., & Edafe, O. (2020). Challenges of accountability and development in Nigeria. *Journal of Money Laundering Control*, *23*(2), 387–402. doi:10.1108/JMLC-10-2019-0086

Maulidi, A. (2020). Storytelling of bureaucratic white-collar crimes in Indonesia: Is it a matter of reciprocal norm? *Journal of Financial Crime*, *27*(2), 573–586. doi:10.1108/JFC-07-2019-0087

MLCA. (1986). *The Money Laundering Control Act of 1986: Creating a New Federal Offense or Merely Affording Federal Prosecutors an Alternative Means of Punishing Specified Unlawful Activity?* Retrieved from https://scholarship.law.nd.edu/cgi/viewcontent.cgi?article=1014&context=law_faculty_scholarship

Montes, G. C., & Paschoal, P. C. (2016). Corruption: What are the effects on government effectiveness? Empirical evidence considering developed and developing countries. *Applied Economics Letters*, *23*(2), 146–150.

Nasir, M. A. (2020). The Relevance of Maqasid al Shari'ah to Anti-Money Laundering and Terrorism Financing. In A. Rafay (Ed.), *Handbook of Research on Theory and Practice of Global Islamic Finance* (pp. 179–194). IGI Global.

Nofianti, L., & Suseno, N. (2014). Factors affecting implementation of good government governance (GGG) and their implications towards performance accountability. *Social and Behavioral Sciences*, *164*, 98–105.

Okunlola, O. C. (2014). Money Laundering: A Threat to Sustainable Democracy in Nigeria. *Journal of Economics and Sustainable Development*, *5*(2), 85–98.

PERC. (2018). Political & Economic Risk Consultancy. Hong Kong: Corrupt Practices Investigation Bureau.

Poormazahaeri, M., Geravand, Z., & Hematfar, M. (2013). Money laundering and its effect on social and political economy in Iran. *European Online Journal of Natural and Social Sciences: Proceedings*, *2*(3 (s)), 607.

Rahman, A. A. (2015). Corporate governance and anti-money laundering measures in the banking industry: Malaysian experience. *International Academic Research Journal of Social Science*, *1*(2), 48–52.

Reganati, F., & Oliva, M. (2018). Determinants of money laundering: Evidence from Italian regions. *Journal of Money Laundering Control, 21*(3), 402–413.

Rodrick, D., & Subramanian, A. (2003). The primacy of institutions (and what this does and does not mean). *Finance and Development, International Monetary Fund*, 31-34. Retrieved from https://www.imf.org/external/pubs/ft/fandd/2003/06/pdf/rodrik.pdf

Saleemi, M. W., & Amir-ud-Din, R. (2019). *How does quality of governance influence occurrence of crime? A longitudinal analysis of Asian countries* (MPRA Paper 94142). Retrieved from https://mpra.ub.uni-muenchen.de/94142/

Savona, E. U., & Riccardi, M. (2019). Assessing the risk of money laundering: Research challenges and implications for practitioners. *European Journal on Criminal Policy and Research, 25*(1), 1–4.

Schneider, F. (2008). Money laundering and financial means of organised crime: Some preliminary empirical findings. *Global Business and Economics Review, 10*(3), 309–330.

Unger, B. (2013). Can money laundering decrease? *Public Finance Review, 41*(5), 658–676.

United Nation. (2009). *Millennium Development Goals Report 2009*. United Nations, Department of Economic and Social Affairs.

UNODC. (2011). *World Drug Report 2011*. United Nation Office of Drug and Crime.

Vaithilingam, S., & Nair, M. (2007). Factors affecting money laundering: Lesson for developing countries. *Journal of Money Laundering Control, 10*(3), 352–363.

Zia, M. A., Abbas, R. Z., & Arshed, N. (2020). *Money laundering and terror financing: Issues and challenges in Pakistan. Journal of Money Laundering and Control*. Early Print.

Chapter 5
Anti-Money Laundering in the Insurance Sector:
The Turkish Case

İsmail Yıldırım
Hitit University, Turkey

Abdul Rafay
https://orcid.org/0000-0002-0285-5980
University of Management and Technology, Pakistan

ABSTRACT

The insurance sector mainly consists of insurance companies, insurance agencies, brokers, and reinsurers. For many years, false damages, without being linked to money, have undoubtedly been the most attractive aspect of the insurance industry. However, for quite some time, the insurance sector is also used by money launders to launder crime revenues due to the increasing volume of money transactions day by day. In order to mitigate the risk of money laundering, the insurance sector in Turkey is implementing the compliance program of Turkish Law No: 5549 on "prevention of laundering proceeds of crime." The main components of this compliance program are the identification of the customers and reporting of suspicious transactions. It is concluded that the risk of money laundering should also be considered during damages and compensation payments, especially in life and pension companies. Policy and contract cancellations should be periodically reviewed, and the reasons for cancellations should be documented well.

DOI: 10.4018/978-1-7998-8758-4.ch005

INTRODUCTION

Money laundering is generally defined as the actions to disclose the "assets obtained from crime" as "income obtained from a legitimate source" in order to hide the illegal source. Money laundering is also expressed in the form of actions and activities aimed at hiding, covering or showing the nature, source, location, status, movement and identity of the assets obtained from the crime (Nasir, 2020). This is either in order to hide their crimes or to create legality of revenues obtained from crimes (Alp, 2000). The insurance sector is one of the most fundamental elements of the financial institutions. The ability of insurance companies to fulfill their commitments to the insured in full and on time, depends on the existence of an active functional market. Financial institutions, including insurance companies, are an important target for money launderers, as they offer customers the opportunity to use a wide range of investment tools and transfer funds from one place to another (Swiss Re, 2013). Although the insurance sector has not been used in money laundering transactions as compared to other financial sectors, the increase in global money transfers causes this sector to be used more and more for money laundering. Since ancient times, without being linked to money, false damages have undoubtedly been the most attractive aspect of insurance for money launders.

RELATED KEY INDICATORS AND INSURANCE SECTOR IN TURKEY

The insurance sector mainly consists of insurance companies, insurance agencies, brokers and reinsurers. In general, insurance companies are large companies that provide insurance coverage and undertake the risks specified in the policy against a certain premium. Insurance agents and brokers are intermediaries selling insurance companies' policies. Some of these agents and brokers only work for one insurance company and sell its policies, while others sell the products of multiple insurance companies. In addition to these two main components of the market, related organizations such as insurance experts and assistance companies that provide supportive services are also included in the market (Aykın, 2010).

Insurance companies assume the risks in the insurance policies and in return calculate the amount to be paid to them as a premium. Insurance companies clearly state the terms and duration of the contract, exactly what risks it covers, the premium and compensation amount in the policies (Çuhacı, 2003). How much premium will be paid is calculated based on the economic value of the goods in non-life insurances, and in the life insurances based on the insured's own value. Insurance companies direct the premiums collected from the insured to the investment in order to pay the insured's damages and compensations on time and completely. Life insurance companies prefer long-term investments due to the long duration of most of the life insurance products.

There are two types of insurance companies: Direct premium companies and reinsurance companies. Direct insurance companies are companies that issue policies and have direct contact with the insured. These companies provide the insured the relevant guarantee and receive a premium in return. Reinsurance companies, on the other hand, are companies that share the risks of the policies issued by insurance companies to the insured. Reinsurance is a kind of insurance company insuring itself, its portfolio. The insured does not have any contact with the reinsurance company. The premium is collected by the insurance company. Risks are transferred to the reinsurance company by the insurance company, provided that they waive a certain rate or amount of the premiums. Reinsurance companies also pay the insurance company upon payment to the insurer at the rate of their responsibility at the time of damage.

Table 1 depicts a comparison of companies in Turkish insurance. Two of the non-life companies established abroad continues to operate as branches of insurance companies of Turkey (Hazine Müsteşarlığı, 2020).

Table 1. Number of Companies in the Turkish Insurance Sector

	31.12.2018	**31.12.2019**
Out of Life	38	38
Life	4	4
Life / Pension	18	18
Reinsurance	2	3
Total	**62**	**63**

Source: Hazine Müsteşarlığı, 2020

There are 25 domestic and 38 foreign companies in the sector if companies are classified according to their capital structures. Foreign shareholding with more than 50% (direct or indirect) share are considered to classify an insurance company as a foreign company. As of December 31, 2019, 66.5% of the total capital of insurance companies is owned by foreigners, while 53% of the total premium is produced by foreigners. During same period, gross premium of insurance companies increased by 26.9% as compared to the previous year (Undersecretariat of Treasury, 2020).

RISKY TRANSACTIONS IN INSURANCE

Company employees and agents pay special attention to premium payments, high-level cash transactions and necessary information. Special attention is paid to the provision of insurance services to sectors and occupational groups where cash movements are intense. It is ensured that the identity, introductory documents and sector information of the insured are recorded completely and carefully. Occupational groups and sector classes that require special attention are specified and updated within the scope and framework of implementation principles.

Risks related to certain transactions are considered as risky transactions. Examples are Fire, loss of profit, theft insurances of goods in warehouses, transportation of imported and exported goods, export credit insurances etc. In the damages transactions, it is essential to make transactions over the original documents and to confirm the documents to the maximum possible extent. Special attention is given to the transactions of nonprofit charitable organizations keeping in view the fact that these can be exploited by terrorist organizations and criminals.

In the domestic and international electronic transfers it is mandatory to disclose the sender's name, surname, the title of the legal person registered in the trade registry, the full name of the other legal entities and non-legal entities, the account number, the address, the birthplace, date of birth, customer number, citizenship number, passport number, tax identification number etc. Any transaction above 2,000 Turkish Lira (TL) must be carried out by the company.

MONEY LAUNDERING AND INSURANCE SECTOR

The insurance sector is one of the fundamental components of the financial markets. The ability of insurance companies to fulfill their commitments to the insured in full and on time depends on the existence of a healthy market. It is a necessity for the insurance company to use the funds collected from the insured for its purpose and to operate smoothly in order to maintain the economic order and the general public order. Insurance is primarily a business activity based on trust. In this regard, the financial adequacy of the insurance companies has been continuously controlled and monitored. The public interest in the insurance sector's safe operation and development has been monitored and insurance companies have been subjected to state supervision (FATF, 2003).

Financial institutions, including insurance companies, are an important target for money launderers, as they offer customers the opportunity to use a wide range of investment tools and transfer funds from one place to another. The possibility that insurance companies are used as a means of money laundering is to confront them with risks such as reputational risk, financial risk, operational risk or criminal sanction both within and outside the country. As discussed above although the insurance sector has been used less in money laundering transactions, false damages have undoubtedly been the most attractive aspect of insurance for money launders. In the UK alone, considering that the fraud in damages related to automobile insurance and fire package policies is at the level of 1.6 billion dollars a year, it becomes clearer to what extent the insurance sector has potential in money laundering (FATF, 2003). Showing the insurance cost higher than the real value with various fraudulent transactions, insuring the insurance subject to more than one insurance company, causing deliberate damage, showing the uninsured damages as insured, etc. are few examples. Corruption after the damage is one of the few methods that money launderers use.

In Turkey, the insurance companies and private pension companies also go through processes such as the recognition of the customer within the framework of the regulations. Following types of suspicious transactions regarding insurance and pension transactions are mentioned by MASAK (Financial Crimes Investigation Board) (MASAK, 2020):

- The client proposes to purchase an insurance policy on the behalf of a third party who is not related to his or her account and is explicitly unrelated by issuing a check on someone else's account or transferring insurance compensation to the account of an unrelated party. It is also obvious that the third party, which is obviously irrelevant, requests change of beneficiaries
- The premiums of the life insurance or pension insurance policy are paid by the customer in high amounts and in cash.
- The customer, who pays a small amount and a regular payment-based policy, offers to purchase a substantially large policy with cash payment while there is no sudden and extraordinary development.
- The customer requests that the policy be repaid before its due date or be paid in favor of a third party without any reasonable reason.
- Payment in the policy is made through EFT from a bank account located in the country where it can be considered risky.
- Client's application for a pension plan or life insurance contract, although his age and health status are not favorable.
- The customer applies to insure a risk that is not related to his business area.
- It has been determined that the customer has policies from other companies and this situation is essentially incompatible with the customer's financial profile.
- A high amount of regular repayments are requested, but this is not compatible with the customer's overall condition and regular income.

Laundering Through Life Insurance

Life insurances enable the customer to transfer large amounts of funds into the financial system and transfer them without leaving a trace to hide their resources. These may include:

- An instrument of investment and fund accumulation,
- Cash participation value,
- Shown as collateral in credit transactions,
- Insurance policies within or without the knowledge of the insurer (bearer policies) to be transferred to the person,
- Early cancellation cost,
- Cancel the insurance policies before the deadline,
- Pay the amounts in excess of the insurance premiums in various ways and then to request the refund of the overpaid part etc.

For reasons, it is more favorable to laundering crime income than non-life insurances.

Laundering Through Non-Life (Elementary) Insurance

Non-life insurance premiums, funded by proceeds from crime, are requested to be returned to the insurance company by requesting claims from the insurance company. This process is working by creating false claims, or by creating damages through collusive activities. Thus, it is possible to get back the illegal funds laundered. When the assets that are insured by the insurance company at a price less than the real value of the assets are shown to third parties as insured at the real value, the damage is to be shown as being covered by the real insurance value of the assets (Kaya, 2010). In reality, the difference between the missing insurance cost and the actual insurance cost is laundered crime revenues.

Insurance intermediaries operating in the fields of life / non-life insurance also play an important role in laundering or preventing money laundering. Insurance brokers working under the insurance company or working independently from the insurance company are in direct contact with the policyholder. For this reason, they can observe some activities that can be considered as laundering indicator at the initial stage. In fact, most of the time, unknown issues about the policyholder are known by the brokers. Since insurance intermediaries (agents, brokers) do not have knowledge about the need and methods of combating money laundering, they have little or no interest in these matters. Placement of crime revenues in the insurance sector can be easily achieved through these people. Insurance intermediaries can create channels for themselves to place their crime revenues in the system. For this reason, it is considered by all countries that insurance intermediaries are informed about combating crime revenues and that some preventive measures are applied to them.

Laundering Through Reinsurance

Reinsurance laundering methods include to establish false reinsurance companies to carry out the laundering process, to establish counterfeit insurance companies to complete the laundering process together with legal reinsurance companies and to ensure that crime revenues are involved in normal reinsurance transactions in order to save the source of funds. Reinsurance has no cash participation value and does not allow transfer of an accumulated value to third parties. There is no direct link between the insurance policyholder and the insured and the reinsurer. Therefore, the procedures for the use of reinsurance companies for laundering create a natural barrier against laundering due to complexity. The use of reinsurance will be possible by the launderers themselves establishing an insurance agency or insurance company and thereafter signing a contract with the reinsurance company. This process is very costly and troublesome so there is a very low risk money laundering. Through reinsurance.

Laundering Through the Private Pension System

During the retirement contract period, the participant can get out of the private pension system at any time for example in case of permanent incapacity to work. In case the participant requests to leave, the savings in the private pension account are paid according to the provisions of the pension contract. The participant suffers a financial loss in such a situation. However, as in life insurances, despite the cost to be incurred, it seems possible to use the system in terms of launderers by choosing an early cancellation path. The participant has the right to withdraw before the pension contract enters into force. It seems possible that the possible crime income transferred to the company in this way will return to the launderers in a very short time, as a check or a bank transfer from a reputable pension company. However, the fact that the money, whose characteristics can be changed by using this method, is limited to "contribution fee or entrance fee" does not make the method very attractive in terms of laundering. In line with the general acceptance that pension policies are not too open to be abused by launderers, it has been stated that exemptions have been made in pension policies regarding identification, and facilitated by the facilitated CDD (Customer Due Diligence) measures.

SCENARIOS OF MONEY LAUNDERING IN THE INSURANCE INDUSTRY

Scenario 1

There is a laundering use of the insurance sector in many cases where insurance intermediaries step in and make first contact with the customer. The identity information of the customers is detected by the intermediaries. The parent company lacks the opportunity to confirm this information or the intermediary firm neglects it because they think it has somehow done thus makes the job of launderers easier. In this way, the launderer who has taken the policy leaves the system after a few months, by terminating the policy on the grounds that the conditions have changed. Even though he endures some damage, he has laundered his money. Sometimes the policy is held for a few years and then invested in a financial institution with the request to make the payment to a different third party, and this institution does not suspect the transaction by not requiring any examination of the funds from a reliable insurance company (FATF, 2018).

Scenario 2

In some countries, when the life insurance policy holder dies, the purchaser has the right to claim all his rights of the policy from the insurance company if he sold the policy. With the increase in AIDS disease, a secondary market for policies owned by patients has emerged. Since the patients know that they will die, they sell their policies in order to spend their remaining days well. The policy buyers earn as much profit as they buy at a discount. The launderers buy these policies by paying more than the price of cash and second-hand markets that is, at lower discounts compared to their real value (FATF, 2019).

It should be kept in mind that launderers may not make any discounts, or even give a price above the nominal value (Aleksoski & Aleksoski, 2015). The time value of the money (and the difference, if taken above its nominal value) in the period until the patient's death constitutes the laundering commission. Naturally, the patient is paid in cash. However, since the patient will continue his daily expenses with the income he earns from the sale, he will spend the cash he earns, without the need for laundering (Defossez, 2017). The launderers (just like the villagers or street vendors who produce the raw materials of drugs) have two advantages. The first advantage is the profit from purchases below nominal value, even if not the main objective. (In case of taking it from nominal value, it will have as much profit as the average laundering commission incurred in other techniques) (Doyle, 2017). The second advantage is that when the patient dies, the money in return for the policy will be paid to the launderer as a check from the insurance company, so there will be no use of cash and this transaction can be done without drawing anyone's attention.

Scenario 3

Another scenario is the laundering of organized crime proceeds by life insurance policies. This is revealed by an investigation by country X's customs authorities into a drug gang that used the insurance industry in money laundering. After joint studies carried out with the contributions of other relevant countries, it was revealed that the drug gang laundered the money they obtained from drugs through the Z insurance company established in the offshore region. Z insurance company was offering its clients instruments similar to mutual funds. Since the rate of return of these instruments is indexed to the world's major stock markets, insurance policies were traded as investment instruments. Policy holders over-funded their accounts, they were providing money movements with various deposit / withdrawal transactions, taking into account the penalty of converting their funds into cash early. As a result, the funds were withdrawn from the account either by a check or money transfer, and then laundered through the insurance company. Within the scope of the investigation, it was determined that 29 million dollars had been laundered by this method until that day, and 9 million dollars of this was seized. In addition, as a result of the joint efforts of countries Y and Z, arrest warrants have been issued for many individuals associated with insurance company Z for laundering activities (FATF, 2016).

FIGHT AGAINST MONEY LAUNDERING OF INSURANCE COMPANIES IN TURKEY

In Turkey Law no: 5549 on "Prevention of laundering proceeds of crime" was adopted on 11/10/2006 and published in the Official Gazette dated 18/10/2006 with the number 26323. In this regard, Financial Crimes Investigation Board (MASAK) reported that suspicious transaction are mostly sent electronically (99.7%), and non-institutional liabilities such as those dealing with the purchase and sale of land vehicles (motor vehicle galleries) or those who sell and sell precious metals, stones and jewelry. (MASAK, 2020). Suspicious transaction reports are subjected to strategic or operational data analysis both on an incident / organization basis and on risk criteria. The number of suspicious transaction reports per year is presented in Figure 1 and the distribution of the obliged groups is presented in Table 2.

In 2018, suspicious transaction reports from banking, electronic money / payment services, effective foreign exchange or precious metal / stone trading transactions has been increased as compared to other years.

Figure 1. Distribution of Suspicious Transaction Report Numbers by Years (2014-2018)

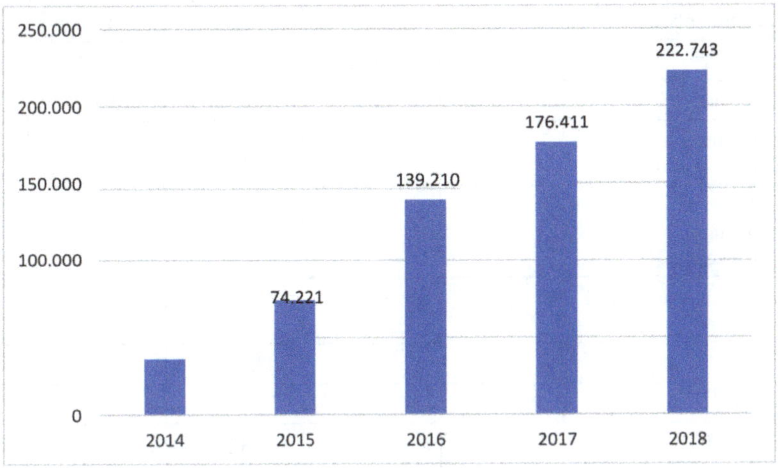

Turkey is experiencing various problems in the fight against money laundering. Penalties cannot be fully implemented due to various problems. One of the characteristics of black money is that it is unrecorded, another characteristic is its connection with crime. In this context, for the evaluation of the reasons, the causes of the informal economy and crime in Turkey, should be evaluated together with the reasons. The criminal sociology deals with the behaviors of people and / or general moral values. According to the information revealed by the data obtained from various studies, the reasons are as follows (Aydin, 2018);

1. poverty in economic terms,
2. feeling victimized in the style of perceiving and interpreting the living conditions he / she is in
3. unhealthy family environment, unemployment of father, substance addiction of father and / or mother, divorce, domestic violence,
4. the close friendship group and the family's environment being in regions with high crime rates and the preference of illegal lifestyle being the dominant values.

Table 2. Distribution of Suspicious Transaction Reports by Obliged Groups (2014-2018)

Incumbents	2014	2015	2016	2017	2018
Banks	31.146	66.719	117.006	159.076	195.803
Factoring Companies	1.925	2.520	6.870	4.399	5.098
Payment Institutions and Electronic Money Institutions	-	-	703	3.382	13.796
Insurance and Pension Companies, and Insurance and Reinsurance Brokers	693	451	1.980	1.487	735
Precious Metals with Authorized Institutions	498	603	899	1.323	1.924
Organizations	194	424	845	693	948
Cargo Companies	39	32	201	631	74
Financing Companies	209	151	371	332	172
Capital Market Intermediary Institutions	101	45	181	78	69
Financial Leasing Companies	-	35	51	37	52
Those dealing with the purchase and sale of all types of marine, air and land transport vehicles, including construction equipment	-	-	-	14	1
Freelance Accountant and Sworn Financial Advisors	-	-	-	4	5
Those Operating in the Field of Fortune and Betting Games	-	-	-	2	-
Independent Audit Firms	1	-	2	1	-
Notaries	-	-	-	1	-
Investment Partnerships	-	-	-	-	43
Precious Metals, Stone and Jewelry Buyers	-	1	-	-	-
Asset Management Companies	-	-	1	-	2
Institutions Providing Clearing and Custody Services	-	-	-	-	3
Portfolio Management Companies	1.677	3.240	3.460	4.951	4.018

Source: MASAK, 2020

Table 3. Distribution of the Number of Financial Institutions SIB Submitted by Years (2014-2018)

Financial Institutions	2014	2015	2016	2017	2018
Banks	33	34	34	32	34
Capital Market Intermediary Institutions	30	25	38	34	32
Insurance and Pension Companies, and Insurance and Reinsurance Brokers	34	34	42	36	35
Factoring Companies	51	48	44	45	42
Financial Leasing Companies	16	12	16	14	11
Financing Companies	5	7	8	9	8
Authorized Institutions and Precious Metal Intermediary Institutions	12	18	25	20	24
Payment Institutions and Electronic Money Institutions	-	-	8	12	24
Institutions Providing Clearing and Custody Services	-	-	1	-	1
Investment Partnerships	-	-	-	1	-
Portfolio Management Companies	-	-	-	-	1

Source: MASAK, 2020

Figure 2. Distribution of Financial Institutions by Years (2014-2018)

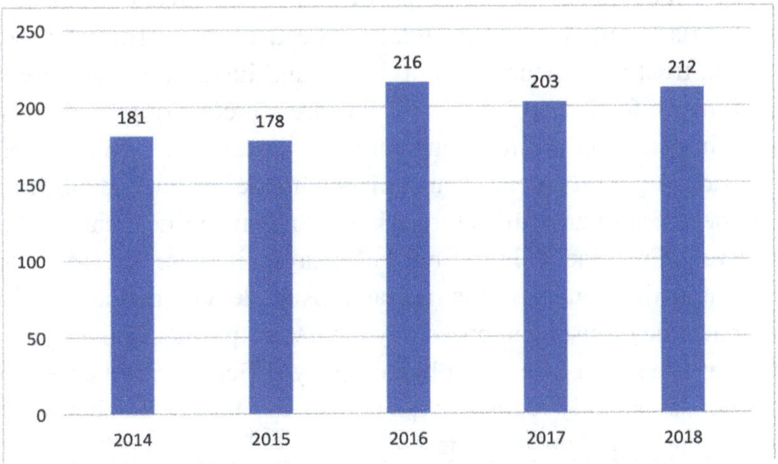

PRECAUTIONARY MEASURES TO AVOID MONEY LAUNDERING

Customer Recognition and Acceptance

Within the scope of the principle of recognition of the customer, it is necessary to provide sufficient information about the activities of the customers and customers. This is important to the determine the transactions related to illegal activities by reducing and controlling the risk of laundering, and to ensure the integrity of the financial system by reducing the possibility of being used as an intermediary in financial crime (Kaya, 2010).

Following measures are required for the recognition of the customer in the insurance industry (MASAK, 2020);

- Identifying the customer
- Obtaining information about the purpose and nature of the business relationship
- Continuity of the business relationship
- Determining the fact that who is the real beneficiary
- Creating a risk profile of the customers by taking into consideration their profession, work history, financial status, accounts, commercial activities, country of residence and other relevant indicators

It is essential to conduct more intensive examinations for high-risk customers. The acceptance of customers with the approval of the managers responsible for the relevant process is essential. Customer relations need to be based on mutual exchange of information, trust and openness. Individuals and institutions who are reluctant to fill in customer information and forms, who are reluctant or provide misleading, unconfirmed information are not considered as customers. While establishing a business relationship with potential customers who are seriously doubtful that they do not earn their wealth and funds through legal means, utmost care and attention should be given. Customers should not be engaged if there are information and documents that justify doubts. In the transactions made with the power of attorney, the power of attorney must be approved by the notary public. The original copy of the power of attorney must be taken by company official, and in cases where the customer is not sufficiently recognized, a confirmation must be obtained from the notary public who issued the document.

MONITORING CUSTOMER STATUS AND TRANSACTIONS

In order to recognize its customers and measure their risks, risk profile is measured for money laundering and terrorist financing, taking into account their customers' address information, profession, business history, financial status, commercial activities, country of residence and other relevant information. The purpose of the risk profile is to identify high-risk customers, business relationships and transactions and to follow them continuously (Kander, 2001). The customer's risk profile assessment needs to be done at the beginning of the business relationship with the customer. However, some clients' comprehensive risk profile can be clarified when transactions start. This necessitates monitoring of customer risks and making necessary reviews continuously (Şentürk, 2009).

In the risk policies of the insurance companies, risky business lines, geographical regions, situations that can be / cannot be guaranteed, coverage limits are specified on the basis of branches, agencies and regional directorates. Regional directorates and agencies are obliged to get authorization from the general directorate in transactions exceeding their limits or in transactions related to risky business lines. While making the risk acceptance, the previous damages of the risk are explored (Usluoğlu, 2002). When deemed necessary, a risk inspection report is prepared. In this context, those customers are monitored:

- who are operating in the risky business line
- who are working in the risky countries
- whose name is being mentioned in the press or watch lists
- who are maintaining a portfolio exceeding the certain size
- who demand transactions against the risk acceptance criteria
- who are facing counterfeit or suspicious damage transactions, etc.

REPORTING OF SUSPICIOUS TRANSACTIONS

According to the first paragraph of Article 4 of Law No. 5549, it is mandatory to notify MASAK, if any suspicious information is found about the assets subject to the transactions made or attempted to be carried out by or through them are used illegally or used for illegal purposes or related to terrorist organizations, terrorists or terrorist financiers (MASAK, 2020). Pursuant to the second paragraph of Article 4 of the Law No. 5549, the obliged parties cannot explain to the MASAK that no suspicious transaction reports have been made to anyone other than those involved in the transaction, the audit staff assigned with the obligation audit and the courts during the trial.

APPOINTMENT OF COMPLIANCE OFFICER

In Article 5 of the Law No. 5549, it is foreseen as an obligation to appoint an administrative level official who is equipped with the necessary authority to comply with the obligations imposed by this Law (Üstün, 2003). With the "Regulation on Compliance with Obligations Regarding Prevention of Laundering Crime Revenues and Financing of Terrorism" the procedures and principles regarding the appointment of a compliance officer have been determined. Following are obliged to appoint a compliance officer.

- Banks,
- Capital market intermediary institutions,
- Insurance and pension companies,
- Postal and Telegraph Organization Inc. (limited to banking activity)
- Institutions that have the authority to issue debit or credit cards other than banks,
- Authorized institutions specified in the exchange legislation,
- Financing and factoring companies within the scope of the legislation on lending operations,
- Reinsurance companies,
- Financial leasing companies and
- Institutions providing clearing and custody services within the framework of capital market legislation
- Futures brokerage companies

CONCLUSION

The insurance sector mainly consists of insurance companies, insurance agencies, brokers and reinsurers. In general, insurers are large companies that provide insurance coverage and take on the risks specified in the policy. Insurance agents and brokers are intermediaries selling insurance companies' policies. Some of these agents and brokers only work for one insurance company and sell its policies, while others sell the products of multiple insurance companies. In addition to these two main components of the market, related organizations such as insurance experts and assistance companies that provide supportive services are also included in the market.

Insurance companies offer their customers a large number of insurance products such as life insurance, disability insurance, health insurance, annuity (*irait* insurance), liability insurance, automobile or home insurance. In addition to individual insurance products, group insurances are also available. Group insurances can cover a few people or millions of people. Group policies are generally sold to employers for their employees or professional organizations for their members. The most common group insurance policies are life and health insurance group policies. The insurance sector offers products with risk transfer, savings and investment characteristics to many groups, from real persons to legal entities, from multinational companies to governments, globally. Therefore, the insurance sector, which may be attractive for those who are seeking to clear their crime revenues by investing in a financial product, is under threat of money laundering, as in other financial sectors. If a money launderer can direct revenues from crime to an insurance product and receive a refund from the insurance company in return, then he will have the function of giving his funds a legal appearance.

The issues such as counting insurance, pension and reinsurance companies among the obliged parties of the Law on the Prevention of Laundering of Crime Revenues No. 5549, identifying the identity stipulated in the International Insurance Auditors Association (IAIS) Guidelines, storing the records, and making suspicious transaction reports has also made it a liability for insurance companies. According to the Regulation on Preparing a Compliance Program based on Law No. 5549, the obligation to prepare a compliance program for insurance and pension companies has made it compulsory for companies to identify the factors that pose a risk in terms of money and to inform MASAK what measures they have taken against these risks.

Companies try to be aware of the risk of money laudering through these compliance programs. However, the possibility of money laundering in insurance companies operating in non-life branches is relatively low. Therefore, there is less obligation to prepare a compliance program for insurance companies operating in non-life insurance sector. With this, all companies operating in the insurance and pension sector, excluding reinsurance companies, are obliged to prepare a compliance program. Fighting against money can only be successful when preventive measures are taken. Detection of laundered money can only play a complementary role in the fight against money. The main measures that companies can take as a preventive measure in the fight against money are integrating the compliance requirements into their workflow processes.

Companies must know their customers. The customers must be duly identified. Suspicious transaction reporting should be placed in workflows. Compliance officers should create a "transaction guide" and plan their work flow processes. A customer acceptance policy focused on clean money, not just sales, should be established. For this purpose, the importance given to the customer profile in life insurances should also cover the commodity or risk subject to insurance in non-life insurance. In cases where the commodity is physically stored or avoided to be shown, the insurer should perceive the situation as a risky transaction and make sufficient examinations on whether there is a suspicious transaction and if necessary, engage the compliance officer. The risk of money laundering should also be taken into account during damages and compensation payments, especially in life and pension companies, policy and contract cancellations should be periodically reviewed, and the reasons for cancellations should be weighed well. Also, damage and compensation payments must be made through the bank.

Agencies are the most important premium production channels of companies and agents are the ones who have the most direct information about customers. Therefore, companies should include their agents in their anti-money programs, and they should explain to their agents how to implement the "know your customer" principle, the measures they need to take in this area, which they are also responsible for. Effective use of Insurance Technologies (InsurTech) can also play a significant role in achieving these goals (Yildirim, 2019).

DISCLAIMER

The contents and views of this chapter are expressed by the authors in their personal capacities. It is not necessary for the Editor and the Publisher to agree with these viewpoints and they are not responsible for any duty of care in this regard.

ACKNOWLEDGMENT

The authors extend sincere gratitude to:

- The Editor-in-Chief and International Editorial Advisory Board (IEAB) of this book who initially desk reviewed, arranged a rigorous double/triple blind review process and conducted a thorough, minute and critical final review before accepting the chapter for publication.
- All anonymous reviewers who provided very constructive feedbacks for thorough revision, improvement, extension and finetuning of the chapter.
- All colleagues, assistants and well-wishers who assisted the authors to complete this task.

REFERENCES

Aleksoski, S., & Aleksoski, O. (2015). Money laundering as a type of organized crime. *Journal of Process Management. Nuclear Technology*, *3*(3), 44–54.

Alp, İ. A. (2000). Paranın Karası, Kara Paranın Makroekonomik Etkileri [Black Money, Macro Economic Effects of Black Money]. *Maliye Dergisi*, *134*, 13–15.

Aydin, H. (2018). TBB-MASAK Çalıştayı Açılış Konuşmaları [TBB-MASAK Workshop Opening Speeches]. *Bankacılar Dergisi, 105*.

Aykın, H. (2010). *Aklama ve Terörün Finansmanı ile Mücadelenin Küresel Boyutu* (Yayın No:2010/406) [The Global Dimension of the Fight against Laundering and Terrorist Financing ((Publication No: 2010/406)]. T.C. Maliye Bakanlığı Strateji Geliştirme Başkanlığı.

Çuhacı, K. (2003). Kara Para Aklama ve Sigortacılık Sektörü [Money Laundering and Insurance Sector]. *Reasürör Dergisi*, *48*, 15–18.

Defossez, D. (2017). The Current Challenges of Money Laundering Law in Russia. *Journal of Money Laundering Control*, *20*(4), 367–385. doi:10.1108/JMLC-09-2016-0041

Doyle, C. (2017). *Money Laundering: An Overview of 18 U.S.C. § 1956 and Related Federal Criminal Law*. CRS.

FATF. (2003). *Financial Action Task Force on Money Laundering, Report on Money Laundering Typologies 2002-2003*. The Financial Action Task Force.

FATF. (2016). *Anti-Money Laundering and Counter-Terrorist Financing Measures*. United States: Fourth Round Mutual Evaluation Report, Paris: The Financial Action Task Force.

FATF. (2018). *Anti-Money Laundering and Counter-Terrorist Financing Measures*. United Kingdom: Fourth Round Mutual Evaluation Report, Paris: The Financial Action Task Force.

FATF. (2019). *Anti-money Laundering and Counter-Terrorist Financing Measures*. Turkey: Fourth Round Mutual Evaluation Report, Paris: The Financial Action Task Force.

FATF / GAFILAT. (2018). *Anti-Money Laundering and Counter-Terrorist Financing Measures*. Mexico: Fourth Round Mutual Evaluation Report, Paris: The Financial Action Task Force.

IAIS. (2004). Anti-Money Laundering and Combating the Financing of Terrorism (Guidance Paper No: 5). International Association of Insurance Supervisors.

Kander, R. (2001). *Türkiye'de Hususi Sigorta Hukuku* [Private Insurance Law in Turkey]. Beta Publications.

Kaya, M. (2010). Suç Gelirlerinin Aklanmasında Bir Araç Olarak Sigortacılık Sektörünün Kullanılması [The Use of Insurance Sector as a Tool in Laundering Proceeds of Crime]. *Sosyal Güvenlik Dünyası Dergisi*, *68*, 1–10.

MASAK. (2020). *Financial Crimes Investigation Board*. Retrieved from https://en.hmb.gov.tr/fcib-presentation

Müsteşarlığı, H. (2020). Sigortacılık ve BES Faaliyet Raporu-2020 [Insurance and BES Annual Report-2020]. Ankara, 2020. Hazine Müsteşarlığı, 2020 Yılı Sigortacılık ve Bireysel Emeklilik Faaliyet Raporu Basın Özeti, Ankara.

Nasir, M. A. (2020). The Relevance of Maqasid al Shari'ah to Anti-Money Laundering and Terrorism Financing. In A. Rafay (Ed.), *Handbook of Research on Theory and Practice of Global Islamic Finance* (pp. 179–194). IGI Global. doi:10.4018/978-1-7998-0218-1.ch010

Şentürk, Ş. S. (2009). *Sigortacılıkta Kara Para ile Mücadele* [Fight against Black Money in Insurance] (Unpublished Master's Thesis). Marmara University Banking and Insurance Institute, Istanbul.

Swiss Re. (2013). *World Insurance in 2013: Steering Towards Recovery*. Retrieved from http://media.swissre.com/ documents / sigma3_2014_en.pdf

Undersecretariat of Treasury. (2020). *Insurance and BES Annual Report-2014*.

Usluoğlu, Ç. (2002). Dünyada Ve Türkiye'de Kara Paranın Aklanmasının Önlenmesine İlişkin Düzenlemelerin Türk Sigorta Sektörü Açısından Genel Bir Değerlendi [An Overview of Turkish Insurance Sector in terms of the Regulations for the Prevention of Money Laundering in the world and in Turkey]. *Reasürör*. Retrieved from http://tsrsb.org.tr/private/trk/sayi37/ince37.htm

Üstün, O. (2003). Mali Eylem Görev Gücü"nün Yeni Kırk Tavsiye Kararı Neler Getiriyor? [What Do the Financial Action Task Force's New Forty Recommendations Bring?]. *Bankacılar Dergisi, 47*.

Yildirim, I. (2019). Emergence of Insurance Technologies (InsurTech): The Turkish Case. In A. Rafay (Ed.), *FinTech as a Disruptive Technology for Financial Institutions* (pp. 42–60). IGI Global. doi:10.4018/978-1-5225-7805-5.ch003

KEY TERMS AND DEFINITIONS

Black Money: Black money means money earned in ways and methods that the state would not allow.

Crime: It is the deliberate and deliberate violation of legal values that should be protected in terms of the continuity of the social order.

Insurance: An insurance is a bilateral contract that requires the insurer to compensate for the damage in the event of an event that damages a person's interest that can be measured with money, which is worth protecting by law in return for a premium to be received by the insurer.

Insurance Company: A company that deals with the management, operation and sales of insurance businesses.

Insurance Premium: In the insurance system, premium is the insurance fee paid by the insured in order to purchase the coverage provided by the selling officer of the insurance.

Pension Mutual Fund: It is a mutual fund created by the pension company to evaluate the contributions collected within the framework of the pension contract and monitored in the individual pension accounts on behalf of the participants.

Revenue of Crime: The proceeds of crime can be expressed as all kinds of economic benefits and values obtained from the acts deemed crime by law.

Chapter 6
Factors Influencing the Outcome of Money Laundering Investigations

Salwa Zolkaflil
https://orcid.org/0000-0002-1039-3448
Universiti Teknologi MARA (UiTM), Malaysia

Normah Omar
Universiti Teknologi MARA (UiTM), Malaysia

Sharifah Nazatul Faiza Syed Mustapha Nazri
Universiti Teknologi MARA (UiTM), Malaysia

ABSTRACT

Money laundering is a global issue that must be effectively mitigated across the nation. Despite various initiatives, investigation outcome either in the form of prosecution, conviction, or confiscation remains low. Therefore, this study aims to investigate the factors influencing money laundering investigating outcome, based on rational choice theory. The study conducted focus group interviews with 15 investigating officers to have an in-depth understanding of factors and challenges faced by investigating officers in conducting money laundering investigation which influences their investigation outcome. The findings demonstrate that money laundering investigation outcome is influenced by three factors, which are cost-benefit analysis, individual belief, and organizational context. The findings of the study provide significant contributions in confirming the theoretical foundations underpinning this research and suggest recommendations for the relevant regulators in improving money laundering investigation and prosecution decision making.

DOI: 10.4018/978-1-7998-8758-4.ch006

INTRODUCTION

Money laundering is a term generally used by practitioners and researchers to illustrate the process by which offenders disguise the illegal proceeds of crime as if it is obtained from a legitimate source (Hamin, Wan Rosli, Omar, & Pengiran Mahmud, 2013; Mohamed & Ahmad, 2012; Ping, 2008; Shanmugam, Nair, & Suganthi, 2003). In most cases, illegal proceeds derived from offences such as fraud, corruption, bribery, criminal breach of trust, human trafficking, sales of drugs will be laundered through creative means. Tax evasion is also a major cause of ill-gotten money (Rafay & Ajmal, 2014)

Globally, a lot of initiatives have been taken to mitigate money laundering offences (Nasir, 2020). This includes the passing of anti-money laundering legislations, issuance of international anti-money laundering standards, establishments of guidelines and the introduction of international cooperation between countries. The Financial Action Task Force (FATF) recommendations were then introduced as a guideline for countries to promote effective implementation of legal, regulatory and operational measures for combating money laundering, terrorist financing and the financing of proliferation, and other related threats to the integrity of the international financial system. However, its implementation varies depending on the member countries. Therefore, the countries have diverse legal, administrative, and operational frameworks and different financial systems, and so cannot all take identical measures to counter the financial threats.

Despite efforts undertaken by various countries and international agencies, the United Nation statistics implicated that around 2% to 5% of the global Gross Domestic Products (GDP) which are equivalent to USD 1 to 2 trillion per year are at lost due to global money laundering transactions. However, less than 1% of the global illicit financial flows are successfully seized by the authorities (United Nations Office on Drugs and Crime (UNODC), 2011). This estimations represents just the tip of the iceberg in showing money laundering's true global scale (PWC, 2014). The negative outcomes of money laundering offences are not only economically implicated, but also the reputational implication that a country needs to negate as both are costly and risky.

Due to such risks, regulators and law enforcement agencies are treating money laundering as a priority issue to be effectively tackled by governments across the nation. *Recommendation 30 of FATF Recommendations (2012),* specifically addresses the *"Responsibilities of Law Enforcement and Investigative Authorities"*, include the need for a country's competent authority to ensure that money laundering predicate offences are properly investigated through the conduct of a financial investigation. In such investigation, law enforcement agencies should be able to identify, trace, and initiate confiscation process through the different provisions of freezing, seizing and forfeiting of property involved in money laundering offences.

One of the most controversial reports on money laundering was issued by the Global Financial Integrity (GFI), a non-profit Washington DC-based research and advisory organisation. Based on the GFI Report (2019), a 10-year study (2006 to 2015) on illicit financial flows of 148 developing countries implicated an increasing trend in money laundering activities. Illicit financial flows are essentially money laundering in a form of illegal financial leakage or capital flight when money is illegally earned, transferred, or spent.

GFI report has named and ranked Malaysia as one of the countries that has been implicated with money laundering activities. Indeed, Malaysia was ranked at the 4th position after China, Russia and Mexico for countries with highest amount of illicit financial flows or financial leakages over a ten-year period of 2002 to 2011 (Kar & LeBlanc, 2013). Financial leakages are increasing from year to year due to the uncurbed money laundering activities which are happening all around the world. Over the period of 2009 to 2013, the report claimed that Malaysia has accumulated total illicit financial flows of USD 242.6 billion. Table 1 summarises the GFI statistics for the year 2009 to 2013.

Table 1. Illicit Financial Flows for Malaysia 2009 to 2013

Year	2009	2010	2011	2012	2013	Total
Illicit Financial Flows (USD Billion)	34.4	62.1	50.2	47.8	48.2	**242.6**

Source: Global Financial Integrity (GFI) Website

The figure has been challenged by Bank Negara Malaysia (BNM) in 2017, stating that the figures reported by the GFI were distorted and which include "unrecorded financial flows" leading to overstated of illicit flows (The Malaysian Reserve, 2017). Nevertheless, even if only a fraction of the statistics is true, the figure is indeed still very alarming. Improvement actions must therefore be taken to mitigate money laundering activities in order to improve Malaysia's economic management (The Star, 2013), as well as to improve Malaysia reputation.

In addressing the money laundering threat, an international agency Financial Action Task Force (FATF). FATF has developed the anti-money laundering standards, known as FATF 40 Recommendations as a guideline for member countries in mitigating money laundering activities. As part of monitoring process, FATF also conducts periodical evaluation on its member countries to assess the compliance and effectiveness of a country in combating money laundering. The assessment includes the compliance and effectiveness of Anti-Money Laundering Regime (AML Regime) of respective countries and results are presented in the report named Mutual Evaluation Report (MER).

Malaysia's Mutual Evaluation Report (MER) (2015) stated that Malaysia has a sound AML Regime, yet the number of prosecution and convictions remained low. During the periods between 2009 until 2013, only 16% of the total investigations proceeded with prosecution, while only 7% of the prosecuted cases ended with conviction, as summarised in Table 2.

Table 2. Money laundering Investigation and Prosecution in Malaysia for 2009 to 2013

	2009	%	2010	%	2011	%	2012	%	2013	%	Total	%
Investigations	138		94		124		230		235		821	
Prosecutions	22	15.9	16	17.0	19	15.3	15	6.5	60	25.5	132	16.1
Conviction	12	8.7	5	5.3	12	9.7	8	3.5	19	8.1	56	6.8

Source: FATF MER Malaysia (2015)

The numbers of money laundering investigation and prosecution in Malaysia is lower as compared to statistics of the USA, as summarized in Table 1.3. The conviction rate for the USA is 53% during the periods between 2010 until 2014.

Table 3. Money laundering Investigation and Prosecution in USA for 2010 to 2014

	2010	%	2011	%	2012	%	2013	%	2014	%	Total	%
Prosecutions	3081		3757		3754		3466		3369		17427	
Conviction	1703	55.3	1802	48.0	1884	50.2	1935	55.8	1967	58.4	9291	53.3

Source: FATF MER USA (2016)

Based on the two reports (Global Financial Integrity and Mutual Evaluation Report) alone it can be seen that whilst money laundering cases including perverted unreported cases are high, the outcome of money laundering investigation is alarming. Since it involves huge number of losses to a small country like Malaysia, it can be concluded that money laundering is a critical issue which need to be tackled in this country. Hence, it leads to the following questions.

1. What are the factors influencing law enforcement agencies to initiate money laundering investigation?
2. Following the initiative to investigate any money laundering cases, what are the factors or challenges faced by the investigating officers to proceed to the next step – i.e., prosecution, conviction and confiscation?

In view of the above issues, this study discusses on the factors influencing money laundering investigation outcome in fighting money laundering activities, from the perspective of the law enforcement agencies in Malaysia. According to the Malaysia's AML Regime, the law enforcement agencies are one of the key players in combating money laundering activities in Malaysia, as they are responsible in conducting the money laundering investigation.

LITERATURE REVIEW

Financial Action Task Force (FATF)

In addressing the money laundering threat, an international agency Financial Action Task Force (FATF) was established in 1989 during a G-7 Summit in Paris by the Finance Ministers of seven countries namely Canada, United Kingdom, Japan, France, Italy, United States of America and Germany. As the leading standard setter against money laundering and financial terrorist financing. FATF has issued 40 recommendations to regulate the global money laundering regime (AML).

At first, FATF only focuses on money laundering activities, however, it has widened the scope to terrorist financing due to the September 11 incident happened in the United States of America. After the 2008 financial crisis, the FATF has highlighted on the vulnerabilities of the global financial system. The FATF regulates and supervises the global AML regime by publishing reports and assess the country's AML enforcement. Although FATF recommendation is accepted by various countries, it is considered as soft law until the recommendation is regulated and included in the country's legislation. Yet, its implementation in member countries varies since it is not mandatory for the countries to strictly follow FATF recommendation (FATF website). This is one of the flaws in fighting against money laundering, because fighting against money laundering should be conducted at global level, by closing and fulfils all the gaps which allow the money launderers to launder their illegal gotten gains.

As part of monitoring process, FATF also conducts periodical evaluation on its member countries to assess the compliance and effectiveness of a country in combating money laundering. The assessment includes the compliance towards the

FATF Recommendations (as shown in Table 4 below) and the effectiveness of Anti-Money Laundering Regime (AML Regime) of respective countries and results are presented in the report named Mutual Evaluation Report (MER). To date, Malaysia has gone through the mutual evaluation twice, in 2007 and 2015. A brief finding from the evaluation will be discussed further in the next sub-section.

Table 4. FATF 40 Recommendations

FATF 40 Recommendation	
1. Assessing risks & applying a risk-based approach	2. National cooperation and coordination
3. Money laundering offence	4. Confiscation and provisional measures
5. Terrorist financing offence	6. Targeted financial sanctions related to terrorism & terrorist financing
7. Targeted financial sanctions related to proliferation	8. Non-profit organisations
9. Financial institution secrecy laws	10. Customer due diligence
11. Record keeping	12. Politically exposed persons
13. Correspondent banking	14. Money or value transfer services
15. New technologies	16. Wire transfers
17. Reliance on third parties	18. Internal controls and foreign branches and subsidiaries
19. Higher-risk countries	20. Reporting of suspicious transactions
21. Tipping-off and confidentiality	22. DNFBPs: Customer due diligence
23. DNFBPs: Other measures	24. Transparency and beneficial ownership of legal persons
25. Transparency and beneficial ownership of legal arrangements	26. Regulation and supervision of financial institutions
27. Powers of supervisors	28. Regulation and supervision of DNFBPs
29. Financial intelligence units	30. Responsibilities of law enforcement and investigative authorities
31. Powers of law enforcement and investigative authorities	32. Cash couriers
33. Statistics	34. Guidance and feedback
35. Sanctions	36. International instruments
37. Mutual legal assistance	38. Mutual legal assistance: freezing and confiscation
39. Extradition	40. Other forms of international cooperation

Financial Intelligence and Law Enforcement Agencies

In response to the continuing and evolving money laundering and terrorism financing threats globally, Malaysia has taken steps to develop a comprehensive Anti-Money Laundering and Counter Financing of Terrorism Regime (AML/CFT Regime)[1]. Malaysia has established a comprehensive AML Regime covering four important elements as summarised in Figure 1 involving; (i) the legal and regulatory framework, (ii) preventive measures for reporting institutions, (iii) financial intelligence unit and law enforcement agencies, and (iv) domestic and international cooperation. These are important to ensure the effectiveness of a country in mitigating money laundering activities.

Figure 1. AML Regime Malaysia
Source: Bank Negara Malaysia Website

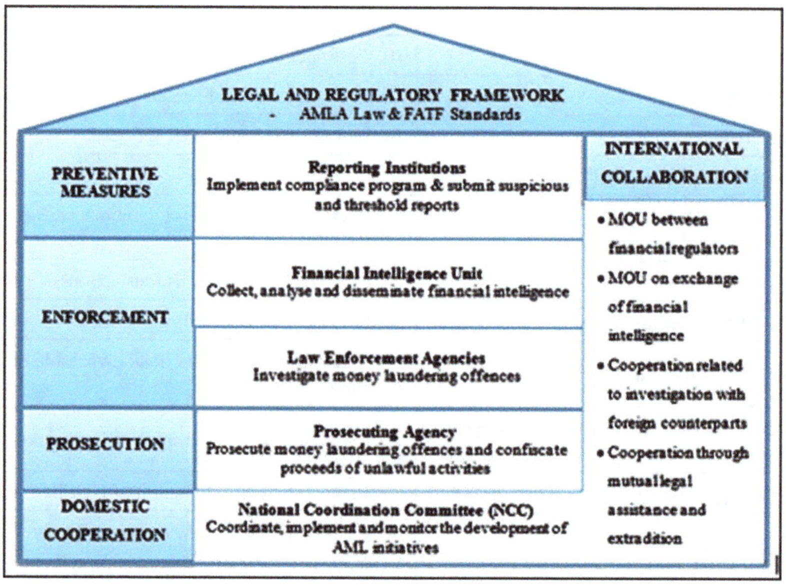

Although there are four elements under AML Regime in Malaysia, this study will only focus on the third element, which is the enforcement of money laundering activities. The enforcement responsibility is placed on the financial intelligence unit (FIU) and law enforcement agencies. The Financial Intelligence Unit (FIU) of Bank Negara Malaysia is established to manage and provide comprehensive analysis on the financial intelligence information received by reporting institutions. The information received may come from various sources such as STRs and CTRs received from the reporting institutions, local law enforcement agencies and foreign FIUs. They contain information which are helpful to the law enforcement agencies in assisting their money laundering investigation. The information will then be disseminated to respective law enforcement agencies. FIU has the responsibility to provide financial intelligence information to the law enforcement agencies when required.

Part V of the AMLA 2001 provides power to the law enforcement agencies to investigate on money laundering activities that is committed or when they have reasons to suspect the commission of an offence under their respective purview. The law enforcement agencies may also request for information from the FIU. According to the Malaysia's AML Regime, the law enforcement agencies are among the main key players in combating money laundering activities in Malaysia. They are responsible in investigating money laundering and its related predicate offenses, with the assistance from the FIU.

Figure 2. Financial Intelligence Gathering
Source: Bank Negara Malaysia Website

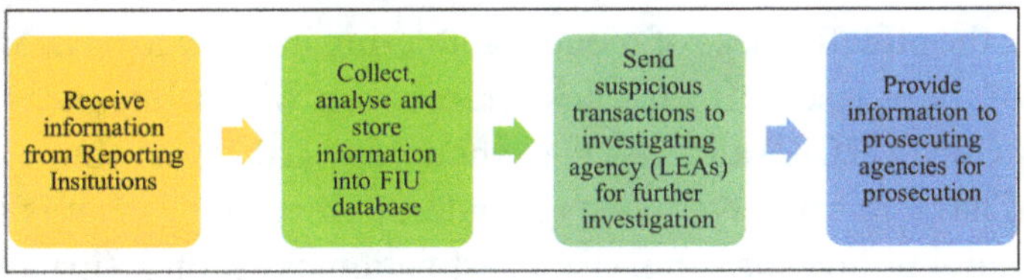

Figure 2 summarises the process of financial intelligence gathering under Malaysia's AML regime. The FIU is responsible in gathering reports submitted from reporting institutions, analysing to produce the intelligence information, and maintaining the information in the database. Throughout the analysis process, FIU also requests information from foreign FIU and relevant agency when necessary. The financial intelligence is then submitted to the investigating agency such as the law enforcement agencies for further investigation. The law enforcement agencies will then conduct investigation based on the financial intelligence and may involve further information from reporting institutions through FIED. Due to complexity and borderless nature of money laundering activities, there is a need for domestic and international cooperation among the authorities in combating money laundering.

Although Malaysia has a comprehensive AML Regime, the country's performance (investigation outcome) remains low (FATF MER, 2015). This is fundamentally reflected on (i) the relatively low number of money laundering prosecutions and convictions and (ii) the low financial value of illegal proceeds confiscation as compared to the actual "financial loss" in money laundering offences. Therefore, this study seeks to understand the factors influencing money laundering investigation outcome in fighting money laundering activities. However, this study focuses on the perspective of the law enforcement agencies in Malaysia since they are the key player responsible in conducting the money laundering investigation.

In understanding the factors influencing money laundering investigation outcome, this study refers to the measurement outlined by Cheng (2012) and FATF Evaluation Methodology (2013) in assessing the effectiveness of AML Regime of member countries.

Money Laundering Effectiveness Framework

Cheng (2012) conducted a comparative study on the effectiveness of a money laundering investigation in the US and Hong Kong in combating money laundering activities. He conducted content analysis of the FATF MER and interviews with respective authorities who were involved in the money laundering investigation in the two countries. However, there are additional effectiveness assessment criteria which was introduced by FATF in 2013, which are used during the assessment. In understanding the effectiveness of money laundering investigation in Malaysia, this study refers to the revised effectiveness framework which integrates the criteria mentioned by Cheng (2012) and FATF Methodology (2013), as outlined in Table 5.

In order to have an effective money laundering investigation, it is important to have; (i) clear aim of investigation, (ii) investigation capability, (iii) asset recovery mechanism, (iv) financial intelligence capability, and (v) domestic and international collaboration (Cheng, 2012; FATF Evaluation Methodology, 2013). Therefore, this study will refer to these elements in understanding the factors which influences the money laundering investigation outcome in Malaysia, using the rational choice theory as the underpinning theory. The criteria is in line with rational choice theory used by Li et al., (2010) and Paternoster & Simpson (1996) which consist of three premises; the cost-benefit of the choice, individual moral belief and organisational contextual factors.

Rational Choice Theory

Rational choice theory was used by criminologists in their studies when analysing financial crime using the economic analysis approach. Prior studies mostly focus on the perspective of the offenders, on the reasons for their commission of criminal act. There are three dimensions of rational choice perspective as relate to current theory of criminology (Akers, 1990), which are (i) the 'rationality' of criminal acts and careers; (ii) the actual or perceived balance of rewards and costs associated with committing crime; and (iii) background and other relevant variables.

Table 5. Operationalisation for Effectiveness of Money Laundering Investigation

Construct	Definition	Keywords
Money Laundering Investigation Capability	It covers the powers and responsibility of the law enforcement in conducting money laundering investigation., are outlined in the legislation or policies	empowerment, investigative power, investigative tools, special investigation technique, power to investigate
Aim of the Investigation	Objective of money laundering investigation, whether for prosecution or revenue recovery.	Revenue Recovery, Confiscation, Prosecution, Investigation, Out of Court Settlement
Freeze, Seizure and Forfeiture features	The practice of asset freeze, seize and forfeiture of the proceeds of crime in money laundering investigation and prosecution.	Freeze, Seize, Seizure, Forfeiture, Confiscation, Criminal Forfeiture, Civil Forfeiture, Administrative Forfeiture, Proceeds of Crime
Domestic Collaboration and Integrated Task Force	A collaboration of the local law enforcement agencies and other entities in combating money laundering activities	Special task force, multi-agency, interagency cooperation, sharing information, sharing expertise
International Cooperation	A collaboration of the local law entities with other countries in combating money laundering activities, especially when it involves cross border transaction.	International cooperation, multi-country cooperation, special task force, mutual legal assistance, bilateral cooperation, multi-lateral cooperation, exchange of criminal intelligence,
Management of Asset Recovery	The process of managing asset obtained through seizure, confiscation and out of court settlement	Law enforcement agencies, centralized agency, own entity, asset management agency, court
Financial Intelligence Capability	Investigative powers and capabilities which enable the law enforcement to cultivate, collect, collate, and develop financial intelligence from different sources.	Financial Intelligence Unit, intelligence information, reporting institutions, financial institutions, suspicious transaction report, cash transaction report, intelligence analysis, suspicious report

Source: Cheng (2012), FATF Evaluation Methodology (2013).

However, in this study, the theory is used to understand the rationale behind the choices made by the enforcement agencies in punishing the criminal offenders. FATF (2012) has mentioned that there are two expected outcomes for conducting money laundering investigation: namely (i) criminalisation of money laundering offenders, and (ii) recovering the illegal proceeds. The decision is made after considering few factors, as what has been outlined under the theory of Rational Choice.

Initially, the rational choice theory explains that the reasons or factors which influences a choice or action by weighing the cost of benefits of the deviant behaviour (Becker, 1968). The theory was mostly used to understand the factors which influence deviant behaviour in deciding whether to commit an offence. The offenders decide to offend after considering two premises, which are the cost-benefit of offending and decision maker's perception or beliefs on the offence.

Paternoster and Simpson (1996) further refined the theory in the context of corporate crime, by considering the organisational context. They found that there are three factors which influences their decision, which are the cost-benefit of offending, individual's perception or beliefs on the offence, and organisational contextual factors. Li, Zhang, & Sarathy (2010) then applied and expended the theory in the context of the internet policy abuse. They discovered that the decision is influenced by three premises, which are cost-benefit of the action, individual moral beliefs and organisational contextual factors. The moral belief of an individual plays a major role on their intention to commit the offence. Although the research is conducted at organisational level, they believe that employees are the representative of the organisation (Li et al., 2010). Therefore, employees' belief is considered as organisation's belief. However, they found that strong personal beliefs against internet abuse together with formal sanction and facilitating conditions override the benefits of internet abuses, which results to high behavioural intention to follow the internet policy.

Therefore, this study applies the theory used by Li, Zhang, & Sarathy (2010) and Paternoster & Simpson (1996) to understand the factors which influences the money laundering investigation outcome. The following sub-section discusses the research methodology used in the study.

RESEARCH METHODOLOGY

A phenomenological study has been conducted in this study to understand the factors influencing money laundering investigation outcome in Malaysia. Phenomenological study constitutes a wide range of philosophical and sociological approaches, sharing the common characteristics of understanding and explaining the social world from the perspective of the actors who are directly involved in the social process (Howell, 2012). In this study, the actors refer to the investigating officers who conduct money laundering investigation. Philosophical idea derived from phenomenological study plays a huge role in a research setting, as it provides guidance to the researcher on the investigator's belief and feeling about the world and how it should be understood and studied (Denzin & Lincoln, 2008). Similar approach has been adopted in a recent study by Korystin, Nekrasov, Krivolapchuk, & Sviridyuk, (2019) in relation to the phenomenology of money laundering in Ukraine.

The study uses qualitative approach for its data collection in understanding the money laundering investigation practices, by referring to the research conducted by Cheng (2012). As discussed in the literature review section, Cheng (2012) has developed a money laundering investigation effectiveness framework. Therefore, this study replicates and extends the study conducted by Cheng (2012), by including additional measurement as shown in Table 5. In trying to understand options to be taken by investigating officers, the rational choice theory is introduced to provide possible explanation for the money laundering investigation outcome.

Money laundering investigating officers are highly specialized in the sense that they have adequate experience and knowledge in financial investigation and the ability to identify predicate offences related to money laundering. They are the officers placed in the money laundering unit or department of their respective law enforcement agencies. These law enforcement agencies have been identified and selected because they were named in the Malaysia's FATF Evaluation Report in 2007 and 2015 for contributing related prosecution and confiscation data on money laundering in Malaysia. Each agency sent two to four investigating officers for the focus group interview sessions. They were the selected interviewees nominated by their respective law enforcement agencies to discuss the challenges faced by the law enforcement agencies in investigating money laundering cases. However, names and identities of the respondents were not disclosed in accordance with ethical disclosure requirement.

The data collection process involves three focus group interviews with fifteen money laundering investigating officers, using interview protocol instrument as a guideline related to the types of preliminary questions asked. The participants were also encouraged to provide opinions and feedback to open-ended questions. The data collection stops at the third interview of focus group interview, as it reached the level of saturation. This approach of deciding on the "saturation point" is supported by Guest, Namey, & McKenna (2017) who stated that "three focus groups were enough to identify all of the most prevalent themes within the data set". The focus group interviews ranged in length of two hours to three hours (Dilshad & Latif, 2013). During the focus group interview, this study managed to follow the time schedule and avoid from taking interviewees' additional time. All interviews were recorded using two voice recorders, pictures were taken along the process and notes were taken by two note takers.

The interviews were, then transcribed verbatim and analyzed using the NVIVO software. The software allowed this study to compare information from different sources. The data of the study were then analyzed using thematic analysis based on the codes and themes developed from the transcriptions. The text was then coded and assigned to its coding labels (categorizing). Coding and categorizing refers to the process of attaching one or more keywords to a text segment in order to permit later identification of a statement, whereas categorization entails a more systematic conceptualization of a statement (Kvale, 2008). Once categorized, the categories and themes were then conceptualized through pattern matching.

Pattern matching is used during the analysis to focus on building the interpretations. It refers to interrogating the meaning units in terms of the specific purpose of the study. Extensive analysis was undertaken by looking for natural meaning units and explicating their main themes. The patterns are then compared with the framework or underpinning theories used in the study to ensure theoretical refutation and consistency (Denzin & Lincoln, 1994). In this study, the emerging pattern is consistent with the rational choice theory and money laundering effectiveness framework (refer Table 5), that help to strengthen the validity of the current study.

FINDINGS AND DISCUSSION

In understanding the factors influencing money laundering investigation outcome, this study refers to rational choice theory as its underpinning theory. The theory focuses on three important elements namely cost-benefit analysis, individual's own beliefs and organizational contextual factors. The findings of this study are then discussed based on the three elements of rational choice theory.

Cost-Benefit Analysis

In deciding the investigation outcome, the investigating officers and prosecutors must take into consideration the investigation costs and benefits in their decision-making process. In money laundering investigation, cost-benefit analysis is considered at two point of time, which are (i) during opening of investigation paper (preliminary investigation) and (ii) upon completion of the investigation (to forfeit property with or without prosecution).

When an investigation paper is opened, AMLA 2001 (sections 48 and 52) allow the freezing and seizure of asset to be undertaken by the investigating officers without proceeding to prosecution. The nature of asset involved will contribute significantly to the decision-making process. For example, in cases of movable assets (e.g., cash, jewelries, car), the option to freeze and seize is given higher priority by the investigators. Since they are given a time frame of 12 months to gather further evidence for the next step of prosecution (investigation timeframe), the decision to freeze and seize the illegal proceeds is often seen as a suitable immediate measure. It is also a good deterrence measure for the offense and offenders. During freezing and seizure, the investigators may prevent offenders from tempering or disposing the evidence.

When money laundering investigation is completed, the decision must be made whether to forfeit property with prosecution (section 55 of AMLA 2001) or to forfeit property without prosecution (section 56 of AMLA 2001). In both cases, decisions can be made by the law enforcement agencies through the Deputy Public Prosecutor (DPP). In Malaysia, public prosecutors are often stationed at respective law enforcement agencies and they facilitate the agencies in making decisions on money laundering investigation. If forfeiture of property with prosecution is chosen, the property will be forfeited at the end of the prosecution or court trial. The proceeds will no longer be able to cover the investigation and prosecution cost incurred.

Therefore, it is a risk which should be carried by the prosecuting agencies once they decided with prosecution. This risky situation may be a factor which influences the low prosecution and recovery for money laundering cases in Malaysia. In contrast, if forfeiture without prosecution is chosen, "*the focus of the application is the recovery of property and not the innocence or guilt of the persons subjected to the application*" (Sittlington & Harvey, 2018). It can be achieved by an order of the High Court that has to be satisfied that the conditions in the provision have been met. Hence, it involves lower risk as compared to forfeiture of property with prosecution.

As such, in making decisions, both investigating officers and DPPs normally consider that the benefits outweigh the cost involved. This notion is supported by Saperstein, Sant, & Ng (2015), who studied on the cost and benefit analysis used by the financial institutions in complying with money laundering initiatives. Although the focus is different, both studies have the same objective, which is preventing and mitigating money laundering activities. Based on the interviews, the investigating officers often choose the option to forfeit without prosecution because it provides faster revenue recovery as it does not involve a long prosecution process. This is because the prosecution process in Malaysia takes more than one year. However, it has a disadvantage in the sense that the amount or value of forfeiture without prosecution is usually much smaller (based on what was believed to be available at that point in time of investigation) compared to a situation if the offence and the actual illegal proceeds had been deliberated in court and more evidence were discovered.

In this study, the findings show that the investigating officers and prosecutors take into consideration the investigation cost (financial resources to support the investigation cost), economic benefit (availability of the illegal proceeds to achieve asset recovery) and chances of winning based on the sufficiency of the evidence to support the charges in court. These are the three main elements which they will consider in making both the investigation and prosecution decisions.

Individual Belief and Capability

Investigators' "individual belief" and professional competency also play an important role in determining their investigation outcome. The rational choice theory posited that people usually act in the light of the beliefs they hold. Interestingly, by observing the outcomes of their actions, people often change their beliefs. The findings of the study showed that the investigating officers sometimes face difficulties when there is lack of motivation and competency in using money laundering legislation. This happened due to lack of clarity in understanding the aim(s) of conducting money laundering investigation and their professional competency in utilizing provisions of AMLA 2001.

Aim of Investigation

Although FATF standards provide two very specific investigation objectives (i.e., prosecution and asset recovery), AMLA 2001 on the other hand provides options to the investigating officers; to forfeiture without prosecution (section 56) or forfeiture with prosecution (section 55). There were circumstances where a money laundering case was recommended for prosecution by the law enforcement agencies (and supported by the DPP) but was not seconded by the Attorney General Chambers (AGC). As such, forfeiture without prosecution may still a better option as it would provide faster and realistic result.

Criminalizing offenders through prosecution takes longer period and more effort to provide sufficient evidence to support the charges. However, some of the interviewees agree on the importance of prosecution as a more effective deterrence method. The conflicts arise when they are bounded by the goal of their respective agency, which is the fast asset recovery, as forfeiture is believed to be a better measure to cripple the money laundering activity. This indirectly showed that the investigating officers' belief on money laundering prosecution itself is lower as compared to asset recovery. This conflict in the decision making is seen as a problem not only in money laundering area but also in other financial crimes (Green & Roiphe, 2016).

Professional Competency

Individual capability (or simply competency) is another element that has been mentioned by the interviewees as contributory to the investigation outcome. The enforcement's capability used in this study referred to the capabilities and competencies of the law enforcement agencies in managing the money laundering investigation.

Since the FATF standards require that money laundering must be "investigated through the conduct of a financial investigation" (Interpretive note to Recommendation 30), it is important to note that not all members within the money laundering investigation loop have accounting background or related experiences. In some cases, the inability of the investigation papers to fulfil all the requirements (especially those related to financial evidence) set by the DPP resulted in the inability to proceed the cases towards prosecution.

The investigating officers' professional competence (especially financial and technological advancement) is determined as one of the factors which influences the money laundering investigation outcome. Globalization and change in technology have made it difficult for the activities to be detected, and that calls for advanced skills and knowledge among the investigating officers. As such, their skills and knowledge must be in line with the current situation to be able to detect illegal activities. Most of the interviewees emphasized on their difficulties in following the money trail, especially when it involves the latest modus operandi. It was also found that the interviewees were not satisfied with the opportunities for training and development and knowledge sharing across investigating officers, departments, and agencies.

The difficulties in criminalizing the offender on money laundering charges may also arise due to lack of knowledge among the investigating officers in understanding the perspective of the prosecutors in defending his or her prosecution. Investigating officers mentioned that they are facing difficulties to convince the prosecutors and judges to understand the money laundering modus operandi. This shows that the law enforcement agencies and deputy prosecutors have different understanding on prosecution criteria in making decision whether to proceed with the money laundering charges or not. The study found that there is an expectation gap between the investigators (from the law enforcement agencies) and public prosecutors. This is because the prosecutors have certain requirements which they must fulfil before they can proceed with the charges. The prosecutor focuses more on cases which are accurate, convincing and has strong evidences and analysis since it has higher winning rate (Petty & Raiborn, 2016).

Therefore, it can be concluded that clear aim of investigation and professional competency do influence the money laundering investigation outcome.

Organisational Context Factor

Organizational context factor refers to the facilities provided by the organisation and AML Regime in facilitating money laundering investigation process. The findings showed that investigation support system, leaders' support, judicial support, and asset recovery management system do influence the investigating officers' decision making. These four elements are important to ensure that the investigation process is performing well in producing good investigation outcome. This is also in line with previous studies which mentioned that organizational context factors such as leader's support, knowledge management, and use of information and communication technology (ICT) do influence an investigation outcome (Ask, Granhag, & Rebelius, 2011; Fahsing & Ask, 2013; Gottschalk, 2006).

Investigative Support System

The findings show that the investigation outcome is influence by the investigative support system provided in assisting their money laundering investigation. A comprehensive investigative support system is helpful in ensuring the effectiveness of money laundering investigation process through its timely response in providing information to the investigating officers. One of the officers mentioned that they were unable to proceed with money laundering prosecution due to insufficient evidence to support the charges and this resulted in non-prosecution decision, resulted from lack of investigative support system. Evidence gathering is difficult since it required the investigating officers to seek information from various agencies. The findings is supported by previous studies that also concluded on the lack of investigative support system as a challenge towards successful money laundering investigation (Belaisha & Brooks, 2014; Bell, 2001; Fitzpatrick, 2017; Man-wai, 2005).

The investigative support system is crucial, especially in gathering information from a third party. The information kept by the FIU is limited to financial information only (for example, CTR and STR). The nature of money laundering is complex. The money laundering offenders make use of entities as their intermediaries which are less regulated in facilitating the illegal act, such as DNFBP, real estate, gold, shell companies and cryptocurrencies (Dostov & Shust, 2014; He, 2010; Irwin, Choo, & Liu, 2012; Simser, 2013; Teichmann, 2017; Unger & den Hertog, 2012). As a result, the investigating officers are required to retrieve information from other agencies to support the money trail. Lack of accessibility to the information from the third parties also impose challenges to the investigating officers.

Hence, a comprehensive investigative support system should be established. However, the investigation support system can only be established with support from the leader of the law enforcement agencies.

Leader's Support

Findings of the study show that there is inconsistent organizational direction in terms of expected investigation outcome by the leader of the law enforcement agencies. Investigating officers are given the option to decide on the best course of action. A study by Lone, Garnås, Myklebust, Bjørklund, Hoff, & Bjørkli (2017) found that good planning, clear goal setting, and task focus behaviours would increase investigation performance. Since the prosecution process took a longer time, investigating officers sometimes feel unmotivated to pursue with money laundering prosecution because of lack of support from their leader. Recognition and empowerment from the leader do influence the motivation of the investigating officers, that indirectly influences the money laundering investigation outcome.

One of the interviewees mentioned that the role of the AML unit is sometimes perceived as *'Ah-Long'* or a debt-collector.

"We receive break of demand (BOD) cases, which are the unresolved cases. It normally involves taxpayers who refused to pay their penalty upon request made by the agency. Once the case is submitted to our department, we investigate and proceed with account freezing, which makes the tax offenders appeal and settle the unsettled penalties. Once the payment is made, we then release the offenders upon instruction from the head department." (Interviewee K).

The statement shows that the investigating officers have not fully utilised their investigative power as money laundering investigating officers, due to lack of support or empowerment given by the top management. This statement was also agreed by another interviewee, as mentioned in following excerpt.

"AMLA is a powerful tool, but we never fully utilise the Act. Since we focus on collecting revenues, we use the act to collect the penalties. We are satisfied if it helps us to gain revenue for our agency". (Interviewee L).

Although leader's support contributes to the money laundering investigation outcome, there are other factors which also influence the outcome, which is the availability of asset recovery facility for asset management. Asset management is also one of the factors which influence the decision making.

Asset Recovery Facility

AMLA 2001 stated that the seized or forfeited assets are to be managed by respective agencies. However, it is costly due to high maintenance cost incurred in managing the recovered assets. This is because the respective law enforcement agencies are deemed responsible in ensuring that the assets are well-kept and maintained to initiate the market value of the assets. Besides the maintenance cost, expertise in handling the assets has also been one of the factors considered in their decision-making. Due to this, certain law enforcement agencies have higher preference to focus on freezing and seizing of cash and the bank accounts instead of assets. Furthermore, it requires certain expertise to manage the large assets, such as ships.

"We focus on seizing cash and freezing their accounts. This is because we do not have a store to keep all the forfeited and seized assets, like Agency A. We still consider economic factor in making the decision, which the current economic condition". (Interviewee M)

"We also use the same method under section 46 of AMLA 2001. We conduct a temporary seizure or full seizure. We think that others may also use this method in managing the seized or forfeited assets". (Interviewee N).

"We are facing the same problem, as there are a lot of things to be considered before we can decide whether to seize the assets or proprietor not. For now, we are still deciding whether to seize a ship or not. If we proceed with the seizure, we are not sure where to park the ship and we need to learn about how to maintain and manage the ship. It is too costly to us". (Interviewee J).

The issue of asset management then requires immediate action. The investigating officers also shared on ways to solve the problem:

"Asset management has been one of the hot issues in the recent meeting in Bangkok. The agencies suggest establishing a one stop centre to manage the seized or forfeited assets and property". (Interviewee O)

"One of the agencies are considering converting the assets into bonds. For example, instead of seizing the car, they plan to convert the car to bonds according to its market value. So, the offender may use the car and at the same time the agency can hold the bond. It will be a win-win situation". (Interviewee M).

The statements also confirmed that the law enforcement agencies are facing difficulties in managing and maintaining the seized and forfeited assets and property during the confiscation period. The interviewees mentioned that they must take into consideration their capability to manage the recovered assets before investigation decision is made. This happened because the responsibility of managing the recovered assets is placed on the shoulders of the respective agencies. This highlights on the importance of having an asset recovery facility to help manage the recovered assets. This is supported by the book written by Brun, Gray, Scott & Stephenson (2011) on the importance of having asset recovery management in crime prevention.

SUMMARY

The factors which influence the investigation outcome can be categorized into three categories which are cost-benefit analysis, personal belief and organizational context factor which are in line with rational choice theory. This study found that there are eight factors which influence the money laundering investigation outcome.

The eight elements are then categorized under three categories, as outlined under rational choice theory.

It is found that individual beliefs (professional competency and clear aim of investigation) and cost-benefit analysis are not the only factors which influence the money laundering investigation. There are many other factors which affects the investigation outcome, such as facilities provided in evidence gathering, support from leader, and good asset recovery mechanism (organizational context factor).

This study found that the low number of money laundering prosecution, conviction and confiscation are due to these factors. Although they are competent as an investigator, lack of organizational support does influence their investigation income. This is because money laundering investigation is highly dependent on the information reported or placed in the other parties. Following the money trail approach, the investigating officers are required to follow the money trail which involves many entities as its layering and integration platform. Hence, having organisation support is crucial to ensure that the investigating officers can gather the quality evidence in timely manner. This is to ensure that the evidence is sufficient and able to support the money laundering charges in court. The findings of this study are as summarised in the following Figure 3.

Figure 3. Factors Influencing Money Laundering Investigation Outcome

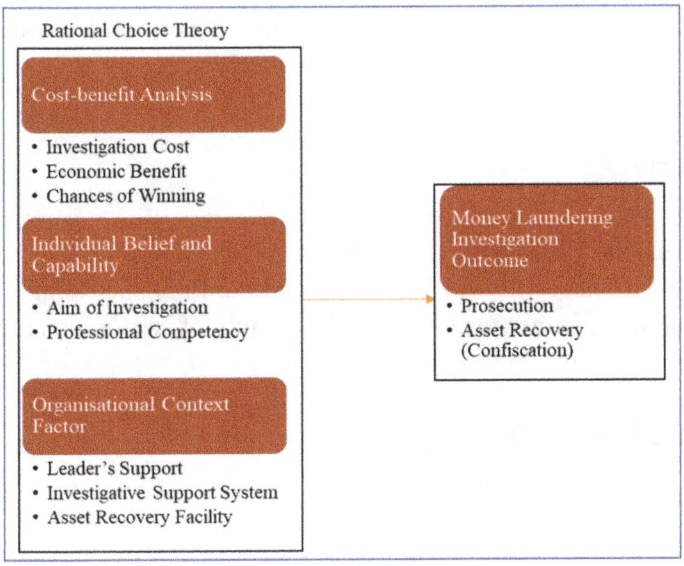

RECOMMENDATIONS

This study highlights on the importance of having good organizational contextual factor in producing good money laundering investigation outcome. It is important for the leaders of the law enforcement agencies to be supportive in assisting the investigation. Having good investigative support system and asset recovery mechanism are also important to ensure that the investigative officers have all the assistance they needed in facilitating their money laundering investigation. The investigative support system here refers to the database which contains all the data needed by the law enforcement agencies, such as the suspicious transaction database in the FIU and other reporting institutions. The database should be made accessible to the investigating officers, and this can be established through memorandum of understanding between respective entities or secondment of officers in the FIU.

Asset recovery mechanism is also one of the factors which influences their decision making. The confiscation decision is made upon when the investigating officers have the confidence to manage the confiscated assets to maintain its value along the confiscation period. It involves considering the cost benefits analysis and their expertise in handling the assets, especially high-value assets such as ship at the harbors and luxury cars. Therefore, it is important for the country to establish a centralized asset recovery center, which will be responsible in managing the confiscation mechanism, starting from reporting, exchanging information, handling assets until its disposal. Future researcher may refer to FATF's guideline on the best practices for countries to facilitate the development of effective asset recovery arrangements.

DISCLAIMER

The contents and views of this chapter are expressed by the authors in their personal capacities. It is not necessary for the Editor and the Publisher to agree with these viewpoints and they are not responsible for any duty of care in this regard

ACKNOWLEDGMENT

The authors extend sincere gratitude to:

- Malaysian Ministry of Education for the grant 600-IRMI/ARI 5/5(026/2019), University Teknologi MARA, Faculty of Accountancy and Accounting Research Institute for funding and facilitating this research.

- The Editor-in-Chief and International Editorial Advisory Board (IEAB) of this book who initially desk reviewed, arranged a rigorous double/triple blind review process and conducted a thorough, minute and critical final review before accepting the chapter for publication.
- All anonymous reviewers who provided very constructive feedbacks for thorough revision, improvement, extension and finetuning of the chapter.

REFERENCES

Akers, R. L. (1990). Rational Choice, Deterrence, and Social Learning Theory in Criminology: The Path Not Taken. *The Journal of Criminal Law & Criminology*, *81*(3), 653–676. doi:10.2307/1143850

Amrani, H. (2012). *The Development of Anti-Money Laundering Regime: Challenging Issues to Sovereignty, Jurisdiaction, Law Enforcement, and Their Implication on the Effectiveness in Countering Money Laundering*. Erasmus University Rotterdam.

Ask, K., Granhag, P. A., & Rebelius, A. (2011). Investigators under influence: How social norms activate goal-directed processing of criminal evidence. *Applied Cognitive Psychology*, *25*(4), 548–553. doi:10.1002/acp.1724

Aurasu, A., & Rahman, A. A. (2016). Money laundering and civil forfeiture regime : Malaysian experience. *Journal of Money Laundering Control*, *19*(4), 337–345. doi:10.1108/JMLC-08-2015-0033

Bank Negara Malaysia. (n.d.). *Malaysia Anti-Money Laundering & Counter Financing of Terrorism Regime*. Retrieved from http://amlcft.bnm.gov.my/AMLCFT02b.html

Becker, G. S. (1968). Crime and Punishment: An Economic Approach. *Journal of Political Economy*, *76*(2), 169–217. doi:10.1086/259394

Belaisha, B. (2014). Money laundering in Dubai: Strategies and future directions. *Journal of Money Laundering Control*, *17*(3), 343–354. doi:10.1108/JMLC-10-2013-0038

Bell, R. E. (2001). Discretion and Decision Making in Money Laundering Prosecutions. *Journal of Money Laundering Control*, *5*(1), 42–51. doi:10.1108/eb027292

Brown, R., & Gillespie, S. (2015). Overseas financial investigation of organised crime. *Journal of Money Laundering Control*, *18*(3), 371–381. doi:10.1108/JMLC-03-2014-0010

Brun, J. P., Gray, L., Scott, C., & Stephenson, K. (2011). *Asset recovery handbook: a guide for practitioners*. The World Bank. doi:10.1596/978-0-8213-8634-7

Buchanan, B. (2004). Money laundering - A global obstacle. *Research in International Business and Finance*, *18*(1), 115–127. doi:10.1016/j.ribaf.2004.02.001

Cheng, N. Y. (2012). *The Effectiveness of Money Laundering Investigations in Fighting Transnational Crime : A Comparison of the United States and Hong Kong*. Retrieved from https://www.brookings.edu/research/the-effectiveness-of-money-laundering-investigations-in-fighting-transnational-crime-a-comparison-of-the-united-states-and-hong-kong/

Choo, H. C., Amirrudin, M. S., Adura, N., Noruddin, A., & Othman, R. (2014). Anti-Money Laundering and its Effectiveness. *Malaysian Accounting Review*, *13*(2), 109–124.

Denzin, N. K. (1978). *Studies in Symbolic Interaction*. JAI Press.

Denzin, N. K., & Lincoln, Y. S. (2008). *Handbook of qualitative research*. SAGE Publications.

Department of the Treasury Financial Crimes Enforcement Network. (2010). *Advisory to Financial Institutions on Filing Suspicious Activity Reports regarding Trade-Based Money Laundering*. Author.

Dhillon, G., Ahmad, R., Rahman, A., & Miin, N. Y. (2013). The viability of enforcement mechanisms under money laundering and anti-terrorism offences in Malaysia: An overview. *Journal of Money Laundering Control*, *16*(2), 171–192. doi:10.1108/13685201311318511

Dilshad, R. M., & Latif, M. I. (2013). Focus Group Interview as a Tool for Qualitative Research: An Analysis. *Pakistan Journal of Social Sciences*, *33*(1), 191–198.

Dostov, V., & Shust, P. (2014). Cryptocurrencies: An unconventional challenge to the AML/CFT regulators? *Journal of Financial Crime*, *21*(3), 249–263. doi:10.1108/JFC-06-2013-0043

Egmont Group. (2017). *Financial Intelligence Units Operational Guidance for FIU Activities and the Exchange of Information*. Retrieved from www.egmontgroup.org

Evans, J. L. (1999). *Money Laundering Investigations : Practices of Interest To the Asia/Pacific Region*. Retrieved from https://icclr.org/publications/money-laundering-in-the-asia-pacific-working-paper-no-3-money-laundering-investigations-practices-of-interest-to-the-asia-pacific-region/

Fahsing, I., & Ask, K. (2013). Decision Making and Decisional Tipping Points in Homicide Investigations: An Interview Study of British and Norwegian Detectives. *Journal of Investigative Psychology and Offender Profiling, 10*(2), 155–165. doi:10.1002/jip.1384

FATF. (2006). Trade Based Money Laundering. *Financial Action Task Force*. Retrieved from https://www.fatf-gafi.org/

FATF. (2008). *Best Practices on Trade Based Money Laundering*. Retrieved from https://www.fatf-gafi.org/

FATF. (2012a). *FATF Guidance Document Best Practices Paper Best Practices on Trade Based Money Laundering*. Retrieved from https://www.fatf-gafi.org/

FATF. (2012b). *Operational Issues Financial Investigations Guidance*. Retrieved from https://www.fatf-gafi.org/

FATF. (2012c). *The FATF Recommendations*. Retrieved from https://www.fatf-gafi.org/

FATF. (2013). *Methodology for Assessing Technical Compliance with the FATF Recommendations and the Effectiveness of AML/CFT Systems*. Retrieved from https://www.fatf-gafi.org/

FATF MER. (2015). *Mutual Evaluation Report on Malaysia Anti-Money Laundering and Counter-Terrorist Financing Measures*. Retrieved from https://www.fatf-gafi.org/

FATF MER. (2016). *Mutual Evaluation Report on USA Anti-Money Laundering and Counter-Terrorist Financing Measures*. Retrieved from https://www.fatf-gafi.org/

Fitzpatrick, D. (2017). A "think piece" on intelligence, investigation and prosecution. *Journal of Financial Crime, 24*(3), 449–460. doi:10.1108/JFC-03-2017-0018

Global Financial Integrity. (2019). *Illicit Financial Flows to and from 148 Developing Countries: 2006-2015*. Global Financial Integrity.

Global Financial Integrity. (2020, January 22). Retrieved from https://gfintegrity.org/about/

Gottschalk, P. (2006). *Knowledge Management Systems in Law Enforcement: Technologies and Techniques*. IGI Global.

Green, B., & Roiphe, R. (2016). Rethinking Prosecutors' Conflicts of Interest. *Boston College Law Review. Boston College. Law School, 58*(2), 463.

Guest, G., Namey, E., & McKenna, K. (2017). How Many Focus Groups Are Enough? Building an Evidence Base for Nonprobability Sample Sizes. *Field Methods*, *29*(1), 3–22. doi:10.1177/1525822X16639015

Hamin, Z., Wan Rosli, W. R., Omar, N., & Pengiran Mahmud, A. A. (2013). Following the Dirty Money : Legal Issues in Legislating against Money Laundering in Malaysia. *International Conference on Governance, Management & Financial Criminology (ICGMF)*, 2–5.

He, P. (2010). A typological study on money laundering. *Journal of Money Laundering Control*, *13*(1), 15–32. doi:10.1108/13685201011010182

Howell, K. E. (2012). *An Introduction to the Philosophy of Methodology*. SAGE Publications.

INCB. (2001). *Globalization and New Technologies : Challenges to Drug Law Enforcement in the Twenty-first Century*. INCB.

Irwin, A. S. M., Choo, K.-K. R., & Liu, L. (2012a). An analysis of money laundering and terrorism financing typologies. *Journal of Money Laundering Control*, *15*(1), 85–111. doi:10.1108/13685201211194745

Irwin, A. S. M., Choo, K.-K. R., & Liu, L. (2012b). Modelling of money laundering and terrorism financing typologies. *Journal of Money Laundering Control*, *15*(3), 316–335. doi:10.1108/13685201211238061

Kim, Y.-C. (2003). *The Effective System of Criminal Investigation and Prosecution in Korea* (No. Resource Material Series No. 60).

Korystin, O. Y., Nekrasov, V. A., Krivolapchuk, V. O., & Sviridyuk, N. P. (2019). The Phenomenology of Money Laundering in Ukraine. *Financial and Credit Activity: Problems of Theory and Practice*, *2*(29), 374–382. doi:10.18371/fcaptp.v2i29.171949

Kvale, S. (2008). *Doing Interviews Qualitative Research Kit*. SAGE Publications.

Kwok, D. (2016). New developments in Hong Kong's anti-money laundering laws. *Journal of Money Laundering Control*, *19*(3), 291–297. doi:10.1108/JMLC-06-2015-0023

Li, H., Zhang, J., & Sarathy, R. (2010). Understanding compliance with internet use policy from the perspective of rational choice theory. *Decision Support Systems*, *48*(4), 635–645. doi:10.1016/j.dss.2009.12.005

Lone, J. A., Garnås, A., Myklebust, T., Bjørklund, R., Hoff, T., & Bjørkli, C. (2017). Organizational climate and investigation performance in the Norwegian police: A qualitative study. *Journal of Investigative Psychology and Offender Profiling*, *14*(3), 227–245. doi:10.1002/jip.1474

Madinger, J. (2012). Money Laundering: A Guide for Criminal Investigators. CRC Press.

Man-wai, T. K. (2005). *Visiting Experts Papers: Investigation of Money Laundering and Corruption*. Academic Press.

Masciandaro, D., Takats, E., & Unger, B. (2007). *Black Finance: The Economics of Money Laundering*. Edward Elgar Publishing.

Maylam, S. (2002). Prosecution for money laundering in the UK. *Journal of Financial Crime*, *10*(2), 157–158. doi:10.1108/13590790310808754

McCarthy, B., & Chaudhary, A. (2014). Rational choice theory and crime. Encyclopedia of Crime and Criminal Justice.

Moamil. (2014). Money Laundering and Its Global Modes. A Serious Challenge to Law Enforcement Agencies. Some Observations. *International Journal of Humanities and Social Science Invention*, *3*(12), 40–44.

Mohamed, Z. M., & Ahmad, K. (2012). Investigation and prosecution of money laundering cases in Malaysia. *Journal of Money Laundering Control*, *15*(4), 421–429. doi:10.1108/13685201211266006

Muller, W. H., Kalin, C. H., & Goldsworth, J. G. (2007). *Anti-Money Laundering: International Law and Practice*. Wiley and Sons.

Nasir, M. A. (2020). The Relevance of Maqasid al Shari'ah to Anti-Money Laundering and Terrorism Financing. In A. Rafay (Ed.), *Handbook of Research on Theory and Practice of Global Islamic Finance* (pp. 179–194). IGI Global. doi:10.4018/978-1-7998-0218-1.ch010

Omar, N., Johari, R. J., & Sathye, M. (2015). Malaysian DNFBPs' Perceptions on Awareness, Perceived Impact and Views on the AML/CFT Requirements. *Procedia Economics and Finance*, *31*(15), 595–600. doi:10.1016/S2212-5671(15)01146-6

Palmiotto, M. J. (2012). Financial Investigation. In M. L. Birzer & C. Roberson (Eds.), *Introduction to criminal investigation* (pp. 199–207). CRC Press.

Park, J. H., Gu, B., Leung, A. C. M., & Konana, P. (2014). An investigation of information sharing and seeking behaviors in online investment communities. *Computers in Human Behavior*, *31*(1), 1–12. doi:10.1016/j.chb.2013.10.002

Paternoster, R., & Simpson, S. (1996). Sanction Threats and Appeals to Morality: Testing a Rational Choice Model of Corporate Crime. *Law & Society Review*, *30*(3), 549–583. doi:10.2307/3054128

Petty, B., & Raiborn, C. (2016). Helping Law Enforcement Secure Successful Financial Crime Prosecutions. *Management Accounting Quarterly*, *17*(2), 21–29.

Ping, H. E. (2008). The measures on combating money laundering and terrorism financing in the PRC: From the perspective of financial action task force. *Journal of Money Laundering Control*, *11*(4), 320–330. doi:10.1108/13685200810910394

Pok, W. C., Omar, N., & Sathye, M. (2014). An Evaluation of the Effectiveness of Anti-Money Laundering and Anti-Terrorism Financing Legislation: Perceptions of Bank Compliance Officers in Malaysia. *Australian Accounting Review*, *24*(4), 394–401. doi:10.1111/auar.12054

Pratt, T. C. (2008). Rational Choice Theory, Crime Control Policy, and Criminological Relevance. *Criminology & Public Policy*, *7*(1), 43–52. doi:10.1111/j.1745-9133.2008.00489.x

PWC. (2014). *Goods Gone Bad: Addressing Money-Laundering Risk in the Trade Finance System*. PWC.

Rafay, A., & Ajmal, M. M. (2014). Earnings Management through Deferred Taxes Recognized under IAS 12: Evidence from Pakistan. *Lahore Journal of Business*, *3*(1), 1–19. doi:10.35536/ljb.2014.v3.i1.a1

Rahman, A. A. (2008). An Analysis of the Malaysian Anti-Money Laundering Laws and their Impact on Banking Institutions. University of Western Australia.

Reiter, K. (2018). *Time Limits on Assignments in Law Enforcement*. Sam Houston State University. Retrieved from http://shsu-ir.tdl.org

Ryder, N. (2012). *Money Laundering-an Endless Cycle? A Comparative Analysis of the Anti-money Laundering Policies in the United States of America, the United Kingdom, Australia and Canada*. Routledge. doi:10.4324/9780203126783

Sanusi, Z. M., Sabri, S. S., Isa, Y. M., & Nassir, M. D. M. (2014). *Money Laundering Risk Assessment by Investment Bankers: How good are they?* Academic Press.

Saperstein, L., Sant, G., & Ng, M. (2015). The Failure of Anti-Money Laundering Regulation: Where is the Cost-Benefit Analysis? *Notre Dame Law Review Online, 91*(1), 12. Retrieved from https://scholarship.law.nd.edu/ndlr_online/vol91/iss1/4

Schroeder, W. R. (2001). Money Laundering: A Global Threat and the International Community's Response. *FBI Law Enforcement Bulletin, 70.*

Shanmugam, B., Nair, M., & Suganthi, R. (2003). Money Laundering in Malaysia. *Journal of Money Laundering Control*, *6*(4), 373–378. doi:10.1108/13685200310809699

Simser, J. (2013). Money laundering: Emerging threats and trends. *Journal of Money Laundering Control, 16*(1), 41–54. doi:10.1108/13685201311286841

Sittlington, S., & Harvey, J. (2018). Prevention of money laundering and the role of asset recovery. *Crime, Law, and Social Change, 70*(4), 1–21. doi:10.100710611-018-9773-z

Talatona, C., & Centre, C. (2014). *28th Task Force of Senior Officials and the 14th Council Of Ministers' Meeting Ccta Talatona Convention Centre Typologies Report on Money Laundering and Terrorist Financing through the Money Remittance and Currency Exchange Sector in the Esaamlg Region*. Academic Press.

Teichmann, F. M. J. (2017). Twelve Methods of Money Laundering. *Journal of Money Laundering Control, 20*(2), 130–137. doi:10.1108/JMLC-05-2016-0018

Transparency International (UK). (2009). *Combating Money Laundering and Recovering Looted Gains : Raising the UK's Game*. Retrieved from https://star.worldbank.org/corruption-cases/sites/corruption-cases/files/documents/arw/Transparency_Intl_UK_Recovering_Looted_Gains_June_2009.pdf

Unger, B., & den Hertog, J. (2012). Water always finds its way: Identifying new forms of money laundering. *Crime, Law, and Social Change*, *57*(3), 287–304. doi:10.100710611-011-9352-z

United Nations Office on Drugs and Crime. (2011, October). *UNODC estimates that criminals may have laundered US $ 1.6 trillion in 2009*. Retrieved from https://www.unodc.org/

ENDNOTE

1 Since this chapter is mainly focusing on the anti-money laundering investigation initiative, the aspect of the counter financing of terrorism regime will not be discussed in this study. AML/CFT Regime will then referred to as Anti-Money Laundering Regime (AML Regime).

Chapter 7
Financing as a Livewire for Terrorism:
The Case of North-Eastern Nigeria

Usman Sambo
Yobe State University, Nigeria

Babayo Sule
Federal University of Kashere, Gombe, Nigeria

ABSTRACT

Terrorism is a global security concern that dominates the theatre of intellectual discourse in the contemporary world. This chapter is taking the case of one of the deadliest insurgents and a terrorist group in the history of Nigeria and also examined various sources of finances of this group in detail. From radical preaching, this group transformed into a terrorist group attacking security, innocent citizens, and all and sundry. As a qualitative study, the social conflict model is adopted in explaining the framework of the existing literature. The data obtained was analyzed critically using content analysis. The study discovered that insurgents sourced their finances through internal and external sources, legal and illegal engagements. The study recommends among several others that the Nigerian Government and security operatives should intensify the process of identifying, tracing, and blockage of the sources of finances for terrorism.

DOI: 10.4018/978-1-7998-8758-4.ch007

INTRODUCTION

Terrorism has won a heavyweight belt of championship in the global arena of contemporary security discourses (Hall, 2009). The subject matter of terrorism is not a new phenomenon in the history of the world since ancient, medieval and modern times (Erlich, 2010). However, the Cold War ideological battle and the post-Cold War era ushered in a new dimension of terrorism with a formidable, pervasive and vehement nature beyond the ordinary perception of many security experts (Smith, 2012). Terrorism in any form denotes an attempt to send a signal of fear and terror in the minds and lives of the innocent souls for economic, political, religious, social, cultural and other motives (Heintze, 2016). Terrorism has been attributed to the movement of armed groups, which caused severe destruction of lives and properties in addition to economic effects world over. For over two decades now, the global terrorism has taken a new shape where intensified attacks led to the declaration of global war against terrorism (Shultz Jnr. & Dew, 2006).

There are several causative factors that manifest terrorism worldwide. Ideology, perceived injustice, untamed widespread of Small Arms and Light Weapons, political uprisings in many countries of the world leading to leadership vacuum that hatched armed groups with impunity, political injustice, double standard and political economic interest of global powers known sometimes as 'Rogue States' are all factors that set the ball rolling powerfully for the terror groups (Deflem, 2004). There is not any specific number that can be identified for the casualties of global terrorism except perhaps, an estimate. However, one certain issue is that terrorism is responsible for the death of hundreds of thousands across the world and a destruction of properties worth billions of US Dollars (Solomon, 2015).

Nigeria is one of the countries that is affected by terrorism in recent years. The Global Terrorism Index (GTI) (2019) reported Nigeria ranking as the third most terrorized country in the world after Iraq and Syria. Nigerian version of terrorism emanated from a radical preaching by a group with an ideology of despising Western socioeconomic and political values which earned them the name of '*Boko Haram*' meaning that 'Western education and values are prohibited' (Thurston, 2018). The group later metamorphosed into a full-blown insurgent group in Northeastern Nigeria carrying sophisticated weapons against the Nigerian security personnel and innocent harmless citizens. Within a short period of time, the insurgency consumed thousands of lives and properties worth billions of dollars were destroyed in the process (Iyi, 2018). The insurgents undertake their activities using various means including weapons, finances and logistics. This chapter examined critically how the *Boko Haram* insurgents secured sources of funding for undertaking their activities (Anugwom, 2019). In doing so, it is pertinent to examine the background of the area of study: Northeastern Nigeria, framework of analysis; which is the use of

Social Conflict Theory; perspectives on *Boko Haram* insurgency in Northeastern Nigeria and sources of financing for *Boko Haram*. In doing so, the study utilised relevant documents such as books, journal articles, newspaper sources, reports and internet sources. The data gathered were analyzed, discussed and interpreted using content analysis. The main objective of the chapter is to establish empirically that financing is the livewire of terrorists' activities and henceforth, identifying the sources including sponsors, means and strategies are vital in cutting the nerves of terrorists' groups existence and survival. The study aimed at narrowing the subject with an empirical study of *Boko Haram* group in Northeastern Nigeria which have its insurgent activities earned Nigeria the rank of 3rd in the 2020 Global Terrorism Index (GTI).

NORTHEASTERN NIGERIA: AN OVERVIEW

The geographical territory that constitutes the present-day Nigeria was part of the British Colony of Northern Nigeria from 1902 to 1914 until the amalgamation in 1914 which led to the proclamation of the region as part of the British Nigerian Colony. Initially, the Northeast zone was part of the Kanem Bornu and Adamawa Empires prior to the advent of colonialist. Most parts of the Northeast including Borno, Yobe and Adamawa were provinces under the Bornu Empire, while Gombe, Bauchi and Taraba formed parts of the neighborhood with the Hausaland and Northern Cameroon. Later in the 18th century, Adamawa, Bauchi, Gombe and Taraba became parts of the Sokoto Caliphate and important centers of the Sokoto *Jihad* (Campbell & Page, 2018).

Currently, Northeastern Nigeria is one of the six (6) geopolitical zones and Federal Capital Territory Abuja (FCTA). The zone comprises of Adamawa, Bauchi, Borno, Gombe, Taraba and Yobe States. Northeast Nigeria has the capacity of nearly one-third of the total land in Nigeria which covers 280,419km^2 of the total Nigeria's land area (909, 890km2). The total population of Northeastern Nigeria is 27,828,844 (13.5%) of the total Nigerian population of 206,139,589 (Worldometer, 2020). The Northeast shares three international borders with Cameroon from the parts of Adamawa and Borno, Chad from Borno and Yobe States and Niger from Yobe and Borno States. The Zone is a major producer of agricultural products including rice, maize, beans, groundnuts, millet, wheat, tomatoes, vegetables and fish. Around 70% of the inhabitants are agrarian farmers engaged in peasant farming. Rearing of livestock is another important occupation of the people of Northeast (McEachern, 2018). The Zone is a host to one of the major Lakes in the world: The Lake Chad which serves the triple purpose of irrigation farming, fishing and rearing of livestock and cross-border transportation among Nigeria, Niger, Chad and Cameroon (Sule *et al.*, 2019). The Zone has porous borders, which enabled for an easy passage of people and goods without being noticed by the international border guards and that has propelled the illicit flow of Small Arms and Light Weapons, funds and other logistics for armed groups in recent years (Sambo *et al.*, 2020). Unfortunately, the Northeast Zone is the poorest, backwards and the most negatively affected by all indices of Human Development Index according to National Bureau of Statistics (2020). The map below shows the geographical location of the six (6) states that formed the geographical zone.

Figure 1. Map Showing the Six (6) Northeastern States of Nigeria
Source: Adopted from Google Map 2020

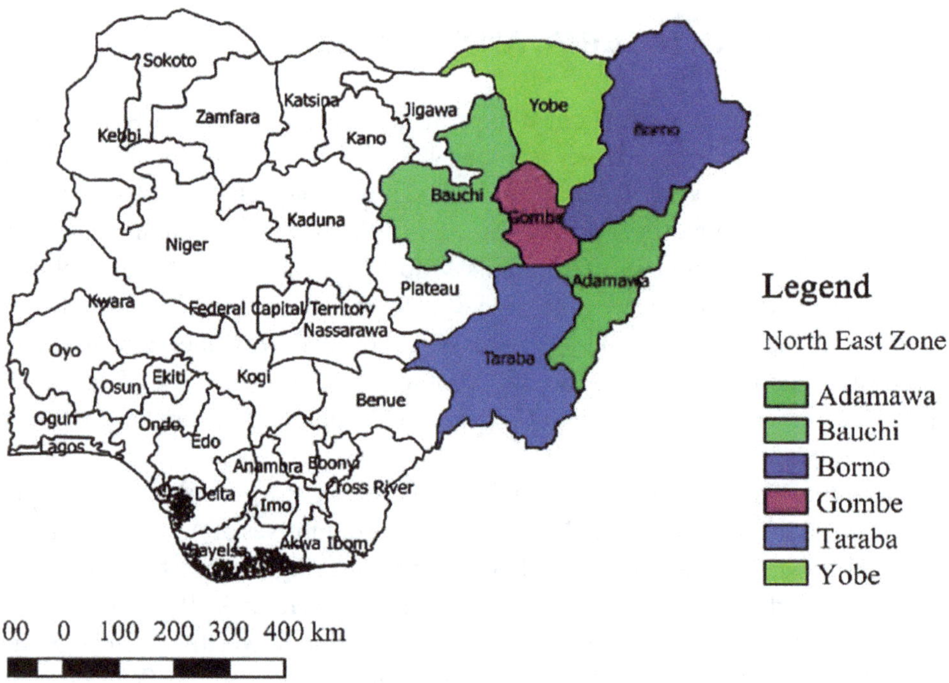

FRAMEWORK OF ANALYSIS

The study employed the framework of Social Conflict Theory in explaining the context of the work. Social Conflict Theory is a Sociological approach to understanding and explaining the causes of grievances and dissatisfaction with the existing social order leading to uprisings and social movements that may escalate to violence and other forms of social disorder. Contributions towards the building of this analytical discourse emanated from classical scholars such as Alfred Marshal, Emile Durkheim, Vilfredo Pareto, Robert Merton and Talcott Parson. The model was later followed by Political Economists like Karl Marx and Max Weber. The framework suggests that conflict is an inevitable part of the society that cannot be escaped no matter the level of justice and equality in the society. In a situation where injustice and inequality prevail in the society, conflict becomes more assertive and necessary. This is because competition for scarce resources and political control are the dominant events that occupied the attention of humankind in the society from time immemorial (Haralambos & Heald, 2015). Issues relating to ideology, class, ethnicity, religion, poverty, inequality, injustice, unemployment, geography, resources and power are the major sources of conflicts in our society. Furthermore, the framework identifies that for a better understanding and management of conflicts, there should be specific analysis and study of causal and related factors of each type of conflict to avoid putting a round hole in a square peg (Haralambos *et al.*, 2015).

One of the general ways suggested by this framework towards preventing and countering conflicts in the society is managing and reducing the gap of inequality, poverty accompanied with intelligence gathering. Furthermore, any conflict resolution should be approached by using a specific model or structure that is suitable and practical to its peculiar nature and environment (Haralambos *et al.*, 2015). The theory has potentials in the sense that it has a strong philosophical backing with a tendency for interdisciplinary interpretations. Additionally, the theory tends to be realistic in practical terms by suggesting that no society can prevent the occurrence of conflict being an inevitable part of social composition. However, the theory quickly identified that the conflicts are solvable once clear measures in their isolated terms are identified and applied. The major weakness of the theory is the submission that conflicts takes different dimensions. As true as this may be, all conflicts have one root, which is dissatisfaction with the social order as promoted by Karl Marx. Hence, a comprehensive approach towards managing all forms of conflicts should have been devised by the postulates of this framework.

The framework is applicable within the context of this study because the subject matter of terrorism is categorized as a disenchantment and a social response against perceived injustice by a particular group. The armed group conflict in form of the *Boko Haram* insurgency reflects the long-term exacerbated injustice, inequality, impoverishment, deprivation and most importantly, above all, ideological and religious extremism. The foundation of armed conflict in Northeastern Nigeria was set as a time bomb for several decades. All warnings by experts were ignored intentionally by policymakers until the time that the bomb was defused. Terrorists must find a way of survival, which consists of sourcing of weapons, finances and logistics to execute their mission and continuously undertake their activities. The aspect of financing of terrorism is what this study is much interested in.

Figure 2. Model of Social Conflict Theory
Source: Designed by the Authors, 2020

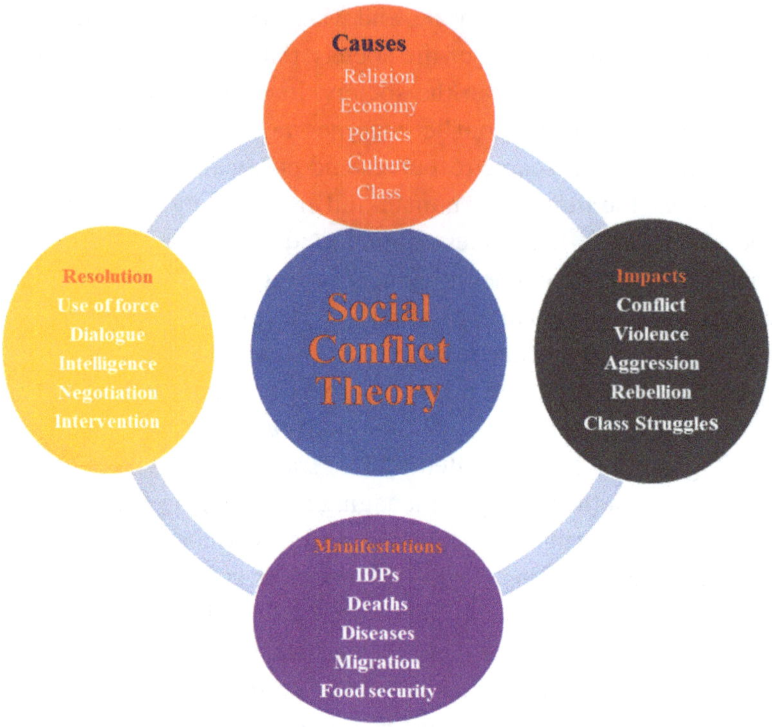

DISCOURSES ON GLOBAL TERRORISM

The actions and manifestations of terrorism across the globe is ancient. However, the modern usage of the term was coined in the 17th century during the French Revolution in describing the brutality unleashed by the Jacobins. The term was linked to Robesier and his colleagues in the 'Appalling Court' committee involving Jacob Baradai and his followers who used a campaign of terror that claimed between 16,000 and 40,000 lives. The reign of terror inflicted by the French revolutionaries was identified as the root behind the modern terror (Al Hageel, 2002). In the post-Cold War era, private groups, individuals, religious organizations and political pressure groups found the use of terror tenable for their goals (Nathanson, 2010). Contemporarily, there are over two hundred (200) variant definitions of the term terrorism according to Simon (1994). Simon (1994) further added that 90 of these definitions are used by governments and organizations while other researchers and institutions are using the other conceptualizations. Terrorism is an attempt at instilling fear and terror upon innocent citizens, security establishments, governments and organizations by any armed group that is not constitutionally mandated with the task of the usage of the apparatus of coercion (Webel & Arnaldi, 2012). Fundamentally, problem of definition is the major issue with the term terrorism. It is simply defined by the user and his sentiment (Asuelime & David, 2015). The Western world, for instance, is comfortable with identifying Islam and Islamic actions as terrorism but it is quick to dismiss same action conducted by its citizens as gunmen or insane acts by lunatics who are in mental dementia. Terrorizing acts perpetrated by the West during their colonial expedition are perceived by the colonized as terrorism but are never accepted as such by the perpetrator countries (Whittaker, 2004).

Terrorism is an organised crime initiated by a gang of criminals across the world (Small & Gilling, 2010). The definition and recognition of terrorism depends on who is throwing the bomb or perpetrating the act. For instance, the Lebanese who bombed the Americans perceived the America's colonization of the world and subjugation as a terror act while the Americans saw the act of the Lebanese as terrorism (Erlich, 2010). Terrorism involves dying for faith in the name of religion accompanied by politics and violence in search of identity that may culminate in the usage of violence (Al-Rashed & Shterin, 2009). Terrorism is a description of the method and a group. It is a form of violence, which is, distinguished from its same kind in another perspective. Nation-states, military and other forms of aggression and wars are also violence in the nature of terrorism but they are given a decent name or an official clearance to depart it from the act of terror in which it is not in practice (Webel & Arnaldi, 2012). Global violence or terrorism is any act that has the potential to cause harm to human beings. The ethical and moral question of how such violence and its perpetrators are handled determine how successful or unsuccessful the war against violence can be across the globe (Heintze, 2016). Terrorism has taken its battle into the limelight of global arena of information warfare. Terrorists in contemporary world utilised information as a source of their activities, which necessitates the responses in information warfare by all actors in the game (Kirpekar, 2009). Terrorism has taken a new dimension as a new form of war after the Cold War where tribal insurgents in places like Somalia, Chechnya, Afghanistan and Iraq organised themselves into armed groups and attack based on their ideology (Shultz Jr. & Dew, 2006). Piracy is a form of terror undertaken by sea gods and criminals who terrorized seafarers by taking their possession as booty or kidnapping them for ransom (Burkart, 2014).

Historically, terrorism is an ancient act emerging from the Jewish nationalist zealots known as '*Sicarii*' movement in AD 66-70, which created a mass insurgency in the Roman Province of Judea leading to obliteration of Jerusalem and Second Temple as well as mass suicide of Zealots in the encircled Masada fortress. The second group of terrorists that followed historically in the ancient time was the Isma'ili '*Hashashins*' known in English as 'Assassins' in AD 1090-1256 which is a group of *Fedayeen* cult of assassins who executed a terror campaign against the *Abbasid* Islamic Empire until when the cult was exterminated by the Mongols during their invasion of the Islamic Kingdom. The French Revolution set the foundation for modern world terrorism in AD 1793 when about 300, 000 suspected enemies of the Revolution were arrested and over 17, 000 were executed led by the leader of the Jacobins, Robespierre. In AD 1865, Ku Klux Klan is founded in Pulaski, Tennessee by a Confederate Civil War veteran, which unleashed several unpalatable terror acts on Americans. In 1878 AD by January, Catechism of the Revolutionist spearheaded by Sergey Nechayey inspired several terror acts in Europe (Anderson & Sloan, 2009).

From January 1878 to March 1881 Narodnaya Volta (People's Will) Russian terrorist group conducted massive bombings against Tsarist Government in its efforts towards staging a revolution that failed. However, it resulted in the assassination of Tsar Alexander II on the sixth effort. In June 1914, Austrian Archduke Francis Ferdinand was assassinated by a Serbian terrorist in Sarajevo, Bosnia Herzegovina, setting the foundation for the Frist World War between 1914-1918, which claimed an estimated 20 million lives. In 1931, the first plane hijack was recorded when rebel soldiers in Peru forced two American pilots to fly them about to drop propaganda pamphlets over Lima in Brazil. By 1938, German Nazis undertook 'Kristallnacht' (ethnic cleansing) against German Jews leading to 'Holocaust' claiming millions of lives of the Jews in Germany until the defeat of the Third Reich in May 1945. From 1939 to 1940, the Irish Republican Army in Ireland, a terrorist group, executed major bombing campaigns within England recording over 50 bombings within just a period of 13 months. In 1948, Hindu terrorist killed Mohandas Gandhi in a terror act. By 1955, Algerian National Liberation Front (FLN) terrorists undertook a manslaughter of 37 European colonizers who were terrorizing the natives in Algeria under the guise of colonialism. The South African white supremacist massacred over 69 blacks' demonstrators in Sharpeville incident under the Apartheid policy (Anderson & Sloan, 2009).

In the 1960s and beyond, the *Al Qaeda* and other groups emerged in the limelight of modern global terrorism; bombing, killing and terrorizing various targets in the West, Middle East and Africa (Mamdani, 2000). *Al Qaeda* received the active financial and logistical support of the United States during the Cold War under the Ronald Reagan's policy of countering Communism (Mamdani, 2004). The *Al Qaeda* is an alumnus from the CIA's school of terrorism according to Blum (2002). Chossudovsky (2005) argued that terror was globalized by the United States and her allies during the colonial exploitation, later expanded in the Cold War race and consolidated in the post-Cold War period. Ever since the resurgence of global terrorism at large scale in the September 11, 2001 attacks, terrorism and terror acts intensified in various shapes and across the continents of the world including the *Al*

Qaeda, *Al Shabab*, Red Brigade, Apocalypse, ISIS, *Boko Haram* and several other terror groups. They pursue political, economic, religious and cultural objectives against individuals, groups, states and organizations (Sule, Yahaya & Sambo, 2019). Chomsky (1989) suggested that the culture of the US elites of global domination is the catalyzer for sponsoring and breeding of internationally renowned terrorist in modern times. Chomsky (2000) suggested that there are the visible hands of the 'Rogue States' with the US qualified as first among its galleries in various acts of global terrorism either undertaken by individuals, groups or nation-states, while some of the acts were directly carried out by the States itself in places like Cambodia, Laos, Nicaragua, Vietnam and other places.

In another view, Livingstone (2007), argues that terrorism in modern times is the reminiscent of the covert conspiratorial clandestine activities of the bloodline of the illuminati. The secret activities of these covert groups paved the way for contemporary counter-responses in aggression and violence because of their insatiable desire to control the world economy and politics. Owing to the defying nature of terrorism, a scholar, Godlewski (2007), suggested that there is a strong need for training the targets of terrorism such as plane passengers, groups, governments, organizations and crowded places on survival techniques including how to relate with the hijackers, distance, posture and responses. In another study, Chomsky (2013), postulated that terrorism was carried out by all sets of human races not only the Islamic or Middle East terrorism. Building his thesis on that basis, he mentioned that Western terrorism in modern times emanated from Hiroshima to the 'Drone War'. Chomsky (2013) reported the murderous legacy of colonialism, concealment of the war crimes of the West, media propaganda, direct and indirect intervention in Asia, Latin America, Eastern Europe and Africa as well as blowing the Arab uprising as acts of terror perpetuated by the West. New terrorism in form of the global *Jihad* was sometimes state sponsored in the Muslim world by states like Pakistan (Casaca, 2017 and Wolf, 2017).

Failed states are the foundation of terrorism. Individuals resort to violence and rebellion when they perceived a clear act of deprivation, which precipitates aggression that may be tantamount to political violence and other forms of violence (Howard, 2014). Another factor that proliferates the emergence of terrorism globally is mass hate, which is metamorphosing into genocide as in the case of orchestrated genocide of Muslims in Bosnia, Rwandan Hutu-Tutsi mishap and an intensified propaganda of Hitler that ushered in the famous ethnic cleansing of the German Jews popularly known as 'Holocaust' (Rieff, 1995). Current economic and political climate are seen as the drivers that fuel insurgency and terrorism in various parts of the world (USDHS, 2009; Adebajo, 2020). Helmus (2009) observed that some people became terrorist emanating from association with radical groups, desire for political change, religious change, environmental and social factors and peer group influence.

Terrorism has an economic cost. For instance, the United States alone spent about 3 trillion dollars in the war against terrorism from 2001 to date. Europe too is another actor that is spending billions of Euro in their counter-terrorism response within and outside of the continent. In Africa, the economic cost of terrorism is unbearable. In 2016, the economic cost of terrorism in Africa was reported as USD1.54 billion. The Africa's share of the global cost of terrorism rose from 4.2% in 2007 to 20.3% in 2016 signifying an increase beyond imagination (UNDP, 2019). Solomon (2015) supported the above assertion in his view because he believed that terrorism has pose a serious security threats to Africa with the likes of *Al Shabab*, AQIM, *Boko Haram* and *Ansaruddin* operating across the continent with a terrible approach and a huge casualty.

TERRORIST FINANCING

Terrorist financial needs mostly anchored around purchase of weapons, recruit of new members, procurement of medical supply and daily needs. Most of these finances are raised through charity of international agencies, black market, theft, kidnapping of important figures for ransom and support of local civilians (Faluyi, Khan &Akinola, 2019). Three major sources of funding for terrorists are identified as direct intentional funding, criminal activities and legitimate commerce. Such pattern of financing was observed in the Chechen armed group who have been operating in the border of Georgia. Substantial funding emanates from the sympathizers of the terrorist group. For instance, the Chechen group obtained their funding from Arab/Islamic countries including Saudi Arabia, Qatar, Kuwait, Yemen and Pakistan (Wittig, 2011). In the case of *Al Qaeda*, the funds for establishment, recruit and operation were all supplied by the CIA from the United States of America. Mamdani (2004), argued that the Reagan Administration found the Afghan-Russian war as a perfect alibi to fight the communist to the last resort. He instructed the CIA to release money for the recruitment of *Al Qaeda* fighters under the supervision of the Pakistani secret security agents. Recruits from Saudi Arabia, Pakistan, Egypt, Sudan, Algeria and Syria were attracted and paid a sum of USD1,700 monthly to fight the Russians. The University of Nebraska received a grant of USD50 million to publish Mathematics books for the Afghan elementary schools under the United States Agency for International Development (USAID). A fourth-grade textbook ups the ante: "*The speed of a Kalashnikov [the ubiquitous Soviet-made semiautomatic machine gun] bullet is 800 meters per second. If a Russian is at a distance of 3200 meters from a Mujahid, and that Mujahid aims at the Russian's head, calculate how many seconds it will take for the bullet to strike the Russian in the forehead.*" (Mamdani, 2004). The correlation between the publication of the books with terrorism financing is that radical *Talibans* that later joined *Al Qaeda* were recruited and taught with the books on *Jihad*. Financing terrorists is not only about the movement of funds but also about the ability to store them and disburse them for final use. Understanding terrorists financing is problematic because it involves the issues of epistemology, identifying the actors or sponsors and the channel of the flow of financial assistance to the terrorists' groups (Wittig, 2011).

In identifying terrorist financing, it is good to discover the root of religious terrorism, which emanates from Middle East, United States of America, Indian Sub-Continent, Northern Ireland and South America. Terrorists are financed via various channels (Nasir, 2020). One of these channels is state sponsored terrorism linked with several Middle East countries and the case of *Al Qaeda* by the United States during the Afghan-Russian War. Individual/corporate contributions are another main source from where terrorists get their finances. According to US prosecutors, Osama Bin Laden was not only recognized as the mastermind of several terror attacks in the US but he was found to have donated around USD250 million for terrorist organizations. Non-profit organizations are another source of terrorist organization (D'Souza, 2012). The Interpol reported that several charity corporations were involved in sponsoring terrorist groups in disguise. Sometimes government programs are responsible for financing terrorism where in countries like Iraq, Iran, Syria and Libya, state policies and programs aided terrorists' groups indirectly. Additionally, terrorists secure their finances through illegal means including drugs and extortion, organised theft, hacking of accounts, cyber fraud, money laundering, tax evasion, and fraud (D'Souza, 2012; Nasir, 2020).

Terrorist organizations sometimes secure their funds through established businesses of multi-million or even billion dollars for reasonable profits that are channeled into financing terrorism (Vittori, 2011). Terrorism is sponsored in some cases using organised crimes. Financing of terrorism including the procurement of explosives and weapons for their operations are conducted in an illicit and a clandestine way. Thus, the evolution of criminal enterprises enabled for the survival and continuation of financing terrorist organizations worldwide (Thacuk & Lal, 2018). Hence, since financing terrorism is the sole aspect that is given fresh blood to the veins of terror groups to continue to survive, it is pertinent to identify the root sources and block them. In this regard, the United Nations General Assembly took a stern position on anti-terrorism making laws that will indict any state, group, organization or individual found as an accomplice to face international law. The Security Council also adopted a measure towards tracing and blockage of the sources of funds for terror groups after the Lockerbie incident (Koh, 2006). Financing terrorism is not conducted in a transparent way and so also tracing and identifying the sources are difficult task that require an utmost cooperation of all actors in the globe.

OVERVIEW OF *BOKO HARAM* INSURGENCY IN NORTHEASTERN NIGERIA

The *Boko Haram* insurgency is one of the radical responses of the restive youth in Nigerian Northeast. Bedeviled by a long-term impoverishment and deprivation from the parasitic ruling class in the country that is ravaging the economy with looting and pilfering, the youth became aggressive in their dealings with the Nigerian state (Sule, Sambo & Tal, 2018). The *Boko Haram*, a 'Hausa' term referring to 'Western education and values are forbidden', is a nomenclature that is linked to the group of preachers in Northeastern Nigeria in the early 2000. Officially, the group named itself "*Jama'atu Ahlul Sunnah Lil Da'awati Wal Jihad*" (meaning 'People Committed for Prophetic Teaching and Proselytisation). There is no specific or exact consensus on when the *Boko Haram* started (Sule, Ahmed, Alhaji, Yahaya & Gambarawa, 2019). In one of the seemingly accurate narrations, Muhammad Yusuf, who was believed to have been the founder of the group, was a student of one, Abubakar Lawan, who initiated the movement in its infancy stage but later secured admission in University of Madina to study theology (Kassim & Nwankpa, 2018). On his departure, he appointed Muhammad Yusuf to become the leader of the group. In another narration, the movement was started by Muhammad Yusuf as early as 2000 but it was manifested in 2002 when they attacked Kanama in Geidem, Yobe States. The group re-appeared in 2007 when it attacked Panshekara Police Station in Kano State. Ever since the 2007 attacks, the group became more radical, anti-Western and anti-Nigerian Government openly (Sule, Yahaya & Sambo, 2019).

The group, unlike the pure *Ahlul Sunnah*, who are critical of any rebellion against the constituted authorities, proclaimed to be *Ahlul Sunnah* and named its center in Maiduguri 'Markazu *Ibn Taymiyyah*' meaning 'Centre for *Ibn Taymiyyah*', adopting the footstep of the *Sunni* radical scholars. However, actions of *Boko Haram* revealed that they are parallel with the teaching and philosophy of *Ibn Taymiyyah* because he belongs to the school of thought, which forbids any form of protest against leaders, rebellion and disrespect for constituted authorities rigidly (Sule *et al.* 2019). The zenith of *Boko Haram*'s tragedy began in 2009 when a clash between the members of the group and the security outfit, 'Operation Flush' in Maiduguri city emanating from the use of helmet on motorcycle riders that the group refused to adhere to led to the killing of some *Boko Haram* members. In retaliation, the group came out in totality armed with sophisticated weapons and attacked the security men especially the Mobile Police Officers. The skirmish led to the death of several members of the sect including the leader, Muhammad Yusuf, who was killed by the Police in extrajudicial manner (Religious Literacy Project, 2018). The 2009 tragedy set the foundation for insurgency by *Boko Haram*. The successor of Muhammad Yusuf, Abubakar Shekau, a radical and an extreme fellow declared a *Jihad* against the

Nigerian security men and by extension, the Nigerian state. By 2013, the *Boko Haram* controlled over eighteen local governments in Adamawa, Borno and Yobe States. Police Stations, Army Barracks and other security outfits were bombed and attacked by the insurgents. Churches, mosques, market gathering and crowded places were attacked, while several villages and towns were ransacked and chased by the activities of the insurgents.

The *Boko Haram* insurgency caused several implications on political, economic and social settings of Northeastern Nigeria. Poverty escalated in the already poverty-ridden zone being the poorest in the country (Foyou, Ngwafu, Santoyo & Ortiz, 2018). Corruption and a weak security architecture contributed to the emergence and flourishing of *Boko Haram* in Northeastern Nigeria (Ibrahim & Bala, 2018). The Global Conflict Tracker (2020) reported that an estimated 37,000 lives were destroyed by the activities of *Boko Haram* insurgency and the report attributed the cause of the attacks to poverty and corruption. The International Crisis Group (2020) relates the cause of *Boko Haram* to the sharp effects of climate change, population bulge and rapid spread of Small Arms and Light Weapons (SALW). The study further narrated that the conditions were compounded by the displacement of the inhabitants in the Northeast leading to over 2.5 million Internally Displaced Persons (IDPs) across the region. Inequality, structural imbalance and negligence of the impoverished groups contributed to the establishment of the *Boko Haram* insurgency as observed by Okoli (2019), while humanitarian assistance became difficult owing to the direct assault on the humanitarian workers (Ewang, 2020). Other studies (Walker, 2016; Uwaisu, 2018; Allen, 2019; Brechenmacher, 2019; Idika-Kalu, 2019; Okolo & Akubo, 2019 and Olukoya, 2019) linked the causes and impact of *Boko Haram* to poverty, corruption, climatic change, the depletion of Lake Chad, structural socioeconomic imbalance, lack of religious censorship and tendency towards fundamentalism. Others included inefficient and ineffective security response to the crisis and mishandling of the situation by the Nigerian Government.

Boko Haram is believed to have caused one of the worst humanitarian crises in Nigeria. After 2009, the insurgents increased their assaults on security outposts, army barracks, police stations, mosques, churches, marketplaces and parks, using mass and sporadic shootings, bombings, kidnapping and propaganda. Within a short period, the Northeast was flooded with IDPs and other vulnerable groups emerging from the activities of the *Boko Haram* group. According to *Shehu Musa Yar'adua* Foundation, from 2009 to 2018, the *Boko Haram* sect had carried out 1, 639 violent attacks in Northeast, with 14,436 casualties, 6,051 injured victims, and 2,063 hostages with over 2 million IDPs (Okolo *et al.* 2019). In another study, Allen (2019) reported that between 2011 and 2019, *Boko Haram* group recorded over four thousand deadly attacks with about 13,000 casualties. The CNN reported 75 deadly attacks with over 20,000 deaths and above 6,000 injured victims. Apart from killings and victims of injuries, about 13.5 million inhabitants of Northern Nigeria currently require intervention from humanitarian assistance due to their critical situation. About 1.3 of them could not be reached for humanitarian assistance because of the terrain of their environment. Children estimated at 900,000 below the age of five suffering from acute malnutrition, malaria fever and cholera outbreak could not be contained in Northeastern region due to humanitarian crisis. About 2.8 million children need education in emergencies in three-conflict affected states of Adamawa, Borno and Yobe. At least 802 schools remained closed and over 497 classes were burned or destroyed by the insurgents (UNICEF, 2019).

In any case of humanitarian crises and violent conflicts, it is expected that both the domestic government and international community will respond in many ways such as rescue mission, prevention, protection, negotiation, identifying the root causes and addressing them and most importantly in the case of insurgency, using several strategies. One of the strategies adopted by the Nigerian government is the use of coercion and traditional/military response. Security personnel were deployed in the Northeast to counter insurgency. Unfortunately, that aim has been defeated because in most cases, the insurgents tend to be holding superior firepower and are more combatant ready than the Nigerian security agencies. This has been one of the motivations behind this work. This work felt that the measures put in place are inadequate in fighting an insurgency of this nature in Northeastern Nigeria. the work opined that other viable options should be utilised among which it identified one which is; a non-traditional or non-military approach. Nevertheless, the responses are briefly analyzed below to justify why they are inadequate and why the suggested approach in this study is necessary. The Nigerian government adopted responsive method which is to respond militarily towards the crisis. The current security situation and laws in the country in addition to weak political institutions all made the responses inadequate. The challenges faced by security personnel include, among many, are lack of synergy and cooperation among the various security operatives, obsolete weapons and equipment, lack of proper intelligence gathering, hostile community relationship and low level of motivation (Sule *et al.*, 2019).

HOW *BOKO HARAM* FINANCED ITS ACTIVITIES: SOME EVIDENCES

A study by Sule & Sani (2020) unpublished, examined based on fieldwork how the *Boko Haram* sourced for their finances. From the various interviews conducted with informants, many narrations revealed various sources. One of these sources is that the insurgents pay membership dues especially during the early stage of the movement. Respective members of the sect were instructed to pay their dues according to the size of their income. Among the followers were businesspersons, artisans, civil servants and farmers. They were encouraged to give no matter how little because the donations would be channeled in striving for the cause of *Allah*. This was the early source of finance for the activities of the insurgents. Other sources revealed by the informants comprised of both the internal and external sources. The internal sources involved contributions by members and sympathizers, loans, farming, fishing, trading, businesses and personal efforts. The external sources consist of kidnapping for ransom where they sometimes kidnapped foreign workers in return for a ransom in dollars. The insurgents exchanged hostages and innocent citizens captured for cash from the government and organizations. The sect also received donations from other terror groups such as *Al Qaeda*, ISIS, AQIM and *Ansaruddin*.

Additionally, the group earned a huge fortune from kidnapping of the Chibok girls in 2013 and Dapchi girls in 2017 (Ibrahim & Hoffman, 2017). Narrations revealed that the Nigerian Government had to pay billions of Naira to secure the release of some of them (Sesay, 2019). Furthermore, sometimes the insurgents released Nigerian security men in their custody and other essential workers in exchange for their members and money from the government to secure finance for their operation. The *Boko Haram* is believed to be a well-funded criminal organization in West Africa and beyond. The US Government reported that *Boko Haram* sourced for their funding from criminal activities especially kidnappings for ransom. Another source from the US identified that the *Boko Haram* insurgents used the Nigerian porous border in West Africa to transport huge cash into Nigeria (Rock, 2016).

In a study, Rock (2016), reported eight (8) major sources of funding for *Boko Haram* group. The first group is microfinancing where loans are offered to members for repayment (Ibrahim, 2020). The Mercy Corps disclosed that the *Boko Haram* offered loan worth N10, 000 up to N1 million in recent years for its members to be repaid in tranches. The second source is membership fees. Inter-Governmental Action Group against Money Laundering in West Africa (GIABA) and the Financial Action Task Force (FATF) reported that, even after Yusuf's death in 2009, membership fees were collected towards 2012 (FATF, 2016). The third source of finance for *Boko Haram* is external support from sister organizations such as AQIM, *Al Qaeda* and ISIS. The fourth source is robbing of banks for carting away of cash. It was estimated that the *Boko Haram* sect robbed banks in Northeastern Nigeria worth 2.7 billion naira (USD6 million). The fifth source is extortion and ransom from kidnappings. The sixth source is illicit trafficking and smuggles of weapons and other contraband for profit (Hathorn & Abbott, 2015). The seventh source is funding from politicians and other individuals in the country who benefit politically from the proceeds of the crisis. The last source is the rampage on shops and business centers where expensive wares are sold. They later resell in the market and cash the proceeds (Eme, 2016).

Apart from the cash, the sect also sourced for other logistics related to cash such as foods, medical supply, clothing, shelter and other daily needs through attacks on towns, taking enough for their needs and burning the shops (Moses, 2017). They raid villages, take foodstuffs, raid hospitals, and abduct nurses and doctors who are forced to stay with them for medical treatment. In other cases, the group bribed the Nigerian security to pass the Northeast porous borders with weapons and other logistics. They also bribed and threatened the local communities against any hostility or release of intelligence report that will expose them (Nowak & Gsell, 2018). The *Boko Haram* possessed expensive weapons including improvised explosive devices (IEDs), bullets, anti-aircraft (AA) guns, general-purpose machine guns (GPMGs) and other munitions of war, which cost billions of Naira. They also rode in a convoy of new brand Toyota Hilux. It is believed that they possessed around 700 Hilux for their operation. Apart from the cost of weapons and logistics, they also pay salaries for their fighters. They also pay expensively for their suicide bombers and cater for the cost of propaganda that they disseminate through YouTube and other platforms of media. How did they secure all these? Ekhomu (2020) responded in his work by presenting the ways in which they earned their funding through some political figures in the country. The identified figures denied the accusations and it is expected because no one will agree to have a link with terrorist. They also exploit the 2.5% Zakat as stipulated by Islam in which it is collected from the rich and redistribute to the poor (Adebayo, 2020). The money is transferred through the porous borders in Northeast and the instrument is mainly cash. Kidnapping keeps on providing a better source of finance for the insurgents. For instance, the group abducted over 200 Chibok schoolgirls in 2013 and partly released some of them after they were paid a huge sum of money. Some of them are still under their custody. Similarly, in 2017, they abducted Dapchi schoolgirls and were also paid a huge ransom. This is putting aside the daily reports of one or two incidences of kidnappings from the sect. it was reported that they ended up securing a deal of billions of Naira before they released the victims (Sule, Sambo & Tal, 2018).

However, there are issues and controversies surrounding *Boko Haram* financing in Northeastern Nigeria. In the last hour of the former ruling People's Democratic Party (PDP), it accused some top northern politicians of deliberately financing the armed group to destabilize the country particularly the region to secure an easy ride for capturing power in 2015. In another way, the northern leaders and its inhabitants pinpointed the former President Jonathan's Administration as the sponsor of *Boko Haram* as alleged by the then, Presidential aspirant, Muhammadu Buhari in an interview that the Federal Government is the *Boko Haram*. Issues that are linked to the emergence and activities of *Boko Haram* such as poverty, unemployment, ignorance are sometimes dismissed as genuine reasons for the radical armed groups. This is perhaps, because the group is reported to have acquired weapons worth

N2 billion in 2018, it has many higher certificate holders of Western education and many learned men in Islamic education and many of them were former civil servants and businessmen who relinquished their occupations to join the group. If poverty, unemployment and ignorance are the major factors for the group, it would not have secured such a huge finance running in billions to execute its activities. They could have used the funds to refurbish themselves and renounce the crime. Furthermore, the recent controversy in 2019, where the Nigerian Government accused some international donors including Mercy Corps, Action Against Hunger and even the United Nations of sponsoring and shielding *Boko Haram* members led to controversial decision of suspending them except the UN from operation in the Northeast for several months. Besides, the position above that the insurgents secured finances through microfinance, personal donation and other sources could not provide billions that they spent in procuring weapons and other logistics for undertaking their crimes (Thurston, 2018).

Some efforts were made in blocking sources of financing terrorism in Nigeria. One of these efforts is the establishment of the Economic and Financial Crimes Commission (EFCC) which is saddled with the task of monitoring corrupt practices, watching of money laundering, illegal financial transactions, advanced fee fraud, crimes pertaining to transactions above the set individual and organizational limit and other related offences. The EFCC was established in 2002 and it has succeeded severally in identifying and blocking dubious and suspicious deal and it has connected in leading to top arrest of criminal sponsors. Another effort is the Money Laundering Act in 2015 which was enacted to trace and punish illicit money transfers abroad and into the country which is helping in blocking crimes. The Cybersecurity Act 2015 is another effort in blocking digital transactions and cybercrimes relating to illicit financial flows to armed groups in Nigeria. The 2018 Nigerian Financial Intelligence Unit (NFIU) is another effort towards gathering classified information on cybercrimes, illicit financial flows and other financial crimes (Sule, Yahaya, Rabi'u, Ahmad & Hussaini, 2019).

The Nigerian Government is unable to block the sources of finance of *Boko Haram* due to several factors. One of them is corruption. Nigerian state developed a notorious reputation in corrupt practices globally. The financial institutions are sometimes accused of shielding illegal and suspicious transactions for fear of losing customers and profits. Through this process, *Boko Haram* easily transfer money and transact within and from abroad undetected (McEachern, 2018). The second factor is the nature of Nigeria's porous borders. According to the former Minister of Internal Affairs in Nigeria, Abba Moro, there are over 1,449 illegal borders in Nigeria making surveillance much difficult considering the inadequacy of security personnel and manpower to monitor the borders. Insurgents move sometimes freely with heavy cash from abroad and outside the country undetected (Onuoha, 2013). Other factors are weak financial monitoring institutions. The Nigerian Financial Intelligence Unit (NFIU) was just established in 2018. This has been the reason why sponsors from abroad are hardly detected. A case to reckon here is the recent arrest of *Boko Haram* sponsors in Dubai. According to Daily Trust Newspaper, six Nigerians were sentenced to ten years and life imprisonment in United Arab Emirates for sponsoring *Boko Haram* from Dubai. The accused were initially arrested 2017 and convicted in November 2020 for their crimes. The court in Abu Dhabi Monday sentenced Surajo Abubakar Muhammad and Saleh Yusuf Adamu to life in prison. Ibrahim Ali Alhassan, AbdurRahman Ado Musa, Bashir Ali Yusuf and Muhammad Ibrahim Isa were each given a ten-year sentence. The newspaper said the court judgement said that between 2015 and 2016, the accused transferred USD782,000 from Dubai to Nigeria to benefit *Boko Haram* even as associates defended their actions, saying there was nothing criminal about the transaction. Related to the above is the ineffective cybersecurity and digital surveillance. Activities of online and digital transactions are carried unmonitored by the Nigerian Government. Additionally, the nature of weak cooperation between Nigeria and its immediate Francophone neighbors of Benin Republic, Cameroon, Chad and Niger Republic made a strict regulations and monitoring of international cash movement and transfers difficult (Sule *et al.*, 2019). The above is attributed as the major reasons why the Nigerian Government failed to monitor and block the sources of finance of *Boko Haram*.

Thus, it is glaring that like other terrorist organizations, as observed in the early section of this study, terrorist survived by a sophisticated and well-designed finance undertaken by criminal syndicate as observed in this section. The *Boko Haram* are surviving because their sources of finances are not identified and blocked by the authorities concerned. Any attempt at ending the nemesis should start genuinely with blockage.

CONCLUSION

Terrorism is glaringly a global security headache in contemporary world and the root causes are divergent and multi-lateral beyond one single purpose or ideology. As observed in this study, the term terrorism itself is a subject of controversy and interpretation by different actors depending on where they are coming from and their perception. However, one certain view that is indisputable in the discourse of terrorism is the motive and impact. Terrorism of whatever kind has the implication of sending fear and instability on the target. Terrorism is propelled by various factors inclusive of political, economic, social, cultural, religious and geographical. Terrorism is an ancient act of humankind emerging from the medieval period to modern times and all race, nations, religions and regions are involved in it. However, contemporary discourse on global terrorism tend to single out Islam and Muslims as terrors with terrorist act despite the several scientific narrations that proved otherwise. In essence, without funding, terrorism will not thrive and flourish. Terrorist source for their funding through both legal and illegal ways and internally and externally. Legally, terrorist organizations are involved in legitimate businesses undetected, which culminated profits for them. Illegally, they are involved in money laundering, drug pedaling, black markets, extortion, kidnapping and other sources. They also secure their sources of financing through external support by member organizations and through internal efforts by members' contributions and support. Hence, this study concludes that terrorists are able to survive and continue with their operations because they have a secured means of financing and *Boko Haram* survived through this process. The study therefore recommends that identification, tracing and blockage of the sources of finances are the long-term panaceas for addressing the conflict in the Northeast. The sources of finance can be blocked through various ways. One of them is the full utilization of the NFIU to intelligently monitor the inflow and outflow of money in Nigeria and outside Nigeria. Digital settings can be used by identifying the mode of online financial illicit transactions. Additionally, the porous borders should be closely monitored using reconnaissance and drones to spy on the activities at the borders to detect suspicious movement of goods, services and people. Also, international cooperation should be sought with global financial agencies and world countries in giving classified information on Nigerians staying abroad or coming from Nigeria or into Nigeria with any suspicious finances. Additionally, the study further recommends that the root long-term causes of *Boko Haram* insurgency such as poverty, deprivation, corruption, inequality, joblessness, injustice and poor educational system in addition to tendency for extremism should be addressed squarely in future to block any such movement.

DISCLAIMER

The contents and views of this chapter are expressed by the authors in their personal capacities. It is not necessary for the Editor and the Publisher to agree with these viewpoints and they are not responsible for any duty of care in this regard.

ACKNOWLEDGMENT

The authors extend sincere gratitude to:

- The Editor-in-Chief and International Editorial Advisory Board (IEAB) of this book who initially desk reviewed, arranged a rigorous double/triple blind review process and conducted a thorough, minute and critical final review before accepting the chapter for publication.
- All anonymous reviewers who provided very constructive feedbacks for thorough revision, improvement, extension and finetuning of the chapter.
- All colleagues, assistants and well-wishers who assisted the authors to complete this task.

REFERENCES

Adebajo, K. (2020). *Terrorism, COVID-19, Flooding and the Growing Humanitarian Crises in Northern Nigeria*. OSIWA/HumAngle Media.

Adebayo, R. I. (2020). Zakat Distribution in the Context of Shari'ah Corporate Governance: Evidence from South-Western Nigeria. In A. Rafay (Ed.), *Handbook of Research on Theory and Practice of Global Islamic Finance* (pp. 161–178). IGI Global.

Al Hageel, S. A. (2002). *The Virtual Position of Islam on Extremism and Terrorism*. King Fahad National Library Cataloguing Publication Data.

Al-Rashed, M., & Shterin, M. (2009). Between Death of Faith and Dying for Faith: Reflections on Religion, Politics, Society and Violence. In M. Al-Rashed & M. Shterin (Eds.), *Dying for Faith: Religiously Motivated Violence in Contemporary World* (pp. 1–3). I.B. Tauris. doi:10.5040/9780755625024.0006

Allen, N. (2019). *How Boko Haram Regained the Initiative and What Nigeria Should do to Stop It*. Texas National Security Review.

Anderson, S. K., & Sloan, S. (2009). *Historical Dictionary of Terrorism*. The Scarecrow Press.

Anugwom, E. E. (2019). *The Boko Haram Insurgence: Perspective from Within*. Palgrave Macmillan. doi:10.1007/978-3-319-96959-6

Asuelime, L. E., & David, O. J. (2015). *Boko Haram: The Socio-Economic Drivers*. Springer Nature.

Blum, W. (2002). *Rogue State: A Guide to the World's Only Superpower*. Zed Books.

Brechenmacher, S. (2019). *Stabilising North East Nigeria After Boko Haram*. Carnegie Endowment for International Peace.

Burkart, P. (2014). *Pirate Politics: The New Information Policy Contents*. MIT Press. doi:10.7551/mitpress/9205.001.0001

Campbell, J., & Page, M. T. (2018). *Nigeria: What Everyone Needs to Know*. Oxford University Press. doi:10.1093/wentk/9780190657970.001.0001

Casaca, P. (2017). The Conceptual Discussion on Terrorism. In P. Casaca & S. O. Wolf (Eds.), *Terrorism Revisited: Islamism, Political Violence and State-Sponsorship*. Springer Nature. doi:10.1007/978-3-319-55690-1_1

Chomsky, N. (1989). *The Culture of Terrorism*. Pluto Press.

Chomsky, N. (2000). *Rogue States: The Rule of Force in World Affairs*. Pluto Press.

Chomsky, N. (2013). *On Western Terrorism: From Hiroshima to Drone Warfare*. Pluto Press.

Chossudovsky, M. (2005). *America's War on Terrorism*. Centre for Research on Globalisation.

D'Souza, J. (2012). *Terrorist Financing, Money Laundering and Tax Evasion: Examining the Performance of Financial Intelligence Units*. CRC Press.

Deflem, M. (2004). Introduction: Towards a Criminological Sociology of Terrorism and Counter-Terrorism. In M. Deflem (Ed.), *Terrorism and Counter-Terrorism: Criminological Perspective*. Elsevier. doi:10.1108/S1521-6136(2004)0000005002

Ekhomu, O. (2020). *Boko Haram: Security Considerations and the Rise of Insurgency*. CRC Press.

Eme, C. (2016). Terrorist Financing in Nigeria: A Case of *Boko Haram. Specialty Journal of Psychology and Management*, *2*(3), 41–52.

Erlich, R. (2010). *Conversation with Terrorists: Middle East Leaders on Politics, Violence and Empire*. Routledge.

Ewang, A. (2020). *Attacks on Aid Workers in Northeastern Nigeria: Insurgent Attacks Against Civilian Constitute War Crimes*. Human Rights Watch.

Faluyi, O. T., Khan, S., & Akinola, A. O. (2019). *Boko Haram's Terrorism and the Nigerian State: Federalism, Politics and Policies*. Springer Nature. doi:10.1007/978-3-030-05737-4

FATF. (2016). *Terrorist Financing in Central and West Africa*. Retrieved from http://www.fatf-gafi.org/media/fatf/documents/reports/Terrorist-Financing-West-Central-Africa.pdf

Foyou, V. E., Ngwafu, P., Santoyo, M., & Ortiz, A. (2018). The *Boko Haram* Insurgency and its Impact on Border Security, Trade and Economic Collaboration Between Nigeria and Cameroon: An Exploratory Study. *African Social Science Review*, *9*(1), 66–77.

Global Conflict Tracker. (2020). *Recent Development*. Council on Foreign Relations. Retrieved https://www.cfr.org/global-conflict-tracker/

Global Terrorism Index. (2019). *Measuring the Impact of Terrorism*. Sydney: Institute for Economics and Peace. Retrieved from https://visionofhumanity.org/reports

Godlewski, R.J. (2007). *Manual of the Independent Counter Terrorist*. US Air force.

Google Map. (2020). *Map of Nigeria Showing Northeastern Zone and Six States*. Retrieved from www.googlemap.com

Hall, J. R. (2009). Apocalypse, History, and the Empire of Modernity. In M. Al-Rashed & M. Shterin (Eds.), *Dying for Faith: Religiously Motivated Violence in Contemporary World*. I.B. Tauris. doi:10.5040/9780755625024.ch-001

Haralambos, M., & Heald, R. M. (2015). *Sociology: Themes and Perspectives*. Oxford University Press.

Hathorn, S., & Abbott, C. (2015). Intelligence brief: Reducing the Supply of Weapons to Boko Haram. *Open briefing*. Retrieved from https://www.openbriefing.org/publications/intelligence-briefings/reducing-the-supply-of-weapons-to-boko-haram/)

Heintze, E. A. (2016). *Global Violence: Ethical and Political Issues*. Routledge. doi:10.4324/9781315684642

Helmus, T. C. (2009). Why and How Some People Become Terrorists. In P. K. Davis & K. Cragin (Eds.), *Social Science for Counter Terrorism: Putting the Pieces Together*. RAND Corporation.

Howard, F. (2014). *Failed States and the Origins of Violence: A Comparative Analysis of State Failure as a Root Cause of Terrorism and Political Violence*. Routledge.

Ibrahim, B. A. (2020). Interest-Free Micro-Finance without any Religious Connotation: An Inclusive Global Model. In A. Rafay (Ed.), *Handbook of Research on Theory and Practice of Global Islamic Finance* (pp. 196–215). IGI Global. doi:10.4018/978-1-7998-0218-1.ch011

Ibrahim, J., & Bala, S. (2018). *Civilian Led-Governance and Security in Nigeria After Boko Haram*. United States Institute for Peace. Retrieved from www.usip.org

Ibrahim, P., & Hoffman, A. C. (2017). *A Gift from Darkness: How I Escaped with my Daughter from Boko Haram*. Other Press.

Idika-Kalu, C. (2020). *The Socioeconomic Impact of the Boko Haram Insurgency in the Lake Chad Basin Region*. Intech Open., doi:10.5772/intechopen.89905

International Crisis Group. (2020). *Boko Haram: Executive Summary*. International Crisis Group.

Iyi, J. (2018). On the Brink? The Nigerian State and the Making of *Boko Haram*. In J. Iyi & H. Strydom (Eds.), *Boko Haram and International Law*. Springer Nature. doi:10.1007/978-3-319-74957-0_1

Kassim, A., & Nwankpa, M. (2018). *The Boko Haram Reader: From Nigerian Preachers to the Islamic State*. Oxford University Press. doi:10.1093/oso/9780190908300.001.0001

Kirpekar, U. (2009). *Information Operation in Pursuit of Terrorists*. Master's Thesis Submitted to The Naval Postgraduate School, Monterrey, CA.

Koh, J. (2006). *Suppressing Terrorist Financing and Money Laundering*. Springer.

Livingstone, D. (2007). *Terrorism and the Illuminati: A Three Thousand Year History*. BookSurge LLC.

Mamdani, M. (2000). Good Muslim, Bad Muslim: America, Cold War and the Root of Terror. Washington: Oxford.

Mamdani, M. (2004). *Contemporary Political Terror: Its Origins in the Late Cold War*. Ahmadu Bello University.

McEachern, S. (2018). *Searching for Boko Haram: A History of Violence in Central Africa*. Oxford University Press.

Moses, J. (2017). Small Arms and Light Weapons Proliferation in the Early 21st Century: The Nigerian Case. *International Journal of Development and Sustainability*, *6*(11), 1638–1652.

Nasir, M. A. (2020). The Relevance of Maqasid al Shari'ah to Anti-Money Laundering and Terrorism Financing. In A. Rafay (Ed.), *Handbook of Research on Theory and Practice of Global Islamic Finance* (pp. 179–194). IGI Global. doi:10.4018/978-1-7998-0218-1.ch010

Nasir, M. A. (2020). The Relevance of Maqasid al Shari'ah to Anti-Money Laundering and Terrorism Financing. In A. Rafay (Ed.), *Handbook of Research on Theory and Practice of Global Islamic Finance* (pp. 179–194). IGI Global. doi:10.4018/978-1-7998-0218-1.ch010

Nathanson, S. (2010). *Terrorism and the Ethics of War*. Cambridge University Press. doi:10.1017/CBO9780511845215

National Bureau of Statistics. (2020). *Population of Nigeria*. Retrieved from www.nbs.org

Nowak, M., & Gsell, A. (2018). *Handmade and Deadly Craft Production of Small Arms in Nigeria*. Palgrave Macmillan.

Okoli, A. (2019). *Boko Haram Insurgency and the Necessity for Trans-Territorial Forestland Governance in the Lower Lake Chad Basin*. ACCORD, AJCR 2019/1.

Okolo, B.I., & Akubo, A. (2019). *Boko Haram Insurgency in Nigeria: Implications for National Security and Restorative Justice*. ACCORD, AJCR 2019/2.

Olukoya, S. (2019). *How Climate Change is Fueling Insurgency of Nigeria's Militant Boko Haram*. Relief Web. Retrieved from https://reliefweb.int/report/nigeria/how-climate-change-fuelling-insurgency-nigeria-s-militant-boko-haram

Religious Literacy Project. (2018). *The Maitatsine Riots*. Cambridge: Harvard Divinity School. Retrieved from https://rlp.hds.harvard.edu/faq/maitatsine-riots

Rieff, D. (1995). *Slaughterhouse: Bosnia and the Failure of the West*. Simon & Schuster.

Rock, J. L. (2016). *The Funding of Boko Haram and the Nigeria's Action to Stop it*. Master's Thesis Submitted to University of Indiana in Pennsylvania.

Sambo, U., Sule, B., Deribe, A. U., & Ahmed, A. (2020). The Impact of Small Arms and Light Weapons (SALW) in the Proliferation of Armed Group Conflicts in Northeastern Nigeria: Interrogating the *Boko Haram* Phenomenon. *International Journal of Humanities, Arts and Social Sciences*, *6*(4), 151–161.

Sesay, I. (2019). *Beneath the Tamarind Tree: A Story of Courage, Family, and the Lost School Girls of Boko Haram*. Harper Collins.

Shultz, R. H. Jr, & Dew, A. J. (2006). *Insurgents, Terrorists and Militias: The Warriors of Contemporary Combat*. Columbia University Press.

Simon, R. (1994). *What is Globalisation?* The Helen Kellogg Institute for International Studies.

Small, C., & Gilling, T. (2010). Blood Money: Bikies, Terrorists and Middle Eastern Gangs. Crows Nest: Allen & Unwin.

Smith, P. (2012). Violence and Terrorism: The Two Constants. *Journal of International Relations Research, 1*(1), 1–6.

Solomon, H. (2015). *Terrorism and Counter-Terrorism in Africa: Fighting Insurgency from AlShabab, Ansar Dine and Boko Haram*. Palgrave Macmillan. doi:10.1057/9781137489890

Sule, B., Ahmed, A., Alhaji, A. U., Yahaya, M. A., & Gambarawa, K. I. (2019). The Challenges of the Fight Against Insurgency in Northeastern Nigeria. *Journal of Techno Social, 11*(1), 7–15. doi:10.30880/jts.2019.11.01.002

Sule, B., & Gombe, S. Y. (2020). *Overview of the Sources of Finance, Weapons and Logistics of Boko Haram*. (Unpublished)

Sule, B., Sambo, U., & Tal, M. K. (2018). Islamic Militants and Insurgency in Northeastern Nigeria: A Comparison of the Ideology and Methodology of Maitatsine and *Boko Haram. Journal of Academia, 7*(2), 76–91.

Sule, B., Yahaya, M. A., Rabiu, A. A., Ahmad, M., & Hussaini, K. (2019). Strategies of Combating Insurgency in Northeastern Nigeria: A Non-Traditional Approach. *Journal of American Studies, 16*(2), 54–75.

Sule, B., Yahaya, M. A., & Sambo, U. (2019). Global Agenda and the Politics of Double Standard: War Against Terrorism or War of Terrorism. *International Journal of Religion and Civilisational Studies, 2*(2), 172–205.

Thacuk, K. L., & Lal, R. (2018). *Terrorist Criminal Enterprises: Financing Terrorism Through Organised Crimes*. Praeger.

Thurston, A. (2018). *Boko Haram: The History of an African Jihadist Movement*. Princeton University Press. doi:10.1515/9781400888481

UNDP. (2019). *Measuring the Economic Impact of Violent Extremism Leading to Terrorism in Africa*. United Nations Development Programme.

UNICEF. (2019). *Education: Nigeria*. Abuja: UNICEF. Retrieved from https://www.UNICEF.org/nigeria/education

USDHS. (2009). *Rightwing Extremism: Current Economic and Political Climate Fueling Resurgence in Radicalisation and Recruitment*. United States Department of Homeland Security.

Uwaisu, I. (2018). Experts Say Nigeria Must Change its Strategy to Defeat *Boko Haram. AFP Reuters*. Retrieved from https://p.dw.com/p/3ANl8

Vittori, J. (2011). *Terrorists Financing and Resourcing*. Palgrave Macmillan. doi:10.1057/9780230117716

Walker, A. (2016). *Eat the Heart of the Infidel: The Harrowing of Nigeria and the Rise of Boko Haram*. Hurst and Company.

Webel, C. P., & Arnaldi, J. A. (2012). The Global War on Terrorism: How Ethical and Effective. *Journal of International Relations Research, 1*(1), 8–18.

Whittaker, D. J. (2004). *Terrorists and Terrorism in the Contemporary World*. Routledge. doi:10.4324/9780203003824

Wittig, T. (2011). *Understanding Terrorist Financing*. Palgrave Macmillan. doi:10.1057/9780230316935

Wolf, S. O. (2017). Pakistan and State-Sponsored Terrorism in South Asia. In P. Casaca & S. O. Wolf (Eds.), *Terrorism Revisited: Islamism, Political Violence and State-Sponsorship*. Springer Nature. doi:10.1007/978-3-319-55690-1_5

Worldometer. (2020). *World Population Statistics by Countries*. Retrieved from https://www.Worldometers.info/world-population/nigeria-population/

Chapter 8
Effect of Terrorism Financing on Selected Global Indices:
The Case of 2015 Paris Attacks

Laila Memdani
ICFAI Business School, Hyderabad, India

Tasiu Tijjani Kademi
Rabiu Musa Kwankwaso College of Advance and Remedial Studies, Nigeria

Abdul Rafay
https://orcid.org/0000-0002-0285-5980
University of Management and Technology, Pakistan

ABSTRACT

Investment is a part and parcel of life. There are various avenues to invest and one of those is the stock market. But the decision of the investor depends on various factors and one of these factors is terrorism. The chapter focuses on the long and short-run association (LSA) and the influence of terrorism on major global stock indices and gold. The Paris attacks of 2015 are taken as a base, and the ARDL model is used to study the long and short-run impact on the selected stock indices. An attempt is also made to study the impact of terrorism on the stock returns using the Miller and Modigliani model. The study reveals a short-run impact of terrorism on the five selected global indices, but there is no long-run impact.

DOI: 10.4018/978-1-7998-8758-4.ch008

INTRODUCTION

Terrorism has a lengthy history and in recent years, extremely disastrous terrorist attacks were observed in the west and world at large. Apart from direct loss of human life and property, the act has a number of indirect effects on society and economy in general. Thus, it is expected to have an adverse impact on investor confidence, leading to wide ranging impact on financial markets (Nikkinen & Vähämaa, 2010).

There has been an attack in New York, Madrid, London, Boston, Paris, Brussels, Nice and Berlin cities in the years 2001, 2004, 2005, 2013, 2015, 2016, 2016 and 2016 respectively all are western nations. Does all these attacks induce abnormal stock markets prices and at what time? (Bonekamp and Van Veen, 2017). In the year 2015 in Paris in particular on 13 November, there has been a series of three synchronous attacks which claim the lives of 137 people with 368 injured and the government placed a state of emergency carrying a series of raids. IS was said to be responsible for the radicalization of the undertakers of the attacks. The media believed that the attacks will have greater economic repercussions in the time to come (Bonekamp & Van Veen, 2017).

With increasing globalization, countries of the world are integrated allowing investors both individual and institutional to trade freely across nations as an occurrence in one country may have an impact in other countries of the world (Memdani & Shenoy, 2019). Stock markets reflect investors' expectations and worries about the future. Unwanted incidences (like terrorists' attacks) have an effect on the economy and have serious effects on capital markets (Memdani & Shenoy, 2019). When information is available about a terrorist attack, investors often flee the market in search of safer heaven which leads to panic selling with its consequences (Chen and Siems, 2004). Thus, the panic leads to chaos that will have a long or short term bearish trend. The markets in other countries where these investors go in the expectation of safer investment may tend to become a bull market.

Most of the researchers focused on the volatility of the benchmark with respect to terrorism economic impact, aftermath of international indices after the major terror attacks, impact of terrorist attack on US stock markets. Others discussed and observed the duration, magnitude and investors' risk diversification as a result of some of the worst terrorist attacks on Global Stock indices like S&P, DAX, IBEX, NIKKEI, FTSE, CAC and BEL (Chen and Siems. 2004; Schepers, 2016; Bonekamp & Van Veen, 2017; Chesney, 2017; Chaudhry *et al.*, 2018). Moreover, some argued that a non-parametric approach is the most appropriate method for analyzing the impact of terrorism on financial markets (Chesney, Reshetar, & Karaman, 2011; Chaudhry *et al.*, 2018). However, some researchers like Hammoudeh and Li (2008) and Inclan and Tiao, (1994) studied market volatility using Cumulative Sum of Squares (ICSS), ARCH and GARCH models.

This chapter mainly focuses on the LSA between the indices of terror affected country and selected global indices and Gold. It also compares the pre and post terror attack with stocks performance of terror affected country's index as compared to selected global indices and Gold.

LITERATURE REVIEW

Researchers discussed a lot how the world financial markets are effected by the waves of terrorism. The most important terrorist attack of Nine Eleven was widely discussed in the literature by Nikkinen *et al.* (2008), Jackson (2008), Charles and Darné (2006) and Chen and Siems (2004). All are of the view that these attacks negatively affected the global stock markets.

Barry and Nedelescu (2006) highlighted the international awareness of the danger of terrorism on financial markets. The study argued that a sound, diversified and liquid markets counter the effects of terrorist attacks within short time frame. Thus, matured stock exchanges absorbed terrorist attacks more efficiently. Similarly, for the period 1990-2003, Eldor and Melnik (2004) discussed the impact of 639 attacks in Israel. The study found a significant adverse impact of suicide attacks on capital markets. However, swift government intervention and nature of the market helps in efficient market operation.

Javaid and Kousar (2018) determined the effect of terror incidents, political stability and rate of exchange variation on the volatility of stock prices in Pakistan PSX market from 2000-2015. The EGARCH model revealed a significant adverse relation of terrorist attack on stock prices while a democratic government presence reduces the volatility of the market although there is no effect of foreign exchange movement on the capital market. An event study on the daily price movement indicates the PSX market resilience as the negative terror attack effect fades within the day of the attack. This is in line with Meng Yun *et al.* (2017) that examined the terrorism and political instability impact on the market equity premium of Pakistan on the panel data of 306 non-financial companies for a period of 14 years. The regression results revealed a significant adverse effect of terrorism on the equity premium while a positive significant effect was found when there is law and order and a stable government. Similarly, Chaudhry *et al.* (2018) studied the impact of terror attack in SAARC countries for the period 2000-2015 using event study methodology and fixed effect regression analysis. They observed that the stock returns of highly affected countries differ from countries that are least effected by terrorism. Moreover, Hadi, Katircioglu and Adaoglu (2019) analyzed the effect of terrorist act on major global tourist attracted countries' tourism industries stock performance with the help of event study technique from 1995-2017. The study found a considerable adverse effect of terrorism on tourist, travel and leisure industries' stock prices. However, Narayan *et al.* (2018), examined the terrorist activities and fear for eight OECD countries for the period 2001-2014 using dynamic conditional correlations (DCC) methodology. They concluded that DCCs of France and seven OECD countries are not much affected due to terrorism over time. The flight for safety was found for other seven countries.

In order to analyse the effect of terrorism on capital markets, Koščo (2017) used multifactor model, a differential equation and logit model. He mainly worked on the world's 20 largest markets from 2000 to 2015. It is concluded that, in the short-run, stock market is negatively affected by terrorism while a high return is envisaged in the long-run. However, Schepers (2016) worked to know the effect of attacks by terrorist on the stock and bond market of United Kingdom, Germany, Spain, France and Belgium. The time span of the research was from 1994 to 2014. There was a significant impact on bond market but not for stock market. It is also found that different targets of the terror attack have different impacts on the stock and bond market. Moreover, Chesney, Reshetar, & Karaman (2011), conducted an empirical study about the impact of terrorism on the behaviour of stock market, bond market and commodity markets. It They observed 25 countries' terror attack for the time period of more than 11 years. It is documented that a non-parametric approach is the most appropriate method in examining the effect of terrorism on financial markets. The study, while providing investors with possible risk diversification alternatives, also found a negative impact of terrorism on stock markets.

Kumar and Liu (2013) examined the impact of terrorism on global capital markets comprising 70 countries' stock indices for a period of 20 years from 1990-2010 although 7 countries were dropped due to issues of unstable government or unavailability of information. Terror attack records were collected from worldwide terrorism database. Using event study and logit regression techniques it is found that a trading partner's stock market will have a significant adverse effect the moment a terrorist attack hit a country. However, although impact is more eminent on a smaller trading partner than a bigger one. Moreover, Kousar *et al.* (2019) examined the south Asian countries stock market: India, Pakistan, Sri Lanka and Bangladesh with the help of DCC GARCH Model for a period of 17 years from 2000-2016. The study opined that there is a negative spillover effect of terrorist act on to a peer country and three stock markets of India, Pakistan and Bangladesh are significantly and positively correlated. Furthermore, Mnasri and Nechi (2016) examined the market of 12 Middle East and North African countries volatility relationship with terrorist attacks. The event study shows considerable market volatility up to the 20 days after the attack and it is found that there is contagion effect of the attack in the region. While, Jackson (2008) that investigated the overall economic impact of 9/11 terrorist attack on the U.S. economy and it is demonstrated that the U S stock market showed an alarming resilience tackling the shocks to a bare rest point at the time. Moreover, Chen and Siems (2004) examined 14 terror attacks and global capital market including Kuwait attack of 1990 and 9/11 America attack. The study found that U.S market recovered soon than any other capital markets due to stability in banking sector and sufficient liquidity of the market. Furthermore, Gok, Demirdogen, and Topuz (2019) examined the major terrorist attack impact on the Turkish stock market using daily market prices and E-GARCH model and no significant impact was seen. Event study model applied on intraday data revealed a significant negative mid-day impact on the prices although it recovers before the closing hour of the day. A case by case analysis of the attacks shows market resilience to the attacks as very few of the attacks confer negative effect and only one of the 35 major attacks has an effect after the 6-11 days of the attack.

Bonekamp and Van Veen (2017) analysed the western world terrorist attacks effect on the stock indices with the help of an event study technique and found that, there is a negative impact on stock prices although it is short lived as it normally goes back to normal within a short period. Similarly, Irshad, Hussain and Saba (2019) examined the stock indices of six high, middle and low income countries (US, UK, China, Turkey, Pakistan and India) for a period of 18 years from 1999-2016 using fully modified least square (LS) regression, fixed effects regression and Pedroni panel co-integration models. The resarchers documented a significant adverse impact of terrorism on the stock market indices in the short run. Contrarily, Apergis and Apergis (2016) studied the effect of Paris terror attack on twenty four global defence companies' stock prices for a period of 12 months using event study technique and found a significant positive impact of the attack on the defence industry share prices. Similarly, Arif and Suleman (2017) examined the long-run terrorist attacks impact on Pakistani stock exchange for a period of 10 years from 2002-2011. The co-integrated panel data revealed a mixed effect of terror attacks on share prices Scanlon (2019) investigated the implication of both foreign and domestic terrorist attacks on the US stock market. Price variation was analyzed using GARCH model while reallocation of capital was examined using OLS model. The results shown a significant negative impact of domestic attack on stock price although disappears within short time period while, there is no significant changes on stock prices when foreign country was hit. It is also documented that a significant capital reallocation is seen especially on the shares of underperformed small companies. This further confirms the level of investor awareness on the short live impact of terrorist attacks on companies share prices over time.

Tauringana *et al.* (2020) investigated the influence of terrorism on the business performance of 173 nations, employing fixed effect estimation model for a period of 7 years. The study reveals that there is no significant relation between terror incidents and performance of the global businesses even when the data was divided into developed, developing and fragile nations although there is a significant adverse effect of terrorism on fragile countries' business performance. Moreover, Moussa and Talbi (2019) investigated the influence of political uncertainty and terror attack on the Tunisian stock market subdivided into two point in time: before and after the revolution. The periods are 1998-2010 and 2010-2017, using event study it is found that, in both periods there is a significant impact of terrorism and political uncertainty on the stock prices and its volatility although it is low before the revolution.

Paris Attacks of 2015

Paris sustained serious organized attacks on a painful day of thirteenth November 2015 that leads to the death of 130 and injuring 368 people. It was started at around 9:15 pm by three suicide bombers in front of the Stade de France stadium gate in Saint-Denis due to the fact that the bombers were prevented access into the stadium while an international football match was being played. The second group attacked crowded cafes and restaurant shooting massively in which one of the attackers blew in the attack. And finally, the third set of the terrorist hit Bataclan theatre at around 9:40 pm shooting indiscriminately on people. This was the deadliest among the three coordinated attacks taking over 1500 people hostage while killing 90 people (www.bbc.com)

In the history of France since the World War II, the attacks of Friday thirteenth November 2015 were the biggest and deadliest that has both direct effects: killing and injuring people and indirect impact on the economy of a country. On Monday fifteenth November 2015 after the attacks, the financial market dropped with share price of some of the French companies reduced adversely although stabilized quickly. It was also evident that, the attacks has an indirect consequence in the form of increased military/police expenditure, enhanced taxation and shortage of funds for other infrastructural need of French economy due to the European union borrowing limit on member countries (Schepers, 2016).

The chapter focuses on LSA and influence of terrorism on major global stock indices and Gold. Paris attacks of 2015 are considered as base and ARDL model is used to study the short-run and long-run impact on the selected stock indices. An attempt is also made to study the impact of terrorism on the stock returns using Miller and Modigliani model.

HYPOTHESIS

H_0: No LSA exists between the terror affected country's benchmark and other selected global indices and Gold.

H_1: No linkages exist between terrorism and the returns in the selected stock markets.

METHODOLOGY

Autoregressive Distributed Lag (ARDL) Model is used to investigate the above hypothesis. short-run and the long-run relationship between Paris attacks and its impact on world's major stock indices. The ARDL model is a LS regression which includes the lags of dependent variables (DVs) and the independent variables (IVs) (Pesaran and Shin 1997). The following ARDL model shows whether there is any association between the CAC-France (DV) and the particular indexes (IVs); DJI (US), FTSE (UK), N225 (Japan), DAX (Germany) and BSE (India). Serial Correlation LM Test, CUSUM Test and Wald test are applied, wherever required.

Following is the equation of the ARDL model:

yt = μ + Xpi=1 γiyt−i + Xr j=0 βjxt−j + εt, ε ∼i.i.d∀ t C(L)yt = μ + B(L)xt + εt,

where

C(L) = 1 − γ1L − γ2L 2 − · · · − γpL p and B(L) = β0 + β1L + β2L 2 + · · · + βrL r

To calculate the returns' performance of the indices, Miller Modigliani Performance measure is used to calculate and analyse the Pre and Post returns on stock indices of top five global indices and gold. Historical data is extracted from relevant websites. Research papers, journals, newspapers, expert views, websites and other various sources are taken into consideration for the further analysis of this research. Paris Attack and the CAC 40 index is used for this study. The data period is one year daily data from November 14, 2016 (date of attack) to November 24, 2017.

RESULTS AND DISCUSSION

For Tables 1-6, the F-statistic for the model is observed to be significant at 5% level i.e., p-value seems to be less than 0.05. Model has no serial correlation because in all cases, for LS, the probability value is greater than 0.05. These tables illustrate the LSA between CAC and other major wold indices (DJI, FTSE, N225, DAX and BSE) by using ARDL model and bound test.

The ARDL model results of Paris attacks on the DJI are summarized in Table 1.

The foregoing table shows that model is fit for Lag 3 (being optimal) deriving the values of AIC (12.86) and SIC (12.99).

Table 1. ARDL Model for CAC and DJI

DV: D(DJI)
Method: LS
Sample (adjusted): 5 252
Included observations: 248 after adjustments

Variable	Coefficient	Std. Error	t-Statistic	Prob.
C	648.82	298.95	2.17	0.03
D(DJI(-1))	-0.10	0.07	-1.58	0.12
D(DJI(-2))	-0.07	0.07	-0.98	0.33
D(DJI(-3))	-0.01	0.07	-0.09	0.93
D(CAC(-1))	0.11	0.17	0.65	0.52
D(CAC(-2))	-0.01	0.16	-0.07	0.95
D(CAC(-3))	0.18	0.16	1.13	0.26
DJI(-1)	0.00	0.01	-0.20	0.84
CAC(-1)	-0.13	0.06	-2.20	0.03
R-squared	0.04	Mean DV		4.43
Adjusted R-squared	0.00	S.D. DV		147.76
S.E. of regression	147.50	Akaike info criterion		12.86
Sum squared resid	5199827.00	Schwarz criterion		12.99
Log likelihood	-1585.78	Hannan-Quinn criter.		12.91
F-statistic	1.11	Durbin-Watson stat		2.00
Prob(F-statistic)	0.36			

Source: Compiled through Eviews

From Figure 1, the plotted points fluctuate between the upper and lower limit i.e., between the red line which signifies that the model is in control limit to check LSA between the variable.

It is observed that F-statistic (2.94) is more than upper bound value (4.85). Hence it is concluded that DJI with CAC have a short-run association. This is in line with the study of Kumar and Liu (2013) and Kousar *et al.* (2019).

The ARDL model results of Paris attacks on the FTSE are summarized in Table 2.

The foregoing table shows that model is fit for Lag 4 (being optimal) deriving the values of AIC (11.30) and SIC (11.46).

Figure 1.

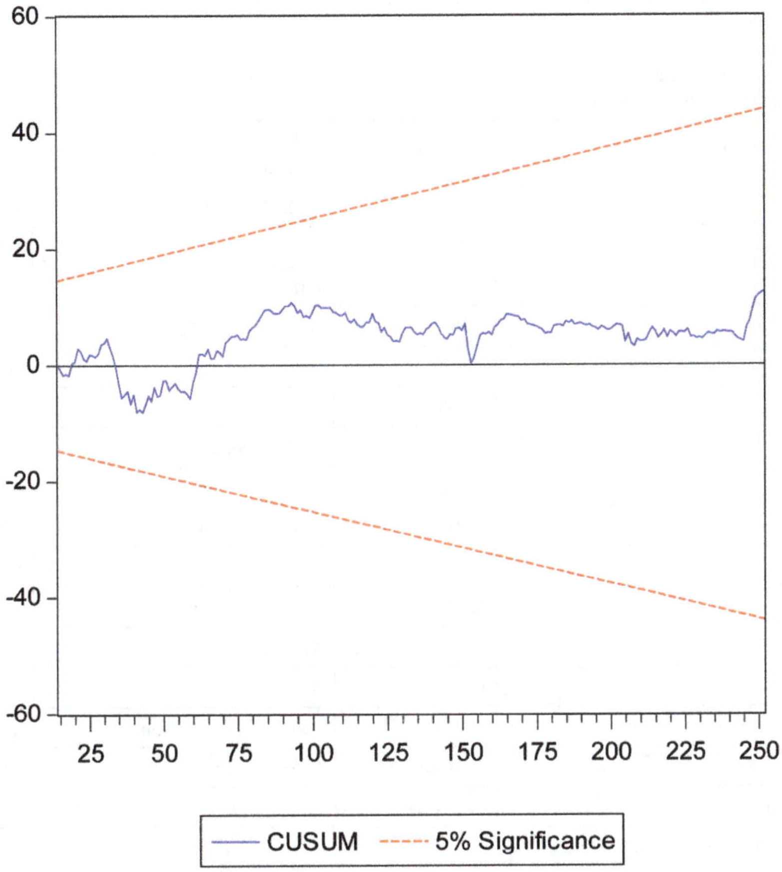

Box 1.

Wald Test			
Test Statistic	**Value**	**Df**	**Probability**
F-statistic	2.941789	(2, 239)	0.0547

Source: Compiled through Eviews

Table 2. ARDL Model for CAC and FTSE

DV: D(FTSE) Method: LS Sample (adjusted): 6 252 Included observations: 247 after adjustments				
Variable	**Coefficient**	**Std. Error**	**t-Statistic**	**Prob.**
C	-8.66	130.22	-0.07	0.95
D(FTSE(-1))	0.12	0.06	1.85	0.07
D(FTSE(-2))	-0.12	0.06	-1.83	0.07
D(FTSE(-3))	0.06	0.06	1.02	0.31
D(FTSE(-4))	-0.15	0.06	-2.31	0.02
D(CAC(-1))	-0.05	0.07	-0.67	0.50
D(CAC(-2))	0.05	0.07	0.68	0.50
D(CAC(-3))	-0.11	0.07	-1.45	0.15
D(CAC(-4))	-0.05	0.07	-0.67	0.51
FTSE(-1)	-0.02	0.01	-1.75	0.08
CAC(-1)	0.03	0.03	1.15	0.25
R-squared	0.07	Mean DV		-2.33
Adjusted R-squared	0.03	S.D. DV		68.48
S.E. of regression	67.34	Akaike info criterion		11.30
Sum squared resid	1070261.00	Schwarz criterion		11.46
Log likelihood	-1384.67	Hannan-Quinn criter.		11.36

Source: Compiled through Eviews

In these results, the plotted points fluctuate between the upper and lower limit i.e., between the red line which signifies that the model is in control limit to check the LSA between the variable.

It is observed that F-statistic (1.92) is more than upper bound value (4.85). Hence it is concluded that FTSE and CAC have a short-run association.

The ARDL model results of Paris attacks on the NIKKEI are summarized in Table 3.

The foregoing table shows that model is fit for Lag 4 (being optimal) deriving the values of AIC (14.16) and SIC (14.29).

In this result, the plotted points fluctuate between the upper and lower limit i.e., between the red line which signifies that the model is in control limit to check the LSA between the variable.

Figure 2.
Source: Compiled through Eviews

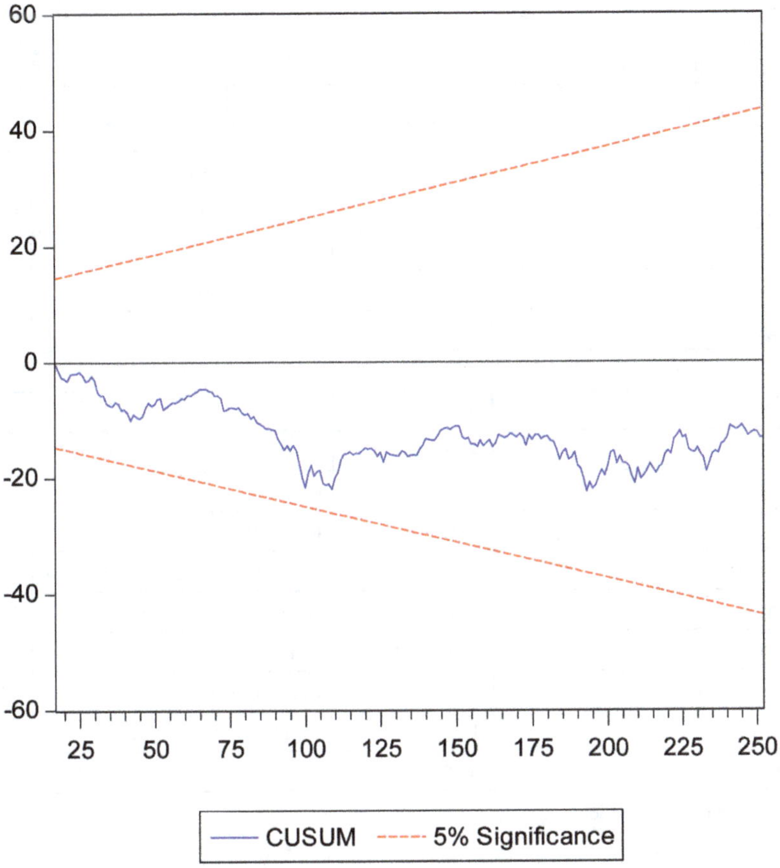

Box 2.

Wald Test			
Test Statistic	**Value**	**Df**	**Probability**
F-statistic	1.929613	(2, 236)	0.1475
Chi-square	3.859226	2	0.1452

Source: Compiled through Eviews

Table 3. ARDL Model for CAC and NIKKEI

DV D(N225) Method: LS Sample (adjusted): 5 252 Included observations: 248 after adjustments				
Variable	**Coefficient**	**Std. Error**	**t-Statistic**	**Prob.**
C	234.70	504.80	0.46	0.64
D(N225(-1))	-0.07	0.07	-1.08	0.28
D(N225(-2))	0.02	0.07	0.37	0.71
D(N225(-3))	-0.02	0.06	-0.30	0.76
D(CAC(-1))	0.09	0.32	0.27	0.79
D(CAC(-2))	0.33	0.31	1.05	0.29
D(CAC(-3))	0.22	0.31	0.69	0.49
N225(-1)	-0.08	0.03	-2.47	0.01
CAC(-1)	0.24	0.19	1.26	0.21
R-squared	0.06	Mean DV		-5.96
Adjusted R-squared	0.03	S.D. DV		286.63
S.E. of regression	282.34	Akaike info criterion		14.16
Sum squared resid	19051744	Schwarz criterion		14.29
Log likelihood	-1746.80	Hannan-Quinn criter.		14.21
F-statistic	1.95	Durbin-Watson stat		2.01
Prob(F-statistic)	0.05			

Source: Compiled through Eviews

It is observed that F-statistic (3.03) is more than upper bound value (4.85). Hence it is concluded that NIKKEI and CAC have a short-run association.

The ARDL model results of Paris attacks on the DAX are summarized in Table 4.

The foregoing table shows that model is fit for Lag 6 (being optimal) deriving the values of AIC (0.49) and SIC (1.13).

In this result, the plotted points fluctuate between the upper and lower limit i.e., between the red line which signifies that the model is in control limit to check the LSA between the variables.

It is observed that F-statistic (2.91) is more than upper bound value (4.85). Hence it is concluded that DAX and CAC have a short-run association.

The ARDL model results of Paris attacks on the BSE are summarized in Table 5.

The foregoing table shows that model is fit for Lag 6 (being optimal) deriving the values of AIC (1.62) and SIC (2.36).

Figure 3.
Source: Compiled through Eviews

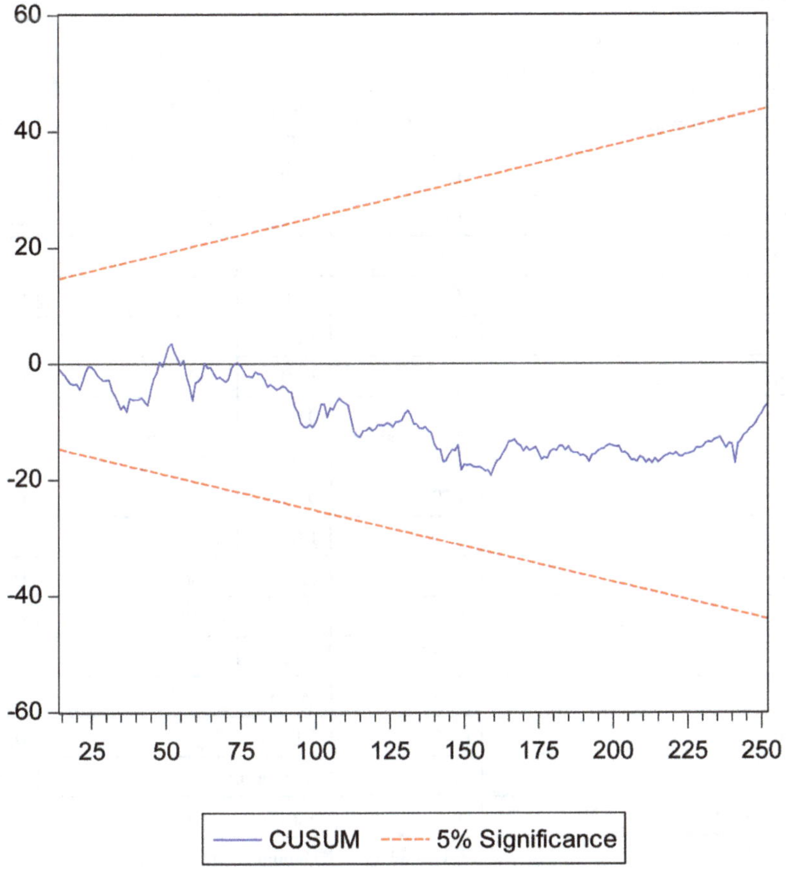

Box 3.

Wald Test			
Test Statistic	**Value**	**Df**	**Probability**
F-statistic	3.03503	(2, 239)	0.0189
Chi-square	8.07006	2	0.0177

Source: Compiled through Eviews

Table 4. ARDL Model for CAC and DAX

DV: D(DAX)
Method: LS
Sample (adjusted): 7 25
Included observations: 19 after adjustments

Variable	Coefficient	Std. Error	t-Statistic	Prob.
C	0.40	0.49	0.81	0.45
D(DAX(-1))	0.26	1.32	0.20	0.85
D(DAX(-2))	0.01	0.97	0.01	0.99
D(DAX(-3))	-0.78	1.16	-0.68	0.52
D(DAX(-4))	-1.05	1.51	-0.70	0.51
D(DAX(-5))	3.76	1.59	2.37	0.06
D(CAC(-1))	0.08	0.69	0.12	0.91
D(CAC(-2))	0.38	0.66	0.57	0.59
D(CAC(-3))	0.70	0.90	0.77	0.47
D(CAC(-4))	0.55	1.03	0.53	0.61
D(CAC(-5))	-2.01	0.85	-2.36	0.06
DAX(-1)	-3.89	1.62	-2.40	0.05
CAC(-1)	1.74	0.72	2.41	0.05
R-squared	0.97	Mean DV		-0.01
Adjusted R-squared	0.92	S.D. DV		0.98
S.E. of regression	0.28	Akaike info criterion		0.49
Sum squared resid	0.463738	Schwarz criterion		1.139618
Log likelihood	8.312483	Hannan-Quinn criter.		0.602785
F-statistic	18.03817	Durbin-Watson stat		1.821683
Prob(F-statistic)	0.000992			

Source: Compiled through Eviews

In this result, the plotted points fluctuate between the upper and lower limit i.e., between the red line which signifies that the model is in control limit to check the LSA between the variables.

It is observed that F-statistic (3.47) is more than upper bound value (4.85). Hence it is concluded that BSE and CAC have a short-run association.

The ARDL model results of Paris attacks on the Gold are summarized in Table 6.

The foregoing table shows that model is fit deriving the values of AIC (1.08) and SIC (1.82).

Figure 4.
Source: Compiled through Eviews

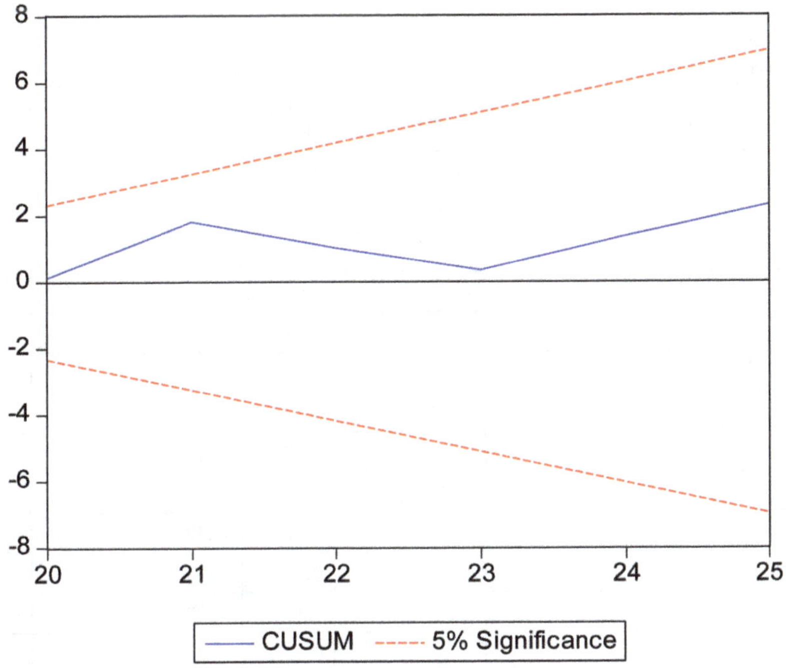

Box 4.

Wald Test		Equation: Untitled	
Test Statistic	**Value**	**Df**	**Probability**
F-statistic	2.917327	(2, 6)	0.1303
Chi-square	5.834655	2	0.0541

Source: Compiled through Eviews

Table 5. ARDL Model for CAC and BSE

DV: D(BSE) Method: LS Sample (adjusted): 8 25 Included observations: 18 after adjustments				
Variable	**Coefficient**	**Std. Error**	**t-Statistic**	**Prob.**
C	-1.59	1.29	-1.23	0.31
D(BSE(-1))	-0.20	1.53	-0.13	0.90
D(BSE(-2))	-0.41	1.64	-0.25	0.82
D(BSE(-3))	-1.02	1.62	-0.63	0.57
D(BSE(-4))	-0.84	2.68	-0.31	0.78
D(BSE(-5))	-0.56	1.81	-0.31	0.78
D(BSE(-6))	-2.21	2.41	-0.92	0.43
D(CAC(-1))	-1.84	0.87	-2.12	0.12
D(CAC(-2))	-0.94	0.94	-1.00	0.39
D(CAC(-3))	-0.39	1.01	-0.38	0.73
D(CAC(-4))	-0.68	0.72	-0.94	0.42
D(CAC(-5))	-0.10	1.30	-0.07	0.95
D(CAC(-6))	-1.00	0.62	-1.62	0.20
BSE(-1)	-0.47	1.13	-0.42	0.71
CAC(-1)	0.93	0.61	1.54	0.22
R-squared	0.94	Mean DV		0.06
Adjusted R-squared	0.65	S.D. DV		0.98
S.E. of regression	0.58	Akaike info criterion		1.62
Sum squared resid	1.01	Schwarz criterion		2.36
Log likelihood	0.40	Hannan-Quinn criter.		1.72

Source: Compiled through Eviews

In these results, the plotted points fluctuate between the upper and lower limit i.e., between the red line which signifies that the model is in control limit to check the LSA between the variable.

It is observed that F-statistic (1.36) is more than upper bound value (4.85). Hence it is concluded that GOLD and CAC have a short-run association.

In the next stage a comparison of pre- and post-attack returns is conducted using Miller Modigliani Approach. Table 7 shows the comparison of pre and post Paris attack returns.

Figure 5.
Source: Compiled through Eviews

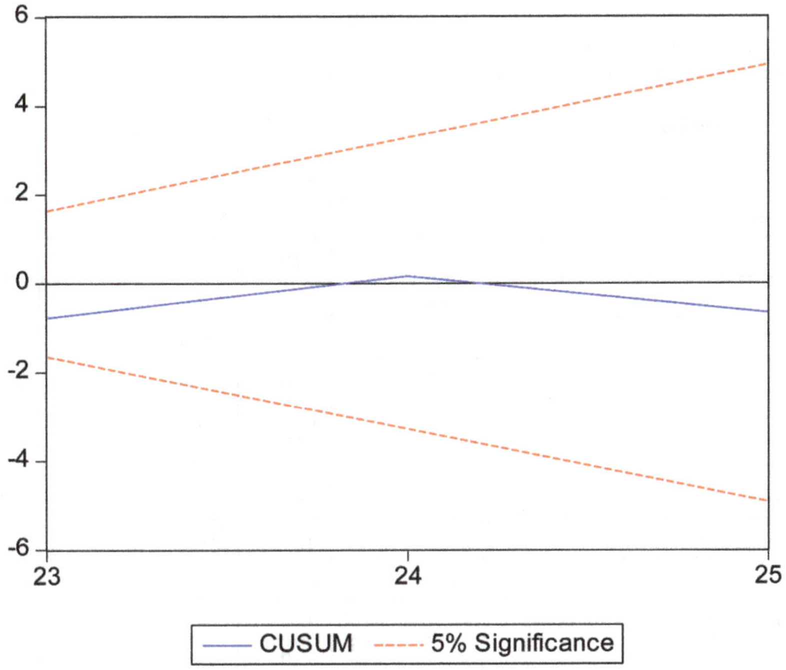

Box 5.

Wald Test		Equation: Untitled	
Test Statistic	**Value**	**df**	**Probability**
F-statistic	3.472498	(2, 3)	0.1657
Chi-square	6.944995	2	0.031

Source: Compiled through Eviews

The study found in the case of DJI a slight decline in returns in Dec 2015 and in January 2016 the returns were negative but it picked up after that and for almost all the months except January, the returns were higher. The yearly average returns were also higher than the pre-attack period. FTSE also shows similar results. There was a decline in January but overall there was an increase. NIKKEI recorded a decline in December and January but later on stabilised and overall average result for the

Table 6. ARDL Model for CAC and Gold

DV: D(GOLD)
Method: LS
Sample (adjusted): 8 25
Included observations: 18 after adjustments

Variable	Coefficient	Std. Error	t-Statistic	Prob.
C	-0.42	3.40	-0.12	0.91
D(GOLD(-1))	0.17	4.62	0.04	0.97
D(GOLD(-2))	0.08	4.16	0.02	0.99
D(GOLD(-3))	-0.02	3.85	0.00	1.00
D(GOLD(-4))	-2.45	3.07	-0.80	0.48
D(GOLD(-5))	-1.40	1.80	-0.78	0.49
D(GOLD(-6))	1.20	1.37	0.88	0.45
D(CAC(-1))	-0.70	1.04	-0.67	0.55
D(CAC(-2))	-0.36	1.00	-0.36	0.74
D(CAC(-3))	-0.93	0.74	-1.25	0.30
D(CAC(-4))	-0.72	0.66	-1.09	0.36
D(CAC(-5))	-0.30	0.65	-0.46	0.68
D(CAC(-6))	-0.49	0.80	-0.61	0.59
GOLD(-1)	-1.30	4.86	-0.27	0.81
CAC(-1)	0.28	0.87	0.32	0.77
R-squared	0.96	Mean DV		0.04
Adjusted R-squared	0.79	S.D. DV		0.97
S.E. of regression	0.44	Akaike info criterion		1.08
Sum squared resid	0.58	Schwarz criterion		1.82
Log likelihood	5.24	Hannan-Quinn criter.		1.18

Source: Compiled through Eviews

year increased. DAX and CAC also depicted similar results but BSE recorded an increase during December while marginal increment was observed in Gold.

CONCLUDING REMARKS

It has been observed that, terrorist attack of November 13, 2015 in Paris have a short term impact on the stock indices of five selected countries including Paris stock market. Similarly, a short-run negative impact on returns has been recorded although

Figure 6.
Source: Compiled through Eviews

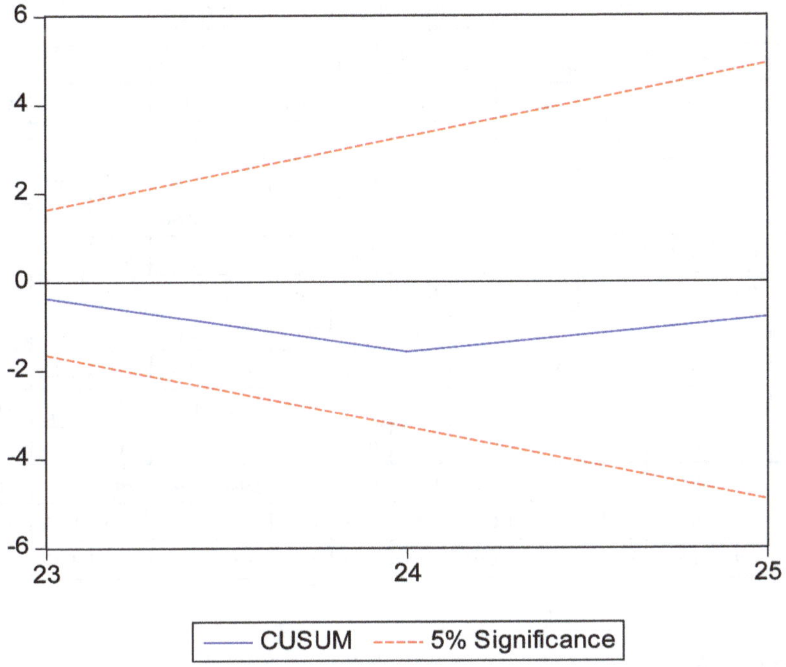

Box 6.

Wald Test		Equation: Untitled	
Test Statistic	**Value**	**Df**	**Probability**
F-statistic	1.366964	(2, 3)	0.3784
Chi-square	2.733928	2	0.2549

Source: Compiled through Eviews

in the long-run there is no impact either on stock indices or returns. This study has an important implication on the investors' decision making i.e. it suggests that in case of any such eventuality when returns are negative and indices are falling rather than losing hope and squaring their positions in losses, they should wait for some time when the impact eventually tapers out and indices are back on growth path.

Table 7. Returns Performance Pre and Post Paris Attack

Returns Performance Based on Miller and Modigliani Approach														
Impact of Paris Attacks on Selected Global Indices and Gold														
	DJI		FTSE		NIKKEI		DAX		BSE		CAC		GOLD	
	Pre	Post	Pre	Post	Pre	Post	Pre	Post	Pre	Post	Pre	Post	Pre	Post
November	0.2	0.3	0.02	0.31	0.08	0.35	0.15	0.37	0.03	0.2	0.11	0.31	0.1	0.3
December	0.1	0.26	0.16	0.32	0.22	0.07	0.44	0.09	0.28	0.48	0.42	0.03	0.19	0.31
January	0.3	-0.05	0.32	0.19	0.38	0.06	0.42	0.23	0.24	0.54	0.39	0.19	0.17	0.38
February	0.1	0.51	0.2	0.57	0.34	0.39	0.26	0.2	0.24	0.09	0.3	0.32	0.21	0.41
March	0.3	0.81	0.17	0.3	0.3	0.66	0.17	0.62	0.08	0.54	0.24	0.65	0.24	0.43
April	0.2	0.67	0.33	0.32	0.16	0.4	0.18	0.45	0.28	0.09	0.16	0.4	0.24	0.37
May	0.1	0.37	0.24	0.4	0.28	0.42	0.14	0.48	0.26	0.46	0.16	0.43	0.18	0.43
June	0.1	0.53	0.02	0.48	0.21	0.35	0.2	0.51	0.32	0.32	0.21	0.55	0.15	0.45
July	0.1	0.64	0.23	0.35	0.23	0.58	0.07	0.28	0.15	0.32	0.01	0.22	0.21	0.36
August	0.4	0.53	0.23	0.45	0.17	0.48	0.34	0.65	0.08	0.42	0.4	0.6	0.62	0.44
September	0.6	0.4	0.04	0.45	0.31	0.52	0.25	0.51	0.19	0.54	0.26	0.62	0.19	0.33
Yearly	0.9	1.55	0.95	1.55	0.97	1.55	0.96	1.55	0.95	1.55	0.96	1.55	0.96	1.54

DISCLAIMER

The contents and views of this chapter are expressed by the authors in their personal capacities. It is not necessary for the Editor and the Publisher to agree with these viewpoints and they are not responsible for any duty of care in this regard.

ACKNOWLEDGMENT

The authors extend sincere gratitude to:

- The Editor-in-Chief and International Editorial Advisory Board (IEAB) of this book who initially desk reviewed, arranged a rigorous double/triple blind review process and conducted a thorough, minute and critical final review before accepting the chapter for publication.
- All anonymous reviewers who provided very constructive feedbacks for thorough revision, improvement, extension and finetuning of the chapter.
- All colleagues, assistants and well-wishers who assisted the authors to complete this task.

REFERENCES

Apergis, E., & Apergis, N. (2016). The 11/13 Paris terrorist attacks and stock prices: The case of the international defense industry. *Finance Research Letters*, *17*, 186–192. Advance online publication. doi:10.1016/j.frl.2016.03.002

Arif, I., & Suleman, T. (2017). Terrorism and Stock Market Linkages: An Empirical Study from a Front-line State. *Global Business Review*, *18*(2), 365–378. doi:10.1177/0972150916668604

Barry, J. R., & Nedelescu, O. M. (2006). The impact of terrorism on financial markets. *Journal of Financial Crime*, *13*(1), 7–25. doi:10.1108/13590790610641233

Bonekamp, B., & Van Veen, T. (2017). *Terrorist Attacks and Financial Markets*. Retrieved from https://papers.ssrn.com/sol3/papers.cfm?abstract_id=2924459

Charles, A., & Darné, O. (2006). Large shocks and the September 11th terrorist attacks on international stock markets. *Economic Modelling*, *23*(4), 683–698. doi:10.1016/j.econmod.2006.03.008

Chaudhry, N., Roubaud, D., Akhter, W., & Shahbaz, M. (2018). Impact of terrorism on stock markets: Empirical evidence from the SAARC region. *Finance Research Letters*, *26*, 230–234. doi:10.1016/j.frl.2018.02.024

Chen, A. H., & Siems, T. F. (2004). The effects of terrorism on global capital markets. *European Journal of Political Economy*, *20*(2), 349–366. doi:10.1016/j.ejpoleco.2003.12.005

Chesney, M., Reshetar, G., & Karaman, M. (2011). The impact of terrorism on financial markets: An empirical study. *Journal of Banking & Finance*, *35*(2), 253–267. doi:10.1016/j.jbankfin.2010.07.026

Eldor, R., & Melnick, R. (2004). Financial markets and terrorism. *European Journal of Political Economy*, *20*(2), 367–386. doi:10.1016/j.ejpoleco.2004.03.002

Gok, I. Y., Demirdogen, Y., & Topuz, S. (2019). The impacts of terrorism on Turkish equity market: An investigation using intraday data. *Physica A*, *540*, 123484. doi:10.1016/j.physa.2019.123484

Hadi, D. M., Katircioglu, S., & Adaoglu, C. (2019). The vulnerability of tourism firms' stocks to the terrorist incidents. *Current Issues in Tourism*, *23*(9), 1138–1152. doi:10.1080/13683500.2019.1592124

Hammoudeh, S., & Li, H. (2008). Sudden changes in volatility in emerging markets: The case of Gulf Arab stock markets. *International Review of Financial Analysis*, *17*(1), 47–63. doi:10.1016/j.irfa.2005.01.002

Inclan, C., & Tiao, G. C. (1994). Use of cumulative sums of squares for retrospective detection of changes of variance. *Journal of the American Statistical Association*, *89*(427), 913–923.

Irshad, H., Hussain, H., & Saba, I. (2019). Terrorism and Stock Markets: Cross-Country Evidence. *Pakistan Journal of Social Sciences*, *39*(4), 1295–1306.

Jackson, O. A. (2008). The impact of the 9/11 terrorist attacks on the US economy. *Journal of 9/11 Studies*, *20*(1), 1-27.

Javaid, M. E., & Kousar, S. (2018). Impact of Terrorism, Political System and Exchange Rate Fluctuations on Stock Market Volatility. *Iranian Journal of Management Studies*, *11*(3), 519–546.

Koščo, M. (2017). *Impact of Terrorism on Stock Markets*. Unpublished Dissertation. Charles University. Retrieved from https://dspace.cuni.cz/handle/20.500.11956/91443

Kumar, S., & Liu, J. (2013). Impact of terrorism on international stock markets. *The Journal of Applied Business and Economics*, *14*(4), 42.

Memdani, L., & Shenoy, G. (2019). Impact of terrorism on stock markets across the world and stock returns: An event study of Taj attack in India. *Journal of Financial Crime*, *25*(3), 793–807. doi:10.1108/JFC-09-2018-0093

MengYun, W., Imran, M., Zakaria, M., Linrong, Z., Farooq, M.U., & Muhammad, S.K. (2017). Impact of Terrorism and Political Instability on Equity Premium: Evidence from Pakistan. *Physica A*, *492*, 1753–1762.

Mnasri, A., & Nechi, S. (2016). Impact of Terrorist Attacks on Stock Market Volatility in Emerging Markets. *Emerging Markets Review*, *28*, 184–202. doi:10.1016/j.ememar.2016.08.002

Moussa, F. B., & Talbi, M. (2019). Stock Market Reaction to Terrorist Attacks and Political Uncertainty: Empirical Evidence from the Tunisian Stock Exchange. *International Journal of Economics and Financial Issues*, *9*(3), 48–64. doi:10.32479/ijefi.7968

Narayan, S., Le, T. H., & Sriananthakumar, S. (2018). The influence of terrorism risk on stock market integration: Evidence from eight OECD countries. *International Review of Financial Analysis*, *58*, 247–259. doi:10.1016/j.irfa.2018.03.011

Nikkinen, J., Omran, M. M., Sahlström, P., & Äijö, J. (2008). Stock returns and volatility following the September 11 attacks: Evidence from 53 equity markets. *International Review of Financial Analysis*, *17*(1), 27–46. doi:10.1016/j.irfa.2006.12.002

Nikkinen, J., & Vähämaa, S. (2010). Terrorism and stock market sentiment. *Financial Review*, *45*(2), 263–275. doi:10.1111/j.1540-6288.2010.00246.x

Pesaran, M. H., & Shin, Y. (1998). An autoregressive distributed-lag modelling approach to cointegration analysis. *Econometric Society Monographs*, *31*, 371–413. doi:10.1017/CCOL0521633230.011

Scanlon, K. (2019). *Effects of Terrorism on the U.S. Stock Market: Evidence from High Frequency Data* (Paper 781). Honors College Capstone Experience/Thesis Projects. Retrieved from https://digitalcommons.wku.edu/stu_hon_theses/781

Schepers, M. (2016). *Effect of terror attacks on the bond and stock market of European countries*. Nijmegen School of Management, Radboud Universit. Retrieved from https://theses.ubn.ru.nl/handle/123456789/2791

Tauringana, V., & Tingbani, I. (2020). Terrorism and global business performance. *International Journal of Finance & Economics*. Retrieved from https://onlinelibrary.wiley.com/doi/full/10.1002/ijfe.2085

Section 2

Financial Governance and Risk Management

Chapter 9
Risk-Based AML/ CFT Regulations for Effective Supervision

S. G. Sisira Dharmasri Jayasekara
https://orcid.org/0000-0001-8006-3252
Central Bank of Sri Lanka, Sri Lanka

ABSTRACT

Money laundering is a global threat that requires an urgent attention of policymakers to protect financial systems from criminals. A jurisdiction is required to develop a regime to control or mitigate the impact of crimes that have multi-dimensional impacts on global economies. Prevention of global crimes is a challenge not only to jurisdiction but also to the global standard setters. The final impact of these crimes hit the financial system and other regulated institutions. Anti-money laundering/ combating the financing of terrorism (AML/CFT) supervision is an emerging area; therefore, a sound regime of AML/CFT supervision is essential to support global initiatives in this regard. This chapter discusses the implementation of a sound risk-based AML/CFT supervision of financial institutions as well as designated non-finance business and professions. This is important for AML/CFT regulators to strengthen the AML/CFT regime of a country.

1. INTRODUCTION

Money Laundering (ML) is a global threat, which requires the urgent attention of policymakers to protect financial systems from criminals. Money laundering is a crime, justified by the fact that whoever launders money is pursuing a way to legitimize their

DOI: 10.4018/978-1-7998-8758-4.ch009

ill-gotten gains which are accumulated by illegal activities and it allows criminals to enjoy the proceeds of their crime (Baldwin, 2003). Rapid developments in financial innovation, information technology, and communication processes pave ways for money to move anywhere in the world with speed and ease, which makes the task of combating money laundering a daunting task more than ever. UNODC (2019b) estimates that the amount of money, laundered globally in a year is around 2-5% of global GDP or USD800 billion to USD2 trillion in current US dollar terms. On the other hand, terrorism and terrorist financing make instabilities in jurisdictions in different aspects. Money laundering and terrorist financing[1] (ML/TF) are global issues that need jurisdictions to strengthen their domestic legal frameworks and implement the legal framework effectively to safeguard financial systems and economies from criminals. This, however, is not an easy process due to the continuous innovations in financial technology, the rapid evolution of information technology such as blockchain and internet-based payment methods such as cryptocurrencies. For example, McCahill (2019) reports that a terrorist organization has converted cryptocurrency into physical currency shortly before carrying out the deadly Easter-Sunday suicide attacks on several locations in Sri Lanka on April 21, 2019.

In this background, a global initiative to prevent ML/TF has been taken by the Financial Action Task Force (FATF). The FATF is the international standard-setter on anti-money laundering and the countering the financing of terrorism (AML/CFT). Initially the FATF has issued 40 recommendations to combat money laundering and later addition 9 special recommendations to combat terrorist financing. In 2012, combining all the 49 recommendations, the FATF has issued 40 recommendations to promote effective implementation of legal, regulatory and operational measures for combating money laundering, terrorist financing and other related threats to the integrity of the international financial system. Accordingly, jurisdictions are required to strengthen the AML/CFT regime of the country by introducing laws covering the scope of the FATF recommendations and to implement the legal framework effectively to achieve the global objectives.

AML/CFT supervision is a very important component of the effective implementation of AML/CFT regime of a country (Nasir, 2020). The supervision includes financial institutions[2] (FIs) as well as designated non-finance business and professions[3] (DNFBPs). The effectiveness of the AML/CFT supervision of a country is also assessed as a part of mutual evaluations. These mutual evaluations are periodically carried out by the FATF or FATF style regional bodies which focus on assessing the AML/CFT regime of a country in terms of technical compliance with FATF recommendations and effectiveness of the implementation of the legal framework of the country in terms of eleven immediate outcomes that are focused on safeguarding global financial systems from criminals. The level of strength of the AML/CFT regime of a country is determined based on the results of mutual evaluation. The countries that show poor results are recognized as countries with strategic AML/CFT deficiencies which are subject to continuous monitoring until they comply with international standards. Therefore, a country should develop an effective AML/CFT supervisory framework to protect the financial system from the criminals.

2. GLOBAL IMPACT OF BLACK MONEY AND FINANCIAL CRIMES

A jurisdiction is required to develop a regime to control or mitigate the impact of predicate offences indicated in FATF recommendations. UNODC (2018) states that the nature of financial crimes such as tax evasion, money laundering, bribery, and other forms of corruption means that the same activity may violate several laws. Therefore, combating these offences is challenging for any jurisdiction as well as to the global standard setters. The FATF recommendations identify 21 such offences as shown in Table 1.

The crimes identified by the FATF are challenging global financial systems and development agendas of jurisdictions. This section analyses the global impact of

Table 1. List of predicate offences

No	Offence	No	Offence
1	Participation in an organised criminal group and racketeering	12	Environmental crime
2	Terrorism, including terrorist financing	13	Murder, grievous bodily injury
3	Trafficking in human beings and migrant smuggling	14	Kidnapping, illegal restraint and hostage-taking
4	Sexual exploitation, including sexual exploitation of children	15	Robbery or theft
5	Illicit trafficking in narcotic drugs and psychotropic substances	16	Smuggling; (including in relation to customs and excise duties and taxes)
6	Illicit arms trafficking	17	Tax crimes (related to direct taxes and indirect taxes);
7	Illicit trafficking in stolen and other goods	18	Extortion
8	corruption and bribery	19	Forgery
9	Fraud	20	Piracy
10	Counterfeiting currency	21	Insider trading and market manipulation
11	Counterfeiting and piracy of products		

Source: (FATF, 2019)

predicate offences based on the information available in public domains. INTERPOL (2020) reports that organized crime networks are billion-dollar businesses operating in many crime areas. They are involved in many different types of criminal activities spanning several countries which may include trafficking in people, drugs, illicit goods and weapons, armed robbery, counterfeiting and money laundering. On the other hand, terrorism financing is a global phenomenon that not only threatens the security of countries but can also undermine economic development and financial market stability. Therefore, it is of paramount importance to stem the flow of funds to terrorists (UNSC, 2018). Ritchie *et al.* (2020) provide the dark side of terrorism that over the previous decade the average number of annual deaths was 21,000. In most countries, terrorism accounts for less than 0.01% of deaths, but in countries of high conflict, this can be as much as several per cents.

Human trafficking also has become a threat to many countries and also it is a serious violation of human rights. This has become a very lucrative business to traffickers through the acquisition and exploitation of human beings by improper means such as force, fraud or deception. UNODC (2020) reports that smuggling of migrants involves the facilitation of illegal entry of a person into a state of which that person is not national or resident, for financial or other material benefits. UNODC (2018) reports that compared to the most frequently detected cases of trafficking in persons for sexual exploitation and forced labour, there are relatively few detected cases of trafficking in persons for organ removal. This shows the brutality of human trafficking and the money-minded behaviour of criminals. The report further adds that over the last 13 years, UNODC has collected information on about 700 victims of trafficking in persons for the removal of organs detected in 25 countries as compared to 225,000 victims of trafficking in persons for all other purposes. These crimes are also related to drug trafficking. UNODC (2019b) reports that globally, some 35 million people suffer from drug use disorders and require treatment services. It further reveals that 585,000 people had died in 2017 as a result of drug use. Corruption and bribery are also becoming a threat because of their consequences on sustainable development. Therefore, World Bank (2020) considers corruption a major challenge to its twin goals of ending extreme poverty by 2030 and boosting shared prosperity for the poorest 40 per cent of people in developing countries. The report emphasises that corruption has a disproportionate impact on the poor and most vulnerable, increasing costs and reducing access to services, including health, education and justice. The example given in the report on corruption is an eye opener in view of the quality of life of the people. It suggests thinking of the effect of counterfeit drugs or vaccinations on the health outcomes of children and the life-long impacts that may have on them. The other side of the corruption is bribery. World Bank (2020) shows that the poor pay the highest percentage of their income in bribes. According to the report, for example, in Paraguay, the poor pay

12.6 per cent of their income to bribes while high-income households pay 6.4 per cent. The comparable numbers in Sierra Leone are 13 per cent and 3.8 per cent, respectively. Therefore, corruption erodes trust in government and undermines the social contract while deteriorating the living standards of the people.

Frontier (2020) studies the impact of counterfeiting and piracy of products on social and economic impacts on displaced economic activity, investment, public fiscal losses and criminal enforcement, and concludes that these costs could reach an estimated USD1.9 trillion by 2022. It also projects that the negative impacts of counterfeiting and piracy may drain USD4.2 trillion from the global economy and put 5.4 million legitimate jobs at risk by 2022.

Environment protection has become a slogan for many countries. However, they have failed to prevent environmental crimes. UNEP (2018) states that environmental crimes are widely recognized as among some of the most profitable forms of transnational criminal activity which the monetary value was estimated in 2016 at between USD91-259 billion annually. The report emphasises that environmental crime is most likely the fourth largest criminal area in the world after drugs, counterfeits and human trafficking. The increased profitability motivates entrepreneurs to avoid taxes. Therefore, tax evasion most often involves bribery and other forms of corruption which may violate several laws. OECD (2019) quoting a World Bank study of 25,000 firms in 57 countries, states that firms pay more bribes to evade more taxes. More broadly, where corruption is prevalent in society, this can foster tax evasion.

Arms trafficking is another area where countries are focussing on in order to keep peace and a stable economy. Illicit arms trafficking fuels civil wars as well as terrorism and promote other types of crimes. SAS (2020) reports that between 2004 and 2009, at least 208,300 violent deaths were recorded in the armed conflicts-an average of 52,000 people killed per year based on recorded deaths. However, the actual number may be much higher.

Sexual exploitation including sexual exploitation of children is a serious concern of a civilised society and a crime. UN News (2018) reports that every day, across all countries and levels of society, millions of girls and boys face the alarmingly common childhood experience of sexual abuse and exploitation. Pereznieto *et al.* (2014) estimates that the global economic impacts and costs resulting from the consequences of physical, psychological and sexual violence against children can be as high as USD7 trillion. They also report that this massive cost is higher than the investment required to prevent much of that violence.

Insider trading and market manipulation is a serious concern of developing a capital market in a country. This is a common issue irrespective of the level of development of a country. Illegal insider trading generally occurs when a security is bought or sold in breach of a fiduciary duty or other relationship of trust and confidence while in possession of material, non-public information. Securities and Exchange Commissions of countries reveal information on the sizable number of instances and cases related to insider dealing. For example, US SEC (2020) provides details of many cases and states that in recent years, the SEC has filed insider trading cases against hundreds of entities and individuals, including financial professionals, hedge fund managers, corporate insiders, attorneys, and others whose illegal tipping or trading has undermined the level playing field that is fundamental to the integrity and fair functioning of the capital markets.

Counterfeiting currency is another area of challenged faced by many jurisdictions. However, the actual value of these crimes cannot be obtained because unless a seizure happens information is not available to anybody. Criminals always target powerful currencies to counterfeit and it is a good opportunity for terrorists. RCMP (2020) reveals that the total value of counterfeit currencies passed into circulation in Canada was USD1.6 million in 2019 and the corresponding figure for 2018 was USD1.8 million.

The above analysis shows how the identified crimes affect the peace and living standards of people all over the world. Therefore, the FATF has provided a framework through the recommendations for countries to develop their AML/CFT regimes and implement it effectively to combat ML/TF. The responsibility of enhancing the quality of life depends on the jurisdictions by controlling the identified crimes. Jayasekara (2020b) suggest that the effective implementation of the AML/CFT legal framework is important to combat ML/TF. The existence of a sound AML/CFT legal framework alone will not be sufficient to combat ML/TF. Therefore, countries are required to implement their legal framework effectively to achieve the AML/CFT goals of the country as well as the global policymaker. The dirtily proceeds come into the formal economy through two kinds of institutions namely, financial institutions and DNFBPs. These institutions are required to supervise and monitor to prevent the misuse of criminals. Therefore, AML/CFT supervision of these institutions is an important aspect of an effective AML/CFT regime.

3. WHY AML/CFT SUPERVISION?

The criminals target to place the proceeds generated from the crimes in the formal financial systems to make it appear as legal. However, we have to keep in mind that the appearance will not make the proceeds legal. Typically, money laundering involves a three-stage process which includes placement, layering, and integration. At the placement stage, criminals focus on financial institutions to place dirty money. The financial institutions are required to be vigilant at the layering stage because criminals use various mechanisms to transfer funds to make them appear as legal proceeds. The possibility of exposing DNFBPs to ML/TF risk is high at the integration stage because criminals used laundered proceeds to purchase luxury assets as well as financial products. Therefore, countries are required to supervise both financial institutions and DNBBPs to strengthen the AML/CFT regime of the country. The first step in this process is to identify the financial institutions and DNFBPs which require supervision in terms of global standards. A clear definition of the institutions within the AML/CFT regime is important in order to implement global standard effectively. Otherwise, deficiencies will result in recognizing a country with strategic AML/CFT deficiencies which may result in various negative implications (Jayasekara, 2020a). The global standards broadly categorise institutions into two groups, namely, financial institutions and DNFBPs.

3.1 Financial Institutions

A country needs to identify a set of entities that are recognized as financial institutions to implement AML/CFT responsibilities within the jurisdiction. The beginning of the identification process starts with the definition or list of institutions given in FATF Recommendations. Accordingly, financial institution means any natural or legal person who conducts as a business one or more of the following activities or operations for or on behalf of a customer (FATF, 2019).

1. Acceptance of deposits and other repayable funds from the public. This also captures private banking
2. Lending which includes inter alia: consumer credit; mortgage credit; factoring, with or without recourse; and finance of commercial transactions (including forfeiting).
3. Financial leasing. This does not extend to financial leasing arrangements in relation to consumer products
4. Money or value transfer services. It does not apply to any natural or legal person that provides financial institutions solely with message or other support systems for transmitting funds
5. Issuing and managing means of payment (e.g., credit and debit cards, cheques, traveller's cheques, money orders and bankers' drafts, electronic money).
6. Financial guarantees and commitments
7. Trading in:
    a. money market instruments (cheques, bills, certificates of deposit, derivatives etc.).
    b. foreign exchange.
    c. exchange, interest rate and index instruments.
    d. transferable securities.

   e. commodity futures trading
8. Participation in securities issues and the provision of financial services related to such issues
9. Individual and collective portfolio management
10. Safekeeping and administration of cash or liquid securities on behalf of other persons
11. Otherwise investing, administering or managing funds or money on behalf of other persons.
12. Underwriting and placement of life insurance and other investment related insurance. This applies both to insurance undertakings and to insurance intermediaries (agents and brokers).
13. Money and currency changing

The financial institutions are assumed to be the soundest entities that comply with the requirements of AML/CFT regime. The scope of operations of financial institutions are broader because the operations of financial institutions involve transactions among international institutions as well as networks. These transactions require financial institutions to establish and adhere to sound AML/CFT systems and controls to minimise the exposed ML/TF risk. The regulators closely monitor the level of compliance of financial institutions under a risk-based AML/CFT supervision. The non-compliances will result in huge monetary as well as administrative penalties. For example, London-based HSBC Bank has been fined by the United States regulator for almost USD2 billion for failing to stop Mexican drug traffickers from using its banking system to launder money (Mclaughlin & Pavelka, 2013). Therefore, compliance self-discipline with the AML/CFT regime has been established within the financial institutions.

3.2 DNFBPs

Under a sound AML/CFT regime, financial institutions as well as DNFPBs are required to identify, assess and take effective action to mitigate the exposed ML/TF risk. However, when it comes to DNFPBs, the implementation of the AML/CFT regime is not so easy because most jurisdictions do not regulate DNFBPs. Often jurisdictions rely on the categories of businesses and professions which have been designated by the FATF to implement the AML/CFT regime of the country. The FATF Recommendations identify the following businesses and professions as DNFPBs.

1. Casinos
2. Real estate agents
3. Dealers in precious metals

4. Dealers in precious stones
5. Lawyers, notaries, other independent legal professionals and accountants
6. Trust and company service providers

A jurisdiction has to identify DNFBPs based on the vulnerability of the relevant businesses and professions for ML/TF risk. The countries should not limit the AML/CFT regime to the FATF defined categories. The level of ML/TF risk depends on the environmental context of the country in which business is operating. Accordingly, it is important to designate additional businesses and professions s DNFBPs based on the ML/TF risk of the country.

Some jurisdictions have identified additional other businesses and professions as DNFBPs within their jurisdictions to combat ML/TF.

Strengthening the compliance level of international standards on AML/CFT has become one of the top priorities in many global jurisdictions. If a jurisdiction is identified as high risk and non-cooperative country in respect of AML/CFT regime, they will need to take enhanced due diligence. AML/CFT supervision is one of the immediate outcomes assessed in mutual evaluations. Therefore, sound supervision of FIs as well as DNFBPs, (institutions) in terms of AML/CFT has become a global priority.

4. AML/CFT SUPERVISION

Each institution is exposed to inherent ML/TF risk that comes from customers, countries or geographic areas of operations, products and services, and transactions or delivery channels of financial institutions (FATF, 2019). The Institutions are required to develop and implement appropriate systems and controls to mitigate ML/TF risks. On the other hand, the AML/CFT Supervisors[4] are required to carry out supervision in terms of the risk-based approach. Assessing inherent risks of the institutions has become a critical component of the risk management process as a result of the rapid speed of innovation in banking and financial technology (Rafay, 2019). An effective regime of AML/CFT supervision includes licensing and registration requirements preventing criminals and their associates from entering the financial system, identification of ML/TF risk in different sectors, risk-based AML/CFT supervision, remedial actions, and understanding of the institutions of their obligations. According to the FATF recommendations, a sound regime of AML/CFT supervision has to cover the following areas.

Table 2. Country Specific DNFBPs

Country	Additional DNFBPs
Belize	• Vehicle dealers • Non-Profit Organizations and Non-Governmental Organizations • A business operating in a free zone area as DNFBPs.
Uruguay	• Real estate developers • Construction companies • Auctioneer • Natural or legal persons engaged in intermediation or mediation in transactions involving the purchase and sale of antiques, works of art • Exporters and direct and indirect users of free trade zones • Any non-profit organisation
Bermuda	• Car Dealers • Boat Dealers • Motorcycle Dealers • Antique Dealers and Auctioneers.
The Turks and Caicos Islands	• The High Value Dealer sector -car dealers
Solomon Islands	• Dealers in high value assets • Dealers in Motor vehicles
Greece	• Auction houses • Dealers in high value goods
Haiti	• Borlette operators
Senegal	• Real Estate Developers • Car dealers • A national lottery company
Burkina Faso	• Dealers in antiquities and works of art
Zambia	• Dealers in second-hand motor vehicles.

Source: Various Mutual Evaluation Reports (https://www.fatf-gafi.org/publications/mutualevaluations)

4.1 Licensing and Registration

Licensing and registration regime are required to prevent criminals from holding and controlling the institutions. The supervisors or other authorities should establish licensing, registration or other controls to prevent criminals and their associates from holding or being the beneficial owner of a significant or controlling interest or holding a management function within institutions. The regime has to be strengthened limiting the abilities to breach the licensing or registration requirements. The regime has to cover the identification of beneficial ownership as well. Understanding of the regulators on the requirement is also an important consideration in implementing a sound licensing and registration regime.

4.2 Identification of ML/TF Risks in Different Sectors

Identification of sector-wise ML/TF risk is another key area. The ability of supervisors to identify and maintain an understanding of the ML/TF risks in the financial and other sectors as a whole, between different sectors and types of institution, and individual institutions are considered broadly. Therefore, conducting a national risk assessment (NRA) is a particularly important initiative to identify ML/TF risks in different sectors. In addition to the identification, countries are required to prioritise the identified sectors in NRA for supervision.

4.3 Risk -Based Supervision

Risk-based supervision is an important component in AML/CFT supervision. Implementation of RBA in terms of AML/CFT supervision has to be extended to DNFBPs in addition to the FIs complying with AML/CFT requirements. The countries are required to designate AML/CFT supervisors for each category of institutions. The supervisors should have a proper understanding of the ML/TF risk of the relevant sector. The RBA of prudential supervision is not adequate, and countries should include ML/TF risk. In addition to the involvement with the process of NRA, supervisors have to improve their understanding of the ML/TF risk. The frequency, scope, and intensity of AML/CFT supervision has to be determined based on the exposed risks.

4.4 Remedial Actions and Sanctions

The implementation of a range of proportionate and dissuasive sanctions for non-compliance with the AML/CFT requirements is a particularly important aspect of effective supervision. Jurisdictions are required to implement effective remedial actions that are proportionate, and dissuasive in imposing sanctions in practice. The remedial actions taken by the regulators should not be characterized by a 'one size fits all' approach, typically consisting of allowing the institutions a certain timetable to address breaches. These sanctions should have to include administrative sanctions as well. For this purpose, a legislation should give sanctioning powers to the regulators.

4.5 Effective Supervisory Actions

Under the effective supervisory actions, the supervisors should demonstrate to what extent the supervisory actions affect the compliance level of the institutions. Supervisory actions often have a largely positive effect on compliance by reporting entities. Therefore, supervisors have to increase guidance and feedback to enhance awareness and understanding of risks and compliance obligations of the institutions in different sectors. Focussing on regular warning letters and remedial actions to rectify gaps will not be sufficient to implement supervisory actions and such actions may have a relatively limited effect. The regulators should provide feedback on compliance with AML/CFT requirements including trends and typologies.

4.6 Understanding AML/CFT Obligations

Improving the understanding of FIs and DNFBPs on the AML/CFT obligations is a prerequisite to implementing a sound AML/CFT strategy within different sectors. Therefore, regulators promote a clear understanding of the AML/CFT obligations among the reporting institutions. The proper understanding will enhance the compliance obligations of the institutions. A program of continuous awareness and training has to be conducted by the regulators and participation of institutions in such program is a must to enhance the awareness of AML/CFT obligations. Often, regulators conduct awareness program for FIs. However, the focus on the outreach of DNFBPs is minimal. In addition to the awareness sessions, regulators can use different media to outreach sectors using press notices, advertisement, and publishing guidelines, among others.

5. RISK-BASED APPROACH

Before moving into risk-based AML/CFT supervision, we have to understand the concept of a risk-based approach. A risk-based approach is a process of recognizing exposed risks, undertaking an assessment of risks and developing strategies to manage and mitigate the identified risks. Identification of ML/TF risk has to be performed at three levels namely; national risk assessment, sectoral supervisors' level, and individual institutional level to implement a sound risk-based approach. FATF has issued guidance notes to each catogories of institutions to facilitate jurisdictions to implement asound risk-based approach. FATF (2019) states that countries should identify, assess, and understand the ML/TF risks for the country, and should take action, including designating an authority or mechanism to coordinate action to assess risks and apply resources, aimed at ensuring the risks are mitigated effectively. In the second level, countries have to apply a risk-based approach to ensure that measures are taken to prevent or mitigate money laundering and terrorist financing in terms of the identified level of risks. AML/CFT supervisors have to use the results of the national-level assessment as an essential foundation to allocate resources efficiently across the AML/CFT regime and the implementation of risk-based measures. Where a country identifies higher risks, they should ensure that their AML/CFT regime adequately addresses such risks. Where countries identify lower risks, they may decide to allow simplified measures for some of FATF Recommendations under certain conditions. In the third level, countries should require FIs and DNFBPs to identify, assess and take effective action to mitigate their ML/TF risks.

Inherent risk assessment of an institution has become an important event under a sound risk-based approach to manage risk utilising resources economically and effectively. Institutional level ML/TF risk assessment focuses on inherent risk in terms of supervisory requirements. Therefore, RBA is intended to offer a less time-consuming and cost-effective alternative to prudential supervision, enabling institutions to focus their resources on high-risk customers. This approach will enhance the level of compliance of institutions tly and supervisors can effectively use their resources to strengthen the AML/CFT regime of the country.

The risk-based approach allows countries to allocate resources efficiently giving priority to identified high-risk areas and taking timely supervisory actions while complying with international standards.

6. RISK-BASED AML/CFT SUPERVISION

The main objective of risk-based supervision is to create both a common understanding of risk-based supervision and to establish consistent and effective supervisory practices across different sectors. The supervisory authorities are required to take specific account of the nature and size of a business and lay down specific measures in an appropriate manner and proportionate to the scale and complexity of its business. Risk-based supervision is characterized as an ongoing and cyclical process as shown in figure 2.

6.1 Offsite Risk Assessment

The process shown in figure 2 is useful for sector-specific supervisors to conduct risk-based AML/CFT examinations. Typically, two kinds of examinations can be identified in order to strengthen AML/CFT supervision under the risk-based approach. The supervisors first have to develop a comprehensive tool to identify the exposed inherent risk of the institutions and the quality of systems and controls in place to mitigate exposed inherent risk. This process is recognized as the off-site examination. Based on the risks identified at the offsite assessment, the supervisors have to conduct on-site examinations.

Off-site risk assessment is the foundation of a comprehensive ML/TF risk-based supervisory process for which the supervisors have to allocate supervisory resources efficiently to high-risk areas. The sectoral risk assessment will be the starting

Figure 1. Process of a risk-based approach
Source: Compiled by the author

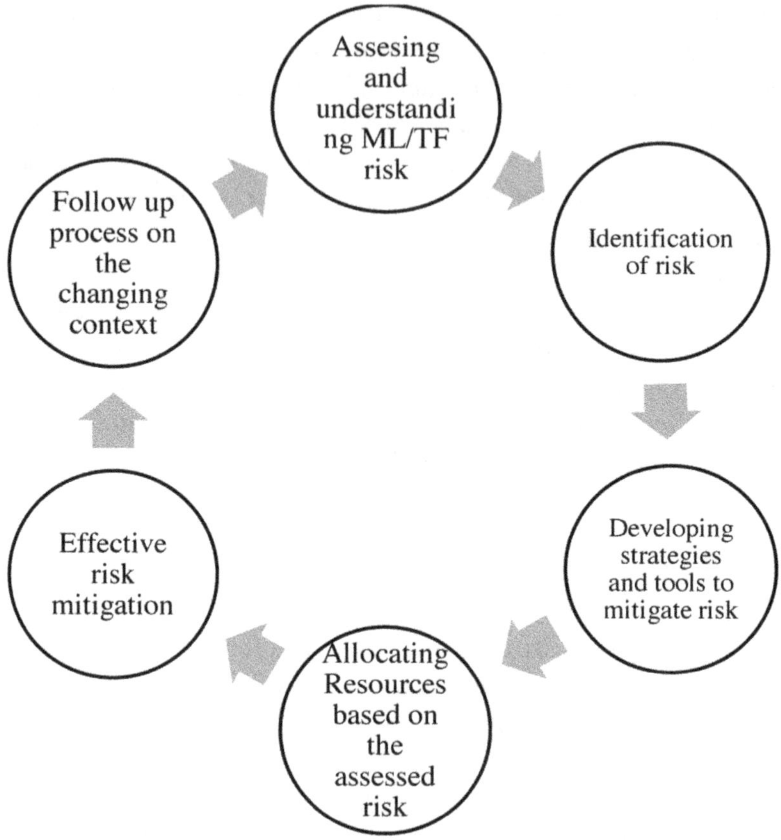

point of commencing the assessment of ML/TF risk of individual institutions. Understanding the structural factors of FIs considering the size, corporate structure whether the capital is foreign or local, and group structure will be extremely useful to determine structural risks. In assessing inherent risk, supervisors have to consider the customers, products or services offered by an institution, geographic locations where the institution operates or customers come from, and the methods or delivery channels by which the institutions offer their products and services to customers. The common sources of ML/TF risk faced by the institutions are shown in figure 3.

Supervisors have to consider profiles of customers giving attention to their legal form whether a natural or legal person and the residence status whether a local or foreign customer at the preliminary stage. Then the preliminary data has to be analyzed using different products and services, geographical locations, and delivery channels. The comprehensive assessment will provide the details of the inherent

Figure 2. Process of risk-based AML/CFT supervision
Source: Compiled by the author

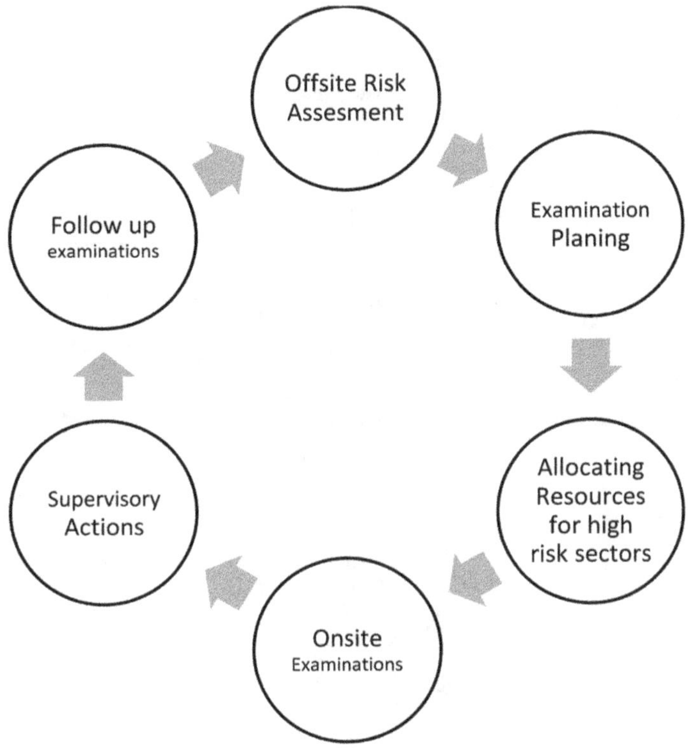

risk pattern of an institution. In addition to the inherent risk, supervisors have to consider the risk-mitigating measures adopted by the institution. These systems and controls may include corporate governance and risk management practices, AML/CFT policies and procedures, internal controls and compliance function, threshold and suspicious transactions reporting mechanisms, and training provided to improve awareness of having a sound AML/CFT framework within institutions. The net risk profile has to be determined considering the overall inherent risk and quality of risk mitigation process. The combination of inherent ML/TF risk and risk-mitigating measures will produce the net ML/TF risk exposure of the institution.

The supervisors have to plan onsite examinations based on the results of a combined assessment of inherent risk and the risk mitigation factors. Accordingly, the institutions are categorized into groups based on the overall net risk profiles such as high risk, moderate risk and low risk. This identification is important to allocate resources to high-risk institutions that show high vulnerabilities. The frequency and intensity of on-site and offsite AML/CFT supervision of institutions will be determined based on the identified level of ML/TF risk. For instance, high-risk institutions are

Figure 3. Common Sources of Inherent ML/TF Risk
Source: Compiled by the author

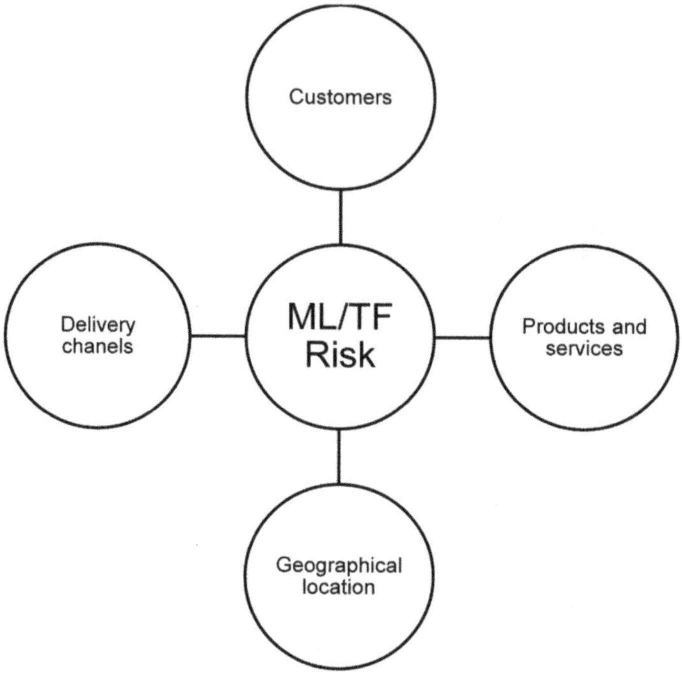

supervised most intensely and monitored closely allocating more resources. The low-risk institutions are not subject to more frequent onsite examinations and off-site supervision will be useful for lower-risk sectors and institutions. The supervisor will review the assessment of the ML/TF risk profile of an institution periodically as well as when there are major events or developments in the management and operations of the institution.

The integration of AML/CFT supervision into the broader framework of prudential supervision can leverage synergies, expertise, and resources to enhance the effectiveness of the overall supervision of institutions. Also, the integration of AML/CFT supervision with financial intelligence functions may provide strong synergies, allowing a more targeted supervision based on identified ML/TF risks.

6.2 Examination Planning and Allocating Resources

The examination planning is a particularly important part of the supervision. One of the main objectives of an offsite risk assessment is to prepare an examination plan and examination strategy for each institution. The examination plan has to be prepared considering the available resources to the supervisor. Priority has to be given to high-risk institutions and other institutions have to be determined based on the available resources. The following hypothetical example is given below to further elaborate on the examination planning process.

EXAMINATION PLANNING AND STRATEGY FOR ABC BANK INC.

Name of the Institution: ABC Bank Inc.
Supervisory Strategy for the year: 20xx.
Prepared by: Examiner in charge
Reviewed by: Head of Examinations
Authorized by: Director
Date of Preparation: 01.01.20xx
Overall Risk Rating (Net risk Profile) of the institution: High risk

The following examination objectives have been determined based on the results of the offsite assessment and information provided by ABC Bank Inc.

1. The bank is required to strengthen the governance framework in relation to the management of AML/CFT risk by revising and updating its AML/CFT policies and procedures.
2. The bank is required to revise its CDD/KYC policies and procedures and the revised policies and procedures must be reviewed and tested for compliance.
3. The bank is required to implement a customer account and transaction monitoring system and improve the recognition and reporting of suspicious transactions.
4. The bank is required to undertake an ML/TF risk assessment.

The examiners are required to develop offsite and onsite activities for each of the objectives. Some examples of activities for the above objectives are given below.

Requirement 1: The Bank Must Update Its AML/CFT Policies and Procedures

Offsite Activities

1. Request the bank to submit revised AML/CFT policies and procedures by [insert date]

2. Review whether the bank has revised policies incorporating all identified deficiencies and they are consistent with the AML/CFT Law.
3. Communicate with the bank accepting the revised policy or requiring the bank to make further amendments or provide clarification matters that may arise from the review of the supervisor.
4. Arrange meetings with management to discuss areas that need further review.
5. Request the bank to provide minutes of the board meetings confirming approval/adoption of revised policies and procedures.

Onsite Activities

1. Meet with the board of directors of the bank to discuss its role in AML/CFT risk management.
2. Meet with key management to discuss changes in policies and procedures and how these have been implemented across the bank.
3. Meet with staff to confirm that new policies and procedures have been introduced and that staff has received adequate training.

Requirement 2: Revise CDD/KYC policies and procedures and ensure that these are subject to assessment for compliance.

Offsite Activities

1. Request the bank to submit revised CDD/KYC policies including all supporting documents such as account opening forms by [insert date]
2. Conduct a review of these policies to ensure that all deficiencies have been addressed and consistent with the AML/CFT Law.
3. Write to the bank accepting the revised policy or requiring the bank to make further amendments or provide clarification matters that may arise from the review.
4. Review the internal audit plan to determine if CDD/KYC has been included as a review area.
5. Arrange meetings with management to discuss areas that need further review.

Onsite Activities

1. Meet with relevant staff (account opening and compliance) to discuss new requirements.
2. Review sample of newly opened accounts to ensure that new requirements are being implemented.

3. Review a sample of old accounts to determine how the bank is obtaining any missing information
4. Meet with internal audit and review copies of any reports generated (this also can be done offsite).

Requirement 3: Implement a new customer transaction and account monitoring system.

Offsite Activities

1. Request the bank to submit revised AML/CFT policies and procedures by [insert date]
2. Conduct a review of these policies to ensure that all deficiencies have been addressed and consistent with the AML/CFT Law.
3. Write to the bank accepting the revised policy or requiring the bank to make further amendments or provide clarification matters that may arise from the review.
4. Arrange meetings with management to discuss areas that need further review.
5. Request the bank to provide the minutes of board meetings confirming approval/ adoption of revised policies and procedures.
6. Review the account monitoring system to determine whether the bank has placed appropriate parameters to generate 'red-flags' given the risk assessment of the bank and the supervisor's view of risk.

Onsite Activities

1. Meet with key management to discuss changes in policies and procedures and how these have been implemented across the bank.
2. Meet with staff to ascertain the level of understanding of requirements/internal policies and procedures.
3. Review a sample of accounts/transactions to determine that the monitoring system is functioning and identifying.
    a. High- risk customers
    b. Customers such as politically exposed persons (PEPs) that should be subject to enhanced CDD
    c. Transactions with high-risk jurisdictions
    d. Transactions involving jurisdictions on TFS lists.
4. Meet with the Compliance Officer to discuss the transaction monitoring system and review process.
5. Review the register of suspicious transactions reporting

The supervisor has to determine the approximate time required to undertake the activities to complete the identified tasks. The number of examiners required for the tasks may vary depending on the size of the bank and the scope of supervision. Considering the risk level of institutions and the available resources, the supervisors have to allocate them for the examinations to get the maximum output from the limited resources.

6.3 On-site Examinations

On-site examinations are conducted based on the results of an off-site assessment. At the preliminary level, the examination strategy for the sector has to be prepared with the results of national risk assessment. The examination plan for the year has to be prepared, based on the results of the off-site assessment of individual institutions and available resources to the supervisor. However, examiners have to give particular attention to the areas that have been identified as high risk or deficient. And also, attention has to be given to the areas where FATF has identified as high risk in terms of the standards. In this regard, examiners may consider systems and controls in place for politically exposed persons, non-profit organizations, wire transfers, non-face to face customers, processing transactions with high-risk jurisdictions etc. After the fieldwork of examination, examiners have to update the results of the off-site assessment as a continuous process.

6.4 Supervisory Actions

Supervisory actions are vital after completing the examination in order to improve the overall AML/CFT framework of the institutions as well as the overall supervisory effectiveness of the country. In order to improve overall effectiveness in AML/CFT supervision, a jurisdiction has to develop its AML/CFT legal framework with adequate provisions to implement sanctions in accordance with international standards. This involves providing feedback for further improvements and imposing sanctions. The supervisors have to issue guidelines and provide feedback, which will assist institutions in applying national measures to combat ML/TF, and, in particular, in detecting and reporting suspicious transactions. Same time, countries have to ensure that there is a range of effective, proportionate, and dissuasive sanctions to be imposed on institutions that fail to comply with AML/CFT requirements. Sanctions have to be structured in order to apply not only to the institutions but also to their board of directors and senior management of such institutions. In addition to the sanctions, the supervisors can give time-bound action plans to the institutions to be completed to rectify the identified deficiencies.

6.5 Follow Up Examinations

After completing the first-round onsite examinations, the supervisor has to consider conducting follow up examinations. The scope of the follow-up examinations has to be limited to the identified deficient areas of the onsite examination. The follow-up examination can be used to monitor the progress of time-bound action plans. The onsite follow up examinations are useful to enhance the level of compliance of the institution.

7. EXAMINATION PROCEDURES

The documentation of the examination procedures is important to enhance the quality of examinations. The documented examination manual can be used as a guidance note and to train new examiners. Frequent update of the examination manual with new developments is also important to enhance the quality of examinations. The supervisor has to explain all the activities involve in examinations up to taking supervisory actions for noncompliance in the examination manual. The examination manual has to cover the obligations of the scope of the institutions under the AML/CFT law of the country. In addition to the obligations, the examination procedures have to be developed for scoping and planning of examinations. A typical examination manual includes the following areas among other things.

- AML/CFT Compliance Framework
- Offsite ML/TF risk assessment
- Scoping and planning
- Compliance Officer
- Staff Training
- Record Keeping
- ML/TF Risk Assessment the institution
- Assessment of AML/ CFT Framework/ Policies and Procedures/ Compliance Programme
- Customer Due Diligence
- Suspicious Transaction Reporting
- Information Sharing
- Purchase and Sale of Monetary Instruments
- Wire Transfers
- Correspondent banking
- Electronic Banking
- Electronic Cash

- Non-resident and foreign individuals
- Politically Exposed Persons
- NGOs and Charities
- Cash intensive business
- Targeted Financial Sanctions
- Beneficial Ownership
- Developing conclusions and finalizing examination
- Supervisory actions including sanctions

The scoping procedure and one examination procedure are discussed below for the benefit of readers.

7.1 Scoping Procedure

The main objective of the scoping is to identify the ML/TF risk of an institution and develop the examination scope and document the plan for the examination. This process includes determining the number of staff and technical expertise required for the examination and selecting examination procedures to be adopted at the examination. In order to facilitate the Examiner's understanding of the risk profile of the institution and to adequately establish the scope of AML/CFT examination, the Examiner is required to carry out the following steps in conjunction with the review of the ML/TF risk assessment of the institution:

1. Review prior examination or inspection reports, related working papers and responses of management to any previously identified ML/TF regulatory issues.
    a. Identify the procedures adopted during the completed AML/CFT examination of the institution.
    b. Identify, in the reports, the processes the institution uses to detect unusual transactions or activities.
    c. Identify previously noted higher-risk areas of operations of the institution.
    d. Review the progress of previously made recommendations in order to assess the progress made by the institution giving particular attention to outstanding issues.
2. In addition, contact the appropriate management of the institution to discuss its:
    a. AML/CFT Compliance Program;
    b. ML/TF Risk Assessment;
    c. Suspicious transaction monitoring and reporting systems; and
    d. Level and extent of its AML/CFT systems automation.

3. Develop a list of AML/CFT regulatory items to be incorporated into the integrated examination request letter. The examiners are required to send their request letter to the institution in order to commence the examination.
4. Review correspondence between the institution and its primary regulator and review correspondence received from or sent to outside regulatory and law enforcement agencies relating to AML/CFT compliance
5. Review number of suspicious transaction reports (STRs), cash transaction reports (CTRs), and electronic fund transfers (EFTs) obtained from AML/CFT reporting database. The number of STRs, CTRs and EFTs should be obtained for a defined period that covers the duration of the AML/CFT examination as determined by the examiner. Consider the above information and analyze the data for unusual patterns, considering the following:
    a. The volume of activity and whether it is commensurate with the customer's occupation or type of business;
    b. Number and volume of transactions involving higher-risk customers;
    c. The volume of CTRs in relation to the volume of exemptions (i.e., whether or not additional exemptions have resulted in significant decreases in CTR returns rendered); and
    d. The volume of STRs and CTRs in relation to the size of the institution, asset or deposit growth and geographic location. The examiners should not criticize an institution solely because the number of STRs, CTRs, and EFTs is lower than the reports filed by "peer" institutions. However, as part of the examination, the examiners must review significant changes in the volume or nature of STRs, CTRs and EFTs rendered and assess potential/possible reasons for these changes.
6. Review internal and external audit reports and working papers for AML/CFT compliance as necessary in order to determine the comprehensiveness and quality of audits, findings and management responses and corrective actions (Khan *et al.*, 2020). A review of the scope, procedures and qualifications of the independent audit report will provide valuable information on the adequacy of the AML/CFT Compliance Program.
7. Evaluation of compliance with the provisions of the AML/CFT legal framework must be included in AML/CFT examinations. It is the primary role of the examiner to identify the violations of the various provisions of the AML/CFT laws and regulations and to evaluate the sufficiency of the institution's implementation of policies, procedures and processes to ensure compliance with AML/CFT laws and regulations.
8. Understanding the ML/TF risk profile of the institution to adequately establish the scope of the AML/CFT examination. The examiners are required to:

a. Review the ML/TF risk assessment reports of the institution. The risk assessment has to be considered various types of products, services, customers, entities, transactions and geographic locations in which the institution is engaged, including those that are processed by, though, or to the institution in order to identify potential ML/TF exposures.
b. Review the institution's independent testing of its AML/CFT Compliance Program.
c. Review correspondence received from Supervisory authorities in order to determine whether or not the institution had any warning letters, fines or penalties imposed by them after the most recent AML/CFT examination.
d. Review correspondence between the institution and the financial intelligence unit (FIU).

9. Develop an initial examination plan based on the above procedures and findings made from the review of the ML/TF risk assessment of the institution. The examiners are required to adequately document the examination plan as well as any changes to it that occur during the examination. The scoping and planning process is designed to ensure that the examiners are aware of the institution's AML/CFT compliance program, compliance history and risk profile of the institution's products, services, customers, entities, transactions and geographic locations and ensure that the examination covers all key risk areas.

Additional core and expanded examination procedures may be conducted, where necessary. While the examination plan may change at any time as a result of on-site findings, the initial risk assessment will enable the examiner to establish a reasonable scope for the AML/CFT review. In order for the examination process to be successful, the examiners are required to maintain an open communication line with the management of the institution and discuss relevant concerns as they arise.

7.2 Sample Examination Procedure- Compliance Officer

Introduction

Institutions are required to appoint a compliance officer to coordinate work with FIU in order to carry out AML/CFT obligations under the AML/CFT law of the country. Often the compliance officer has to be a senior management level officer.

Examination Objectives

1. To determine whether the institution has appointed a compliance officer as required by the AML/CFT law.

2. To ensure that the compliance officer or any other person authorised to assist him or act on behalf of him has proper access to all customer records and other relevant information which may be required to discharge their functions.
3. To assess whether the compliance officer of the institution has involved in developing policies, practices and procedures relating to AML/CFT requirements.
4. To determine the adequacy of the authority and responsibilities assigned to the compliance officer in order to implement a sound AML/CFT framework within the institution.
5. To determine whether the institution has provided adequate training and development opportunities to the compliance officer and supporting staff.
6. To determine the effectiveness of the work of compliance officer.
7. To initiate corrective action when policies, practices, procedures or internal controls are deficient or when violations of law or regulations have been noted.

Testing to Be Conducted by Examiners

1. Obtain the organization structure and review for the management level of the compliance officer.
2. Obtain the Job description of the compliance officer and review for the scope of the activities of the compliance officer.
3. Review the number of staff allocated to the compliance division.
4. Review the AML/CFT policy and check whether the compliance officer has given more responsibilities and powers on executing his duties.
5. Review the alert generation and alert handling procedure bay taking a sample of closed alerts.

8. CONCLUSION

AML/CFT supervision has become a significant component of combating money laundering and terrorist financing in many countries in order to protect financial systems from criminals. The approach of supervision has been changed today to a risk-based approach from a rule based-approach to use limited resources of jurisdiction as an effective risk mitigation measure. AML/CFT supervision is also an important component of assessing the overall effectiveness of the AML/CFT regime of a jurisdiction. Implementation of an effective risk-based approach in order to strengthen AML/CFT supervision in order to allocate limited resources is vital for jurisdiction in combating ML/TF. Therefore, countries are required to

Table 3.

Examination Procedure	Supervisors' Findings
Appointment of a Compliance Officer • Has the bank appointed a compliance officer? • Has the institution appoint a separate compliance officer for AML/CFT? • What is the management level of the compliance officer (senior/ middle/Junior)? • Does the compliance officer have adequate legal/risk management and compliance skills? • To whom compliance officer is reporting	
Policies and Procedures • Does the compliance officer engage in the development of AML/CFT policies and procedures? • Does the compliance officer review and update the bank's AML/CFT policies and procedures periodically? • Has the board/senior management developed policies and procedures covered the role of the compliance officer?	
Requirements under the Law and related Rules and Directives • Ensure that the bank has appointed a compliance officer in terms of the FTRA and CDD rules. • Ensure that compliance division has been provided with adequate resources.	
Monitoring measurement and Control (Management Information Systems) • Is the compliance officer evaluated to ensure that it is effective and up to date? • Does the compliance officer communicate new AML/CFT related laws or changes to existing AML/CFT related policies or practices to the senior management /employees? How does this occur? • Does the AML/CFT compliance officer confirm that adequate training is provided to staff and maintain a register of attendance? • Is the board kept informed of the development in AML/CFT regime?	
Internal Control and Audit • Are there adequate arrangements in place for an independent internal review and assessment of the performance of compliance division? • Are reports produced by the independent review function sent to the board or a committee thereof? • Does the financial institution comply with recommendations made by such reports	
Effectiveness of the compliance function • Does compliance officer access to all information on customers, CDD documents electronically and manually? • Does the institution use the AML/CFT software for AML/CFT practices? • What is the time taken for Generated STR escalate to FIU? • Does the compliance division timely report to the board about AML/CFT matters? • What is the Staff strength of the Compliance division?	

identify, assess and manage the ML/TF risk of institutions under a sound risk-based approach. Accordingly, measuring inherent ML:/TF risk assessment and the quality of risk mitigation process employed by institutions are important for the institutions as well as to the supervisors. Overall examination strategy and examination plan have to be prepared based on the results of risk assessment and limited resources to be allocated for high-risk institutions. The AML/CFT examinations should be conducted in a risk-sensitive manner and non-compliances have to be addressed through proportionate and dissuasive sanctions in order to strengthen the AML/CFT framework of institutions. If a country fails to implement a sound AML/CFT regime, such a country will be identified as a jurisdiction with strategic deficiencies in AML/CFT framework and the outcome to the country will not be favorable. Therefore, countries have to adopt sound AML/CFT strategies in order to strengthen the AML/CFT framework of the country and overcome international pressure on failures. On the other hand, institutions are also required to implement a risk-based approach to mitigate ML/TF risk by developing a sound AML/CFT framework. The role of the Board of Directors is imperative and expected to regularly oversee the overall AML/CFT compliance level and commit adequate resources. The regulator should have power to take regulatory actions for the failures of the board of directors in implementing AML/CFT framework within their organizations.

DISCLAIMER

The contents and views of this chapter are expressed by the author in his personal capacity. It is not necessary for the Editor and the Publisher to agree with these viewpoints and they are not responsible for any duty of care in this regard.

ACKNOWLEDGMENT

The author extends sincere gratitude to:

- The Editor-in-Chief and International Editorial Advisory Board (IEAB) of this book who initially desk reviewed, arranged a rigorous double/triple blind review process and conducted a thorough, minute and critical final review before accepting the chapter for publication.
- All anonymous reviewers who provided very constructive feedbacks for thorough revision, improvement, extension and finetuning of the chapter.
- All colleagues, assistants and well-wishers who assisted the author to complete this task.

REFERENCES

Baldwin, G. (2003). The new face of money laundering. *Journal of Investment Compliance, 2003*(Summer), 38–41. doi:10.1108/15285810310812997

FATF. (2019). *International Standards on Combating Money Laundering and the Financind of Terrorism & Proliferation*. Financial Action Task Force.

Frontier. (2020). *The Economic Impacts of Counterfeiting and Piracy*. Frontier Economics Ltd. Retrieved from https://iccwbo.org/publication/economic-impacts-counterfeiting-piracy-report-prepared-bascap-inta/

INTERPOL. (2020). *Organised Crimes*. International Criminal Police Organisation. Retrieved from ttps://www.interpol.int/en/Crimes/Organized-crime

Jayasekara, S. D. (2020a). Deficient regimes of anti-money laundering and countering the financing of terrorism: Analysis of short term economic implications. *Journal of Money Laundering Control, 23*(3), 663–675. doi:10.1108/JMLC-02-2020-0015

Jayasekara, S. D. (2020b). (Forthcoming). How effective are the current global standards in combating money laundering and terrorist financing? *Journal of Money Laundering Control, ahead-of-print*(ahead-of-print). Advance online publication. doi:10.1108/JMLC-05-2020-0047

Khan, N., Rafay, A., & Shakeel, A. (2020). Attributes of Internal Audit and Prevention, Detection and Assessment of Fraud in Pakistan. *Lahore Journal of Business, 9*(1), 33–58. doi:10.35536/ljb.2020.v9.i1.a2

McCahill, E. (2019). *ISIS funded Sri Lanka Easter bombings with Bitcoin donations*. Retrieved from https://www.mirror.co.uk/news/world-news/isis-funded-sri-lanka-easter-14982949

Mclaughlin, J. S., & Pavelka, D. (2013). The use of customer due delligence to combat money laundering. *Accountancy Business and Pbulic Interest*, 57-84. Retrieved from http://visar.csustan.edu/aaba/McLaughlinPavelka2013.pdf

Nasir, M. A. (2020). The Relevance of Maqasid al Shari'ah to Anti-Money Laundering and Terrorism Financing. In A. Rafay (Ed.), *Handbook of Research on Theory and Practice of Global Islamic Finance* (pp. 179–194). IGI Global. doi:10.4018/978-1-7998-0218-1.ch010

News, U. N. (2018). *Child sexual abuse and exploitation: UN event sheds light on the unthinkable*. UN News. Retrieved from https://news.un.org/en/story/2018/10/1022152

OECD. (2019). *Combatting Tax Crimes More Effectively in APEC Economies*. Organisation for Economic Co-operation and Development.

Pereznieto, P., Montes, A., Langston, L., & Routier, S. (2014, September). The costs and economic impact of violence against children. *Child Fund Alliance*, 1-10. Retrieved from https://www.childfund.org/uploadedFiles/public_site/media/Articles/current/2014/ODI%20Report%20%20The%20cost%20and%20economic%20impact%20of%20violence%20against%20children.pdf

Rafay, A. (Ed.). (2019). *FinTech as a Disruptive Technology for Financial Institutions*. IGI Global. doi:10.4018/978-1-5225-7805-5

RCMP. (2020). *Currency counterfeiting statistics*. Royal Canadian Mounted Police. Retrieved from https://www.rcmp-grc.gc.ca/fsis-ssji/statistics-Statistiques-eng.htm

Ritchie, H., Hasell, J., Appel, C., & Roser, M. (2020). Terrorism. *Our World in Data*. Retrieved from https://ourworldindata.org/terrorism

SAS. (2020). *Direct Conflict Deaths*. Small Arms Survey. Retrieved from: http://www.smallarmssurvey.org/armed-violence/conflict-av/direct-conflict-deaths.html

UNEP. (2018). *Environmental crimes are on the rise, so are efforts to prevent them*. United Nations Environment Programme. Retrieved from https://www.unenvironment.org/news-and-stories/story/environmental-crimes-are-rise-so-are-efforts-prevent-them

UNODC. (2018). *Global Report on Trafficking in Persons 2018*. United Nations Office on Drugs and Crimes.

UNODC. (2019a). *United Nations Office on Drugs and Crime*. Retrieved from https://www.unodc.org/unodc/en/money-laundering/laundrycycle.html

UNODC. (2019b). *Global Overview of Drug Demand and Supply*. Vienna: United Nations Office on Drugs and Crimes.

UNODC. (2020). *Human trafficking and smuggling of migrants*. United Nations Office on Drugs and Crime. Retrieved from https://www.unodc.org/westandcentralafrica/en/newrosenwebsite/TIPSOM/Human-trafficking-and-smuggling-of-migrants.html

UNSC. (2018). *United Nations Security Council Counter-Terrorism Committee Executive Directorate: Terrorism Finance*. United Nations Security Council.

US SEC. (2020). *SEC Enforcement Actions; Insider Trading*. U S Securities and Exchange Commission. Retrieved from https://www.sec.gov/spotlight/insidertrading/cases.shtml

World Bank. (2017). *World Bank list of economies.* The World Bank. Retrieved from https://www.worldbank.org/en/search?q=list+of+economies+&currentTab=1

World Bank. (2020). *World Development Indicators.* Retrieved from https://datacatalog.worldbank.org/dataset/world-development-indicators

ENDNOTES

1 Terrorist financing is the financing of terrorist acts, and of terrorists and terrorist organizations (FATF,2019)

2 Financial institutions mean any natural or legal person who conducts as a business one or more of the following activities or operations for or on behalf of a customer (FATF,2019): 1. Acceptance of deposits and other repayable funds from the public. 2. Lending. 3. Financial leasing 4. Money or value transfer services 5. Issuing and managing means of payment (e.g., credit and debit cards, cheques, traveler's cheques, money orders and bankers' drafts, electronic money). 6. Financial guarantees and commitments. 7. Trading in: (a) money market instruments (cheques, bills, certificates of deposit, derivatives etc.). (b) foreign exchange. (c) exchange, interest rate and index instruments. (d) transferable securities. (e) commodity futures trading. 8. Participation in securities issues and the provision of financial services related to such issues. 9. Individual and collective portfolio management. 10. Safekeeping and administration of cash or liquid securities on behalf of other persons. 11. Otherwise investing, administering or managing funds or money on behalf of other persons. 12. Underwriting and placement of life insurance and other investment related insurance60. 13. Money and currency changing

3 Designated non-financial businesses and professions means (FATF,2019): 1) Casinos 2) Real estate agents. 3) Dealers in precious metals. 4) Dealers in precious stones. 5) Lawyers, notaries, other independent legal professionals and accountants – this refers to sole practitioners, partners or employed professionals within professional firms. It is not meant to refer to 'internal' professionals that are employees of other types of businesses, nor to professionals working for government agencies, who may already be subject to AML/CFT measures. 6) Trust and Company Service Providers refers to all persons or businesses that are not covered elsewhere under these Recommendations, and which as a business, provide any of the following services to third parties: a) acting as a formation agent of legal persons. b) acting as (or arranging for another person to act as) a director or secretary of a company, a partner of a partnership, or a similar position in relation to other legal persons. c) providing a registered

office; business address or accommodation, correspondence or administrative address for a company, a partnership or any other legal person or arrangement. d) acting as (or arranging for another person to act as) a trustee of an express trust or performing the equivalent function for another form of legal arrangement. e) acting as (or arranging for another person to act as) a nominee shareholder for another person.

4 AML/CFT Supervisors are the designated competent authorities or non-public bodies with responsibilities aimed at ensuring compliance by financial institutions and/or DNFBPs with requirements to combat money laundering and terrorist financing. Non-public bodies (which could include certain types of SRBs) should have the power to supervise and sanction financial institutions or DNFBPs in relation to the AML/CFT requirements. These non-public bodies should also be empowered by law to exercise the functions they perform and be supervised by a competent authority in relation to such functions (FATF,2019).

Chapter 10
Compliance Monitoring and Testing Seismometer to Detect Compliquake

Sachin Shah
Independent Researcher, India

ABSTRACT

Effective corporate compliance function has been the focus of all the financial institutions (FI) and the regulators across the globe in this fast-changing and dynamic business landscape. The compliance function is a key component of financial institutions' (FIs) lines of defence in terms of managing and mitigating the risks. Compliance monitoring and testing by the compliance departments can act as an effective "seismometer" in detecting the "compliquakes" in the FIs if implemented effectively. If FIs across the globe internalize this philosophy, the author opines that the overall financial services and the financial institution's ecosystem will be a much better world in terms of identification and strengthening of the compliance control framework.

INTRODUCTION

Strong AML/CFT compliance program is an increased focus area for almost all the financial institutions (FIs) and banks across the globe. Various regulators and global watchdogs help the FIs to achieve this objective of having a strong and robust AML/CFT compliance program. The country mutual evaluations conducted by The Financial Action Task Force (FATF) demonstrates the effort by global regulators and the countries to assess the effectiveness of the Anti-Money Laundering/Counter-

DOI: 10.4018/978-1-7998-8758-4.ch010

Financing of Terrorism (AML/CFT) effectiveness (FATF, 2020). The unique approach and the methodology followed by FATF in conducting the mutual evaluations ensure a transparent assessment (FATF, 2020). These assessments and mutual evaluations are done for the technical compliance and adequacy of implementation and considers various elements like AML/CFT program outcomes, indicators, data and various other factors.

These watchdogs also expect that financial supervisors across the countries to assist the FIs in achieving their objective by supervising, monitor, and regulate FIs through appropriate supervisory processes. It is also an ask that all the countries consistently implement and enforce the AML/CFT laws. As a consequence, the FIs are also supposed to design, implement and execute AML/CFT compliance program as a preventive measure which is commensurate with the risks they are exposed to and appropriately file the suspicious activity reports (SARs). In November 2020, the FATF released the consolidated assessment ratings using the 2013 Assessment Methodology which demonstrates the increased focus on the technical compliance and effectiveness of AML/CFT framework across the globe by the FIs and respective regulators (FATF, 2020).

THE COMPLIANCE FUNCTION

The recent enforcement actions on the FIs globally demonstrates how seriously the focus has shifted to the appropriate compliance culture and an effective and robust corporate compliance function in FIs. Regulators are now increasingly emphasizing on the importance of "Tone from the top" to attain the right culture and expecting that the senior stakeholders lead the compliance culture by example. It is the onus of the senior stakeholders like the C suite individuals and senior management to set examples on a continuous basis and assist in establishing and implementing an effective AML/CFT compliance program.

The Board

The ultimate responsibilities for the AML/CFT compliance program lie with the financial institutions board and their activities. The activities of the board of directors include:

- Governance and oversight of the compliance risk in the financial institutions and related actions taken to mitigate these risks.
- Implementing and promoting a culture that encourages adherence to the compliance framework and regulations

- Setting the roles and responsibilities and ensuring that the senior management has required skill sets and has the necessary qualifications and experience to execute the compliance program effectively
- Approving and vetting the internal policies and procedures of the financial institution
- Reviewing and assessing the financial institutions actions, undertaken periodically, to ensure the management of the compliance risk in an effective way.

Senior Management

The responsibility of the financial institutions to effectively manage their compliance risk lie with the senior management. The key role played by them include:

- Taking necessary steps to disseminate and promote the culture of compliance culture by communicating and reinforcing the standards with the respective stakeholders
- Design and implement a robust corporate compliance function as part of robust and effective compliance program
- Assisting the board in the management of compliance risk and governance and oversight of the implementation of the compliance program
- Design and implementing reporting framework to report senior management on critical matters related to compliance and the robustness and effectiveness status of the compliance risk management program
- Overseeing and executing the corrective action plans for breaches identified

Compliance Function

The role of compliance function in any FI is very strategic considering the current scenario and the way things are changing dynamically way globally. The key functions of any compliance function are as follows:

- Providing and maintaining independence on the oversight of compliance activities by ensuring that there is no scope for inherent conflict of interests between competing responsibilities and priorities. They are also required to have inroads to all the necessary information and personnel to carry out their responsibilities appropriately and as per expectations.
- Ensuring sufficient capacity building for the compliance function with an objective of effectively managing the compliance risk within the financial institutions

- Designing, establishing and implementing a robust compliance program, providing appropriate advice, assist in increasing the awareness education, assessing compliance risk, performing appropriate monitoring and testing of the control framework and escalation and communicating the implementation, effectiveness and robustness of control for compliance risk
- Key point of contact for the regulators and external supervisors

The function of compliance is also responsible for conducting the necessary monitoring and testing (M&T) activity by performing the risk-based compliance monitoring and testing (CM&T) program. This is done in-order to ensure the implementation of robust and effective AML/CFT compliance management program and pro-actively identify deficiencies and significant issues in the control framework at entity level. It must be noted that the risk-based approach is the key to attain a robust and effective compliance monitoring and testing program.

A compliance monitoring and testing (CM&T) program consist of various elements which ranges from the understanding and review of the risk assessment performed by the business functions, creating the testing schedules, roll-out annual plans, and review of internal control framework which covers the internal policy, procedures and processes documents and standards across the business lines to ensure adherence of the control framework and the compliance vis-à-vis the internal policy and procedures and the laws and regulations. The outcome of the any monitoring and testing program is to pro-actively identify potential control-gap issues and provide guidance to the respective business function and the internal stakeholders on the corrective steps to be taken to bridge the control gaps identified. This is always beneficial when an FI and the senior management has the visibility of the control gaps before any regulatory and internal inspection is conducted. It is necessary for the FIs to focus on the AML/CFT compliance testing results and the identified weakness in the control framework and the proposed corrective actions to demonstrate robust compliance program and avoiding issues raised by the external audit or inspection which has a risk of reputational, operational and financial damages. It must be noted that CM&T work papers should be articulated and maintained in such a manner which allow for any third party or external supervisor to replicate the monitoring and testing activity and arriving at the same observations which the CM&T team has brought-up or has identified.

COMPLIANCE MONITORING AND TESTING (CM&T) - EVOLUTION AND HISTORY

In the last few decades there are plenty of examples to demonstrate the glaring failures in corporate governance which has also contributed to a larger extent triggering the financial crisis of 2008. Considering the enforcements actions over the last decade by regulators across the globe it is very clear that there is a clear focus required on the enhancements of the internal control framework and the control points for the FIs and the banks so as to mitigate the risks and avoid any regulatory rebuke or penalties. Although there are voices who argued that corporate governance reforms have fallen so far short of what many had expected, however the global financial meltdown of 2008 triggered fresh discussions of the importance of robust internal controls framework. This also prompted the FIs to have a framework in place to introduce robust internal controls, encourage design and execution of effective governance and oversight framework by having the relevant management committees and have a dedicated individual acting as chief risk officer (CRO) who is accountable for the effective identification and management of the entity risks and also assist in having the appropriate and effective internal control framework. Similar thoughts are also be mentioned in the guidelines on corporate governance principles for banks issued by the Basel Committee on Banking Supervision (BCBS) in 2015 (BIS, 2015). If we read the guidance note published by BCBS, we will clearly make out that the focus area is re-iterated in-terms of having robust risk management procedures by having an effective and independent risk management function led by a dedicated senior management official under the capacity of chief risk officer (CRO), having required skills, experience, qualification, resources and the independence. Further, the changing landscape of the business models and the increased threats in-terms of risk posed and its impact on the internal control framework necessitates that FIs risk management program and the control infrastructure should be commensurate with the bank's risk profile, so that the risk can be pro-actively identified, monitored and controlled on business-as-usual basis covering the entity at a holistic level. Similar suggestions are also provided by the The Organization for Economic Co-operation and Development (OECD) where they have also reiterated the importance of having internal policy and procedures and having a dedicated and senior individual in the capacity of CRO to manage the risks posed by the FI (OECD, 2014). There is enough literature in public domain which underlines the gaps and deficiencies related to the risk management which include following risks:

- inappropriate understanding of risks and insufficient risk management,
- insufficient authority provided to internal stakeholders to mitigate the risk,
- absence of real-time information on risks

The above concerns requires the management to focus on re-thinking their approach towards risk management which may include – (i) clearly defining board-level responsibilities and remove any scope of internal conflicts; (ii) formulation of the oversight and governance framework and having a dedicated committee structure; (iii) having a dedicated chief risk management officer with sufficient skills, experience and qualifications; and (iv) closer and high level of coordination, communication and cooperation among the internal stakeholders and the senior management and the board.

While contemplating the implementation of the above data points, the business world and the regulators globally relied on the line of defense approach followed in the military planning and strategy formulation. The idea of defence model has originated from the military setting where multiple layers of defense were erected to tackle the enemy and their attacks. This military strategy of having multiple layers of defence consisted of multiple barriers in the form of live trees with branches, sharped wires which were aimed to defend against the enemy attack. In the similar way for an organization, a line of defense is the layer of people and dedicated function who work towards mitigating the attack of any risk on the FIs control framework. Superimposing the same concept in enterprise risk management, three lines of defense model constitutes of three separate layers of defence with separate roles and responsibilities and with a single aim of managing risk and continuously work on the corrective actions to strengthen the control framework. Academicians have argued for long that the reason for having robust and effective internal control framework is to have a strong defence mechanism to combat the risk and effectively manage it. The idea and the theory are also supported by the Principles of Sound Management of Operational Risk published by Basel Committee of Banking Supervision (BIS, 2011). Considering the military planning and the BCBS principles; it will be very imperative that primary focus of the defence mechanism is "Efficiency" and this is also a common link to all the international standard setters. Following the same approach, any internal control framework with focus on efficiency follows the "5W" approach. That is – (i) What, (ii) Who, (iii) Where, (iv) When and finally (v) How. In other words when the monitoring and testing across the three line of defence is performed, the focus are is to ascertain the "Design Effectiveness" and "Operating Effectives" by identifying the answers to these 5Ws, i.e. What is the control, who perform this control, where is this control performed, when is the control performed and finally how (the test steps) to implement the intended control? This approach holds true for all the banks and FIs. The latest updates of the Committee of Sponsoring Organizations of the Treadway Commission (COSO) Internal Control Framework again elaborates the significance of effectiveness of internal controls which ultimately acts as a foundation of the compliance monitoring and testing framework for an effective compliance program. It will be pertinent here to mention that how COSO defines internal control. The COSO model (COSO, 2020) defines internal control as a process effected by an entity's board of directors, management and other personnel designed to provide reasonable assurance of the achievement of objectives in the following categories:

- Operational Effectiveness and Efficiency
- Financial Reporting Reliability
- Applicable Laws and Regulations Compliance

It further mentions that for a control framework to be effective, it must have five components to assist the FIs to achieve their objective of effectiveness. These components are – (i) Control Environment, (ii) Assessment of Risk, (iii) Control Activities, (iv) Information and Communication and (v) Monitoring. The COSO framework can be depicted as below which clearly showcase the critical components of the control framework:

If one glace through the recent regulatory actions against the banks and the FIs, it will be very clear that there is still a room of improvement to enhance the control framework by the banks and they need to further enhance corporate governance measures and their internal control framework. This has really pushed the Compliance monitoring and testing function to the forefront of the management strategy in risk management. This will result into more focused and pointed internal policy and procedures pertaining to effective compliance framework at banks and also assist in the increased coordination, cooperation and communication between supervisors, and external and internal auditors. Ineffective internal control systems were also one of the primary reasons for many of the recent enforcement actions on banks and FIs. For example, in July 2020 (The Baltic Times, 2020). The Financial and Capital Market Commission (FCMC) fined Signet Bank for breaching AML rules and inadequate internal control system was one of the gaps identified by FCMC for levying fine. Such instances impact the public trust in a big way and this lack of public confidence negatively impacts the stability and integrity of the financial services sector and hence economy at large. To reiterate the ultimate outcome; this resulted into regulators increased attention and focus on the gaps in oversight function and the failure in internal control framework.

OUTLINE OF THE THREE-LINES-OF-DEFENCE MODEL

Following extensive discussions within the industry, Institute of Internal Auditors in 2013 adopted a three-lines-of-defence (LoD-3) model to address the issues outlined in the above section. It provided the FIs a measuring scale to measure the degree of robust internal control framework for the various business functions in an organization. It started with the development of generic model, however gradually transitioned to a full-fledged operational risk model as and when the regulatory dynamics changed. The key feature of the model was the close linkage among various control responsibilities in an effective and efficient manner. This also make it necessary to have clear communication of the roles and responsibilities to all the internal stakeholders so that everyone understands the objective and their responsibility.

Figure 1 depicts the LoD-3 model in a pictorial way.

Figure 1.

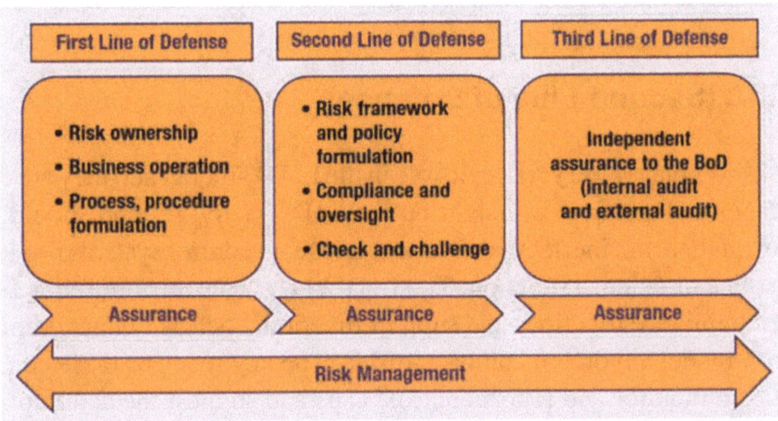

The key features of the LoD-3 model are described in the following sections.

The LoD-1 (First Line of Defence)

The front-line line of businesses is treated as the first line of defence (LoD-1). They are the risk owners. Being the risk owners, there is a lot of onus on the LoD-1 and it is expected that they are aware of the various risks in a holistic manner. As a result, the relevant staff in this layer need to understand the risk very clearly and work closely on the corrective steps to remediate and manage the risks which the business function is exposed to. It is expected that the LoD-1 will assess, understand and implement required corrective steps to have a robust control framework supplemented by details policy and procedure framework. This allows pro-active identification of the control gaps so that it can be escalated to the appropriate management levels for the necessary action and remediation.

The key highlights of the first line of defense include those shown in Table 1.

Table 1.

Responsibilities	Control Validation	Control Inventory	Escalation Practices
Owner of the risks, and accountable for the design and maintenance of internal control frameworks	Leveraging the Control Assessment process, verify the effectiveness of controls and remediate the control deficiencies to ensure that the control framework on BAU is sustainable and addresses all the risks.	Create and maintain updated control inventory for all the business divisions / functions across the organization.	Perform escalation and reporting key risk indicators for senior management review. Also undertake corrective actions on the control deficiencies.

The LoD-2 (Second Line of Defence)

The LoD-2 layer plays a very strategic role in the LoD-3 model and they are expected to maintain an independent oversight on the LoD-1 activities and should identify pro-actively if there are ineffective or lack of adequate control systems implemented by the first line of defence function. The LoD-2 layer consist of multiple functions including compliance functions and support functions such as finance, compliance, risk control, model validation and back office. The key focus of these constituents of LoD-2 is to monitor and report controls gaps and suggest the action plans. The LoD-2 has evolved considerably in organizations over the last two decades and with the introduction of a middle office its scope has expanded exponentially in the FIs strategy and vision statements. FIs over the past 1-2 decade has also strengthened their 2LoD team in-response to the increased regulatory focus and the innovation of more complex products and processes. As such, the LoD-2 defines perform the reviews and assess the design and operating effectiveness of the control framework and independently assess if the firm control framework is in adherence to the internal policies and the applicable laws and regulations. The LoD-2 independently assess the control framework as per the annual plan and provide their recommendations on the corrective action to be taken.

The key highlights of the second line of defense include those shown in Table 2.

The LoD-3 (Third Line Defence)

The LoD-3 function is the ultimate level of control and is entrusted to internal audit function. In the LoD-3 model, internal audit function has also evolved by the

Table 2.

Responsibilities*	Control Validation	Escalation Practices
- Formulation of Compliance Monitoring and testing framework which is risk based and commensurate to FIs risk appetite - Assess whether the elements, processes and controls of the compliance programme are designed appropriately and are operating as designed - Advising business on the gaps in internal control framework and remedial actions to plug the gaps	Perform compliance monitoring and testing and provide independent assurance on adherence to all the laws, regulations, and policies	Escalate control gaps and recommend corrective actions

changing dynamics of the regulations and has played increasing role in providing impartial assurance to relevant stakeholders on the overall control framework across the FI. It must be noted that the main differential between LoD-2 and LoD-3 is the regulatory accountability. Since LoD-3 has a final accountability to the board and the to the regulators; there is little room to have mishaps at this level. The overall USP of the model is that the control gaps cannot be missed at the LoD-3 layer and even if the LoD-1 or LoD-2 miss to identify any control gaps, it can be caught at the LoD-3 level. To achieve the objective and perform the task effectively; the FIs and banks follows the guidance on implementing structures proposed by the IIA Attribute Standards 1100, which include organizational independence, implementation of a direct reporting line for the chief audit executive and unrestricted access to senior management and the board.

The key highlights of the third line of defense include:

Table 3.

Responsibilities	Control Validation	Escalation Practices
Formulation of audit plans for the holistic review of control framework at entity level, providing Impartial assurance on the design and operating effectiveness of the entity control framework.	Perform internal audits to review and assess the existing controls and give assurance on overall effectiveness of controls	Provide corrective actions on the identified issues during the internal audit and reviewing and tracking the action taken by the business on the proposed remedial actions.

To summarize, the entities internal audit function plays a critical role in the LoD-3 model by assessing the design and operating effectiveness of the existing controls and confirm the overall effectiveness of the control framework and providing independent assurance to the relevant stakeholders.

It must be noted that CM&T as a sub-function of the compliance function is responsible to monitor specific risks such as noncompliance with applicable laws and regulations. However Internal audit function provides the assurance on the overall effectiveness of governance, risk management, and internal controls at an entity level.

External Controls

Besides the LoD-3 layers and the existing controls implemented by the three layers there are external controls too that complements the existing set of layers of the internal controls. The most common thing which can be bucketed in this section is external auditors who are required by various regulations for most organizations. Even though they are external to the organization external auditors play a very strategic role in providing assurance to the organization's overall effectiveness of the control framework and if the controls are operating as designed or not. They also confirm the adherence of these controls to the existing policy framework and the external rules and regulations. In some instances, external auditor may take even more important role in some exceptional cases where regulatory issues take center stage in an organization. Below section will complement the LoD-3 by elaborating key regulatory requirements on the monitoring and testing function.

Regulatory Requirements

When one tries to evaluate the regulatory framework around the requirements for CM&T function, the first thing which can be noticed is the definitions put-forth by the Federal Reserve Board's Supervisory Letter SR 08-8 (FRS, 2008). The definition elaborates that to validate the key assumptions, data sources, and procedures; CM&T function takes strategic priority. It further elaborates that work of CM&T function is very critical to measure and monitor the compliance risk. Also, the gaps identified in the controls framework and the recommendations on the corrective action post testing of controls are essential to have a proper oversight on the effective internal control framework." It further mentions that the foundation of such M&T activity starts with the risk assessment exercise which becomes very crucial for an effective CM&T programme.

Bank Secrecy Act (BSA) also talks about the same in CFR 21.21 of procedures which is related to compliance monitoring activity. It mentions that one of the important features of an effective compliance program is to provide an independent assurance for compliance to be conducted by banks or FIs and by the designated individuals.

Last but not the least, Principle 7 of Basel committee of Banking Supervision (BCBS, 2005) also considers monitoring and testing as one of the key compliance function responsibilities. The principle says that the compliance function should monitor and test compliance by performing sufficient and representative compliance testing. The results of the compliance testing should be reported up through the compliance function reporting line in accordance with the bank's internal risk management procedures.

COMPLIANCE MONITORING AND TESTING: ROLE IN EFFECTIVE COMPLIANCE PROGRAM

The CM&T framework or the program plays a strategic role for any bank or FI for the pro-active identification of control gaps and the overall effectiveness of the control framework. The identification of gaps is required to determine the extent of enhancement to be carried in the existing controls and visualizing the overall effectiveness of AML/CFT compliance framework. The program consists of the compliance review plan which includes thematic and targeted reviews involving relevant AML/CFT guidance and standards. The approach of CM&T resembles to that of internal audit function having similarity in-terms of *modus operandi*, objective and the focus areas.

A holistic CM&T programme aims at identifying the effectiveness of controls. To achieve the same objective, the CM&T function performs the thematic and targeted reviews for the business functions which is commensurate to the risk it possesses to the entity. It is thus very critical for the compliance department to create a culture which nurtures the monitoring and testing function and harnesses its effectiveness in the overall compliance program. Few of the elements to be considered to ensure the robustness of CM&T programme are as below:

- Tone at the top
- Corporate culture of integrity
- Well defined roles and responsibilities
- Leveraging on technology
- Apply a robust and consistent methodology
- Ensure buy-in from the business
- Work effectively with other control functions
- Maintain flexibility in the monitoring plan

Organizations need to work on changing the mindsets of the senior management about the importance of CM&T function by making them realize the role it plays in the larger ecosystem. Apart from the senior management, organization at large must accept and understand that robust CM&T provides relevant and reliable information to stakeholders of compliance program in the following manner:

- The CM&T program is viewed as firm's commitment to compliance framework from a regulator's perspective.
- It provides much needed data and management information to senior management so as to take informed decisions and having an effective oversight on the overall compliance program.
- It builds trust and confidence among all the internal and external stakeholders as it evidences the understanding and execution of ethics and compliance programs.

METHODOLOGY TO PERFORM COMPLIANCE MONITORING AND TESTING (CM&T)

Compliance monitoring and testing program has to be very robust and holistic in its coverage. It starts with the assessment of the control environment and identifying the various risk areas across the business functions. Basis the risk assessment undertaken; CM&T conducts the CM&T reviews and covers – (i) Transactions, (ii) Information Systems and (iii) Policy and Procedures. While covering the above elements, the compliance reviewer will identify the various controls points and then assess the overall effectiveness of the control framework. The high-level overview of the compliance monitoring and testing program is presented as below:

Figure 2.

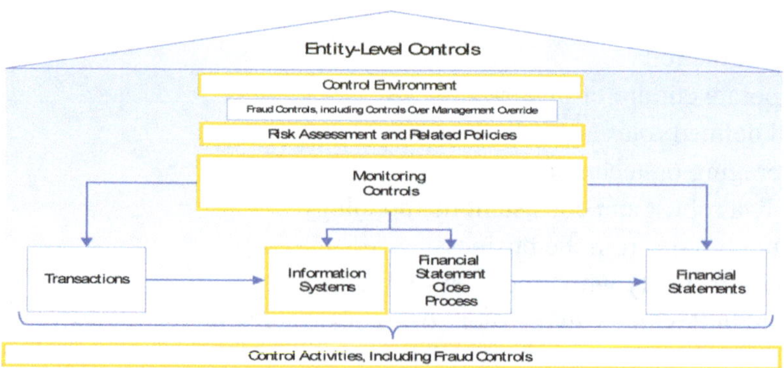

In-terms of the approach, the monitoring and testing will have following steps –

RISK ASSESSMENT

This includes review and assessment of the following

Entity Risk

Based on the geographical and regulatory regime, understand the risks posed to entity and create risk profiles

Business Risk

Assess the risk posed through the business types and related business volumes that are being served by the entity and its impact on process

Transition Risk

Gather the risk emanating from transition of process and assess impact

Compliance Risk

Undertake assessment of existing rules and regulations to understand the impact of the regulatory risk and its coverage including frequency of updates, changes and action

DEVELOPING CM&T PLAN

It includes

Develop and Draft CM&T Plan

Basis the risk assessment and the feedback from internal stakeholders, develop the testing plan to be executed over the year. The same will include thematic as well as target testing reviews considering the criticality of the control failure.

Discuss Plan With Senior Management

The annual testing plan will be discussed with the senior management and the relevant stakeholders for their necessary approval and vetting.

Plan Approval

The annual plan is approved and finalized along with the execution timelines.

Socialization

The approved plan is socialized with the respective business stakeholders and various governance committees.

Planning which includes the following –

- Based on risk assessment conducted and entity risk profiles, define the criteria for the purpose of coverage of entities, frequency and timings
- Schedule discussion with the business and explain the coverage of the CM&T plan to be performed. Take the feedback of the auditee to make the necessary modifications in the scope of the review
- Basis the initial opening meeting, develop the list of deliverables and share with business to provide the same with-in the stipulated time frame. Follow-up to be made, for the deliverables as and when required
- Assess the system access requirements and coordinate with business and IT to obtain the necessary system access for performing the review.

Fieldwork which covers –

- Conduct walk-though sessions with the stakeholders to understand the control framework, processes and policies and the business as usual.
- Perform Design Effectiveness Assessment based on 5 W principle. If there is any deficiency noted in the design of controls, notify the management immediately and perform Substantive testing.
- Perform Operating effectiveness assessment based on risk-based approach
- Identify the Issue, Root Cause and the Risk and assign appropriate risk rating to be shared finally with the business in the form of the report.
- The draft report to be discussed with the Head of CM&T for final review and approval.

Reporting which includes

Report Discussion

Discussion on findings and factual accuracy

Agree on action plans and owners

Reporting

Report containing assessment of current processes for regulatory purposes

Detailed report for management

Recommendations

Recommendations to relevant senior stakeholders

Recommendations emanating from industry best practices

Provide inputs on standards/SOPs based on benchmarking with Local/Global AML regulations

WEAKNESSES AND FAILURES OF THREE-LINES-OF-DEFENCE MODEL

As we are now familiar with the CM&T function, its role in the Three Lines of Defence (LoD-3) model and also the methodology adopted by the CM&T function; let's now move on to understand a bit about the pain-points and the weaknesses of the LoD-3 model and the challenges faced by the CM&T teams across the FIs. CM&T works at par with the internal audit function and addresses that requirement which serves similar purpose but is still independent from the organizations internal audit department. Without the LoD-2 on testing and monitoring, FIs will continue to grapple with the assess the effectiveness of any compliance program and to know what is working and what needs enhancement. It also serves as an early red flag that allows the stakeholders along with the compliance function to identify pro-actively the potential compliance issues.

Despite adopting and scaling-up the LoD-2 model among the financial institutions and banks over the last decade, the number of instances of enforcement actions and penalties by the regulators across the FIs globally evidences the fact that there are still lop of gaps in the model which needs to be looked-upon and plugged. The kind of impact it has on the public trust and the financial strain on the FIs in-terms of monetary penalties make it worth a discussion and focus point so that appropriate action can be taken to plug the gaps. Considering the various instances following are the key gaps of the three-lines-of-defence:

INHERENT CONFLICTS WITHIN LOD-1

1st LoD takes a very important role in-terms of managing the risk, however there is inherent conflict among the business function, i.e., the risk owners to prioritize the risk management and the key result area of generating revenue and profits. As most of the business structures has compensation policy based on achievement of financial goals, this impacts the way risk is understood and managed by the 1st LoD. One of the recent developments to tackle this gap is to introduce a compensation system which is aligned with the performance related to control framework enhancements and the role internal stakeholder plays in strengthening the control framework for his/her respective domain or department.

LACK OF INDEPENDENCE OF LoD-2 LAYER

One of the pain points for the overall effectiveness of the LoD-3 model is the lack of independence provided to the LoD-2 layer / team. As mentioned in the above section, LoD-2 has a very strategic role to play and their independence is very critical in-terms of achieving the overall effectiveness and plugging the gaps of the control framework. The reward structure of the second line of defence function also plays a crucial role. However, FIs faces a big challenge in-terms of compensating the team members of the CM&T teams often prioritizing the reward structure of the front-line staff at the cost of LoD-2 team. Though it can be agreed that the front-line staff generates the revenue, however the specialized task which CM&T performs is often ignored which also gets reflected in their compensation structures.

DEARTH OF RESOURCES IN LoD-2 FUNCTIONS

Another challenge which is faced by the FIs is to lack of resources with appropriate skill sets and competency levels for the execution of LoD-2 activities. It must be noted that in such scenarios, even if LoD-2 functions independently, it may impair their ability to challenge the status-quo which can result into in-effective assessment and testing of the control framework.

LACK OF HOMEWORK BY LoD-3

One of the biggest challenges FIs have faced is the failure in detecting high-risk areas by the internal auditors (LoD-3). This results audit function focusing on the wrong risk areas which undermine the effectiveness of the third line of defence. Though internal audit function is a highly specialized function and heavily relies on the experience and the audit framework, however, still there are numerous instances where the LoD-3 has failed in assessing the risk appropriately.

MISCONCEPTION AND INTERPRETATION ABOUT THE DEFINITION

Many professionals don't know the exact difference between "testing" and "monitoring" and of the use the terms interchangeably. However, it must be noted that although they seem to be same, but they are not interchangeable and cannot be fully optimized without each other. The commonly used definitions (Deloitte, 2015) of each are as follows:

- Testing program: It is a risk based, dynamic and independent compliance oversight process designed to periodically select and review a sample of business products, services, communications, and other areas to gauge and report on the operating effectiveness of compliance controls and/or adherence to stated policies and procedures.
- Monitoring program: The ongoing surveillance, review, and analysis of key business performance and risk indicators that allows the organization to identify potential compliance violations. While many seek to implement "automated" monitoring programs, monitoring activities can be either automated or manual.

The biggest irony in the compliance world is that the CM&T function and related activity are often misunderstood and not given required attention and the priority. The challenge to implement and sustaining efficient and effective CM&T program is still there. It may be due to several reasons and few of them are lack of skilled resources, ineffective design and of driving the program consistently across the enterprise, and the heave dependency on other stakeholders for data and the execution of the programs.

Most of the literature evidence that independent CM&T is one of the key pillars of any good financial crime programme. However, it also faces the similar challenges which an internal audit function faces and also fraught with unique challenges. The most remarkable challenge is that the testing and monitoring are often treated as orphans, lacks the punch which the audit function has, and the M&T reports are not treated the same way as an audit report. To some extent there is also an issue in-term of the mindset due to which senior business managers and the staff in general has a wrong impression about the compliance testing function. Some perceive it as support and non-critical function and hence does not pay heed to the reports issues resulting into diluting the control gaps identified. Moreover, regulators are also now focusing on the quality of output and the activities performed by compliance officers resulting into increased scrutiny and expectations, without increasing or changing the powers delegated to them. In short, a gap is emerging, and a paradigm shift is needed.

In short, such gaps can have a ripple effect on other areas of the compliance program and can trigger a "Compliquake" which can be devastating for any financial institution (FI).

THE COMPLIQUAKE – CHALLENGES FOR EFFECTIVE TESTING AND MONITORING

Despite the entire regulatory framework, CM&T implemented by many FIs is still a "check-box" approach. The assessment of specific compliance process is still getting validated against a list to be ticked and is performed at periodic intervals without visualizing the "big picture" of risks, and with no forward-looking issues being raised. This myopic approach by many of the banks results into "Regulatory tsunami" or "Compliquake" where organizations fail to adequately assess the control framework and hence run the big risk of regulatory censure or inviting hefty fines. Some key triggers for such Compliquakes are mentioned below.

In several instances the compliance monitoring and testing is embedded in business as usual with no or very limited authority or powers to influence the business actions regarding control framework. This results into testing staff not getting positioned in such a manner as the internal audit staff is. This ultimately leads to a situation where compliance testing reports are not taken very seriously.

Often the senior management behaves in an intimidating way towards the compliance testing staff. In some power structures the situation is so worse compliance testing officer's careers are put at stake. There are also instances where one of the scariest things is the intimidation by business management to downplay/ suppress results of their compliance testing or other compliance identified issues.

The alignment of the CM&T activity across the three lines of defence is another pain point for the banks and FIs.

THE FUTURE – ENHANCEMENTS TO THE CHANGING REGULATORY COMPLIANCE LANDSCAPE

Keeping in mind the above weaknesses and the issues faced by FIs in the execution and achieving effectiveness of the LoD-3 model, it is imperative to discuss the probable solution and how it can be made more robust. The numerous regulatory and enforcement actions clearly have a lesson in-terms of the control failures and what enhancements are required. Accordingly, the necessary tweaking can be made to the existing approach and the LoD-3 model. There is plenty of reading material available in public domain in-terms of enhancements required for the improvement of internal control systems. Interesting point to be noted is the ideas in-terms of adding extra layer of defence, i.e., ideating the Four Line of Defence Model (4 LoD) which adds the regulators as the incremental layer of defence.

It can always be debated how effective the 4 LoD model can be and if it will be appropriate to even focus on it in-terms of design and implementation. While having such discussions, one should always be mindful of the constrains and challenges the LoD-3 approach faces. There are concerns in-terms of effectively tacking the issue of corporate governance, risk management and identifying the control gaps in a pro-active manner when leveraging the LoD-3 model. The ever-changing dynamics of the business and the regulatory environment has made the things more challenging. This has also triggered heightened expectations from the regulators in-terms of pro-active stances and having more robust effective internal control review framework in place.

The most logical approach which will also be note very onerous is to strengthen LoD-3 model by embedding the additional layer of external supervisors as an inherent part of the defence framework. In the existing model also, there is an interface of the LoD-3 layers with the external regulators, however by making the model more inclusive will ensure the clear-cut allocation and assignment of roles and responsibilities between respective stakeholders within financial institutions and that of the external regulators and supervisors.

Learning from the past mistakes and the supervisory inspections, there is more focus for a continuous interaction and enhanced dialogue among the internal stakeholders and the senior management on the risk management which includes discussion on the design, implementation, execution and assessment of FIs risk appetite framework and its risk culture. Regulators across the globe are also deliberating and implementing the same in their approach. Classic example is The Federal Reserve who tried addressing the issue by issuing a new section entitled - Enhanced internal audit practices leveraging upon the 2003 Policy statement on the internal audit function. That section promotes the idea that FIs should rely on the reviews and assessment work of the internal audit function and should also enhance their examination procedures through continuous assurance of key elements of internal audit". Such steps will not only help in having an oversight on the expectations made by the supervisory bodies which are relevant to the internal audit function but also projects the benefits of enhanced and continuous communication between supervisors and the internal auditors. This also brings to the forefront an important point that although supervisors remain outside the organization's boundaries, they have the potential to become a critical and key element of compliance M&T, oversight and governance systems.

In other words, the supervisors might provide an independent and impartial assessment of the first three lines which gives overall comfort on the adherence of the FIs compliance with regulatory requirements. Hence impartial M&T by regulators and other supervisors can play a key role in the overall governance and control structure of an FI. Also, such a close relationship between the supervisors and the internal LoD-3 layers will help to enhance the governance of financial institutions by focusing in pro-active rather than reactive and outcome-based supervisory approach.

CONCLUSION: CM&T TURNING OUT TO BE EFFECTIVE SEISMOMETER

Compliance M&T activity by the compliance departments can't be done away with and in-fact can act as effective "Seismometer" in detecting the "Compliquakes" in the FIs if implemented effectively. For that the senior management needs to be convinced that it is an important tool which, if combined with other tools and technologies, can effectively be used to deter and detect the inherent risks and enhance the operating and design effectiveness of the existing control framework. Also, the Board needs to design an effective governance framework which ensures that the compliance testing and monitoring program works in-tandem with other line of defence teams. Also, it must be ensured that compliance testing staff have a high degree of operational independence, even within the compliance department, and have a stature on par with internal audit. A suitable control framework should also be created so that testing staff can do the confidential escalations to audit where compliance testing or other compliance staff have concerns, they believe were unaddressed or bulldozed, alongside a no-retaliation policy.

If FIs across the globe internalize this, it's sure that the overall compliance ecosystem will be a much better world in terms of identification and strengthening of the compliance control framework.

DISCLAIMER

The contents and views of this chapter are expressed by the author in his personal capacity. It is not necessary for the Editor and the Publisher to agree with these viewpoints and they are not responsible for any duty of care in this regard.

ACKNOWLEDGMENT

The author extends sincere gratitude to:

- The Editor-in-Chief and International Editorial Advisory Board (IEAB) of this book who initially desk reviewed, arranged a rigorous double/triple blind review process and conducted a thorough, minute and critical final review before accepting the chapter for publication.
- All anonymous reviewers who provided very constructive feedbacks for thorough revision, improvement, extension and finetuning of the chapter.
- All colleagues, assistants and well-wishers who assisted the author to complete this task.

REFERENCES

BCBS. (2005). Compliance and Compliance Function in banks. *Bank for International Settlements*. Retrieved from https://www.bis.org/publ/bcbs113.htm

BCBS. (2011). Principles for the Sound Management of Operational Risk. *Basel Committee of Banking Supervision*. Retrieved from https://www.bis.org/publ/bcbs195.pdf

BIS. (2015). Basel Committee's revised principles. *Bank for International Settlements*. Retrieved from https://www.bis.org/bcbs/publ/d328.htm

CFR § 21.21 - Procedures for monitoring Bank Secrecy Act (BSA) compliance. *Bank Secrecy Act*. Retrieved from https://www.law.cornell.edu/cfr/text/12/21.21

COSO. (2020). Five Components of the COSO Framework You Need to Know. *KnowledgeLeader Blog*. Retrieved from https://info.knowledgeleader.com/bid/161685/what-are-the-five-components-of-the-coso-framework

Deloitte. (2015). *Building world-class ethics and compliance programs: Making a good program great.* Retrieved from https://www2.deloitte.com/content/dam/Deloitte/no/Documents/risk/ Building -world-class-ethics-and-compliance-programs.pdf

FATF. (2020). Consolidated assessment ratings, FATF Mutual Evaluations. *Financial Action Task Force*. Retrieved from http://www.fatf-gafi.org/publications/mutualevaluations/documents/assessment-ratings.html

FRS. (2008). Compliance Risk Management Programs and Oversight at Large Banking Organizations with Complex Compliance Profiles. *Federal Reserve System*. Retrieved from https://www.federalreserve.gov/boarddocs/srletters/2008/SR0808.htm

OECD. (2014). Risk Management and Corporate Governance. *The Organization for Economic Co-operation and Development*. Retrieved from http://www.oecd.org/daf/ca/risk-management-corporate-governance.pdf

The Baltic Times. (2020, July 16). FCMC fines Signet Bank with EUR 906,600 for breaching AML rules. *The Baltic Times*. Retrieved from https://www.baltictimes.com/fcmc_fines _signet_bank_with_eur_906_600_for_breaching_aml_rules/

Chapter 11
Shariah Governance Systems of Islamic Banks in Bangladesh:
A Comparison With Global Governance Practices

Md. Kausar Alam
University of South Asia Dhaka, Bangladesh

Mosab I. Tabash
Al Ain University, UAE

Md. Farjin Hassan
Putra Business School, Malaysia

Nihad Hossain
Universiti Putra Malaysia, Malaysia

Md. Akib Javed
Universiti Putra Malaysia, Malaysia

ABSTRACT

This chapter explores the Shariah Governance (SG) of Islamic banks in Bangladesh as compared to global SG practices. Applying semi-structured face-to-face interviews, this study finds that Bangladesh is not far behind the global SG system. Most of the countries have enacted Islamic banking regulations, but Bangladesh does not have any separate banking legislation for Islamic banks. Islamic banks are working on their own instead of centralized functioning under the regulations of the central bank.

DOI: 10.4018/978-1-7998-8758-4.ch011

Islamic banks in Bangladesh are mainly dominated by the 'buy and sell mode' which is diminishing the real sense of Islamic finance. Islamic banks are not practicing true Islamic banking because of the predetermined profit rate and violation of the Shariah principles. But the central bank has accepted it due to social demands and people's expectations. The corporate social responsibility functions are broader and more focused in Bangladesh as compared to global practices.

1. INTRODUCTION

The global *Shariah* Governance (SG) practices of Islamic Financial Institutions (IFIs) vary due to countries' legal rules and regulations to monitor the overall functions of Islamic banks and finance (Hassan *et al.*, 2011). The governance structure is the written form of guidelines and practiced by the Board of Directors (BOD) to ensure accountability, fairness, and transparency among the concerned stakeholders (customers, investors, shareholders, management, employees, society, and government). The government and regulators deliver the guidelines for controlling the institutions and safeguard the interest of the numerous stakeholders. Accordingly, Ginena and Hamid (2015) stated that SG is a complete system that outlines how IFIs follow the *Shariah* principles in conducting their business functions. Islamic Financial Service Board (IFSB) (2009) has demonstrated SG systems as "*a set of structural procedures where IFIs assure the Shariah compliance throughout its operational activities*". SG is the backbone of the IFIs because it outlines a comprehensive procedure for ensuring the *Shariah* rules to accomplish the business functions. Without the SG it is impossible to assure a proper Islamic financing system. Thus, a comprehensive SG structure is grounded on four pillars i.e., *Shariah* Supervisory Board (SSB), management and supervision, *Shariah* compliance and review, and lastly, transparency and disclosure (Minhas, 2012; Rafay & Farid, 2018).

However, Bangladesh has started its Islamic banking journey through the inauguration of the 'Islami Bank Bangladesh Limited' in 1983 with combined efforts of the government and general people (Hassan *et al.*, 2017). Currently, Bangladesh has 8 full-fledged Islamic banks (Bangladesh Bank, 2019). Though the Central Bank promulgated a guideline in 2009 still Bangladesh has an absence of a well-defined full-fledged regulatory, supervisory specific and structured governance framework to govern, supervise, monitor, and regulate the Islamic banking activities (Ullah, 2014; Ahmad *et al.*, 2014; Perves, 2015; Alam *et al.*, 2019; Alam *et al.*, 2020a, b; Nomran and Haron, 2020). The study of Alam *et al.* (2020a) found that the intention of the regulators and concerned stakeholders are responsible for the absence of a comprehensive SGF of IBs in Bangladesh. As a result of such lacking and absence of a comprehensive SGF, Islamic banks have developed their SG mechanisms that are flexible in their practices (Hassan *et al.*, 2017; Sohrabuddin, *et al.*, 2020). In the guideline, the central bank stated that the formation of SSB is voluntary rather than compulsory which contradicts the global practices (BMB Islamic, 2011).

The Islamic banks and financial institutions as well as their SG guidelines are developed by the government of the respective country (Hassan *et al.*, 2017; Adam and Muizzuddin, 2020). While the government of the respective countries actively supports the development and expansion of Islamic banking and finance whereas the scenario is different in Bangladesh. The development of Islamic banks and their governance systems are developed by the initiative of the general people and Muslims in Bangladesh (Hassan *et al.*, 2017). As a result, the self-developed SG are diversified in the formation and practices which create confusion among the general people, customers and government (Abdullah and Rahman, 2017). Besides, it is well-known that Islamic banks are violating the *Shariah* principles in the existing practices (Alam *et al.*, 2020b). Besides, the BOD and management influence in the implementations of SG of Islamic banks in Bangladesh (Alam *et al.*, 2020c). Sometimes, the *Shariah* auditors do not conduct a comprehensive *Shariah* audit of large customers. Therefore, it is required to examine the uniqueness, limitations and consequences of the SG of Islamic banks in Bangladesh. This chapter aims to examine the uniqueness, limitations and consequences of SG systems of Bangladesh compare to global SG practices. For doing this we asked the respondents "how do the *Shariah* Governance systems of Islamic banks in Bangladesh are different from global *Shariah* governance practices?"

Starting with the introduction, section 2 illustrates the literature review. Section 3 outlines the methodology of the appear and section 4 narrates the findings and discussions from the respondents. Finally, section 5 concludes with implications and policy recommendations.

2. LITERATURE REVIEW

2.1 Different Shariah Governance Models Adopted by Countries

The legal frameworks governing Islamic banking and finance activities of different countries can fluctuate and influence the practice of SG in IFIs. In global practices, there are three types of SG which are centralized, laissez-faire and hybrid. First, the centralized model is established by the *Shariah* Advisory Council (SAC). Established at the central level, The *Shariah* Advisory Council (SAC) proceeds consolidated *fatwa* on Islamic business agreement, guides the Central Bank on *Shariah* matters and implements consolidated appointment of SSB at the bank level. Comparing to other models, the centralized model is considered to have more extensive instruction, and the particular implementation of SG yet has a stricter requirement to be met by the IFIs (Noordin and Kassim, 2019). Sudan, Indonesia, Iran, Brunei and Malaysia have accepted this model of SG.

Second, the market regulators have no intervention with the laissez-faire or self-regulated approach, which is created in the provision of SSB to the IFIs. Moreover, this model is considered the best as an essential issue by *Shariah* compliance. Hence, the IFIs should construct their specific ways of assuring *Shariah* compliance and decreasing *Shariah* risks related to their banking products to be established as a more flexible SG model. As a result, individual IFIs may have unique rules of maintaining *Shariah* non-compliance issues with no final authority to decide on *Shariah*, matters. Gulf Cooperative Council (GCC) countries, including Kuwait, Qatar, and Saudi Arabia and non-Islamic regimes, including Hong Kong, South Korea, United Kingdom, Germany, and France have more adopted this model than other countries. The third and final model is the hybrid model which is different from other models. IFIs implement rules to the countries which have accepted this model in which IFIs have to establish *Shariah* compliance by themselves and report their efforts to the central regulatory authority. For example, the *Shariah* advisors of Islamic banks of Pakistan have to follow "fit and proper" rules and present a report on *Shariah* compliance to the SSB of the State Bank of Pakistan, which has the highest authority and supervisory roles of ensuring *Shariah* compliance in the country (Rafay, 2020a; Noordin and Kassim, 2019). UAE has also executed the same SG model. National Council of the *Shariah* Supervisory Committees of IFIs of UAE must be reported any arising issues about Sharia compliance.

In addition, numerous standard-setting agencies have been established for the development of Islamic banking and finance as well as their SG. Among these authorities, the Auditing Organization for Islamic Financial Institutions (AAOIFI) and Islamic Financial Services Board (IFSB) were most prominent and established in 1992 and 2004 respectively. AAOIFI works with the individual IFIs and IFSB works on the regulatory policies for the central banks (Dusuki, 2011).

2.2 An Overview of Islamic Banking and *Shariah* Governance in Bangladesh

The regulatory authorities and monitoring bodies (BOD, SSB, and management) monitor and supervise the Islamic banks and their SG activities according to the central bank rules and regulations along with *Shariah* principles. Thus, along with the central bank and the Ministry of Finance, there are several non-government organizations have formed to supervise the functions of the Islamic banks as an advisory basis in Bangladesh. Those bodies are playing an imperative role in the development of the Islamic banks and their SG functions. To assure *Shariah* compliance in the Islamic banks, the central bank has fixed the criteria before starting the bank. The organizers of the bank must ensure the expertise and facilities and confirm all business activities comply with *Shariah* (Bangladesh Bank, 2009). The central bank does not have a separate department to monitor and control the Islamic banks, and it reviews Islamic banks with the inspection of traditional banks' guidelines (Alam *et al.*, 2019). Also, the central bank has formed a competency group to develop the checklist of *Shariah* compliance to observe the supervisory activities of the SSB of Islamic banks. The central bank also suggested to follow the AAOIFI guidelines, but Islamic banks are not following accurately (Alam *et al.*, 2020b; Ullah *et al.*, 2018)

In addition, Islamic Banks Consultative Forum (IBCF) have formed on 11 October 1995, is providing services towards the improvement of Islamic banking. The IBCF considered an effective and efficient institution, which has attained more objective such as policy development, managing the problems and matters concerning Islamic banks, and the development of Islamic banking in Bangladesh. However, the CSBIB, Islamic Insurance Companies, Bangladesh Government Islamic Investment Bond, renovation of new Islamic financial products, and the group investments are the practical accomplishments of IBCF. Besides, in 2016, IBCF has launched the IBCF Research Training Academy for the overall improvement of the talent management process, human capital, and generating future leaders.

The Central *Shariah* Board for Islamic Banks of Bangladesh (CSBIB) established as a private institution in 2002 for the development and assurance of the similar *Shariah* rulings for the Islamic banks in Bangladesh. CSBIB aims to supervise and support Islamic banks, banking branches, and windows to implement *Shariah* guidelines in their overall banking functions. Besides these, CSBIB provides supports to the central bank, government, and all its member banks in disputes issues and *Shariah* issues in conforming *Shariah* rules and regulations in their complete business activities. Sometimes, CSBIB arranges training programs and general discussion programs for bankers and *Shariah* executives. As such, CSBIB plays a vital role in solving the controversial matters between Islamic banks and the customers as well as providing *fatwas* regarding contemporary issues. The government can legalize this body by providing a circular for mandatorily following its guidelines (Alam *et al.*, 2020d).

Figure 1 shown above represents the existing SG structure of the Islamic bank in Bangladesh. In the current practices, SSB provides advisory services and accomplishes *Shariah* audit and review functions and finally provides an annual certificate based on the accomplished tasks which is published in the annual report of the respective bank and submit to the Bangladesh Bank (Abdullah and Rahman, 2017). If the SSBs face any problem in *Shariah* issues to accomplish their functions,

Figure 1. Shariah governance structure of Islamic banks in Bangladesh
Source: Abdullah and Rahman (2017). Modified

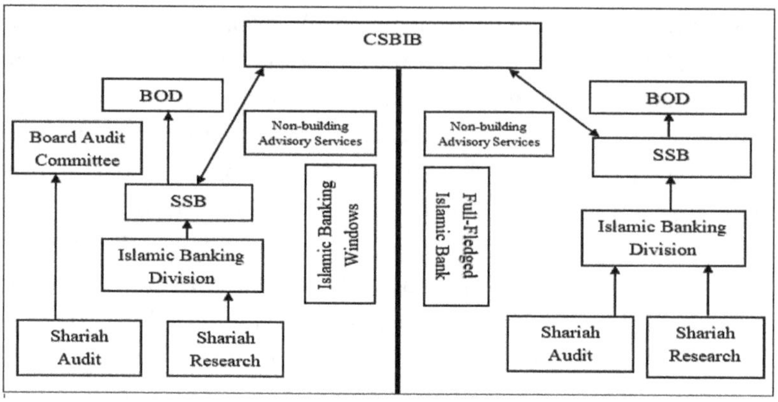

they contact CSBIB for the possible solution. Additionally, SSB also assesses the personal performance of the executives concerning the *Shariah* compliance and performs *Shariah* audit once or twice a year for ensuring proper implementations of *Shariah* principles (Alamgir, 2016). Besides, the board audit committee is responsible for ensuring *Shariah* compliance as per the central bank guideline in the overall functions (Alamgir, 2016). Islamic banks implement internal *Shariah* reviews in the pre and post-operational functions, which are mostly concerned with SSB supervision, monitoring, and controlling (Rahman, 2014).

All the Islamic banks have a respective *Shariah* secretariat or *Shariah* department or *Shariah* Inspection and Compliance Division that prepares files and presents *Shariah* related documents to assist SSB functions. Additionally, if the *Shariah* secretariat faces any problems, suggestions, and opinions, they will communicate with SSB. Therefore, some of the *Shariah* department executives in the Islamic banks conduct *Shariah* research (Abdullah and Rahman, 2017).

Hossain (2012) outlined that Islamic banks need to follow more rules and regulations rather than conventional banks such as AAOIFI standards, IFSB guidelines and *Shariah* principles. Islamic banks in Bangladesh is following some rules and regulations from international standards-setting institutions. Still, Islamic banks don't need to follow the guidelines and standards of AAOIFI and IFSB. The different nature of actions of Islamic banks required applying diverse accounting and reporting systems (Abdel-Magid, 1981; Khan, 1994). Thus, Islamic banks requisite to disclose some adequate information for their stakeholders which is not applicable comparing to conventional banks (Rafay, 2020b).

3. METHODOLOGY

Qualitative research has executed in exploring the SG of Islamic banks compared to global SG practices. Qualitative research permits researchers to understand the experiences of people, the way of constructing their words and the meaning they attribute to their expertise (Merriam, 2009). It is also able to provide detailed information concerning the uniqueness, limitations, and consequences of the SG of Islamic banks in Bangladesh (Weischedel *et al.*, 2005).

This study followed a similar research methodology for accomplishing the research objectives applied by Alam (2021) and Alam *et al.* (2020a, b, c, d, e). They explored the grounds for the not present of a comprehensive SGF for Islamic banks in Bangladesh (Alam *et al.*, 2020a), problems of SGF and regulatory bodies of the Islamic banks in Bangladesh (Alam *et al.*, 2020b), the impact of BOD and management, influence in the SG guidelines, (Alam *et al.*, 2020c), the formation of a central *Shariah* regulatory authority (Alam *et al.*, 2020c), and the relevance of external *Shariah* audit and review committee (Alam *et al.*, 2020e). The study of Alam (2020) stated the overall data collection and data saturation process in the development of a centralized *Shariah* governance framework for Islamic banks in Bangladesh. We applied the purposeful and snowball tactic in the respondents' selection process. Therefore, a probable respondent list has developed before proceeding with final data collections with a combination of SSB members, *Shariah* executives and experts in Islamic banking from the Islamic banks in Bangladesh. The respondents were practically connected with SG functions and activities of the *Shariah* Department of the Islamic banks.

The researchers have chosen the semi-structured interview to expand additional data concerning this research and to have a more comprehensive observation of the experimental feature of the subject issues. This interview is selected for this research because of its flexibility which allows the researchers to discover more entirely the opinions of respondents, which may influence outcomes in more and wide-ranging particulars of the whole gathering of answers (Dane, 1990). Besides, this method delivers the chance to the respondents to provide their thoughts in accordance with their information and practical understandings (Saunders *et al.*, 2007). Contrary to other categories, the semi-structured interview tactic can outline the more in-depth perceptive information based on the prepared questions of the phenomenon (Berg and Lune, 2007). Moreover, Bryman and Bell (2003) emphasized that this method is significant in explaining and understand the events, designs, and procedures of behavior and able to provide a more rigorous image of respondents' perceptions.

A formal consent form was sent to all of the respondents by requesting interviews. Overall, 17 interviewees were subsequently interviews based on study criteria as data was saturated (Alam, 2020; Alam *et al.*, 2020a, b, c, d, e). Among these studies,

Alam (2020) stated the overall data saturation process within 17 respondents over the information redundancy, referring to responses of other respondents and declining of NVivo nodes in the development of a centralized *Shariah* governance framework for the Islamic banks in Bangladesh. The face-to-face interview was executed in which this process can be comfortable the process of getting a transparent understanding of the research issues. When an interview is taken face-to-face, it helps to find out the in-depth responses from the participants. This process assists the participants in understanding the questions more transparently (Sekaran and Bougie, 2016). A face-to-face interview safeguards the personalities of the participants in providing their opinions, which is a widely valued quality in the overall data collection procedure (Kvale, 1996; Gillham, 2000; Sekaran and Bougie, 2016).

The interviews were recorded over mobile for final results and the length of the interview was 45 minutes to 60 minutes. All of the respondents were assured about the privacy of their name and identity in the research and publications. After recording the interviews, it was transcribed word by word accordingly. In the transcription, the respondents have given symbolic identities for protecting their confidentiality which are 'RA' (Regulatory authorities), 'SP' (*Shariah* Practitioners) from the Islamic banks and 'E' (Experts) who are related with the industry and research in this field. For qualitative analysis, NVivo is the most user-friendly software for analyzing numerous textual data, since it allows in-deeper and provides more technologically advanced tools to envisage data. (Gibbs, 2002; Patton, 2002). Using this software, users can make themes, code, and categories (Alam, 2020; Alam *et al.*, 2020a, b, c, d, e; Strauss, 1987; Joffe and Yardley, 2004).

We applied thematic analysis to analyze our interviews as it has more flexibility. This thematic analysis is a procedure of identifying, analyzing, and reporting themes from the perceived data (Braun and Clarke, 2006). Initially, this tactic is applied to generate the codes, categories, and themes from the transcribed data for further explanation and interpretation of the data. We present the generated theme and categories in the next section.

4. FINDINGS AND DISCUSSIONS

Based on the data analysis through NVivo, we found one central theme and six types of categories regarding the uniqueness, limitations, and consequences of the SG systems of Islamic banks comparing with global SG practices. Figure 2 shown below illustrates the identified theme and categories identified from NVivo.

Islamic banks in Bangladesh are self-regulated from their beginning but the global system is different. The countries develop the guidelines and system. But,

Figure 2. Uniqueness of SG Systems of Bangladesh compare to Global SG Practices
Source: Developed by Authors

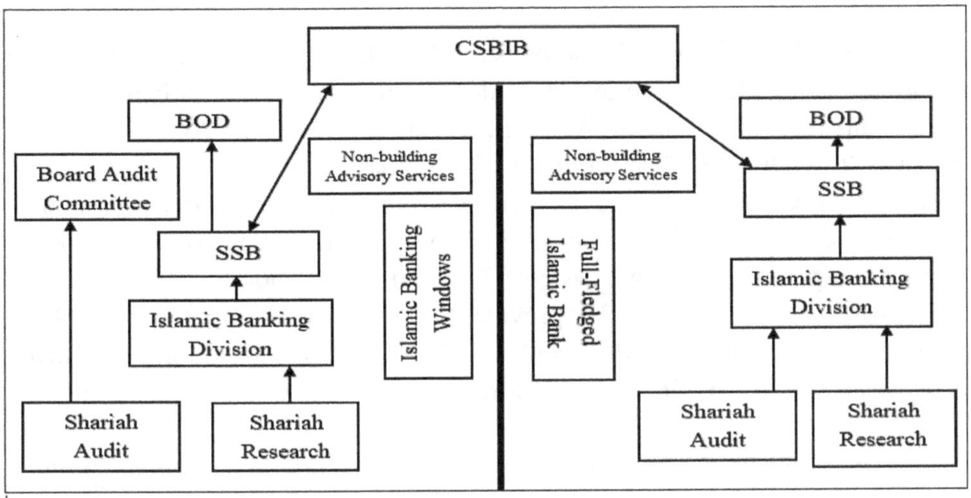

Islamic banks in Bangladesh started the banking functions rather than developing the regulations, banking act, and other infrastructures.

In our current practices, Islamic banks are self-regulated from the very inception, I mean from 1983 and that's why they are done better in terms of assets, deposit, foreign trade business, investment, and whatever. ...... If we look at the Islamic banking industry maximum country firstly prepared the regulation, then they implement it but if we look at the Bangladesh perspective, we see that first, we work practically, and then the regulations have developed. If you look at the Banking Company Act, 1991 last amendment in 2018, you will see that the Shariah terms in finance have been included and discussed with a specific definition. The last amendment is good but for betterness, it is required to develop a separate Islamic banking act. [SP#9]

Moreover, in Bangladesh, Islamic banks are working individually rather than centrally functioning under the regulations of the central bank of the Ministry of Finance. Islamic banks are operating their functions and the internal system through the guideline of the Banking Regulations and Policy Department (BRPD) since their inaugurations (Alam *et al.*, 2020b).

The problem in Bangladesh is the bank here working individually. They are not working through regulations of the central bank of the Ministry of Finance. "We have only Shariah guideline from the central bank and this guideline have been implemented in the banking industry for the Islamic banking for the year 2015 through Banking Regulations and Policy Department (BRPD) circular 15. [RA#3]

The internal policies of Islamic banks in Bangladesh are different because of self-developed practices. The internal rules, regulations and the principles of all Islamic banks are almost similar (Alam *et al.*, 2020b; Hassan *et al.*, 2017). All Islamic banks have their BOD, SSB, and *Shariah* officers for monitoring *Shariah* principles. Islamic banks have internal manual, own *fatwas*, own training institute, individual audit team, *Shariah* audit system, monitoring system and *Shariah* compliance system. Along with the internal systems, the central bank monitors and supervises the Islamic banks where the CSBIB provides the *fatwas* solves the referred problems concerning Islamic finance (Alam *et al.*, 2019). Nearly all the banks have a *Shariah* secretariat which is part-time and full-time basis.

I think in principle or, the rules and regulations of the banks are almost accurate or sufficient for SG. In some cases, there might be some errors, but the framework is okay. We have Shariah council, we have manual, we have fatwas, we have Shariah technical committee, we have the manpower, we have a training center, and we train the manpower, on Shariah compliance on Shariah knowledge. We have a Shariah audit, we have a monitoring system, and we have a compliance system. All we have.. [SP#5]

All the Islamic banks do not mandatorily follow the practices of full-time *Shariah* secretariat which creates a gap between the SSB and management. Therefore, this issue is still controversial because some say if the *Shariah* secretariat is a fulltime member, then the management will try to pressurize and influence them.

But we have the gap between the SSB and management that there is no member who is full time for this bank. [SP#7] .... gaps are continuing like this way and it will not fill-up anymore, and it will be increased. [SP#7]

Every bank has its internal guidelines named 'internal control and compliance guideline' where they described *Shariah* guidelines very effectively and efficiently but in terms of *Shariah* audit, they explained slightly. Therefore, the respondent from the *Shariah* practitioners raised the question about, "*the Shariah principles have described everything completely but what we do*?" However, they do not follow *Shariah* principles in all aspects of SG (Alam *et al.*, 2020b). This is one of the limitations of regulatory monitoring and supervision. Thus, researchers recommended for external *Shariah* audit and review committee concerning Islamic banking in Bangladesh (Alam *et al.*, 2020e).

Every bank has its internal guideline which has been described the SG effectively and structured and there is no system in violating the rules and regulations but in the case of Shariah audit, everything has described floatingly. The depth of the guideline has not been addressed properly. [SP#6]

In addition, the central bank also promulgated some instructions, circulars, and guidelines for the development of overall banking and especially some guidelines for the Islamic banks' SG practices.

Rather than these, Bangladesh Bank sometimes provides some issues, guidelines, circulars, and letters for both types of banking, conventional and Shariah banking and some are only for the Islamic banks. The main thing this that there must be a necessity of framing governance; without governance, an institution cannot run in a mannered way, effective way and a good manner. [SP#9]

In Bangladesh, Islamic banks form their SSBs with a combination of bankers, lawyers, and Islamic economists which is absent in the global SG practices (Abdullah and Rahman, 2017).

In our country, the SSB is also included people of the other professions like the bankers, lawyers, economists preferably those who have Islamic backgrounds of the Shariah. So, this is about the importance of the Shariah regulation committee. [E#3]

Also, numerous voluntary organizations have been formed for monitoring and supervising the Islamic banks who guide and suggest them timely and deal with the corresponding authorities for the development of Islamic banks (Alam *et al.*, 2019; Abdullah and Rahman, 2017).

We see gradual development in the harmonization, uniformity or level of practice in Shariah governance. Moreover, there is a voluntary organization CSBIB, they are also helping these issues and some issues are also referred to them. So, that all banks can operate or practice uniformity. In addition to that, there is a forum like 'Islamic Bank Consultative Forum'. They also take care of every issue; they deal with the problems with the government, central bank and the other regulatory authorities. They also conducted seminars and discussions in this aspect. [E#5]

The CSBIB performs its role in the development of the overall banking and sometimes provides solutions referred by the central banks, courts, and Islamic banks.

"Though the CSBIB does not have the real power but when there is an issue from the court regarding the fatwa or Shariah or banking transaction then the court refers to the CSBIB for their opinion. Islamic banks calculate the Shariah non-compliance income based on the percentage of Shariah violation in a specific deal or investment. [E#5]

Compare to the global SG practices, one of the experts said that Bangladesh is not far behind the SG practices and quality of *Shariah* compliance. The quality of Islamic banking compliance is higher than other countries of the world, but Bangladesh must lack in *Shariah*-based transactions or the *Shariah* compliance products and *Shariah* related issues.

I feel we are not sourced country, or we are not lagging behind for compliance with Shariah. We are doing Islamic banking more compliant than any other country in the world. We are doing banking compliant with the Shariah but most importantly, we should think about the Shariah-based transaction or Shariah-based product and Shariah-based issues. We are more concerned about the Shariah-compliant transaction. [E#1]

Besides, respondents illustrate that Islamic banks are violating *Shariah* principles and practicing improper banking procedures. Islamic banks check *Shariah* principles in the product development and selling stage instead of an investment. The respondents illustrate that the present audit system is inappropriate and incomplete. Islamic banks do not disclose the *Shariah* non-compliance amount in their annual report. As the study of Hassan *et al.* (2017) reported that 55.56% of the IFIs do not disclose anything concerning SSB meeting and 66.67% reported nothing about the audit process and findings.

Just that they present a small report, but how they implement the Shariah rules and regulations in their functions is with no detailed information as a result of vague and irresponsible gaps that have been produced in some cases." [SP#7] "Reporting is the only indicator as to whether banks practice SG truly or not. ..... This is very small, and this report never disclosed any financial matter, whether it is Shariah-compliant or not? [E#4]

In Bangladesh, most of the *Shariah* violations have occurred in foreign transactions, investments, letter of credit, calculation of dollars, and investment rescheduling. Some of the banks are using their SSBs to make their profit maximization by the name of Islam (Alam *et al.*, 2020b).

In opening L/C, foreign currency transactions, dollar conversion rate, pre-assumed rate of dollar is not allowed in Shariah. [SP#7]

Moreover, the Islamic banking practices in Bangladesh are mainly dominated by the buy and sell mode which is diminishing the real beauty of Islamic finance. Therefore, it is urgently required to come out with more *Shariah* compliance products based on *Mudarabah* and *Musharakah* then the beauty of Islamic finance will be seen more rigorously in the view of customers.

If we concentrate only Shariah-compliant product which is mostly dominated by the buy mode, then we do not give the beauty of that Islamic finance. If you want to get the beauty of that Islamic banking, Islamic finance, then we should explore the Shariah-based product that is Mudarabah, Musharakah these issues. To get the Islamic or the beauty of the Islamic finance we should be concentrated or we should try to be Shariah-based product and in that case, we should popularize our Musharaka mode, Mudarabah mode and these modes for the investment part. [E#1]

In addition, Bangladesh does not have a separate Islamic banking law and a central *Shariah* regulatory authority (Alam *et al.*, 2020b; Hassan *et al.*, 2017), which are the fundamental difference compare to the global practices.

Maybe they need to do the Shariah law. So, this is the very difference between Bangladesh and other countries. [E#4]

Furthermore, one of the *Shariah* experts opined that the global practice of SG is a better and higher standard than Bangladesh due to the two main reasons such as higher quality people in the academic and practical field which are entirely absent in Bangladesh (Alam *et al.*, 2019; Alam *et al.*, 2020b). In Malaysia, they have a professional course and degrees in academic and professional life that is why their market growth is higher than we are (Abdullah and Rahman, 2017).

Global practice is much better and high standard than Bangladesh. Why are there high standard people? Because their academic life has similarities with practical life. There is a great similarity between the two lives. But in our country, major problems are that Islamic banking and finance is absent in academic life. If there have that it is limited to one or two courses or one or two classes regarding this but likely Malaysia there have the scope of opportunity to study 3 to 4 years in Islamic banking and finance. That's why they are becoming masters but, in our country, we do not have any courses in our universities. This issue should flourish. [SP#9]

In contrast, the functions of Islamic banks in Bangladesh are more targeted and concerned about Corporate Social Responsibility (CSR) functions. Islamic banks are engaged in more social functions such as tree plantation, study scholarship, orientation program, zakat management and so on. The following response has been outlined below:

Islamic banks CSR much more focused and much more targeted. [RA31]

Finally, this research found that Islamic banks in Bangladesh are more flexible in preparing SG guidelines. Bangladesh is far behind from the research compare to Malaysia and lack of academic courses.

5. CONCLUSION AND RECOMMENDATIONS

Islamic banks in Bangladesh are performing better as for self-developed SG guidelines. Islamic banks are unable to completely follow the *Shariah* principles due to the dual banking system of the country and intention of the BOD and management. In Bangladesh, Islamic banks are broadly engaged with CSR and social functions.

This chapter has outlined the uniqueness, limitations, and consequences of the existing SG of the Islamic banks in Bangladesh which will be more interesting for the global Islamic financial institutions. As the current system is not comprehensive, the regulatory authorities can formulate a complete SG guideline for the development of the Islamic banks by maintaining a global standard. The findings will be beneficial for the regulatory authorities to overcome these limitations of the current practices. The central bank can implement the policy guidelines provided by IFSB to modify or propose a comprehensive SG guideline for Islamic banks in Bangladesh. The regulatory authority can strongly suggest following the guidelines of AAOIFI in the individual practices of SG by Islamic banks.

Our study was limited to the Islamic banks in Bangladesh rather than other countries such as Malaysia, Pakistan, and Indonesia, as well as the Gulf countries such as Saudi Arabia, Qatar, and Iran, which are also practicing dual banking (conventional and Islamic banking). Besides, we did not include Islamic insurance companies in Bangladesh. We are recommending future researchers to examine a comparative study among the SG models in qualitative or quantitative to evaluate the SG quality, indebtedness, and comprehensiveness as well as its application in ascertaining the *Shariah* compliance.

DISCLAIMER

The contents and views of this chapter are expressed by the authors in their personal capacities. It is not necessary for the Editor and the Publisher to agree with these viewpoints and they are not responsible for any duty of care in this regard.

ACKNOWLEDGMENT

The authors extend sincere gratitude to:

- The Editor-in-Chief and International Editorial Advisory Board (IEAB) of this book who initially desk reviewed, arranged a rigorous double/triple blind review process and conducted a thorough, minute and critical final review before accepting the chapter for publication.
- All anonymous reviewers who provided very constructive feedbacks for thorough revision, improvement, extension and finetuning of the chapter.
- All colleagues, assistants and well-wishers who assisted the authors to complete this task.

REFERENCES

Abdel-Magid, M. F. (1981). The theory of Islamic banking: Accounting implications. *The International Journal of Accounting*, *17*(1), 79–102.

Abdullah, M. F., & Rahman, A. (2017). Shari'ah governance of Islamic banks in Bangladesh issues and challenges. *Journal of Islamic Economics. Banking and Finance*, *13*(3), 82–94.

Adam, M. & Muizzuddin. (2020). Banking Governance: Perspective of Islamic Banking. In *Growth and Emerging Prospects of International Islamic Banking* (pp. 263-277). IGI Global.

Ahmad, A. U. F., Rashid, M., & Shahed, A. K. M. (2014). Perception of bankers and customers towards deposit and investment mechanisms of Islamic and conventional banking: Empirical evidence from Bangladesh. *Journal of Islamic Business and Management*, *4*(2), 91–114. doi:10.12816/0019145

Ahmed, M., & Khatun, M. (2013). The compliance with *Shariah* governance system of AAOIFI : A Study on Islamic Banks Bangladesh Introduction. *Journal of Islamic Economics, Banking and Finance*, *9*(3), 177–191.

Alam, M. K. (2021). A systematic qualitative case study: Questions, data collection, NVivo analysis and saturation. *Qualitative Research in Organizations and Management*. Advance online publication. doi:10.1108/QROM-09-2019-1825

Alam, M. K., Ahmad, A. U. F., & Muneeza, A. (2020e). External Sharī'ah Audit andReview Committee vis-a-vis Sharī'ah Compliance Quality and Accountability: A Case of Islamic Banks in Bangladesh. *Journal of Public Affairs, 2364*, 1–10. doi:10.1002/pa.2364

Alam, M. K., Miah, M. S., Siddiquii, N., & Hossain, M. I. (2020c). The Influences of board of directors and management in *Shariah* governance guidelines of the Islamic banks in Bangladesh. *Journal of Islamic Accounting and Business Research, 11*(9), 1633–1647. doi:10.1108/JIABR-08-2019-0155

Alam, M. K., Mustafa, H., Uddin, M. S., Islam, M. J., Mohua, M. J., & Hassan, M. F. (2020b). Problems of *Shariah* Governance Framework and Its Mechanisms: An Empirical Investigation of Islamic banks in Bangladesh. *Journal of Asian Finance, Economics and Business*, *7*(3), 265–276. doi:10.13106/jafeb.2020.vol7.no3.265

Alam, M. K., Rahman, S. A., Mustafa, H., Shah, S. M., & Hossain, M. S. (2019). *Shariah* governance framework of Islamic banks in Bangladesh: Practices, problems and recommendations. *Asian Economic and Financial Review*, *9*(1), 118–132. doi:10.18488/journal.aefr.2019.91.118.132

Alam, M. K., Rahman, S. A., Thakur, O. A., Bashir, M. A., & Hosen, S. (2020a). The reasons behind the absence of a comprehensive *Shariah* governance framework for the Islamic banks in Bangladesh. *International Journal of Economics and Business Administration.*, *8*(1), 134–145.

Alam, M. K., Tabash, M. I., Thakur, O. A., Sahabuddin, M., Hosen, S., & Hassan, M. F. (2020d). A central *Shariah* regulatory authority for the Islamic banks in Bangladesh: Legalization or formation. *Journal of Asian Finance. Economics and Business*, *7*(1), 91–100.

Alamgir, M. (2016). An analysis of Islamic banking activities in Bangladesh: Issues and challenges. *Thoughts on Economics, 25*(3-4), 29-58.

Bangladesh Bank. (2009). *Guideline for conducting Islamic banking.* Bangladesh Bank. Retrieved from https://www.bb.org.bd/aboutus/regulationguideline/islamicbanking/ islamicguide.php

Bangladesh Bank. (2019). *Bangladesh Bank quarterly report on 'Developments of Islamic Banking in Bangladesh' January-March, 2019*. Bangladesh Bank.

Berg, B. L., & Lune, H. (2007). *Qualitative research methods for the social sciences*. Pearson.

Braun, V., & Clarke, V. (2006). Using thematic analysis in psychology. *Qualitative Research in Psychology*, *3*(2), 77–101. doi:10.1191/1478088706qp063oa

Bryman, A., & Bell, E. (2003). *Business research methods*. Oxford University Press.

Dane, F. C. (1990). *Research Methods*. Brooks/Cole Publishing.

Dusuki, A. W. (2011). *Islamic Financial Systems: Principles and Operations*. ISRA.

Gibbs, G. (2002). *Qualitative data analysis: explorations with NVivo*. Open University.

Gillham, B. (2000). *Developing a questionnaire*. Continuum.

Ginena, K., & Hamid, A. (2015). *Foundations of Shari'ah governance of Islamic banks*. John Wiley & Sons.

Hassan, M. K., Ullah, M. H., & Khanam, R. (2017). Shariah governance practices in Bangladesh. In N. Ali (Ed.), Shariah Governance Systems and Practices in a Globalized World. Academic Press.

Hassan, R., Abdullah, N. I., Hassan, A., Ibrahim, U., & Sawari, M. F. M. (2011). A comparative analysis of Shariah governance in Islamic banking institutions across jurisdictions. Kuala Lumpur: ISRA.

Hossain, M. M. (2012). Financial statements of banks under Islamic *Shariah*: Status of regulatory compliance. *Thoughts on Economics*, *22*(1), 53–67.

IFSB. (2009). *Guiding principles on Shari'ah governance systems for institutions offering Islamic financial services*. Islamic Financial Services Board.

Islamic, B. M. B. (2011). *Global Islamic Finance Report (GIFR) (2011)*. BMB.

Joffe, H., & Yardley, L. (2004). *Content and thematic analysis. Research methods for clinical and health psychology*. Sage.

Khan, M. (1994). *Accounting issues and concepts for Islamic banking*. Paper presented at the International Conference on Developing Accounting Standards for Islamic Banks, London, UK.

Kvale, S. (1996). *Interviews: an introduction to qualitative research interviewing*. Sage.

Merriam, S. B. (2009). *Qualitative research: A guide to design and implementation*. Jossey-Bass.

MinhasI. (2012). *Shari'ah governance model (SGM) and its four basic Pillars*. Islamic Finance News Malaysia Published by Red Money Publication. Retrieved from https://ssrn.com/abstract=2153106

Nomran, N. M., & Haron, R. (2020). Shari'ah Governance for Islamic Banking: Evidence from Diverse Regulatory Environments. In A. Rafay (Ed.), *Growth and Emerging Prospects of International Islamic Banking* (pp. 213–244). IGI Global. doi:10.4018/978-1-7998-1611-9.ch012

Noordin, N. H., & Kassim, S. (2019). Does *Shariah* committee composition influence *Shariah* governance disclosure? *Journal of Islamic Accounting and Business Research*, *10*(2), 158–184. doi:10.1108/JIABR-04-2016-0047

Patton, M. Q. (2002). *Qualitative research and evaluation methods*. SAGE publications.

Perves, M. M. (2015). Legal and regulatory framework in Islamic banking system: Bangladesh perspective. *European Journal of Business and Management*, *7*(21), 179–188.

Rafay, A. (Ed.). (2020a). *HandBook of Research on Theory and Practice of Global Islamic Finance*. IGI Global. doi:10.4018/978-1-7998-0218-1

Rafay, A. (Ed.). (2020b). *Growth and Emerging Prospects of International Islamic Banking*. IGI Global. doi:10.4018/978-1-7998-1611-9

Rafay, A., & Farid, S. (2018). Shariah Supervisory Board Report (SSBR) in Islamic Banks: An experimental study of Investors' perception and behaviour. *International Journal of Islamic and Middle Eastern Finance and Management*, *11*(2), 274–296. doi:10.1108/IMEFM-07-2017-0180

RahmanJ. M. (2014). *Cost-Benefit analysis of implementing Shari'ah auditing as a separate discipline in Bangladeshi Islamic banks*. doi:10.2139srn.2538590

Saunders, M., Lewis, P., & Thornhill, A. (2007). *Research methods for business students*. Prentice Hall.

Sekaran, U., & Bougie, R. (2016). *Research methods for business: A skill building approach*. John Wiley & Sons.

Sohrabuddin, S. M., Zoynul Abedin, M., & Afroz, N. (2020). Islamic Financial Inclusion: An Alternative Approach to Reach the Unbanked of Bangladesh. In A. Rafay (Ed.), *Growth and Emerging Prospects of International Islamic Banking* (pp. 155–173). IGI Global.

Strauss, A. L. (1987). *Qualitative analysis for social scientists*. Cambridge University Press. doi:10.1017/CBO9780511557842

Ullah, M. H. (2014). Shari'ah compliance in Islamic banking - An empirical study on selected Islamic banks in Bangladesh. *International Journal of Islamic and Middle Eastern Finance and Management*, *7*(2), 182–199. doi:10.1108/IMEFM-06-2012-0051

Ullah, M. H., & Khanam, R. (2018). Whether *Shariah* compliance efficiency a matter for the financial performance: The case of Islami Bank Bangladesh Limited. *Journal of Islamic Accounting and Business Research*, *9*(2), 183–200. doi:10.1108/JIABR-01-2016-0001

Ullah, M. H., Khanam, R., & Tasnim, T. (2018). Comparative compliance status of AAOIFI and IFSB standards: An empirical evidence from Islami Bank Bangladesh Limited. *Journal of Islamic Accounting and Business Research*, *9*(4), 607–628. doi:10.1108/JIABR-11-2014-0040

Weischedel, B., Matear, S., & Deans, K. (2005). A Qualitative Approach to Investigating Online Strategic Decision Making. *Qualitative Market Research*, *8*(1), 61–76. doi:10.1108/13522750510575444

Chapter 12
Fraud Risk Management in Banks:
An Overview of Failures and Best Practices

Abhishek Sinha
https://orcid.org/0000-0001-6604-5461
Department of Finance, IBS Hyderabd, India

ABSTRACT

White collar crimes refer to the criminal activities by a professional holding a responsible position in the organization. Banking frauds are one of the most pronounced forms of white collar crimes. These frauds impact the reputation of the bank and also effects its financial sustainability. The chapter entails the frauds that happen in banks and identifies reasons for the failure of banks to prevent such frauds. The author pinpoints the best practices in developing fraud prevention frameworks and emphasizes the importance of corporate governance in preventing such frauds. Best practices and future trends are also identified that are important to prevent and detect banking frauds.

INTRODUCTION

White Collar Crimes refers to criminal activities involving a professional holding a responsible position in the organization (Strader, 2011). Most of these crimes involve experts who have been given fair autonomy to make decisions, which may impact the reputation risk of the entity whom the professional represents. Essentially

DOI: 10.4018/978-1-7998-8758-4.ch012

these events do not cause physical harm to anyone, however, it may lead to material economic losses to the affected party. In the case of banks, there is also a risk of the economy being impacted by these crimes.

Most of the white-collar crimes take time to be unearthed and proved because they involve professionals who yield enormous power within the organization where they commit the crime. They are also aware of the weakness and loophole in the risk management system and they exploit it to the best of their abilities. This generally creates a fear in the minds of the victims and tarnishes the reputation of the organization. The tarnished image may then materialize into the business loss. White Collar Crimes are committed by people who are involved in otherwise, lawful businesses and covers a wide range of activities. (Sutherland, 1983).

The perpetrators hold respectable positions in the communities unless their crime is discovered. The laws relating to white-collar crimes depends upon the exact nature of the crime committed.

Following are the different category of white-collar crimes:

Fraud by Employees

It refers to the process of circumventing the risk management mechanism in a business organization to profit from it. This is generally tantamount to breach of trust and due to opaqueness in the functioning of banks, it is difficult to detect them before some material harm has already been done.

Blackmail

Blackmail means demand for money by threatening some person to cause physical injury or exposing his secrets. In the banks, there are very few instances of such frauds. Hence, this kind of fraud is outside the scope of the book.

Bribery

It is the process of offering money to influence the judgment of the professional holding discretionary power in the organization. This leads to partisan behaviour and unduly influences the decision- making process and hence is categorized as a crime. Such crimes are typically a function of the culture existing in the organisation. Over the years, an increase in the level of automation has increased transparency and hence reduced instances of bribery.

Digital Fraud

Frauds involving technologically induced malpractices leading to a financial burden for the aggrieved party are known as a digital fraud. Digital frauds incidences are increasing. It can be attributed to the exponential rate of change in the industry and the vulnerability of digital platforms to security. Digital fraud also has the potential to retard the rate at which the fintech industry is growing. Hence, it is important to curb such incidents.

Embezzlement

It refers to the process where a person who has been entrusted with money or power of attorney misappropriates it without the permission of the authorized party. As can be seen in the Karvy scam in the Indian stock markets. In the Karvy Scam which happened in January 2020, a group of employees of the company used Power of Attorney (PoA) given to the company by the investors and transferred the shares from the investors' account to another account and then pledged Rs. 2,300 crore worth of shares of over 95,000 clients as collateral to get loans from banks and National Banking Financial Corporation (NBFCs) by pretending that the shares belonged to the company.

Extortion

The process of illegally acquiring the property of a person without the permission of the individual. This generally involves an individual who can influence the law enforcement bodies in a country. The banking sector is generally not impacted by the instances of such crime.

Insider-Trading

This refers to the phenomenon where an employee of the entity trades in the market using price sensitive information not available in the public domain. The information asymmetry that exists in case of confidential information and the agency problem are the main factors that lead to this kind of insider trading.

Tax Fraud

When a company or an individual through scrupulous means avoids paying taxes to the local or central authorities in a country it tantamount to tax fraud. This could lead to huge penalties and cause a liquidity problem for the company in question.

For the uninitiated, it is important to note that white-collar crimes have a rippling effect hence could create systemic risk. Thus, it is of utmost importance for risk managers to reduce or negate the occurrence of such incidents to improve the overall efficiency and efficacy at the operational level (Rafay, Sadiq & Mohsan, 2016). The scope of this chapter is restricted to fraud in banks.

FRAUD - DEFINITION

"A deliberate act of omission or commission by any person carried out in the course of a banking transaction or the books of accounts maintained manually or under computer system in banks, resulting into wrongful gain to any person for A temporary period or otherwise, with or without any monetary loss to the bank" – Fraud as defined by Reserve Bank of India

Frauds are thus, events that have a colossal impact on the financial system of the country depending on the size and extent of the fraud conducted. Depending on the type of fraud, fraud can be high frequency or low-frequency events.

Furthermore, it tarnishes the reputation of the organization and impacts the future business prospects of the company. For banks, the raw material is cash, work in process is cash and the final product is also cash. This leads to higher expected returns in the form of one of the most liquid assets – cash at a given level of risk for fraudsters. Hence, there is a higher probability of a person who is acquainted with the flaws of the system to leverage the opportunity.

One major reason for banks' inability to prevent frauds from occurring, stems from banks having a higher level of opaqueness compared to other industries. Due to the size and complexity of operations in the banking industry, frauds occur and at times grow without the risk management system detecting it. Most of these frauds are triggered internally. Furthermore, many times frauds are also a function of internal collusion. Thus, there is a need to create an organizational culture that aims at preventing such frauds.

WHY DO FRAUDS HAPPEN?

Frauds are risk management failures, and these failures are generally man-made (Banerjee, 2015; Ramamoorti, 2008; Hubbard, 2014). As frauds are risk management failures and are manmade it is important to delve deeper and understand why they occur:

Figure 1. Motives for Frauds
Source: Author (2020)

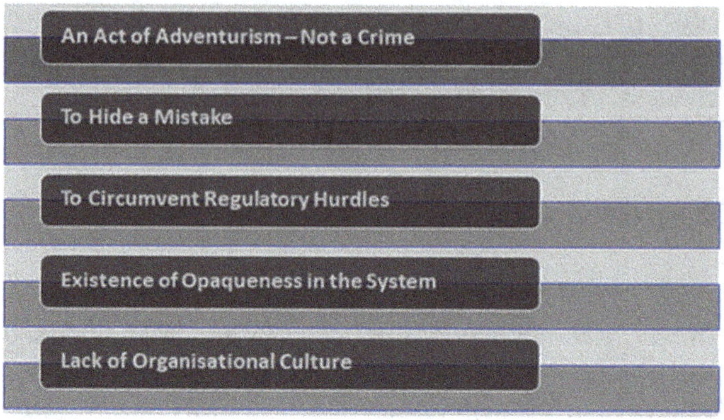

To Hide a Mistake

Frauds often start with an operational manager entering a wrong transaction inadvertently and then the manager trying to camouflage his mistake. In the process, he discovers lacuna in the system which enables him to beat the system and so higher profitability for the company and hence pocket higher returns.

An Act of Adventurism – Not a Crime

Too many white collared managers, it appears that this kind of fraudulent activity is a way of getting their dues from the company. They also argue that it has only economic implications and does not cause physical harm to anybody, hence it is alright to indulge in such crimes.

To Circumvent Regulatory Hurdles

Many a time these crimes are committed to circumventing regulatory hurdles that stand in the way of maximizing profits of the organization. This increased profit also leads to increased incentives for the individuals involved. The common retort here is to break the regulatory system to allow the free-market forces to maximize returns.

Existence of Opaqueness in the System

At times operational managers can create opaqueness and hence beat the system. This is a failure of the risk management system that exists in the organization and there should be an effort to prevent people from creating opaqueness around their roles to prevent such failures.

Lack of Organisational Culture

There is often a lack of organizational culture that promotes risk management and fraud detection. The organization culture at times promotes aggressive reporting and risk-taking and the risk managers are left with no choice but to accept the excess risk the company is taking or to part ways. This creates a system that is bound to fail (Khanna & Arora, 2009).

CASES – FAILURE OF TWO BANKS

Frauds happen and they cause considerable losses to the affected parties. Here is an effort to understand a few cases of fraud that have shaken the financial system in recent times.

Punjab National Bank (PNB) (India)

In 1895, history was created, when for the first time a bank was formed solely with Indian capital. The bank which grew through acquisitions and became one of the largest players to reckon with in the Indian banking space was nationalized in 1969. Over the years Punjab National Bank has grown to become the second-largest public sector bank in India. As of June 2019, the bank serviced 115 million strong clienteles through more than 7,000 branches. The table below shows for the period 2009-2019 how Punjab National Bank has emerged as the largest breeding ground for fraud in India in terms of value. In terms of the number of frauds, the bank accounts for only 3% of the total frauds. However, in terms of the value of frauds in the given period in India, the bank accounts significantly by contributing around 15% of the total value of frauds.

The value of the Nirav Modi scam has dented the reputation of the bank. Hence, it is important to deep dive and draws valuable lessons from the scam (The Economic Times, 2018).

What Happened?

Nirav Modi, a leading jeweler who had a global presence allegedly acquired fraudulent letters of undertaking from Brady House branch (a branch that catered exclusively

Table 1. Frauds by Banks - India (2009-2019)

Bank	No. of Frauds	In %	Value of Frauds (Rs. Cr.)	In %
Punjab National Bank	2,047	3.8%	28,700.74	14.0%
State Bank of India (SBI)	6,793	12.7%	23,734.74	11.6%
Bank of Baroda	2,160	4.0%	12,962.96	6.3%
Indian Overseas Bank	1,115	2.1%	12,644.70	6.2%
Bank of India	1,872	3.5%	12,358.20	6.0%
Central Bank	1,613	3.0%	9041.98	4.4%
IDBI Bank	1,264	2.4%	9041.98	4.4%
Syndicate Bank	1,783	3.3%	5830.85	2.8%
Oriental Bank of Commerce	1040	1.9%	5,598.23	2.7%
Canara Bank	1,254	2.4%	5553.38	2.7%
Axis Bank	1,944	3.6%	5,301.69	2.6%
ICICI Bank	6,811	12.8%	5,033	2.5%
United Bank of India	944	1.8%	3052.34	1.5%
Standard Chartered Bank	1,263	2.4%	1221.41	0.6%
HDFC Bank	2,497	4.7%	1,200.79	0.6%
Rest of India	18,954	35.5%	63,723	31.1%
India	**53,354**	**100.0%**	**205,000**	**100.0%**

Source: (Reserve Bank of India, 2019)

to the mid-sized corporates) of Punjab National Bank for overseas credit from other Indian lenders in Mumbai.

In the words of PNB "It was found through SWIFT trail that one 'junior level' branch official unauthorizedly and fraudulently issued Letter of Undertakings (LoUs) on behalf of some companies belonging to Nirav Modi Group viz. Solar Exports, Stellar Diamonds, and Diamond R US for availing buyers' credit from overseas branches of Indian banks."

For the uninitiated, Punjab National Bank issued a Letter of Undertakings that were issued by the bank on behalf of subsidiaries of the Nirav Modi Group. The letters were written with the intent to enable the client to secure the vendor's credit. These letters were issued by the chief protagonist. He was able to raise INR 30000 million from banks through rolling over the same Letters of Understanding many times.

17 banks lent money to different firms associated with Nirav Modi. Besides PNB, other lenders on the list included Allahabad Bank IDBI Bank, Central Bank of India, Dena Bank, Vijaya Bank, Bank of India, Syndicate Bank, Oriental Bank

of Commerce and Union Bank of India. These lenders relied on the LoUs that was issued by Punjab National Bank.

The red flags that were ignored are:

- The letter of credit was issued by the bank without any collateral. In other words, they were an unsecured letter of credit issued by the bank.
- An employee who had not been transferred for the last seven years was able to commit the crime with abatement from select few confides. The risk management mandates the regular transfer of employees who are in roles which have client exposure. Moreover, it is also advisable to send employees to mandatory15 days' vacation.
- The executive in question was a junior level official and it was surprising that he was not questioned by any of his superiors.
- The risk management team failed to ensure basic checks.
- Some lapses could not be pardoned. Two employees were able to bypass the security and issue payment instruction through the NEFT system.
- This shows that there was no attempt to reconcile the balances of the core system with the NEFT System.
- As the total Letter of Understanding (LOU) has a limit of USD 20 million it can be assumed that there was more than one LOU raised in the given period.
- According to experts such lapses can be committed as there are no checks when data is entered into NEFT. However, reconciliation should have helped find such mismatches.

Financial Implications

The financial implication of such frauds cannot be determined in a hurry. This is because these frauds have a cascading impact on the parties which have given loans to the company based on Letter of Understanding (LoUs) by PNB. As it turns out, investors are paying through their nose as fresh details emerge in the PNB fraud case with each passing day. The alleged fraudulent transactions as disclosed by Punjab National Bank (PNB) earlier this week are pegged at Rs 11,400 crore. But this has so far knocked off nearly Rs 15,000 crore in market capitalization of companies or lenders that are linked to the entire saga some way or the other (The Economic Times, 2018; Khanna & Arora, 2009).

Commonwealth Bank (Australia) (CBA)

The Commonwealth Bank of Australia (CBA) is the largest financial services entity listed in the Australian bourses. The company has a presence in the Australian subcontinent, Asia and England and the United States. The bank started its operation as a public sector bank in 1911, however, it was privatized 85 years after being incorporated. It is one of the four pillars on which the financial system of Australia stands. Founded in 1911 by the Australian government and fully privatized in 1996, the Commonwealth Bank is one of the "big four" Australian banks, with National Australia Bank (NAB), ANZ and Westpac. The bank listed on the Australian Stock Exchange in 1991.

Commonwealth Bank is a leading Australian bank that saw an unprecedented fall in its numbers because of risk management failures. Risk management is generally manmade and the evidence of the same can also be found in the case of Commonwealth Bank. It appears as if the failure is systemic that is the inefficiency in the risk management system flew from top to bottom (Maddock, 2018).

What Happened?

The bank while announcing its 2018 six-monthly results conceded that it had failed to follow regulations required to ensure the plugging of anti-money laundering. This led to the bank anticipating a fine in presenting its 2018 half-yearly profits. The bank decided to keep a provision of AUD 375 million as fine. According to experts, equity investors in the bank will be impacted with lower earnings in the next few years because there is an urgent need to plug the operational risk management failure. The estimated cost of plugging the gaping hole in risk management is estimated at AUD 500 million. These estimates were made earlier however were not executed due to the lack of commitment by the top management of the bank (Australian Financial Review, 2018).

One of the major reasons that can be attributed to this phenomenon is the failure of information technology. This is expected to lead to an increased informational technology cost in the short term. The company's overdependence on "RiskinSite" seemed to have led to its debacle. The application was supposed to track the status of issues and incidents of risk management lases. However, due to its limited capabilities, the system failed miserably. Hence, the bank had to go for a completely new system.

The total penalty that the company is supposed to pay is more than AUD 1.2 billion. The most shocking observation in the whole episode seems to be the complete ignorance of the APRA directives by CBA. The incidence of violating regulations had increased considerably since 2011. The failure was top-down. According to experts, if the board of directors had taken risk management seriously such incidents could have been completely avoided. The blame also fell on the accountability and remuneration committee for not being strict in adherence to the guideline. There was a lack of organizational culture that could take cognizance of the transactions that were taking place.

What Went Wrong?

In hindsight, it has been observed that it was the culture of the organization that was to be blamed for the debacle. According to the regulators following are the major cultural factors that led to the debacle.

Too Big to Fail

There was a consensus within the organization that the bank was too big to fail. This led to complacency among its employees. This was all-pervasive and could be observed at all levels in the organization. The top-level management felt that the bank was well run and there was no need to consider any of the non-financial risks as the bank was conservative in risk-taking. The bankers were inclined on following the processes without having the end goal in sight. This was true at all levels.

Lack of Proactivity

For any growing organization of the size of the CAB, there must be a proactive approach to managing risk. However, in the case of the bank, it was quite contrary. In the dealings with the regulators, the bank was reactive most of the time. They were slow to respond to any queries and they seemed to be trying to satisfy the regulators rather than plug the hole in their system. This along with the too big to fail syndrome was a potent mixture and had a cascading impact on the risk culture of the company.

Absence of Feedback Loop

There was no attempt by the bank management to identify pain points in the system and work towards removing it. This made the organization insular. There was no mechanism of recording failures and disseminating it across teams to prevent future failures.

There was no attempt to get the bigger picture right. Everyone seemed to be running to stand still. Coupled with the absence of risk intelligence among decision-makers in the organization there was a complete disconnect in terms of processes and outcomes. This impacted the risk culture negatively.

Absence of Whistle-Blowers

As already mentioned, there was a sense of complacency and reactivity in the environment. This led to the absence of constructive criticism and there was no one to raise issues about the flouting of processes within the organization. No one seemed to be interested in the bigger picture. There was no one to take accountability of risk issues within the organization. If there was a failure in risk management, the same was readily discounted and ignored due to the "good intentions of the manager" in question.

Lack of Corporate Governance

Most of the board of directors had exceeded their terms and were now more a part of management rather than custodians appointed to protect the interest of the investors. As the bank had not been impacted by the sub-prime crisis of 2008 there was a sense of complacency among the board members. At the time of the scam, it was observed that two of its directors had held their positions for more than 5 years which was not at all acceptable.

Lessons from the Two Failures

Both the white-collared crimes impacted the reputation of the banking sector globally. The role of risk managers involved was questioned and there was a loss of customer faith. Both the failures had something in common. They were manmade and involved the absence of risk management culture in the organizations. Hence, these frauds could have been avoided if the banks had built a culture of getting the bigger picture right in terms of risk management. Hence the lesson drawn from these failures is hinged on developing a risk intelligent banking system that prevents individuals from taking advantage of the loopholes in the system and causing debacle.

The chapter now delves into methods of developing a risk management culture within organizations.

FRAUD AND FRAUD RISK MANAGEMENT

According to the results of a global survey conducted by KPMG on fraud in May 2019, it was established that banking frauds are on the rise. Hence, efforts should be made to manage the risk that arises out of fraud (KPMG, 2019). Furthermore, the losses from fraud are way higher than the amount spent on managing fraud risk. In Europe alone, the size of total fraud in 2019 has been estimated at 1.8 billion Euros according to the European Central Bank. In Asia, according to the Experian Report on Bank Frauds 2019, half of the banks surveyed had seen a growth in the incidence and magnitude of the fraud. In Africa, the main economies of the region suffer from the menace and are trying hard to find a solution to the problem. The situation is said to be grim globally as approximately 55 per cent of the companies surveyed faced a growing risk of financial fraud. With increased technological advancement and tightening regulatory norms, it has become imperative that the banks should not take these incidents lightly.

However, it should be noted that it might not be possible to determine the magnitude of fraud at a given time because banks many a time are reluctant to divulge the details due to the impact of fraud on its reputation. Furthermore, it also impacts the effectiveness and efficiency of the underlined process due to increased checks and balances. Thus, frauds have a cascading impact and may also lead to an adverse impact on the morale of the employees. It also may cause banks not paying the amount of money on time.

Traditionally, a lot of importance has been laid down on auditing processes to detect frauds, however, it is not enough and hence the focus is gradually shifting towards preventing the frauds from occurring rather than assessing and reducing the damage (Khan *et al.*, 2020). To reduce fraudulent incidents in the future the company should focus on fraud risk management. The way ahead is to develop a "risk intelligent" banking environment with minimum tolerance towards fraud.

Developing a Strong Fraud Risk Management System

The way ahead is to develop a strong fraud risk management system. Following are the factors that would play an important role in detecting and preventing frauds:

Corporate Governance and Fraud Risk Management

The intent to create a fraud-free environment should come from the board of directors. The board of director's help must create an environment, where tolerance towards deviation in following risk management protocol is low. Hence, there should be policies and framework in place to help create an environment which shows an intent to help reduce frauds through a proactive and dynamic system.

The following are the steps that can be taken by the banks to develop a more efficient corporate governance structure. It should be noted that the role of the board of directors will be very important in the whole process. A proper corporate governance structure begins with the board of directors, whose job is to:

Create an Environment Which Promotes Business Ethics

Business Ethics or constructive criticism of processes that lack business ethics is of prima facie importance for any organization. The risk of a bank increases exponentially in cases where there is a lack of business ethics. If the employees do not understand the importance of such behaviour, most of the time it is the top management that needs to be blamed. Aggressive selling and creating spurious assets along with large scale deviations from pre-determined risk management can be all attributed to the absence of business ethics in the organization. Business ethics can be imbibed in the culture of the organization by awarding the employees whistleblowing and pointing out anomalies in risk management processes.

Define the Meaning and Build a Framework to Identify Fraud Risks

It is important to define the meaning of fraud consistently for the whole organization. Care should be taken by the board to ensure that there are no cases of deviations in identifying frauds. As has been the case many times, a subjective view is taken of the definition of fraud and sighting the good intention of the banker involved he can continue his practices without any punitive action. Hence it is important to define the frauds objectively.

Once, the fraud has been identified it is important for the board to initiate a framework for identifying fraud risks. This process of identifying fraud risks should be consistent throughout the organization and steps should be taken to prevent a lack of adherence to the process of identifying fraud risks. The whole organization should be aware of the framework and there should be no attempt to circumvent processes in place. This can be assured only if the top-level management is aware and willing to prevent deviations in the framework. The board of directors must play the role of custodians and prevent and mitigate incidents of fraud in the bank.

Retain Control of the Fraud Risk Assessment Process

The fraud risk assessment process should be controlled by the committee appointed and reporting directly to the board of directors. Hence, the fraud risk assessment process should be in direct control of the board of directors. The board of directors should be informed as a matter of practice of any increase in incidences of fraud risk across its branches and functional areas. There should be red flags raised at an appropriate juncture to prevent the snowballing of such incidents. The Chief Risk Officer should be involved in the whole process and he should be reporting directly to the board of directors to prevent frequent aberrations from the set policies due to pressure from operations managers and decision-makers within the organization. This is important and should be followed by a feedback mechanism that needs to be developed by the chief risk officer in cognizance with the board of directors.

Develop a Feedback Loop for Preventing Future Incidents

Any risk intelligent organization needs to keep improving its practices by identifying the key risk management failures and quickly disseminating the same to the operations managers to prevent occurrences of such incidents in the future. To achieve the above objective, it is prudent to have an official feedback loop that aims at preventing future incidents and makes the organization risk intelligence at all levels. The same cannot be achieved if the top-level managers are not involved in the whole process. Hence this feedback loop should mandate the involvement of the board of directors.

Oversee Internal Controls Established by Management

The success of the internal control mechanism to a great extent depends on the ability of the top management's ability to create awareness and ensure strict adherence to the same. The challenge for most of the banks emanates due to their sheer size and number of employees who need to be monitors regularly. Hence without having a culture, it would be impossible to arrest or reduce incidents about risk. It is important to spell out at every level the steps that the bank should be taken in case there is a deviation reported. Such policies need to be adhered to without exception and any intervention from the operations manager.

Set the Appropriate Tone at the Top

The appropriate tone needs to be created at the top and once the tone is created it becomes very easy for the risk management team to control such incidents of fraud. However, if the top-level management is complacent and does not realize the importance of creating a risk intelligent fraud-free organization it would be practically impossible for the risk managers to deliver. The best way to set a tone is to prevent the biases that exist in the system from impacting the process of decision making. It is important to provide autonomy to the risk managers and prevent any form of manual intervention from impacting the fraud detection process.

Outsourcing Risk Management Function Where Necessary

In areas where the bank does not have the expertise and is not able to develop expertise in a short time, it is important to outsource risk management function. In case of frauds if the bank cannot automate the process however the top management feels it is important to outsource risk management function the same needs to be outsourced and the chief risk officer should have control over the implementation of the process.

Provide for External Auditors' Evidence of Active Involvement

External risk auditors should be appointed. These auditors should mandate and establish the extent to which top-level management is involved in the process of risk management. The same should be reported to the board of directors. Increased incidence of lack of involvement of top management should be reported immediately to the board of directors so that they can take remedial actions. It is critical to understand that most of the frauds trigger due to callousness of the top-level management and the same can be arrested with the help of experts.

Awareness of Latest Risk Management Practices

The board of directors must be aware of the latest risk management practices. If the board of directors is not aware of the nitty and gritty involved in the risk management process it becomes difficult for them to keep a tab on the process. Hence, banks should have on their board at least one director who is aware of the nuances of risk management. He should be mandated to set a tone for developing awareness about the risk management practices in the country.

FACTORS THAT DETERMINE THE SUCCESS OF FRAUDS DETECTION AND MANAGEMENT

Once the tone is set at the top it is important to take care of the following factors to ensure the success of risk management practices.

The Autonomy of a Risk Manager

The manager should have enough autonomy to make decisions that are important to curb risk. It is also critical to ensure that the risk managers report directly to the Board of Directors to prevent any coercion from top-level executive managers in case they have colluded to commit the fraud. A risk manager's success depends on his ability to develop an organization that understands the importance of risk. For, achieving the goal he needs to support the top management. The top management should provide enough autonomy to the risk managers to achieve the goal. In many organizations that are aggressive in acquiring clients, risk managers are habituated to creating systems that no one follows. They are akin to toothless tigers and their job is to ensure that regulators do not question. Such systems are created to camouflage risk instead of managing them, hence the success of risk management depends on the autonomy of the risk managers.

Strategic Intent and Anti-Fraud Strategies

Banks should have in place long term strategies to combat fraud. These strategies should be aimed at reducing the incidence of fraud in the long run. They should be built to control fraudulent activities. Hence a system to gauge the regularity and severity of various frauds should be also in place. Based on the incidents of frauds the strategies should be reviewed and appropriate changes in the strategies could be recommended.

Technological Savvy Directors

At least one of the directors should be aware of the technology being used and the security challenges that are involved in the technology being used. This helps plug holes in the risk management system and hence makes it more robust at the end of the day.

Rotation and Forced Vacations

It is important to rotate employees and send employees on forced vacations to detect any irregularities that may exist in the system. This system is generally followed by all leading multinational banks. However public sector banks in India and other developing countries are still not following these best practices. It should be noted that creeping of complacency or the assumption that nothing can go wrong will lead to more undetected frauds and the financial impact of such frauds will also be huge.

Risk Audits and Assessment Framework

A fraud risk audit and assessment framework need are of paramount importance to ensure a fraud-free environment. Stress testing and scenario planning are tools that should be integrated into the process of risk process of assessing the robustness of such a framework. Frauds are accompanied by window-dressing and this magnifies the impact of frauds. In worst scenarios, it culminates into the run on the banks.

Create Awareness among Clients

There should be an intent to create awareness among the clients on how frauds are committed and how the same can be averted. The leading banks such as Citibank and HSBC are quite transparent about the processes they follow to help reduce and mitigate risk arising from frauds that are committed.

Develop a Culture to Encourage Whistleblowing

The corporate governance system of the organization should facilitate whistleblowing. This helps improve the chances of early detection of frauds and hence reduce the severity of the incident. The same can be done by maintaining complete confidentiality about the identity of the whistleblower and awarding people who report fraud.

CRYSTAL GAZING – FUTURE RISK MANAGEMENT PRACTICES

With every new incident of fraud comes an innovation to curb frauds. These innovations in risk management are impacted by technological advancement and best practices in other fields. This has led to large scale transformation in the risk management principles and practices globally. It has also impacted fraud risk management. The huge financial implication of unearthing of fraud is to a great extent responsible for the transformation. The author feels that this is just a tip of the iceberg and there is a large-scale transformation waiting to happen. One of the palatable changes that the function is witnessing is the increased use of technology to automate the process.

The changes in risk management would be necessitated by changing landscape of operations leading to new risks and new risk management practices. However, at this moment because of the rate of changes in risk management and the disruption effect that these changes are causing, it is becoming increasingly difficult to project the changes. However, a broad direction can be provided for understanding the changes taking place. The risk management team needs to have a forward-looking approach to identifying risk. Here is an attempt to capture the six major changes in trends that are going to impact the sector in the future.

Regulators Role Will Become More Pronounced

The regulations across the world to detect fraud are governed to a great extent by the experience of the region. Hence there is a difference in the rate at which regulatory changes take place. Hence there is going to be heterogeneity in the regulator's role. However, the experts believe that the role of regulators will generally become more pronounced.

With the increased incidence of frauds, there is a general tendency among the customers to run away from banks that are more fraud prone. This was evident from the run on the banks that were witnessed in 2008 across the world. This led to regulators role becoming more pronounced. Most of the countries saw a complete overhaul of the regulatory framework aimed at reducing such incidents. There are certain uncertainties regarding operational risk management in the region. These regulatory changes can be attributed to the fact that public sentiments against regulatory failures have increased. The Basel IV norms are a culmination of such pressures after the 2008 crisis.

Governments are exerting regulatory pressure in other forms, too. Increasingly, banks are being required to assist in crackdowns on illegal and unethical financial transactions by detecting signs of money laundering, sanctions-busting, fraud, and the financing of terrorism, and to facilitate the collection of taxes. Governments are also demanding that their banks comply with national regulatory standards wherever they operate in the world. Banks operating abroad must already adhere to US regulations concerning bribery, fraud, and tax collection, for example. Regulations relating to employment practices, environmental standards, and financial inclusion could eventually be applied in the same way.

This leads to a more robust risk management model which is going to be a divorce from the existing traditional risk management model. This model is expected to be more proactive and hence would play a role in reducing the risks to a greater extent. The new model is also expected to have more dependence on different functional areas to capture increasing correlation during recessionary times. There is expected to be a higher role in automation.

Meeting Change in Customer Expectation

There is a change in the customers' expectation. This change is primarily driven by the customers' change in attitude. In countries such as India, China, Brazil, Australia where there is a high population of young learners who are technologically savvy, there is an increase in the rate of technological innovation. This increased technological innovation is leading to new more innovative ways of committing frauds. Hence, risk management is poised to be impacted by the changing profile of clients and customers. To sum up, risk managers need to have a complete understanding of what the customers expect to charter a future road map for risk management.

TECHNOLOGY AND ADVANCED ANALYTICS ARE EVOLVING

The challenge with technology is the disruption that it causes and the rate at which it causes the disruption. The following are some of the major drivers of risk management (Jensen, 1997; Rafay, 2019).

Increase the Ability to Handle the Large Volume of Data

With time, the banks can handle larger sets of data. The following are the areas in which these data can be used:

1. Fraud Detection
2. Surveillance
3. Managing Credit Risk
4. Detecting Crimes by identifying anomalies
5. Predicting future Operating Performance
6. Predicting future defaults
7. Designing Customer payment and prepayment prediction models.
8. Automated Portfolio Monitoring
9. Enhancing precision in balancing and rebalancing of portfolio
10. Using the information on the social platform to predict future customer payment behaviour

Machine Learning

With a leap in technological advancement, there are developments in machine learning that cannot be ignored. It increases accuracy in predicting frauds when the training data set is ample to determine future direction. With time the prediction of these models keeps on improving as they can self-learn and improve results. There is a high probability that the accuracy of detecting frauds will improve as the application of machine learning in fraud detection increases exponentially. Hence, advancements in machine learning need to be followed regularly.

Crowdsourcing

The Internet enables the crowdsourcing of ideas, which many incumbent companies use to improve their effectiveness. Allstate Insurance Company hosted a challenge for data scientists to crowdsource an algorithm for new car-accident insurance claims. Within three months, they improved the predictive power of their model by almost 300 per cent.

Many of these technological innovations can reduce risk costs and fines, and they will confer a competitive advantage on banks that apply them early and boldly. However, they may also expose institutions to unexpected risks, posing more challenges for the risk function. Data privacy and protection are also important concerns that must be addressed with due rigor (Kannangara & Uguccioni, 2013).

NEW RISKS ARE EMERGING

Inevitably, the risk function will have to detect and manage new and unfamiliar risks over the next decade. Model risk, cybersecurity risk, and contagion risk are examples that have emerged.

Model Risk

Banks' increasing dependence on business modelling requires that risk managers understand and manage model risk better. Although losses often go unreported, the consequences of errors in the model can be extreme. For instance, a large Asia-Pacific bank lost $4 billion when it applied interest-rate models that contained incorrect assumptions and data-entry errors. Risk mitigation will entail rigorous guidelines and processes for developing and validating models, as well as the constant monitoring and improvement of them (Fender & Kiff, 2004, Chauhan, Yadav & Choudhary, 2019).

Cybersecurity Risk

Most banks have already made protection against cyberattacks a top strategic priority, but cybersecurity will only increase in importance and require ever-greater resources (Tarter, 2017). As banks store an increasing amount of data about their customers, exposure to cyberattacks is likely to further grow.

Contagion Risk

Banks are more vulnerable to financial contagion in a global market (Schoenmaker, 1996; Aldasoro, Gatti, & Faia, 2017). Negative market developments can quickly spread to other parts of a bank, other markets, and other involved parties. Banks need to measure and track their exposure to contagion and their potential impact on performance. Measures to reduce a bank's total risk can reduce its capital requirements, as contagion risk is one of the main drivers for classification as a global systemically important bank (G-SIB) and for G-SIB capital surcharges.

To prepare for new risks, the risk-management function will need to build a perspective for senior management on risks that might emerge, the bank's appetite for assuming them, and how to detect and mitigate them. And it will need the flexibility to adapt its operating models to fulfil any new risk activities.

Managing Frauds by Removing Biases

According to experts, risk management failures are generally triggered through human emotions which gives rise to biases. Off late, academicians and practitioners are working on developing models that are biased agnostic. It is by no means an easy task to remove biases in the process of fraud detection. For example, many a time a lapse is attributed to the employee being overworked or the employee is new. This can remove objectivity from the process of decision making and hence lead to biased behaviour which can be a breeding ground for fraudsters aware of this loophole in the system.

It should be observed that risk management is about managing uncertainty in the future. Uncertainty can give rise to biased behaviour. For example, a trader in a bank may use subjectivity to justify future actions which may not necessarily be in the best of the bank's interest.

To remove biases, it is important to adopt state-of-the-art analytical methods that help identify any deviations at the earliest and an increase in the incidence of such deviations could indicate there is some fraudulent activity occurring within the organization.

Risk management needs to have members who are strong analytically and at the same time have functional knowledge to arrest deviations and hence fraud. Working in silos is not advisable when it comes to risk management. The focus of risk management should be to prevent any form of biases from impacting an operating manager's ability to decide. Thus, it would make sense for the banks to identify the biases beforehand. The risk management team than through a concerted effort aim at removing the biases.

The Pressure for Cost Savings Will Continue

The world over organizations is being awarded by investors for their ability to show consistent growth. Banks are no exception. This leads to a steady reduction in the costs and as costs diminish there is pressure on banks to find innovative ways of reducing their cost. Risk management is a cost centre and does not directly play a role in increasing profits in the short run. Hence, it is evident that they will be under pressure to reduce cost. The same can be attained through automating processes and reducing human intervention. This will not only help reduce cost it will also help remove biases in decision making. However, for the automation to work in risk management manual intervention is required from time to time to strengthen the system by removing loopholes if any in the system (Schmit & Roth, 1990).

CONCLUSION

From the above discussion, it is evident that fraud risk management is going through a transformation. However, the basic function of fraud risk management remains the same – reduce the incidence of frauds. Banks need to keep learning from their mistakes to improve their fraud risk management. Hence developing a robust risk-intelligent bank with a pervasive fraud risk management system can only help develop sustainable and viable business models for the banks in the future.

DISCLAIMER

The contents and views of this chapter are expressed by the author in his personal capacity. It is not necessary for the Editor and the Publisher to agree with these viewpoints and they are not responsible for any duty of care in this regard.

ACKNOWLEDGMENT

The author extends sincere gratitude to:

- The Editor-in-Chief and International Editorial Advisory Board (IEAB) of this book who initially desk reviewed, arranged a rigorous double/triple blind review process and conducted a thorough, minute and critical final review before accepting the chapter for publication.
- All anonymous reviewers who provided very constructive feedbacks for thorough revision, improvement, extension and finetuning of the chapter.
- All colleagues, assistants and well-wishers who assisted the author to complete this task.

REFERENCES

Aldasoro, I., Gatti, D. D., & Faia, E. (2017). Bank networks: Contagion, systemic risk and prudential policy. *Journal of Economic Behavior & Organization*, *142*, 164–188. doi:10.1016/j.jebo.2017.05.022

Australian Financial Review. (2018). *CBA's risk failures will cost shareholders at least $500m.* Retrieved from https://www.afr.com/chanticleer/cbas-risk-failures-will-cost-shareholders-at-least-500m-20180501-h0zid0

Banerjee, R. (2015). *Who Cheats and How? Scams, Fraud and the Dark Side of the Corporate World*. SAGE.

Chauhan, V., Yadav, R., & Choudhary, V. (2019). Analyzing the impact of consumer innovativeness and perceived risk in internet banking adoption. *International Journal of Bank Marketing*, *37*(1), 323–339. doi:10.1108/IJBM-02-2018-0028

Fender, I., & Kiff, J. (2004). *CDO rating methodology: Some thoughts on model risk and its implications* (Working Paper No. 163). Bank for International Settlement. Retrieved from https://papers.ssrn.com/sol3/papers.cfm?abstract_id=623662

Hubbard, D. W. (2014). *The Failure of Risk Management: Why It's Broken and How to Fix it*. John Wiley & Sons, Inc.

Jensen, D. (1997). Prospective assessment of AI technologies for fraud detection: A case study. In *AAAI Workshop on AI Approaches to Fraud Detection and Risk Management* (pp. 34-38). Retrieved from https://www.aaai.org/Library/Workshops/1997/ws97-07-007.php

Kannangara, S. N., & Uguccioni, P. (2013). Risk management in crowdsourcing-based business ecosystems. *Technology Innovation Management Review*, *3*(12), 32–38. doi:10.22215/timreview/751

Khan, N., Rafay, A., & Shakeel, A. (2020). Attributes of Internal Audit and Prevention, Detection and Assessment of Fraud in Pakistan. *Lahore Journal of Business*, *9*(1), 33–58. doi:10.35536/ljb.2020.v9.i1.a2

Khanna, A., & Arora, B. (2009). A study to investigate the reasons for bank frauds and the implementation of preventive security controls in the Indian banking industry. *International Journal of Business Science and Applied Management*, *4*(3), 1–21.

KPMG. (2019). *KPMG Global Banking Fraud Survey 2019*. Retrieved from https://home.kpmg/xx/en/home/insights/2019/05/the-multi-faceted-threat-of-fraud-are-banks-up-to-the-challenge-fs.html

Maddock, R. (May 2018). *How Commonwealth Bank got itself into such a mess*. Financial Review. https://www.afr.com/opinion/cbas-ordeal-does-australia-a-service-20180502-h0zizj

Rafay, A. (Ed.). (2019). *FinTech as a Disruptive Technology for Financial Institutions*. IGI Global. doi:10.4018/978-1-5225-7805-5

Rafay, A., Sadiq, R., & Mohsan, T. (2016). X-Efficiency in Banking Industry – Evidence from South Asian Economy. *Global Management Journal for Academic & Corporate Studies*, *6*(1), 25–36.

Ramamoorti, S. (2008). The psychology and sociology of fraud: Integrating the behavioural sciences component into fraud and forensic accounting curricula. *Issues in Accounting Education, 23*(4), 521–533. doi:10.2308/iace.2008.23.4.521

Schmit, J. T., & Roth, K. (1990). Cost-effectiveness of risk management practices. *The Journal of Risk and Insurance, 57*(3), 455–470. doi:10.2307/252842

Schoenmaker, D. (1996). *Contagion risk in banking*. LSE Financial Markets Group. Retrieved from https://www.academia.edu/download/61841734/345_contagion_risk_in_banking20200120-107135-1vlz1ta.pdf

Strader, J. K. (2011). *Understanding White Collar Crime*. LexisNexis.

Sutherland, E. H. (1983). *White-collar crime: The uncut version* (Vol. 58). Yale University Press.

Tarter, A. (2017). Importance of cybersecurity. In *Community Policing-A European Perspective*. Springer. doi:10.1007/978-3-319-53396-4_15

The Economic Times. (2018, February). *How did everyone miss the PNB scam? An accountant explains what could have gone wrong*. Retrieved from http://widgets.economictimes.com/industry/banking/finance/banking/how-did-everyone-miss-the-pnb-scam-an-accountant-explains-what-could-have-gone-wrong/articleshow/62928611.cms

Chapter 13
Banking Scams in India:
A Case-Based Analysis

Rohan Prasad Gupta
University of Calcutta, India

Bappaditya Biswas
University of Calcutta, India

ABSTRACT

In today's dynamic world, banking scams and frauds that are committed by willful defaulters are more technical and complex in nature. To tackle these crimes, banks need to improve their working system and technologies. In this chapter, cases of recent banking scams in India have been analyzed to find out the operational loopholes present in the system which led to such a crisis. Further, the measures taken by the Government of India to detect and prevent such scams have been discussed. On the basis of an in-depth study of the cases, researchers suggested certain feasible solutions to overcome such crises in the future. These recommendations shall prove useful to strengthen the banking sector, which is believed to be having considerable socio-economic significance to bring back confidence among the stakeholders and to safeguard the money of the masses.

INTRODUCTION

Banking sector of any country acts as an engine that accelerates the determinants of economic growth and sustainable development. In Indian context, the banking industry have expanded in a fast pace since independence, especially as we stand today. Banking sector plays very significant role for the economic growth in our

DOI: 10.4018/978-1-7998-8758-4.ch013

country and aids in the development of the industry and trade as well (Rafay, Franco & Gilani, 2019). The health of the banking sector in a country replicates the realities of its financial strengths. Almost all sectors, especially the Ministry of Micro, Small and Medium Enterprises (MSME) sector and the small-scale sector industries rely heavily on banks to pull them out of serious problems.

According to Reserve Bank of India Report (RBI, 2020), the Indian banking system consists of 12 public sector banks, 22 private sector banks, 44 foreign banks, 56 regional rural banks, 1,485 cooperative banks in urban areas and 96,000 cooperative banks in rural areas in addition to cooperative credit institutions. The total amount of bank credit provided and deposits received by the Indian banking sector stood at Rs. 102.19 *lakh crore* (USD 1.45 trillion) and Rs. 140.20 *lakh crore* (USD 1.98 trillion), respectively, as on July 31, 2020.

Banks are the engines that drive the operations in the financial sector and growth of an economy (Rafay & Farid, 2018). But with the growing banking industry in India, scams and frauds in banks are also increasing and fraudsters are becoming more sophisticated and ingenious (Bhasin, 2015). The increase in the financial sector scams in India is turning to be a downshifting factor which clearly indicates the risk associated with the Indian financial system. It is evident that big ticket banking sector frauds and scams has potentially increased in recent years. The data released by the RBI revealed that big-ticket frauds against banks have been rising consistently in the last decade. In 2008-09, the average amount involved in advances (loan) related fraud was Rs 75 *lakh* which have been increased to Rs. 9 *crore* in 2017-18 (Kishore, 2018).

The rising Banking frauds and scams in India have distorted the growth of this sector. With soaring levels of scams and consequently increasing Non-Performing Assets (NPAs), it is negatively impacting the entire financial sector and is becoming a source of stress for all the stakeholders. The rising scams and corporate failures mirrors the inefficiencies in mechanisms followed. With this background the objectives of the study is to study the cases related to recent banking sector scams in India and to identify the operational loopholes present in the banking system that led to such scams. The study also aims to formulate suggestions that will aid in protecting the Indian banking sector from scam.

BACKGROUND

The impacts of banking sector scams are most disastrous for any economy. It causes an imbalance in the entire economic system often leading to weakening of the money and securities market, which in turn negatively impacts the investors and common masses. Due to such banking scams, securities market faces huge crashes thereby affecting the economy in a massive way. This results in slowing down the economic growth and which in return often leads to weakening the economy and decreasing the foreign investments. When any banking sector scam came into light or a bank collapses, the whole public sentiment turns towards negative with it. This also leads to a shift in the public trust from the banks to other monetary means of the economy.

Though banking scams might not be new in India but repercussions of a scam are widespread these days. The frauds seem to be innovative in terms of *modus operandi* and are pretty huge by size. With the passage of time the dimensions of scams in the banking industry are changing. Hence, there is a need for a strong international frame to cope up with such emerging challenges and to minimize such scams. The legal structure needs to be strengthened and should be of an international form. The regulation needs to be stricter towards such crisis.

With the advancement of banking industry in India, scams and frauds in banks are also increasing very fast, and fraudsters have started using advanced means to escape from the frauds. It is also true that banks cannot be 100% secure against unidentified threats; a certain level of attentiveness can go a long way in disputing fraud risk (Bhasin, 2015). With this background the present study aims to address the issues and impacts of recent banking sector scams in India and the remedies thereof.

In past few years Indian banking sector is confronted with banking frauds. For a better system, banking sector needs to be prompt in reporting and action. The fraud in this sector is one of the key concerns for the regulator, government and banking industry. Banking business involves risk but with rising frauds, banks must have effective control mechanism. This sector is making huge investments over a period of time on Fraud Risk Management frameworks, systems and controls (Pan, 2020). Sharma and Sharma (2018) used content analysis to significantly measure the impact of prevention techniques on prevention of banking frauds and concluded that there is a significant impact. Jayraman, Lee and Ng (2019) identified and focused on causal factors which comprise macroeconomic as well as bank-specific factors, influencing NPA in Indian commercial banks through a panel approach by using 16 annual observations (from fiscal year 2000–2001 to 2015–2016) for three groups of banks by ownership: public, private, and foreign. They revealed that the macroeconomic and bank-specific factors are important determinants in rising NPAs in India.

Ramana and Krishna (2017) in their research work explained the impact of fraud in Indian banking sector with special reference on retail banking products which includes stolen checks, cheque kiting, forgery and altered cheques, accounting fraud, uninsured deposits, demand draft fraud, rogue traders, fraudulent loans and fraudulent loan applications, forged or fraudulent documents, wire transfer fraud, bill discounting fraud, payment card fraud, booster cheques, stolen payment cards, duplication or skimming of card information, empty ATM envelope deposits, impersonation, prime bank fraud, phishing and internet fraud and money laundering.

George (2020) in his research work tried to cover the timeline from the infusion of Liberalization, Privatization and Globalization (LPG) and how slowly but surely lack of proper monitoring and unrestricted lending policies lead to a financial crisis big enough to halt the entire nation's economy, or the ripple effect of overlooked bad apples in the banking system. He concluded that the Indian banking system is in a Catch-22 situation – trying to balance between credit scores development and dangerous loans and Coronavirus has aggravated the situation.

Jeyanthi, Mansurali and Krishnaveni (2020) focused on different endeavored fake and fraud cases for both internal and external misrepresentation plots in the banking sector. They concluded that bank should consider how their business models will be affected by current and potential future new requirements, and whether their risk management programs have the capacity to answer flexibly to the ongoing process of regulatory change.

Thangam and Bhavin (2019) in their research depict the various types of banking sector frauds in the Indian scenario and also revealed its legal action taken by the investigation agency. They suggested that industry should take zero tolerance towards any form of mismanagement or unlawful activities and the Banks should execute the RBI's fraud controlling measures immediately without any delay and loopholes.

Pande and Prakash (2019) examined the scams in Indian Banking industry through case study of Nirav Modi Scam. In their work, they identified that it is mandatory for the bank that they should improve their risk management system and concluded that banks had been continuously hit by scam which show that the internal risk management system is very weak and non-planned. Gayathri and Mangaiyarkarasi (2018) critically analyzed the factors that led to Punjab National Bank (PNB) Scam and delved into auditing process of the Banks and possible loopholes that led to this fraud. Further they summarized the impact of scam on various Banks and the economy as whole and concluded that the Punjab National Bank fraud exposed many banks to credit risk.

Kaur (2020) identified and analyzed the factors that led to this massive PNB scam. The research work includes full analysis of PNB scam, how it occurred and measures to be taken to avoid such scams. The paper also summarizes the impact of scam on various banks and economy as a whole. In her paper she concluded that the role of the regulator and the auditors of the banks are under question now and suggested that RBI should empower the banks to deal with fraudsters in a swift manner thereby avoiding unwanted red tape. Upadhyay (2018) in her research article analyzed the most significant banking fraud namely the Nirav Modi scam, Vijay Mallya scam, Allahabad bank scam, Rotomac Pens scam, RP Info Systems scam, Simbhaoli Sugar Mills bank fraud, United Bank of India fraud, Karnataka banking sector scam, SBI frauds, etc., which are the banking sector frauds and scams that rocked the Indian banking sector.

Rajan (2019) in his case analysis of different dimensions of Yes Bank crisis revealed that decisions taken by two founders of the bank and other tragic circumstances have ruined the bank. He concluded that due to a family dispute, exposure to bad loans and RBI's audit of the banks in India eventually led to Yes Bank losing its market and eventually declined. Roy and Chatterjee (2018) in their paper examined shadow Banking/Non-Banking Financing Company (NBFCs) within India and outside India along with the financial and legal framework in India regulated by the RBI and SEBI regulations and analyzed the Infrastructure Leasing & Financial Services Limited (IL&FS) crisis in context to shadow banking in India. Their conclusion is that the IL&FS scam has raised serious concerns with regards to the Indian financial system and its regulators and there is an urgent need of restructuring the framework and regulations to curb such crisis.

The present study is exploratory and descriptive in nature and is based on secondary data. Different working papers, case studies, legal proceedings, journals, Government reports, newspapers, magazines, respective bank's annual report and websites are being consulted for this study. Under the study, the researchers intend to perform case-based analysis of the recent banking sector scams in three different categories of banking i.e., public sector banks, private sector banks and NBFCs. The analysis includes the study of the scam of Punjab National Bank from public sector, Yes Bank scam from private sector and Infrastructure Leasing & Financial Services Limited (IL&FS) scam from NBFCs. It is proposed that the researchers will intensify their analysis in identification of the loopholes and mismanagement present in the current system which is giving rise to such scams. Furthermore, the researchers intend to highlight the policies formulated by the government to address such issues and to provide suggestions which will aid in strengthening the Indian banking system.

RECENT BANKING SCAMS IN INDIA

All the banking transactions in India are made under the rules and regulations of the Reserve Bank of India (RBI). RBI foresees every bank operating in the country and also formulates guidelines in relation to Non-Performing Assets (NPAs). The loans given by banks often not returned back on time are known as NPAs. These NPAs when not returned on time often cause a lot of headache to the bank and result in loss of public money. This leads to loss of trust from the bank and the ultimately distress of the bank. According to a former Deputy Governor of the Reserve Bank of India, the number of frauds in private and foreign Banks is at the top, but with regards to amount of money lost, public sector banks are the top rankers. The scams emerged as a large demon in front of the regulators and the government of the country.

Table 1. Credit related frauds reported (amount involved >= Rs. 1 lakh)

Financial Year	Credit Related Frauds			
	No. of Frauds	Percent of Credit Related Frauds to Total Frauds	Amount Involved (in Rs. *crore*)	Percent of Credit Related Frauds to Total Frauds
2014-15	2,251	48.52	17,122	88.01
2015-16	2,125	45.28	17,368	92.88
2016-17	2,322	45.74	20,561	85.91
2017-18	2,525	42.68	22,558	54.8
2018-19	3,606	53.02	64,548	90.22
2019-20	2,438	55.25	110,419	97.39

Source: BI Financial Report 2019 and 2020.

It is evident from the above table that a very high percentage of banking frauds is related with credit and has increased significantly in terms of amount. The above table shows that 97.39% of the total frauds in 2019-20 are related to credit and this in return is the major causes of rising NPAs in the country. The six years period starting from 2013 to 2019 are the worst period in terms of NPAs in the Indian banking sector. According to RBI reports for these periods, Gross NPAs of Public Sector Banks (PSBs) rose approximately four times to Rs. 8.06 *lakh crore* in March 2019 from Rs. 1.30 *lakh crore* in March 2014.

In case of scheduled commercial banks, Gross NPAs climbed to Rs. 9.49 *lakh crore* from Rs. 1.42 *lakh crore* for the same time period. According to the RBI Financial Stability Report 2018, Gross NPA to Gross advances ratio (%) has increased to 11.18% in 2017-2018 from 3.83% in 2013-2014. Profitability of 'All Scheduled Banks' have also declined significantly from profit of Rs. 809.127 billion in 2013-14 to loss of Rs. 324.377 billion. The amount of NPAs upsurge vigorously in recent past which is a matter of concern.

However, according to the RBI Financial Stability Report 2019, the change in the NPA recognition norms by the RBI along with the changes made in the provisioning rules in 2018 and 2019 has led to an increase in NPA amounts in the past years. The rapid rise in NPAs is the consequence of the aggressive and careless lending by the banks to mostly non-productive units along with rise in willful defaulters and economic slowdown. Not a single public sector and even private sector banks and NBFCs have been spared. In the next section, the cases related to the recent banking sector scams have been discussed.

CASE STUDY 1: PUBLIC SECTOR BANK - PUNJAB NATIONAL BANK (PNB) SCAM

Case Details

Punjab National Bank, the second largest Public sector bank of India, reported on 14th February 2018 to the Reserve Bank of India (RBI), the Central Bureau of Investigation (CBI) and the stock exchanges regarding exceptional and illicit transactions of approximate value $ 1.77 billion (around Rs. 11,400 *crore*) tending to be fraudulent at one of its Mumbai branches. The Bank had named the people and business houses associated with this scam. One of them is Nirav Modi and the other one is Mehul Chauksi, uncle of Nirav Modi and owner of *Gitanjali* group who committed massive frauds with the bank officials. Punjab National Bank (PNB) lost approximately $1.77 billion in the scam led by the diamond merchant Nirav Modi and his uncle Mehul Choksi (Kolte and Wagh, 2019; Sudhin, 2018).

The amount of losses incurred by the bank signifies the magnitude of the scam. The event puts serious concerns regarding modus operandi of the scam in the bank which comes out of integration of external and internal banking operations or some other ghost reasons, which remained undefined till date. Analysts and media houses states that the technicalities behind the scam are related to Society for Worldwide Interbank Financial Telecommunications (SWIFT), Core Banking Solutions (CBS), auditing etc., but the role of political intervention cannot be set aside and need serious analysis. The role of RBI is under questions from the stakeholders and general public regarding the inability to detect the illicit transactions during the auditing process.

The investigation probes that this scenario was happening from the past seven years with respect to the diamond merchant Nirav Modi case. According to the First Information Report (FIR) launched with the CBI, two junior employees, of PNB had been held responsible for these unauthorized guarantees for the last seven years. The case bubbled up in the month of January 2018, when a new PNB employee asked for collateral security for fresh loans to the Modi firms, which then found that it has never been asked for in the past. This roused the suspect for the fraud and the scam was discovered.

Operational Loopholes

The crisis emerged due to the issue of fake Letter of Understanding (LoU) by the bank officials of PNB on the basis of which foreign branches of some of Indian banks, including Allahabad Bank, State Bank of India, Union Bank and Axis Bank remitted loans in foreign currency (dollar) to the *Gitanjali* group. Now, PNB is left holding bank guarantee of Rs. 11,400 *crore* which is fraudulent in nature and is held responsible for making payment to other banks as it has received the bank guarantee charges.

Analyzing the case of PNB scam, it is found that since past seven years the collateral free SWIFT transactions were taking place without being identified. The important question here is that how the transactions by passed the Core Banking Solution (CBS) framework and such a big fraud raises serious concerns over the honesty of the bank officials. The entire operational process of the PNB is under question. Lack of proper planning to manage operational risk and negligence of the regulators is prominently seen. The role of RBI is also under question as the entire auditing process of the transactions surpassed the vigilance of the regulators for seven years.

Broad Follow-Up and Impact of the Scam

As an aftermath of the fraud, RBI, on March 13, 2018, issued a directive which imposed a ban on all commercial banks from issuing guarantees in the form of letters of undertaking (LOU) to prevent any further misuse of the facility. The process of issuance of LoUs for trade related credits for imports in India has also been discontinued by the commercial banks as per the directive. RBI directed banks to integrate their CBS with SWIFT system.

In this context, charges of criminal conspiracy, cheating, dishonesty, fraud, breach of trust and breach of contract was lodged against Nirav Modi and has been arrested in London after an arrest warrant was released against him. Assets worth over Rs. 5870 *crore* belonging to Nirav Modi has been seized by the Enforcement Directorate (ED) from Allahabad Bank, Kolkata branch, which is estimated of having an exposure of Rs. 2363 *crore* in connection to this case. (Sarkar, 2018).

The scam had also impacted the entire banking sector. Out of the 39 banks which are listed in stock exchange, 34 listed bank's share prices fell between February 12 to February 15, 2018 while benchmark BSE index lost 1.2 per cent during the same period. Five commercial banks like Union Bank of India, SBI, UCO bank, Axis bank, and Allahabad bank have been directly affected by the scam as they had offered short term buyer's credit to PNB (Sarkar, 2018). The condition of other Public Sector Banks (PSBs) was also in substandard situation during that period. Out of 21 listed Banks, 11 Banks came under RBI's surveillance because of their deteriorating condition of capital, assets return and loans.

CASE STUDY 2: PRIVATE SECTOR BANK - YES BANK SCAM

Case Details

The Yes Bank crisis started in 2018 when RBI demanded the bank's founder Rana Kapoor to step down as Chief Executive Officer (CEO) witnessing severe corporate governance issues and Deutsche Bank AG's former India CEO Ravneet Gill was brought in to replace Rana by the RBI. The plot begins from the founders' dream to become the largest private sector bank in the country and eventually ended up being a bank in distress. The journey of Yes Bank started in 2003 as an Indian private bank under the leadership of three founders, Rana Kapoor, Ashok Kapur and Harkirat Singh. The bank was performing well accordingly as compared to its peers, but in 2018, questionable decisions taken by two founders ruined the bank ultimately and it landed with Rana Kapoor.

The decisions of the promoter regarding aggressive lending led to huge exposures to bad loans and RBI's clean drive and audit process of the banks in India eventually led to Yes Bank losing its sheen and ultimately in distress situation, waiting for its revival. (Adhikari, 2020). "*The meteoritic rise and ultimately the fall of YES bank have scarred the Indian Economy. In 2015, RBI had conducted its first asset quality review (AQR) of banks to find corporate loan accounts having severe financial weakness that were classified as standard accounts on the books of the lenders.*" (Press Trust of India)

RBI proposed a draft plan for the revival of the bank which outlines for a takeover by the government. The draft proposes to form a consortium consisting of State Bank of India (SBI), Life Insurance Corporation of India (LICI) and some other PSBs to rescue yes bank. According to various estimates, Yes Bank needs approximately Rs. 25,000 *crore* capital infusion for its survival. Furthermore, the survival plan proposes to alter the authorized capital for the reconstituted bank to Rs 5,000 *crore* from Rs 800 *crore* and states that any investor including SBI can pick up a 49% stake in the equity of Rs 5,000 *crore* at Rs 10 per share. The draft has been placed in the public domain for review. (Merwin, 2020).

Operational Loopholes

The case analysis of Yes bank reveals that severe misclassification was found regarding bad loans and potential conflict of interests in connection with the promoter Rana Kapoor. In the month of September 2018, RBI directed Yes Bank to disclose the non-performing loans which amounted to Rs. 4,930 *crore*, near about seven times more than the Rs. 750 *crore* that the company reported in its audited accounts for the year ended in March 2016, which in fact is a matter of serious concern. Later in 2019, it was found that the bank's exposure to troubled assets were almost at Rs. 26,000 *crore*, an amount that was significantly larger than the Rs. 17,000 *crore* declared by the bank.

It is considered as a banking scam as the personal interest and conflicts of the promoters of the bank, especially of Mr. Rana Kapoor ruined the entire bank and left the investors and customers nowhere. The alarming problem with this bank is that it has the highest stressed assets among Indian banks (both private and public) with estimated stress of 54.5 percent of the reported net worth of financial year 2018-2019 with total exposure of Rs. 147 billion as of 2018-19. Near about one-sixth of the Bank's total loans and advances were remitted to financial and real-estate firms and coincidentally the two sectors were facing the biggest funding squeezes in India due to the economic slowdown.

These loans include $1.85 billion (approximately Rs. 11,100 *crore*) given to Mr. Anil Ambani's Reliance Telecommunication that was undergoing bankruptcy and a $470 million exposure (approximately Rs. 2820 *crore*) to Subhash Chandra's Zee Entertainment Enterprises which is also facing financial difficulties (Rajan, 2019). Furthermore, Yes Bank also has highest exposure towards those entities which are classified as high-risk by the rating agencies such as ADAG (Finance), Cox & Kings, CG Power, DHFL, Essar Shipping and Mcleod Russel, which was reported as Rs. 102.6 billion. In the month of May 2019, the bank reported stressed assets worth Rs. 10,000 *crore*, which mainly comprises exposure to real estate, entertainment and infrastructure sector-based corporate groups. The financials of the banks depicted that the bank's profits came down from Rs. 4,224 *crore* in FY 2017-18 to Rs. 1,720 *crore* in FY 2018-19. The bank got the title of the world's worst-performing lender in 2019.

JLN US & Co. (JLN), a Vadodara-based auditor was engaged as the bank's audit committee to independently examine the matter. Auditors informed the bank's board that it has not been able to prove some of the allegations raised by the whistleblower. The reason given by the audit firm is limited access to the documents provided by the internal management and bank officials and was unable to accurately trace the transactions done by Rana's family office. This instance was really alarming for the stakeholders (Gopakumar, 2019).

Broad Follow-Up and Impact of the Scam

After the failure of this private sector bank the share market took a great hit. This caused Nifty and Sensex to fall crashing throughout the stock market. The scam negatively impacted the trust of the investors and the depositors which led to the decline of the bank. Millions of people in India and the major institutions who tied-up with Yes Bank in their journey have been affected. The Bank was following a spat over breaches of confidentiality and regulatory guidelines revealed in their inspections. After this the bank witnessed an 81% decline in its market stock price. Till now, nearly 40 brokerage firms' and rating agencies have given negative ratings to Yes Bank stocks.

In the rescue plan for the bank, the State Bank of India (SBI), along with Housing Development Finance Corporation (HDFC), ICICI bank, Axis bank, Kotak Mahindra bank, R.K. Damani, Rakesh Jhunjhunwala and AzimPremji Trust gave it a lifeline by bailing out YES bank and buying a significant share of stake in the bank. This step is significant in the banking sector to revive a major commercial bank and to regain the trust of the people and its customers on the bank and the banking sector.

CASE STUDY 3: NBFC - INFRASTRUCTURE LEASING & FINANCIAL SERVICES LIMITED (IL&FS) SCAM

Case Details

Infrastructure Leasing and Financial Services (IL&FS) scam, which emerged in the month of September 2018 was considered to be a major eye opener about the financial risks in connection with Indian Non-Banking Financial Company (NBFC) sector. IL&FS, being one of the largest shadow banking firms with multiple businesses and highest ratings defaulted certain payments in September 2018 and repeatedly failed to service the commercial papers arising on the due dates. The entire Indian banking system witnessed the largest liquidity freeze due to the collapse of IL&FS. The liquidity crisis emerged due to the failure of IL&FS has led to a situation where most NBFCs are struggling for their survival, which is matter of serious concern.

According to the rating agencies, the company's NPA has increased approximately about 99 percent in a single year, from Rs. 410 *crore* in 2017 to Rs. 816 *crore* in 2018. This indicated that there is a liquidity crunch or is in cash shortage. The first instance of the crisis came into light when the institution postponed the issue of USD 350.00 million bonds in March 2018 because the investors demanded for a higher yield. The other reason for the crisis is the recent increase in infrastructure projects and resulting disputes over contracts made, which resulted into a huge amount, approximately Rs. 9000 *crore* of payments due from the government.

Surprisingly, the central government intervened into the matter and took control of the crippled IL&FS group, which has 358 subsidiaries owing more than Rs. 91000 *crore* from banks and other lenders. The board constituted by the National Company Law Tribunal (NCLT), which is chaired by Uday Kotak. The board reported that involving significant capital infusion from credible and financially strong investors is not a feasible solution for the crisis. According to NCLT, "*it is not possible to find a single solution for the IL&FS crisis and its Rs. 91,000 crore debt*". Furthermore, they added that the resolution demands for breaking off and selling entire business to willing buyers as well as there is a need for significant capital infusion, asset monetization to retire debt and resolution with the creditors.

Operational Loopholes

The scam has raised concerns about the regulatory system in India and its effectiveness to avoid such events in future. Along with RBI, which regulates NBFCs in India, the role of the Securities and Exchange Board of India (SEBI) is also under question as it also regulates some part of the shadow banking in India such as the collective investment companies, mutual funds, and other securities related institutions. As per the charge sheet filed by the Serious Fraud Investigation Office (SFIO) and Ministry of Corporate Affairs (MCA) order dated May 29, 2019, the role of RBI is under serious question with regard to this scam. In this charge sheet, SFIO said that action at the right time may have prevented ballooning of the matter. The auditing process evaluated the role of the various credit rating agencies on various debt instruments in the IL&FS case and concluded that excessive borrowings from money markets by the company had eventually led to such defaults.

The forensic audit by Grant Thornton on the engagement of IL&FS with credit rating agencies reveals that there are instances of manipulating the rating agencies to act in favor of the company. The forensic audit report significantly indicates that the then key employees of IL&FS either delayed the process of rating or delayed the publication of the rating on the public domain, when they found out that ratings wouldn't be in favor of the company. It is also evident in the report that in certain instances, it was found, that the company deliberately provided incorrect or incomplete information to credit rating agencies to avoid a rating downgrade. These instances depict that it is a clear case of scam. (Ghosh, 2019). With the intervention of the National Company Law Tribunal (NCLT), it is expected that it will provide a legal framework for the damage control in the future course of time with respect to this shadow banking crises and the Indian financial system will receive an extra support to protect the economy from such a financial crash any time in the near future.

Broad Follow-Up and Impact of the Scam

The case of IL&FS crisis is an eye opener for the regulators and policy makers with respect to such financial risks in the NBFC sector in India. The serious debt and liquidity crisis emerged due to the failure of the NBFC has created a credit crunch in the Indian financial sector and other NBFCs. The crisis has affected almost all financial sectors as well as the real estate and infrastructure sector, which mostly are dependent for their funding and growth on NBFCs.

The cascading effects of the liquidity crisis created due to the IL&FS scam worried the investors and traders. Default by IL&FS led to panic in the debt market and resulted into a liquidity shortage of Rs. 1 *lakh Crore* in the system. In case of Debt mutual funds, they started to write down their value by 3-5% on their portfolios. Due to this crisis, Sensex shed 2,000 points just in a week just after the news came into light (Pandey, 2019).

In light of this crisis, On November 15, 2019, the Central Government issued a notification to bring NBFC's under the definition of Financial Service Provider which will result in bringing NBFCs with assets worth Rs 500 cores or more under the ambit of Insolvency and Bankruptcy Code (IBC). It is a positive step and is expected to help limit losses for creditors as compared to liquidation.

RECENT MEASURES TAKEN BY THE GOVERNMENT OF INDIA IN DETECTION AND REPORTING OF BANK FRAUDS

The Government of India has taken the following comprehensive steps to address the underlying causes of the scams and to provide for proactive checking and detection of frauds in the banking sector (Ministry of Finance, 2019).

- Government has issued framework for timely detection, reporting and investigation relating to large value bank frauds to public Sector Banks (PSBs) for systematic and comprehensive checking of legacy stock of their NPAs. Government has notified that all accounts exceeding Rs. 50 *crore*, if classified as NPAs accordingly, must be examined by the concerned banks from the angle of possible fraud and a report to be placed before the bank committee for review of NPAs on the basis of the investigation. In depth examination must be initiated for willful defaulters immediately upon reporting fraud to RBI.
- Public Sector Banks (PSBs) have also been advised by RBI to look for a report on the borrower from the Central Economic Intelligence Bureau, in case an account turns NPA. FIRs have been registered and proactive actions have been taken against 2,881 willful defaulters.
- For enforcement of auditing standards and ensuring the quality of audits, the Government of India established a body of independent regulator naming the National Financial Reporting Authority (NFRA). Fugitive Economic Offenders Act, 2018 has been enacted in order to dissuade economic offenders from evading the process of Indian law by remaining outside

the jurisdiction of Indian courts. The act is empowered to attach property of the fugitive economic offender, confiscation of such offender's property and disentitlement of the offender from defending any civil claim. Pursuant to Government's advice to PSBs, they have been obtaining certified copy of passport of the promoters/directors and other authorized signatories of companies availing loan facilities of more than Rs. 50 *crore* and decide on publishing photographs of willful defaulters in consultation with RBI and as per the board approved policy.

- The banks have been directed to strictly ensure zonal transfer of officials/ employees on sensitive posts. The heads of the PSBs are now being empowered to request for lookout circulars against the defaulters. In order to bring transparency and accountability in the Indian and financial system, 3.38 *lakh* bank accounts of inoperative companies were frozen from 2017 to 2019. In March 2018, the Reserve Bank of India rejected the financing instruments that is, the Letters of Understanding (LoU) and Letters of Comfort (LoC), aimed at plugging a proviso and improving banks' expected credit perseverance. In February 2020, the Finance Ministry hiked the bank deposit insurance from Rs. 1 *lakh* to Rs. 5 *lakhs*, which will provide more security to the bank deposits of the general public.

RECOMMENDATIONS

After in-depth analysis of the three above mentioned case studies, the failure of the regulatory system and the fraudulent behavior of the bank officials are clearly evident. In this context it is of utmost importance to chalk out some of the feasible solutions which will help out in early detection and prevention of banking frauds in future. The researchers have given certain recommendations or suggestions in this regard which are discussed below:

Need of Forensic Accounting Along With Forensic Audit in Banking Frauds

With the steep increase in money laundering, banking frauds and willful default cases, RBI has made forensic audit mandatory for banks in case of large advances and restructuring of accounts. In view of the rising levels of financial irregularities, growing NPAs and the increase in willful defaulters as well as regular issues of corporate governance, the requirement for forensic accounting is greater than ever. In this dynamic business ecosystem, forensic accounting and forensic audit are complementary to each other and more the business uses the forensic accounting in general, less the need of forensic audit (Khan *et al.*, 2020).

The concept of forensic accounting is in developing phase. India will be the first country to issue standards on forensic accounting practices. The Digital Accounting Assurance Board of The Institute of Chartered Accountants of India (ICAI) has developed an exposure draft on Standard on forensic Accounting and investigation (FAIS) and has put forward for public comments in the month of September 2020.

Forensic accounting in banking sector is relevant for restoring the stakeholders' confidence in the financial reporting process and corporate governance. Forensic accounting aids in scrutiny and examination of financial payment dealings in the accounting system to decide if they are standard or beyond company policy. It includes forensic processes on a routine schedule in order to reduce fraud perpetration and transaction risks and helps in accessing unusual development in the accounting and financial systems. It is the need of the situation that India inculcates such qualified and experienced forensic accounting skill sets that will definitely help the government, regulators and all stakeholders of the banking sector to restore the confidence in dealing with such banking frauds.

Need for Sustainability and Ethical Banking

Ethical banking is also known as 'sustainable banking' or 'civic banking' or 'clean banking'. *"Ethical banking, in the field of banking and finance, is a business model that responds to emerging approaches to sustainable economy based on the principles of corporate social responsibility. Transparency in reporting is a major value integrated in the fundamentals of ethical banking"*. (Dogra & Dogra, 2019). In theory, ethics can be defined as a convention or norm of behavior considered being correct, which includes rules and cultural values on the grounds of being good or bad; being right or wrong. In case of the financial institutions such as banks and NBFCs, they are expected and required to contribute towards the development of a sustainable economy. In banking sector, the principals of ethical practices are quite general and include the principles of integrity, neutrality, reliability, transparency and respect to the environment in which it operates

Banks are required to follow these principles in true spirit, but there are certain instances such as the cases of PNB scam, the Yes bank crisis and the IL&FS crisis, which has given the bank a major chunk of NPAs and an overriding amount of debt. In all the three cases these norms have been broken, guidelines have been violated and ethics have been compromised to a great extent. Hence, it is expected and desirable for the entire financial and banking sector to strictly follow the ethical norms so that the confidence of the stakeholders is restored in the banking process and the hard-earned money of the general people are safe guarded. In this context, the researchers suggest that incentive linked practice norms can be developed by the banks for its employees for early fraud detection and rewards for proactive practices to avoid such frauds.

Additional Preventive Measures

- Banks must be vigilant while recruiting staff in their branches and the management must watch the activities of its officials on a regular basis and must not rely on any person unduly. Any presents or gift from the borrowers must not be accepted by the bank officials as well as job rotation must be made mandatory in all bank branches.
- The bank must thoroughly check the background of a borrower especially before sanctioning a very heavy loan amount and must pay particular attention whenever any irregularity appears in the account no matter how small the irregularity is. Transactions must be properly authorized.
- The banks should initiate awareness programs among its employees and also take initiate for public awareness programs about bank fraud and legal consequences. The banking sector should collectively introduce continuous training mechanism for its employee's as this will support them to tackle the latest fraudulent practices.
- All the public, private sector banks, NBFCs, and other financial institutions should execute the central bank's fraud controlling measures immediately without any delay and loopholes.

CONCLUSION

In Indian context, slack regulations, baggy strategies, improper risk management practices, false reporting of the auditors and fraudulent practices of the internal management led to the scams. The rising fraud cases have hampered the trust of the common man and only few fraudulent businessmen have been benefited by having loans and guarantees. There was a serious issue of operational loopholes, internal check and internal control in all the three cases that have been discussed in the study. The greed of few top-level bank managers and the failure to detect that at earlier stage has become the major reason behind the scam.

It is important to re-define and re-structure the role of the regulatory institution while dealing with these frauds. Proper coordination and integration among various financial regulators at both national and international level should be maintained to avoid such frauds. The financial industry as well as the regulators should initiate towards zero tolerance policy for the officials who commit any form of mismanagement, or unlawful activities. Public sector banks need to take more care in handling these frauds. There should be a quick mechanism for reporting and follow-ups of such frauds and at the same time any information from the whistleblower should be considered seriously.

As the dimensions of frauds and scams in the banking sector are changing day by day, there is a need for a strong international frame and harmonization of government policies to counter these types of willful defaulters and fraudsters. There is a need to revamp the entire financial system of the country for the speedy recovery and sustainable growth of the Indian financial system. The entire outlook needs to be restructured as even now banking frauds are treated as one of the costs of transacting business in India. But the complexity and inherent costs of frauds and scams have increased manifold resulting in an alarming call for the regulators and policy makers as it is harshly impacting the bank's profitability and consequently on the Indian economy.

At the end, it is the hard-earned money of the masses of the country which are lost in these crises and still now the regulations are not such strong to safeguard the general people from such scams. One has to face many hurdles to withdraw his/ her own funds from his account after such crisis, without knowing his fault, which is really a pathetic situation, as is seen in the PNB and Yes bank crisis. The policy makers must not only impose the policies but must also focus on strongly implementing those policies. The negligent behavior must change otherwise it will lead to a disaster in the near future.

DISCLAIMER

The contents and views of this chapter are expressed by the authors in their personal capacities. It is not necessary for the Editor and the Publisher to agree with these viewpoints and they are not responsible for any duty of care in this regard.

ACKNOWLEDGMENT

The authors extend sincere gratitude to:

- The Editor-in-Chief and International Editorial Advisory Board (IEAB) of this book who initially desk reviewed, arranged a rigorous double/triple blind review process and conducted a thorough, minute and critical final review before accepting the chapter for publication.

- All anonymous reviewers who provided very constructive feedbacks for thorough revision, improvement, extension and fine-tuning of the chapter.
- All colleagues, assistants and well-wishers who assisted the authors to complete this task

REFERENCES

Adhikari, A. (2020, March 23). How to Bust a Bank. *India Today*. Retrieved from https://www.indiatoday.in/magazine/cover-story/story/20200323-how-to-bust-a-bank-1654646-2020-03-13

Agarwal, A. (2020, March 8). Yes Bank Crisis: RBI's Tryst with Large Private Bank Failures. *Bloomberg Quint Opinion*. Retrieved from https://www.bloombergquint.com/opinion/yes-bank-crisis-rbis-trysts-with-large-private-bank-failures

Bhasin, M. (2015). An Empirical Study of Frauds in the Banks. *European Journal of Business and Social Sciences*, *4*(7), 1–12.

Dogra, A., & Dogra, M. (2019). Sustainability and Ethical Banking: A Case Study of Punjab National Bank. *Amity Journal of Corporate Governance*, *4*(1), 15–27.

Gayathri, S., & Mangaiyarkarasi, T. (2018). A Critical Analysis of the Punjab National Bank Scam and Its Implications. *International Journal of Pure and Applied Mathematics*, *119*(12), 14853–14866.

George, R. (2020). Two decades of faulty credit policy later, an unending rippling effect of financial crisis and a staggering economy: Indian financial system in a catch 22 situation. *Journal of Engineering Sciences*, *11*(8), 153–160.

Ghosh, S. (2019, July 20). IL&FS influenced credit ratings in its favour, forensic audit report finds. *Mint*. Retrieved from https://www.livemint.com/companies/news/il-fs-influenced-credit-ratings-in-its-favour-forensic-audit-report-finds-1563611258934.html

Gopakumar, G. (2019, November 13). Yes Bank faces fresh audit into complaints by whistleblower. *Mint*. Retrieved from https://www.livemint.com/industry/banking/yes-bank-faces-fresh-audit-into-complaints-by-whistleblower-11573668757156.html

Jayraman, T. K., Lee, C., & Ng, C. (2019). The Causal Factors behind Rising Non-performing Assets of India's Commercial Banks: A Panel Study. *Advances in Pacific Basin Business, Economics and Finance*, *7*, 201–212.

Jeyanthi, P., Mansurali, A., & Krishnaveni, V. (2020). Significance of fraud analytics in Indian Banking sectors. *Journal of Critical Reviews*, *7*(4), 209–213.

Kaur, L. (2020). PNB SCAM: Shining Diamond Trader Took Away PNB's Shine. *International Journal of Engineering Development and Research*, *8*(1), 51–55.

Khan, N., Rafay, A., & Shakeel, A. (2020). Attributes of Internal Audit and Prevention, Detection and Assessment of Fraud in Pakistan. *Lahore Journal of Business*, *9*(1), 33–58. doi:10.35536/ljb.2020.v9.i1.a2

Kishore, R. (2018, May 26). Reserve Bank of India data shows rise in big-ticket bank frauds. *Hindustan Times*. Retrieved from https://www.hindustantimes.com/business-news/reserve-bank-of-india-data-shows-rise-in-big-ticket-bank-frauds/story-MJio0ibsS1V31reOx1yhdN.html

Kolte, A., & Wagh, P. (2019). Analyzing Punjab National Bank Scam. *Journal of Emerging Technologies and Innovative Research*, *6*(6), 585–592.

Merwin, R. (2020, March 14). YES Bank rescue plan: Will SBI and consortium of private lenders be able to bail out the bank. *The Hindu business Line*. Retrieved from https://www.thehindubusinessline.com/money-and-banking/yes-bank-rescue-plan-will-sbi-and-consortium-of-private-lenders-be-able-to-bail-out-the-bank/article31067637.ece

Ministry of Finance. (2019). *Increase in detection and reporting of bank frauds due to Government's proactive measures* (Release ID: 1573465). Retrieved from https://pib.gov.in/PressReleaseIframePage.aspx?PRID=1573465

Pan, S. (2020). Analysis of Frauds in Indian Banking Sector. *International Journal of Trend in Scientific Research and Development*, *4*(3), 70–73.

Pande, S., & Prakash, V. (2019). Case Study on Scam in Indian Banking industry (NiravModi). *Pramana Research Journal*, *9*(6), 626–630.

Pandey, N. (2019). Infrastructure Development and Financial Services: A Case Study on IL&FS. *International Journal for Research in Engineering Application & Management,* 65-66.

Rafay, A., & Farid, S. (2018). Competitive Environment in Banking Industry: Evidence from an Emerging Economy. *Business and Economic Review*, *10*(3), 65–84. doi:10.22547/BER/10.3.4

Rafay, A., Franco, G., & Gilani, U. J. (2019). Measuring Competition in Banking Industry: Evidence from Latin American Economies. *Pakistan Business Review*, *21*(1), 154–163.

Rajan, T. (2019). The Case of Yes Bank: From the Founders' Dream to a Bank in Distress. *Journal of Advance Research in Dynamical & Control Systems, 11*(11), 674–678. doi:10.5373/JARDCS/V11SP11/20193083

Ramana, S. V., & Krishna, S. G. (2017). A study on impact of fraud in Indian banking sector (With special reference on retail banking products). *International Journal of Academic Research and Development*, *2*(6), 544–547.

RBI. (2020). *Annual Report 2019-2020.* Reserve Bank of India. Retrieved from https://www.rbi.org.in/Scripts/AnnualReportMainDisplay.aspx

Roy, B., & Chatterjee, S. (2018). Shadow Banking in India in Relation to the IL&FS Crisis. *Journal of Banking and Insurance Law*, *1*(2), 1–6.

Sarkar, A. (2018, March 6). PNB Fraud Case: Axis Bank discloses Rs. 200 *crore* exposures to NiravModi, Gitanjali Gems Accounts. *Bloomberg Quint*. Retrieved from https://www.bloombergquint.com/business/pnb-fraud-case-axis-bank-discloses-rs-200-*crore*-exposure-to-nirav-modi-gitanjali-gems-accounts

Sharma, M. (2018, February 16). State Control Has Opened India's Banks to Fraud. *Bloomberg Quint*. Retrieved from https://www.bloombergquint.com/opinion/state-control-has-opened-india-s-banks-to-fraud

Sharma, M. (2018, October 3). The Roots of India's Shadow-Bank Crisis. *Bloomberg Quint Opinion*. Retrieved from https://www.bloombergquint.com/opinion/india-needs-better-model-for-funding-infrastructure

Sharma, N., & Sharma, D. (2018). Rising Toll of Frauds in Banking: A Threat for the Indian Economy. *Journal of Technology Management for Growing Economies*, *9*(1), 71–88. doi:10.15415/jtmge.2018.91003

Sudhin, S. (2018). The Punjab national bank: Nirav Modi Scam, 2018. *International Journal of Advanced Research and Development*, *3*(3), 180–182.

Thangam, M., & Bhavin, P. (2019). Banking Frauds in India; A case analysis. *Journal of Emerging Technologies and Innovative Research*, *6*(1), 29–35.

Upadhyay, D. (2018). Banking Scams in India. *Journal of Banking and Insurance Law*, *1*(2), 7–13.

KEY TERMS AND DEFINITIONS

Forensic Accounting: Forensic accounting is the in-depth investigation of fraud or financial manipulation by performing extremely detailed research and analysis of financial information.

NBFC: Under section 451 (f) of RBI Act, 1934 NBFC means a non-banking financial institution which is company engaged in the business of loans and advances, acquisition of shares/stocks/bonds/debentures/securities or other marketable securities of a like nature, leasing, hire-purchase, insurance business, chit business, etc.

NPA: According to Reserve Bank of India (RBI), a Non-Performing Asset (NPA) is defined as a credit facility in respect of which the interest and/or instalment of principal has remained 'past due' for a specified period of time.

Willful Defaulter: A willful defaulter is a person or an entity that has not repaid the loan despite the ability to repay it.

Compilation of References

ABC Solutions. (2021). *Money Laundering: A Three – stage Process*. About Business Crime Solutions Incorporation. Retrieved from https://www.moneylaundering.ca/public/law /3_stages_ML.php

Abdel-Magid, M. F. (1981). The theory of Islamic banking: Accounting implications. *The International Journal of Accounting*, *17*(1), 79–102.

Abdullah, M. F., & Rahman, A. (2017). Shari'ah governance of Islamic banks in Bangladesh issues and challenges. *Journal of Islamic Economics. Banking and Finance*, *13*(3), 82–94.

Abdulqayumov, S., Arshed, N., & Bukhari, S. (2020). Economic impact of institutional quality on environmental performance on post-soviet countries. *Transition Studies Review*, *27*(2), 13–24.

Abioje, P. O. (2017). Christian prophets and other prophets in Nigeria. The 167th Inaugural Lecture, University of Ilorin.

ACAMS. (2007). Risks and Methods of Money Laundering and Terrorist Financing. In *Study Guide for the CAMS Certification Examination* (pp. 13-110). Miami: Association of Certified Anti-Money Laundering Specialists. Retrieved from http://files.acams.org/pdfs/English_Study_Guide/Chapter_2.pdf

ACCR. (2015). *Australian Crime Commission Annual Report*. Australian Criminal Intelligence Commision.

Adam, M. & Muizzuddin. (2020). Banking Governance: Perspective of Islamic Banking. In *Growth and Emerging Prospects of International Islamic Banking* (pp. 263-277). IGI Global.

Adebajo, K. (2020). *Terrorism, COVID-19, Flooding and the Growing Humanitarian Crises in Northern Nigeria*. OSIWA/HumAngle Media.

Adebayo, R. I. (2016). Dividends of international Islamic organisations in Nigeria. In Y. A. Quadri, R. W. Omotoye, & R. I. Adebayo (Eds.), *Religion in Contemporary Nigeria* (pp. 241–267). Adonis & Abbey Publishers Ltd.

Adebayo, R. I. (2017). *Qur'an*otherapy and the Quest for Islamisation of Yorubaland, Nigeria. In S. D. Mills (Ed.), *Religion: past, present and future perspectives* (pp. 27–61). Nova Science Publishers.

Adebayo, R. I. (2018). Muslim involvement in *Ori-Oke* prayers in Nigeria. In S. N. Yaovi, P. U. Nwosu, A. G. Alamu, L. E. Odeh, & A. Y. Mohammed (Eds.), *Ori-Oke spirituality and social change in Africa: Contemporary perspectives* (pp. 21–44). Langaa Research & Publishing Common Initiative Group. doi:10.2307/j.ctvh9vtpk.6

Adebayo, R. I. (2020). Zakat Distribution in the Context of Shari'ah Corporate Governance: Evidence from South-Western Nigeria. In A. Rafay (Ed.), *Handbook of Research on Theory and Practice of Global Islamic Finance* (pp. 161–178). IGI Global.

Adebayo, R. I., & Hassan, M. K. (2013). Ethical principles of Islamic financial institutions. *Journal of Economic Cooperation & Development, 34*(2), 63–90.

Adetona, L. M., & Raji, M. O. (2016). A study of the misuse of Sūratu Yāsīn among Yoruba Muslims. *Ilorin Journal of Religious Studies, 6*(1), 1–15.

Adetoro, J. E. (1980). *History of West Africa, Bk 2*. African University Press.

Adhikari, A. (2020, March 23). How to Bust a Bank. *India Today.* Retrieved from https://www.indiatoday.in/magazine/cover-story/story/20200323-how-to-bust-a-bank-1654646-2020-03-13

Afolabi, A. (2020, August 14). Boyfriend, pastor nabbed for allegedly using apostle's daughter for ritual in Ondo. *The Guardian.* Retrieved from https://guardian.ng/news/boyfriend-pastor-nabbed-for-allegedly-using-apostles-daughter-for-ritual-in-ondo/

AFP. (2012, December 12). Report Unmasks Tax Evasion Among Pakistan Leaders. *The Express Tribune*. Retrieved from https://tribune.com.pk/story/478812/report-unmasks-tax-evasion-amongpakistan-leaders

Agarwal, A. (2020, March 8). Yes Bank Crisis: RBI's Tryst with Large Private Bank Failures. *Bloomberg Quint Opinion*. Retrieved from https://www.bloombergquint.com/opinion/yes-bank-crisis-rbis-trysts-with-large-private-bank-failures

Agazue, C. (2016). He told me that my waist and private parts have been ravaged by demons:" sexual exploitation of female church members by "prophets" in Nigeria. *Dignity: A Journal on Sexual Exploitation and Violence, 1*(1). Retrieved from https://digitalcommons.uri.edu/dignity/vol1/iss1/10

Ahmad, A. U. F., Rashid, M., & Shahed, A. K. M. (2014). Perception of bankers and customers towards deposit and investment mechanisms of Islamic and conventional banking: Empirical evidence from Bangladesh. *Journal of Islamic Business and Management, 4*(2), 91–114. doi:10.12816/0019145

Ahmed, M., & Khatun, M. (2013). The compliance with *Shariah* governance system of AAOIFI : A Study on Islamic Banks Bangladesh Introduction. *Journal of Islamic Economics, Banking and Finance, 9*(3), 177–191.

Ahtik, M., Pilipovic, O., & Marelja, M. (2019). Economic analysis of money laundering prevention in Croatia and Slovenia. *Journal of Money Laundering Control, 22*(1), 97–109. doi:10.1108/JMLC-01-2018-0009

Akers, R. L. (1990). Rational Choice, Deterrence, and Social Learning Theory in Criminology: The Path Not Taken. *The Journal of Criminal Law & Criminology*, *81*(3), 653–676. doi:10.2307/1143850

Akyay, I. (2001). *Problems Encountered in Money Laundering Investigations* (Unpublished Master's Thesis). University of North Texas, Texas. Retrieved from https://digital.library.unt.edu/ark:/67531/metadc2856/

Al Agha, S. (2007). Money laundering from Islamic perspective. *Journal of Money Laundering Control*, *10*(4), 406–411. doi:10.1108/13685200710830899

Al Hageel, S. A. (2002). *The Virtual Position of Islam on Extremism and Terrorism*. King Fahad National Library Cataloguing Publication Data.

Alamgir, M. (2016). An analysis of Islamic banking activities in Bangladesh: Issues and challenges. *Thoughts on Economics, 25*(3-4), 29-58.

Alam, M. K. (2021). A systematic qualitative case study: Questions, data collection, NVivo analysis and saturation. *Qualitative Research in Organizations and Management*. Advance online publication. doi:10.1108/QROM-09-2019-1825

Alam, M. K., Ahmad, A. U. F., & Muneeza, A. (2020e). External Sharī'ah Audit andReview Committee vis-a-vis Sharī'ah Compliance Quality and Accountability: A Case of Islamic Banks in Bangladesh. *Journal of Public Affairs*, *2364*, 1–10. doi:10.1002/pa.2364

Alam, M. K., Miah, M. S., Siddiquii, N., & Hossain, M. I. (2020c). The Influences of board of directors and management in *Shariah* governance guidelines of the Islamic banks in Bangladesh. *Journal of Islamic Accounting and Business Research*, *11*(9), 1633–1647. doi:10.1108/JIABR-08-2019-0155

Alam, M. K., Mustafa, H., Uddin, M. S., Islam, M. J., Mohua, M. J., & Hassan, M. F. (2020b). Problems of *Shariah* Governance Framework and Its Mechanisms: An Empirical Investigation of Islamic banks in Bangladesh. *Journal of Asian Finance, Economics and Business*, *7*(3), 265–276. doi:10.13106/jafeb.2020.vol7.no3.265

Alam, M. K., Rahman, S. A., Mustafa, H., Shah, S. M., & Hossain, M. S. (2019). *Shariah* governance framework of Islamic banks in Bangladesh: Practices, problems and recommendations. *Asian Economic and Financial Review*, *9*(1), 118–132. doi:10.18488/journal.aefr.2019.91.118.132

Alam, M. K., Rahman, S. A., Thakur, O. A., Bashir, M. A., & Hosen, S. (2020a). The reasons behind the absence of a comprehensive *Shariah* governance framework for the Islamic banks in Bangladesh. *International Journal of Economics and Business Administration.*, *8*(1), 134–145.

Alam, M. K., Tabash, M. I., Thakur, O. A., Sahabuddin, M., Hosen, S., & Hassan, M. F. (2020d). A central *Shariah* regulatory authority for the Islamic banks in Bangladesh: Legalization or formation. *Journal of Asian Finance. Economics and Business*, *7*(1), 91–100.

Albanese, J. S. (2012). Deciphering the linkages between organized crime and transnational crime. *Journal of International Affairs*, *66*(1), 1–16.

Albrecht, C., Duffin, K. M., Hawkins, S., & Rocha, V. M. M. (2019). The use of cryptocurrencies in the money laundering process. *Journal of Money Laundering Control*, *22*(2), 210–216. doi:10.1108/JMLC-12-2017-0074

Aldasoro, I., Gatti, D. D., & Faia, E. (2017). Bank networks: Contagion, systemic risk and prudential policy. *Journal of Economic Behavior & Organization*, *142*, 164–188. doi:10.1016/j.jebo.2017.05.022

Aleksoski, S., & Aleksoski, O. (2015). Money laundering as a type of organized crime. *Journal of Process Management. Nuclear Technology*, *3*(3), 44–54.

Alemika, E. E. (2013). *The impact of organized crime on governance in West Africa*. Friedrich-Ebert-Stiftung.

Al-Ghazaali, M. (1998). Al-Mankhul min ta'liqat al-'Usul (a book on usul al-fiqh). Dar al-Fikr.

Allen, N. (2019). *How Boko Haram Regained the Initiative and What Nigeria Should do to Stop It*. Texas National Security Review.

Alp, İ. A. (2000). Paranın Karası, Kara Paranın Makroekonomik Etkileri [Black Money, Macro Economic Effects of Black Money]. *Maliye Dergisi*, *134*, 13–15.

Al-Rashed, M., & Shterin, M. (2009). Between Death of Faith and Dying for Faith: Reflections on Religion, Politics, Society and Violence. In M. Al-Rashed & M. Shterin (Eds.), *Dying for Faith: Religiously Motivated Violence in Contemporary World* (pp. 1–3). I.B. Tauris. doi:10.5040/9780755625024.0006

Aluko, A., & Bagheri, M. (2012). The impact of money laundering on economic and financial stability and on political development in developing countries. *Journal of Money Laundering Control*, *15*(4), 442–457. doi:10.1108/13685201211266024

Amara, I., & Khlif, H. (2018). Financial crime, corruption and tax evasion: A cross-country investigation. *Journal of Money Laundering Control*, *21*(4), 545–554. doi:10.1108/JMLC-10-2017-0059

Amoh, J. K., & Adafula, B. (2019). An estimation of the underground economy and tax evasion. *Journal of Money Laundering Control*, *22*(4), 626–645. doi:10.1108/JMLC-01-2019-0002

Amrani, H. (2012). *The Development of Anti-Money Laundering Regime: Challenging Issues to Sovereignty, Jurisdiaction, Law Enforcement, and Their Implication on the Effectiveness in Countering Money Laundering*. Erasmus University Rotterdam.

Anderson, S. K., & Sloan, S. (2009). *Historical Dictionary of Terrorism*. The Scarecrow Press.

Anti-Corruption Digest. (2019, July 12). Money Laundering and housing affordability in GTA. *Anti-Corruption Digest*. Retrieved from https://anticorruptiondigest.com/2019/07/12/ money-laundering-and-housing-affordability-in-gta/#axzz6TFHLOLK6

Anugwom, E. E. (2019). *The Boko Haram Insurgence: Perspective from Within*. Palgrave Macmillan. doi:10.1007/978-3-319-96959-6

Apenda, A. Z. (2006). Spirituality or materialism: The dilemma of contemporary church in Nigeria. In M.T. Yahya, A.P. Dopamu, R.A. Raji, E.A. Odumuyiwa, D. Shishima, S.A. Owoeye & P.O. Abioje (Eds.), Issues in the Practice of Religion in Nigeria (pp. 125-139). Nigeria Association for the Study of Religions (NASR).

Apergis, E., & Apergis, N. (2016). The 11/13 Paris terrorist attacks and stock prices: The case of the international defense industry. *Finance Research Letters*, *17*, 186–192. Advance online publication. doi:10.1016/j.frl.2016.03.002

Arif, I., & Suleman, T. (2017). Terrorism and Stock Market Linkages: An Empirical Study from a Front-line State. *Global Business Review*, *18*(2), 365–378. doi:10.1177/0972150916668604

Arnone, M., & Borlini, L. (2010). International anti-Money Laundering programs: Empirical assessment and issues in criminal regulation. *Journal of Money Laundering Control*, *13*(3), 226–271. doi:10.1108/13685201011057136

Arshed, N., Arif, A., Abbas, R. Z., & Hameed, K. (2020). Comparing quality of institutions with happiness of Asian people. *Studies in Applied Economics*, *39*(2).

Ask, K., Granhag, P. A., & Rebelius, A. (2011). Investigators under influence: How social norms activate goal-directed processing of criminal evidence. *Applied Cognitive Psychology*, *25*(4), 548–553. doi:10.1002/acp.1724

Asongu, S., & Kodila-Tedika, O. (2016). Fighting African conflicts and crimes: Which governance tools matter? *International Journal of Social Economics*, *43*(5), 466–485. doi:10.1108/IJSE-11-2014-0233

Asuelime, L. E., & David, O. J. (2015). *Boko Haram: The Socio-Economic Drivers*. Springer Nature.

Auditor General of Canada. (2003). *Canada's Strategy to Combat Money Laundering*. Report of the Auditor General of Canada to the House of Commons. Retrieved from https://www.oag-bvg.gc.ca/internet/docs/20030403ce.pdf

Aurasu, A., & Rahman, A. A. (2016). Money laundering and civil forfeiture regime : Malaysian experience. *Journal of Money Laundering Control*, *19*(4), 337–345. doi:10.1108/JMLC-08-2015-0033

Australian Financial Review. (2018). *CBA's risk failures will cost shareholders at least $500m*. Retrieved from https://www.afr.com/chanticleer/cbas-risk-failures-will-cost-shareholders-at-least-500m-20180501-h0zid0

Aydin, H. (2018). TBB-MASAK Çalıştayı Açılış Konuşmaları [TBB-MASAK Workshop Opening Speeches]. *Bankacılar Dergisi, 105*.

Aykın, H. (2010). *Aklama ve Terörün Finansmanı ile Mücadelenin Küresel Boyutu* (Yayın No:2010/406) [The Global Dimension of the Fight against Laundering and Terrorist Financing ((Publication No: 2010/406)]. T.C. Maliye Bakanlığı Strateji Geliştirme Başkanlığı.

Aziz, O., Grant, K. A., & Arshed, N. (2020). Does entrepreneurial activity assist in alleviation of poverty? *Journal of Applied Business & Economics*, *22*(7), 114–132.

Bajrang, P., Ritika, P., Puneet, & Parashar, N. (2012). Factors Affecting Money Laundering: A Lesson for Developing Countries. *Drishtikon: A Management Journal, 3*(2), 108-139.

Bakare, Y. (2018). Police arrest Muslim cleric with human parts in Lagos. *Vanguard*. Retrieved from https://www.vanguardngr.com/2018/01/breaking-police-arrest-muslim-cleric-human-parts/

Baldwin, G. (2003). The new face of money laundering. *Journal of Investment Compliance*, *2003*(Summer), 38–41. doi:10.1108/15285810310812997

Banerjee, R. (2015). *Who Cheats and How? Scams, Fraud and the Dark Side of the Corporate World*. SAGE.

Bangladesh Bank. (2009). *Guideline for conducting Islamic banking*. Bangladesh Bank. Retrieved from https://www.bb.org.bd/aboutus/regulationguideline/islamicbanking/ islamicguide.php

Bangladesh Bank. (2019). *Bangladesh Bank quarterly report on 'Developments of Islamic Banking in Bangladesh' January-March, 2019*. Bangladesh Bank.

Bank Negara Malaysia. (n.d.). *Malaysia Anti-Money Laundering & Counter Financing of Terrorism Regime*. Retrieved from http://amlcft.bnm.gov.my/AMLCFT02b.html

Barry, J. R., & Nedelescu, O. M. (2006). The impact of terrorism on financial markets. *Journal of Financial Crime*, *13*(1), 7–25. doi:10.1108/13590790610641233

Bartlett, B. L. (2002). *The Negative Effects of Money Laundering on Economic Development*. Asian Development Bank. Retrieved from https://waleolusi.files.wordpress.com /2013/05/the-negative-effects-of-money-laundering-on-econom.pdf

BCBS. (2005). Compliance and Compliance Function in banks. *Bank for International Settlements*. Retrieved from https://www.bis.org/publ/bcbs113.htm

BCBS. (2011). Principles for the Sound Management of Operational Risk. *Basel Committee of Banking Supervision*. Retrieved from https://www.bis.org/publ/bcbs195.pdf

BCGN. (2019a, May 9). Billions in Money Laundering increased B.C. housing prices, expert panel finds. *British Columbia Government News*. Retrieved from https://news.gov.bc.ca/releases/2019FIN0051-000914

BCGN. (2019b, May 10). B.C. government addressing housing affordability challenges. *British Columbia Government News*. Retrieved from https://news.gov.bc.ca/factsheets/bc-government-addressing-housing-affordability-challenges

BCGN. (2019c, June 12). B.C.'s efforts front and centre at anti-Money Laundering meeting. *British Columbia Government News*. Retrieved from https://news.gov.bc.ca/releases/2019FIN0061-001233

BCGN. (2019d, November 12). Single real estate regulator protects people, combats Money Laundering. *British Columbia Government News*. Retrieved from https://news.gov.bc.ca/releases/2019FIN0115-002149

Becker, G. S. (1968). Crime and punishment: An economic approach. In N. G. Fielding, A. Clarke, & R. Witt (Eds.), *The economic dimensions of crime*. Macmillan. doi:10.1007/978-1-349-62853-7_2

Becker, G. S. (1968). Crime and Punishment: An Economic Approach. *Journal of Political Economy*, *76*(2), 169–217. doi:10.1086/259394

Belaisha, B. (2014). Money laundering in Dubai: Strategies and future directions. *Journal of Money Laundering Control*, *17*(3), 343–354. doi:10.1108/JMLC-10-2013-0038

Bell, R. E. (2001). Discretion and Decision Making in Money Laundering Prosecutions. *Journal of Money Laundering Control*, *5*(1), 42–51. doi:10.1108/eb027292

Benoit, K. (2011). Linear regression models with logarithmic transformations. *London School of Economics, 22*(1), 23-36.

Berg, B. L., & Lune, H. (2007). *Qualitative research methods for the social sciences*. Pearson.

Bergström, M., Svedberg Helgesson, K., & Mörth, U. (2011). A new role for for-profit actors? The case of anti-money laundering and risk management. *Journal of Common Market Studies*, *49*(5), 1043–1064. doi:10.1111/j.1468-5965.2010.02167.x

Bhasin, M. (2015). An Empirical Study of Frauds in the Banks. *European Journal of Business and Social Sciences*, *4*(7), 1–12.

BIG. (2020). *Basel AML index 2020: Ranking money laundering and terrorist financing risks around the world.* Basel Institute on Governance. Retrieved from https://baselgovernance.org/sites/default/files/2020-07/basel_aml_index_2020_web.pdf

BIS. (2015). Basel Committee's revised principles. *Bank for International Settlements*. Retrieved from https://www.bis.org/bcbs/publ/d328.htm

Blum, W. (2002). *Rogue State: A Guide to the World's Only Superpower*. Zed Books.

Bonekamp, B., & Van Veen, T. (2017). *Terrorist Attacks and Financial Markets*. Retrieved from https://papers.ssrn.com/sol3/papers.cfm?abstract_id=2924459

Braun, V., & Clarke, V. (2006). Using thematic analysis in psychology. *Qualitative Research in Psychology*, *3*(2), 77–101. doi:10.1191/1478088706qp063oa

Brechenmacher, S. (2019). *Stabilising North East Nigeria After Boko Haram*. Carnegie Endowment for International Peace.

Brown, J. (2018, August 20). Enforcement lacking in anti-money-laundering efforts. *Canadian Lawyer*. Retrieved from https://www.canadianlawyermag.com/news/ general/enforcement-lacking-in-anti-money-laundering-efforts/275393

Brown, A. N. (2009). *Brown Money Laundering*. Green.

Brown, R., & Gillespie, S. (2015). Overseas financial investigation of organised crime. *Journal of Money Laundering Control, 18*(3), 371–381. doi:10.1108/JMLC-03-2014-0010

Brun, J. P., Gray, L., Scott, C., & Stephenson, K. (2011). *Asset recovery handbook: a guide for practitioners*. The World Bank. doi:10.1596/978-0-8213-8634-7

Bryman, A., & Bell, E. (2003). *Business research methods*. Oxford University Press.

Buchanan, B. (2004). Money laundering - A global obstacle. *Research in International Business and Finance, 18*(1), 115–127. doi:10.1016/j.ribaf.2004.02.001

Budget, B. C. (2018). *Homes for B.C: A 30-Point Plan for Housing Affordability in British Columbia.* Retrieved from https://www.bcbudget.gov.bc.ca/2018/homesbc/2018 _homes_for_bc.pdf

Burkart, P. (2014). *Pirate Politics: The New Information Policy Contents*. MIT Press. doi:10.7551/mitpress/9205.001.0001

Burr, R., & Horte, C. (2019, May). British Columbia Landowner Transparency Act becomes law. *Norton Rose Fulbright*. Retrieved from https://www.nortonrosefulbright.com/en / knowledge/publications/deee862a/british-columbia-land-owner-transparency-act-becomes-law#:~:text=In%20its%202018%20budget%2C%20the,of%20land%20in%20 the%20province.

Button, M., & Cross, C. (2017). *Cyber frauds, scams and their victims*. Taylor & Francis. doi:10.4324/9781315679877

Campbell, J., & Page, M. T. (2018). *Nigeria: What Everyone Needs to Know*. Oxford University Press. doi:10.1093/wentk/9780190657970.001.0001

Canada, T. I. (2019). Opacity: Why Criminals Love Canadian Real Estate (And How to Fix it). *Static1. Transparency International Canada.* Retrieved from https://static1.squarespace.com/static/5c8938b492441bf93fdbc536/t/5c92f6ec104c7b75c315b507/1553135372459/BOT-GTA-Report-English.pdf

Casaca, P. (2017). The Conceptual Discussion on Terrorism. In P. Casaca & S. O. Wolf (Eds.), *Terrorism Revisited: Islamism, Political Violence and State-Sponsorship*. Springer Nature. doi:10.1007/978-3-319-55690-1_1

CBC. (2018). Weak regulations make Canada a money-launderer's playground, says report. *CBC News*. Retrieved from https://www.cbc.ca/news/politics/money-laundering-howe-meunier-1.4811911

CF. (2021). Company Formations. *Canada Registered Agent Services*. Retrieved from https://companyformations.ca/canada-registered-agent-service/

CFR § 21.21 - Procedures for monitoring Bank Secrecy Act (BSA) compliance. *Bank Secrecy Act*. Retrieved from https://www.law.cornell.edu/cfr/text/12/21.21

Chaikin, D. (2017). Money laundering and tax evasion–the assisting of the banking sector. In M. S. Aßländer & S. Hudson (Eds.), *The Handbook of Business and Corruption*. Emerald. doi:10.1108/978-1-78635-445-720161012

Chan, A. (2019, May 22). Chinese Canadians. *The Canadian Encyclopedia*. Retrieved from https://www.thecanadianencyclopedia.ca/en/article/chinese-canadians

Chandra, E. M. (2019). Victimless Crime in Indonesia: Should We Punished Them? *Padjadjaran Journal of Law*, *6*(2), 216–232.

Charles, A., & Darné, O. (2006). Large shocks and the September 11th terrorist attacks on international stock markets. *Economic Modelling*, *23*(4), 683–698. doi:10.1016/j.econmod.2006.03.008

Chaudhry, N., Roubaud, D., Akhter, W., & Shahbaz, M. (2018). Impact of terrorism on stock markets: Empirical evidence from the SAARC region. *Finance Research Letters*, *26*, 230–234. doi:10.1016/j.frl.2018.02.024

Chauhan, V., Yadav, R., & Choudhary, V. (2019). Analyzing the impact of consumer innovativeness and perceived risk in internet banking adoption. *International Journal of Bank Marketing*, *37*(1), 323–339. doi:10.1108/IJBM-02-2018-0028

Chen, J. (2020, July 7). Money Laundering. *Investopedia*. Retrieved from https://www.investopedia.com/terms/m/moneylaundering.asp

Chen, A. H., & Siems, T. F. (2004). The effects of terrorism on global capital markets. *European Journal of Political Economy*, *20*(2), 349–366. doi:10.1016/j.ejpoleco.2003.12.005

Cheng, N. Y. (2012). *The Effectiveness of Money Laundering Investigations in Fighting Transnational Crime : A Comparison of the United States and Hong Kong*. Retrieved from https://www.brookings.edu/research/the-effectiveness-of-money-laundering-investigations-in-fighting-transnational-crime-a-comparison-of-the-united-states-and-hong-kong/

Chesney, M., Reshetar, G., & Karaman, M. (2011). The impact of terrorism on financial markets: An empirical study. *Journal of Banking & Finance*, *35*(2), 253–267. doi:10.1016/j.jbankfin.2010.07.026

Chironda, M. (2017, September 29). Nigeria: How Much Did Former Oil Minister 'Steal'? *allAfrica Blog*. Retrieved from https://allafrica.com/stories/201709290489.html

Chomsky, N. (1989). *The Culture of Terrorism*. Pluto Press.

Chomsky, N. (2000). *Rogue States: The Rule of Force in World Affairs*. Pluto Press.

Chomsky, N. (2013). *On Western Terrorism: From Hiroshima to Drone Warfare*. Pluto Press.

Choo, H. C., Amirrudin, M. S., Adura, N., Noruddin, A., & Othman, R. (2014). Anti-Money Laundering and its Effectiveness. *Malaysian Accounting Review*, *13*(2), 109–124.

Chossudovsky, M. (2005). *America's War on Terrorism*. Centre for Research on Globalisation.

Clarke, C. P. (2016). Drugs & thugs: Funding terrorism through narcotics trafficking. *Journal of Strategic Security*, *9*(3), 1–15. doi:10.5038/1944-0472.9.3.1536

Cohen. (2020). Commission of Inquiry into Money Laundering in British Columbia. *Cullen Commission*. Retrieved from https://cullencommission.ca/data/transcripts/2020%2002%20 26%%20Transcripts%20-%20Opening%20Statements.pdf

Cohen, M. A. (2005). *The costs of crime and justice*. Routledge. doi:10.4324/9780203313145

Comply Advantage. (2020). Anti-Money Laundering in Canada 2020. *Comply Advantage*. Retrieved from https://complyadvantage.com/anti-money-laundering-in-canada-2020/

COSO. (2020). Five Components of the COSO Framework You Need to Know. *KnowledgeLeader Blog*. Retrieved from https://info.knowledgeleader.com/bid/161685/what-are-the-five-components-of-the-coso-framework

Cuellar, M. (2003). The Tenuous Relationship between the Fight against Money Laundering and the Disruption of Criminal Finance. *The Journal of Criminal Law & Criminology*, *93*(2-3), 311–466.

Çuhacı, K. (2003). Kara Para Aklama ve Sigortacılık Sektörü [Money Laundering and Insurance Sector]. *Reasürör Dergisi*, *48*, 15–18.

Cullen Commission. (2019, July 1). *Commission of Inquiry into Money Laundering in British Columbia*. Retrieved from https://cullencommission.ca/comm-statements/

Cullen Commission. (2020a, May 25). *Commission of Inquiry into Money Laundering in British Columbia*. Retrieved from https://cullencommission.ca/data/transcripts/Transcript%20May %20 25,%202020.pdf

Cullen Commission. (2020b, Feb 24). *Commission of Inquiry into Money Laundering in British Columbia*. Retrieved from https://cullencommission.ca/data/transcripts/ 2020%2002%2024%20 Hearing%20Transcripts%20-%20Opening%20Statements.pdf

Cullen Commission. (2020c, Feb 26). *Commission of Inquiry into Money Laundering in British Columbia*. Retrieved from https://cullencommission.ca/data/transcripts /2020%2002%2026%20 Hearing%20Transcripts%20- %20Opening%20Statements.pdf

Cullen Commission. (2020d, Jun 2). *Commission of Inquiry into Money Laundering in British Columbia*. Retrieved from https://cullencommission.ca/data/transcripts/Transcript%20June %20 2,%202020.pdf

Cullen Commission. (2020e, Jun 3). *Commission of Inquiry into Money Laundering in British Columbia*. Retrieved from https://cullencommission.ca/data/transcripts/Transcript%20June %20 3,%202020.pdf

Cullen Commission. (2020f, Jun 11). *Commission of Inquiry into Money Laundering in British Columbia*. Retrieved from https://cullencommission.ca/data/transcripts/Transcript%20June %20 11,%202020.pdf

Cullen Commission. (2020g, May 28). *Commission of Inquiry into Money Laundering in British Columbia*. Retrieved from https://cullencommission.ca/data/transcripts/ Transcript%20May%20 28,%202020.pdf

Cullen Commission. (2020h, May 26). *Commission of Inquiry into Money Laundering in British Columbia*. Retrieved from https://cullencommission.ca/data/transripts/Transcript %20May%20 26,%202020.pdf

Cullen Commission. (2020i, July 9). *Commission of Inquiry into Money Laundering in British Columbia*. Retrieved from https://cullencommission.ca/media/?open=19

D'Antuono, S. M. (2018, November 29). Combating Money Laundering and Other Forms of Illicit Finance: Regulator and Law Enforcement Perspectives on Reform. *FBI News*. Retrieved from https://www.fbi.gov/news/testimony/combating-money-laundering-and-other-forms-of-illicit-finance

D'Antuono, S. M. (2019, May 21). Combating Illicit Financing by Anonymous Shell Companies. *FBI News*. Retrieved from https://www.fbi.gov/news/testimony/combating-illicit-financing-by-anonymous-shell-companies

D'Souza, J. (2012). *Terrorist Financing, Money Laundering and Tax Evasion: Examining the Performance of Financial Intelligence Units*. CRC Press.

Dane, F. C. (1990). *Research Methods*. Brooks/Cole Publishing.

Deflem, M. (2004). Introduction: Towards a Criminological Sociology of Terrorism and Counter-Terrorism. In M. Deflem (Ed.), *Terrorism and Counter-Terrorism: Criminological Perspective*. Elsevier. doi:10.1108/S1521-6136(2004)0000005002

Defossez, D. (2017). The Current Challenges of Money Laundering Law in Russia. *Journal of Money Laundering Control*, *20*(4), 367–385. doi:10.1108/JMLC-09-2016-0041

Deloitte. (2015). *Building world-class ethics and compliance programs: Making a good program great*. Retrieved from https://www2.deloitte.com/content/dam/Deloitte/no/Documents/risk/ Building -world-class-ethics-and-compliance-programs.pdf

Denis, J. S., & Ball, D. P. (2019, May 9). $7.4B Money Laundering scheme spiked B.C. home costs 5 per cent, reports find. *Toronto Star*. Retrieved from https://www.thestar.com/ vancouver/2019/05/09/74-billion-in-illegal-cash-drove-up-bc-house-prices-by-5-per-cent-attracted-more-organized-crime-says-report.html

Denzin, N. K. (1978). *Studies in Symbolic Interaction*. JAI Press.

Denzin, N. K., & Lincoln, Y. S. (2008). *Handbook of qualitative research*. SAGE Publications.

Department of Finance Canada. (2015). Assessment of Inherent Risks of Money Laundering and Terrorist Financing in Canada. *Government of Canada*. Retrieved from https://www.canada.ca/content/dam/fin/migration/pub/mltf-rpcfat/mltf-rpcfat-eng.pdf

Department of Finance Canada. (2018, February 7). Reviewing Canada's Anti-Money Laundering and Anti-Terrorist Financing Regime. *Government of Canada*. Retrieved from https://www.canada.ca/content/dam/fin/migration/activty/consult/amlatfr-rpcfa-eng.pdf

Department of Finance Canada. (2019, June 14). *Joint Statement – Federal, provincial and territorial governments working together to combat Money Laundering and terrorist financing in Canada*. Retrieved from https://www.canada.ca/en/department-finance/news/2019/06/joint-statement--federal-provincial-and-territorial-governments-working-together-to-combat-money-laundering-and-terrorist-financing-in-canada.html

Department of the Treasury Financial Crimes Enforcement Network. (2010). *Advisory to Financial Institutions on Filing Suspicious Activity Reports regarding Trade-Based Money Laundering*. Author.

Dhillon, G., Ahmad, R., Rahman, A., & Miin, N. Y. (2013). The viability of enforcement mechanisms under money laundering and anti-terrorism offences in Malaysia: An overview. *Journal of Money Laundering Control*, *16*(2), 171–192. doi:10.1108/13685201311318511

Dilshad, R. M., & Latif, M. I. (2013). Focus Group Interview as a Tool for Qualitative Research: An Analysis. *Pakistan Journal of Social Sciences*, *33*(1), 191–198.

Dogra, A., & Dogra, M. (2019). Sustainability and Ethical Banking: A Case Study of Punjab National Bank. *Amity Journal of Corporate Governance*, *4*(1), 15–27.

Dopamu, A.P. (2009). *In the Service of Humanity*. A Farewell Lecture, University of Ilorin, Ilorin.

Dostov, V., & Shust, P. (2014). Cryptocurrencies: An unconventional challenge to the AML/CFT regulators? *Journal of Financial Crime*, *21*(3), 249–263. doi:10.1108/JFC-06-2013-0043

Doyle, C. (2017). *Money Laundering: An Overview of 18 U.S.C. § 1956 and Related Federal Criminal Law*. CRS.

Draghi, M. (2011). *Le mafie a Milano e nel Nord: aspetti sociali ed economici*. Retrieved from https://www.bancaditalia.it/pubblicazioni/interventigovernatore/integov2011/Draghi-110311.pdf

Duhaime. (2021). Role of FINTRAC. *Duhaime's Anti-Money Laundering Law in Canada*. Retrieved from https://www.antimoneylaunderinglaw.com/aml-law/role-of-regulator

Dusuki, A. W. (2011). *Islamic Financial Systems: Principles and Operations*. ISRA.

Ede, R. E. (2019, November 20). Police parade Enugu pastor for rape, money ritual. *Punch*. Retrieved from https://punchng.com/police-parade-enugu-pastor-for-rape-money-rituals/

Egmont Group. (2017). *Financial Intelligence Units Operational Guidance for FIU Activities and the Exchange of Information*. Retrieved from www.egmontgroup.org

Ekhomu, O. (2020). *Boko Haram: Security Considerations and the Rise of Insurgency*. CRC Press.

Eldor, R., & Melnick, R. (2004). Financial markets and terrorism. *European Journal of Political Economy*, *20*(2), 367–386. doi:10.1016/j.ejpoleco.2004.03.002

Eme, C. (2016). Terrorist Financing in Nigeria: A Case of *Boko Haram. Specialty Journal of Psychology and Management*, *2*(3), 41–52.

Enofe, A. O., Aliu, A. K., & Ombu, A. (2018). Money laundering and the Nigerian Economy. *International Journal of Advanced Academic Research*, *4*(4), 185–210.

Erlich, R. (2010). *Conversation with Terrorists: Middle East Leaders on Politics, Violence and Empire*. Routledge.

ESAAMLG. (2013). *Typologies Report on Money Laundering through the Real Estate Sector in The ESAAMLG Region*. Tanzania: The Eastern and Southern Africa Anti-Money Laundering Group (ESAAMLG). Retrieved from https://esaamlg.org/reports/TYPOLOGIES-REPORT-ON-Money Laundering-THROUGH-THE-REAL-ESTATE-SECTOR.pdf

Essien, D. E. (2018). Ethical audit of prosperity gospel: Psychological manipulation or social ministry. *International Journal of Knowledge-Based Organizations*, *8*(2), 53–64. doi:10.4018/IJKBO.2018040105

European Parliament. (2019). *Understanding Money Laundering through real estate transactions*. Retrieved from https://www.europarl.europa.eu/cmsdata/161094/7%20-%2001%20EPRS_Understanding %20money%20laundering%20through%20real%20estate%20transactions.pdf

Eurostat. (2017). *Commercial Property Price Indicators: Sources, methods and issues*. Luxembourg: Eurostat Statistical Reports. Retrieved from https://ec.europa.eu/eurostat/documents/7870049/8545612/KS-FT-16-001-EN-N.pdf/9e4bbc9b-8c6f-44a9-b686-1083a7a8fa0f

Evans, J. (2018, April 30). Court Hears of Unexplained Millions from China and Toronto Real Estate. *Better Dwelling*. Retrieved from https://betterdwelling.com/city/toronto/court-hears-of-unexplained-millions-from-china-and-toronto-real-estate/

Evans, J. L. (1999). *Money Laundering Investigations : Practices of Interest To the Asia / Pacific Region*. Retrieved from https://icclr.org/publications/money-laundering-in-the-asia-pacific-working-paper-no-3-money-laundering-investigations-practices-of-interest-to-the-asia-pacific-region/

Ewang, A. (2020). *Attacks on Aid Workers in Northeastern Nigeria: Insurgent Attacks Against Civilian Constitute War Crimes*. Human Rights Watch.

Expert Panel on Emerging Crimes. (2005, January 7). *How is crime changing in the 21st Century?* Ottawa: Department of Justice, Canada. Retrieved from https://www.justice.gc.ca/eng/rp-pr/csj-sjc/crime/rr03_20/p1.html

Fahsing, I., & Ask, K. (2013). Decision Making and Decisional Tipping Points in Homicide Investigations: An Interview Study of British and Norwegian Detectives. *Journal of Investigative Psychology and Offender Profiling*, *10*(2), 155–165. doi:10.1002/jip.1384

Faluyi, O. T., Khan, S., & Akinola, A. O. (2019). *Boko Haram's Terrorism and the Nigerian State: Federalism, Politics and Policies*. Springer Nature. doi:10.1007/978-3-030-05737-4

FATF / GAFILAT. (2018). *Anti-Money Laundering and Counter-Terrorist Financing Measures*. Mexico: Fourth Round Mutual Evaluation Report, Paris: The Financial Action Task Force.

FATF MER. (2015). *Mutual Evaluation Report on Malaysia Anti-Money Laundering and Counter-Terrorist Financing Measures*. Retrieved from https://www.fatf-gafi.org/

FATF MER. (2016). *Mutual Evaluation Report on USA Anti-Money Laundering and Counter-Terrorist Financing Measures*. Retrieved from https://www.fatf-gafi.org/

FATF. (2003). *Financial Action Task Force on Money Laundering, Report on Money Laundering Typologies 2002-2003*. The Financial Action Task Force.

FATF. (2006). Trade Based Money Laundering. *Financial Action Task Force*. Retrieved from https://www.fatf-gafi.org/

FATF. (2007). *Money Laundering & Terrorist Financing through the Real Estate Sector*. Financial Action Task Force. Retrieved from https://www.fatf-gafi.org/documents/documents/moneylaunderingandterroristfinancingthroughtherealestatesector.html

FATF. (2008). *Best Practices on Trade Based Money Laundering*. Retrieved from https://www.fatf-gafi.org/

FATF. (2011). Laundering the Proceeds of corruption in FATF Report. *Financial Action Task Force*. Retrieved from http://www.FATF-gafi.org

FATF. (2012a). *FATF Guidance Document Best Practices Paper Best Practices on Trade Based Money Laundering*. Retrieved from https://www.fatf-gafi.org/

FATF. (2012b). *Operational Issues Financial Investigations Guidance*. Retrieved from https://www.fatf-gafi.org/

FATF. (2012c). *The FATF Recommendations*. Retrieved from https://www.fatf-gafi.org/

FATF. (2013). *Methodology for Assessing Technical Compliance with the FATF Recommendations and the Effectiveness of AML/CFT Systems*. Retrieved from https://www.fatf-gafi.org/

FATF. (2016). *Anti-Money Laundering and Counter-Terrorist Financing Measures*. United States: Fourth Round Mutual Evaluation Report, Paris: The Financial Action Task Force.

FATF. (2016). *Terrorist Financing in Central and West Africa*. Retrieved from http://www.fatf-gafi.org/media/fatf/documents/reports/Terrorist-Financing-West-Central-Africa.pdf

FATF. (2016, September). *Anti-Money Laundering and counter-terrorist financing measures -Canada*. Paris: Financial Action Task Force. Retrieved from http://www.fatf-gafi.org/media/fatf/documents/reports/mer4/MER-Canada-2016.pdf

FATF. (2018). *Anti-Money Laundering and Counter-Terrorist Financing Measures.* United Kingdom: Fourth Round Mutual Evaluation Report, Paris: The Financial Action Task Force.

FATF. (2019). *Anti-money Laundering and Counter-Terrorist Financing Measures.* Turkey: Fourth Round Mutual Evaluation Report, Paris: The Financial Action Task Force.

FATF. (2019). *International Standards on Combating Money Laundering and the Financind of Terrorism & Proliferation*. Financial Action Task Force.

FATF. (2020). Consolidated assessment ratings, FATF Mutual Evaluations. *Financial Action Task Force*. Retrieved from http://www.fatf-gafi.org/publications/mutualevaluations/documents/assessment-ratings.html

FATF. (2020). *COVID-19-related Money Laundering and Terrorist Financing – Risks and Policy Responses*. Financial Action Task Force.

Fender, I., & Kiff, J. (2004). *CDO rating methodology: Some thoughts on model risk and its implications* (Working Paper No. 163). Bank for International Settlement. Retrieved from https://papers.ssrn.com/sol3/papers.cfm?abstract_id=623662

Finney, D. (2020, May 10). Mortgage Fraud: Understanding and Avoiding It. *Investopedia*. Retrieved from https://www.investopedia.com/articles/mortgages-real-estate/10/how-mortgage-fraud-affects-markets.asp

FINTRAC. (2019a, June 21). *Penalties for non-compliance*. Financial Transactions and Reports Analysis Center of Canada, Government of Canada. Retrieved from https://www.fintrac-canafe.gc.ca/pen/1-eng

FINTRAC. (2019b, August). *Guideline 7A: Submitting Large Cash Transaction Reports to FINTRAC Electronically*. Financial Transactions and Reports Analysis Center of Canada, Government of Canada. Retrieved from https://www.fintrac-canafe.gc.ca/guidance-directives/transaction-operation/Guide7A/lctr-eng

Fitzpatrick, D. (2017). A "think piece" on intelligence, investigation and prosecution. *Journal of Financial Crime*, *24*(3), 449–460. doi:10.1108/JFC-03-2017-0018

Fossen, A. (2003). Money Laundering, Global Financial Instability, and Tax Havens in the Pacific Islands. *The Contemporary Pacific*, *15*(2), 237–275. doi:10.1353/cp.2003.0058

Foyou, V. E., Ngwafu, P., Santoyo, M., & Ortiz, A. (2018). The *Boko Haram* Insurgency and its Impact on Border Security, Trade and Economic Collaboration Between Nigeria and Cameroon: An Exploratory Study. *African Social Science Review*, *9*(1), 66–77.

Frontier. (2020). *The Economic Impacts of Counterfeiting and Piracy.* Frontier Economics Ltd. Retrieved from https://iccwbo.org/publication/economic-impacts-counterfeiting-piracy-report-prepared-bascap-inta/

FRS. (2008). Compliance Risk Management Programs and Oversight at Large Banking Organizations with Complex Compliance Profiles. *Federal Reserve System.* Retrieved from https://www.federalreserve.gov/boarddocs/srletters/2008/SR0808.htm

Galloway, G. (2019, October 17). Election Special: Parties Target Money Laundering Housing Schemes. *Toronto Storeys.* Retrieved from https://torontostoreys.com/federal-election-toronto/

Gayathri, S., & Mangaiyarkarasi, T. (2018). A Critical Analysis of the Punjab National Bank Scam and Its Implications. *International Journal of Pure and Applied Mathematics*, *119*(12), 14853–14866.

GECF. (2018). Global Economic Crime and Fraud Survey. *German Prevention Congress.*

George, R. (2020). Two decades of faulty credit policy later, an unending rippling effect of financial crisis and a staggering economy: Indian financial system in a catch 22 situation. *Journal of Engineering Sciences*, *11*(8), 153–160.

German, P. M. (2018, March 31). *Dirty money.* Retrieved from https://s3.amazonaws.com/tld-documents.llnassets.com/0019000/19257/german_gaming_final_report.pdf

GFI. (2019). *Illicit financial flows to and from 148 developing countries: 2006-2015.* Global Financial Integrity. Retrieved from https://www.gfintegrity.org/wp-content/uploads/2019/01/GFI-2019-IFF-Update-Report-1.29.18.pdf

Ghosh, S. (2019, July 20). IL&FS influenced credit ratings in its favour, forensic audit report finds. *Mint.* Retrieved from https://www.livemint.com/companies/news/il-fs-influenced-credit-ratings-in-its-favour-forensic-audit-report-finds-1563611258934.html

GIABA. (2010). *Threat Assessment of Money Laundering and Terrorist Financing in West Africa.* Inter-Governmental action group against money laundering in West Africa. Retrieved from www.GIABA.org

Gibbs, G. (2002). *Qualitative data analysis: explorations with NVivo.* Open University.

Gillham, B. (2000). *Developing a questionnaire.* Continuum.

Gilmore, W. (2004). *Dirty money : the evolution of money laundering counter-measures.* Council of Europe Publishing.

Gilmour, N. (2016a). Preventing money laundering: A test of situational crime prevention theory. *Journal of Money Laundering Control*, *19*(4), 376–396. doi:10.1108/JMLC-10-2015-0045

Gilmour, N. (2016b). Understanding the practices behind money laundering - A rational choice interpretation. *International Journal of Law, Crime and Justice*, *44*, 1–13. doi:10.1016/j.ijlcj.2015.03.002

Ginena, K., & Hamid, A. (2015). *Foundations of Shari'ah governance of Islamic banks*. John Wiley & Sons.

Global Conflict Tracker. (2020). *Recent Development*. Council on Foreign Relations. Retrieved https://www.cfr.org/global-conflict-tracker/

Global Financial Integrity. (2019). *Illicit Financial Flows to and from 148 Developing Countries: 2006-2015*. Global Financial Integrity.

Global Financial Integrity. (2020, January 22). Retrieved from https://gfintegrity.org/about/

Global Terrorism Index. (2019). *Measuring the Impact of Terrorism*. Sydney: Institute for Economics and Peace. Retrieved from https://visionofhumanity.org/reports

Godlewski, R.J. (2007). *Manual of the Independent Counter Terrorist*. US Air force.

Godspower-Akpomiemie, E., & Ojah, K. (2018). *Money laundering, Tax havens, Transparency and Board of Directors of Banks* (MPRA Paper No. 89550). Wits Business School, University of the Witwatersrand. Retrieved from https://mpra.ub.unimuenchen.de/89550/https://www.acic.gov.au/sites/g/files/net1491/f/2017/08/oca_2017_230817_1830.pdf

Gok, I. Y., Demirdogen, Y., & Topuz, S. (2019). The impacts of terrorism on Turkish equity market: An investigation using intraday data. *Physica A*, *540*, 123484. doi:10.1016/j.physa.2019.123484

Google Map. (2020). *Map of Nigeria Showing Northeastern Zone and Six States*. Retrieved from www.googlemap.com

Gopakumar, G. (2019, November 13). Yes Bank faces fresh audit into complaints by whistleblower. *Mint*. Retrieved from https://www.livemint.com/industry/banking/yes-bank-faces-fresh-audit-into-complaints-by-whistleblower-11573668757156.html

Gottschalk, P. (2006). *Knowledge Management Systems in Law Enforcement: Technologies and Techniques*. IGI Global.

Government of Canada. (2020, February). Strengthening Corporate Beneficial Ownership Transparency in Canada. *Government of Canada*. Retrieved from https://www.ic.gc.ca/eic/site/142.nsf/eng/00001.html

Green, B., & Roiphe, R. (2016). Rethinking Prosecutors' Conflicts of Interest. *Boston College Law Review. Boston College. Law School*, *58*(2), 463.

Grubel, H. (Ed.). (2009). *The Effects of Mass Immigration on Canadian Living Standards and Society*. Fraser Institute. Retrieved from https://www.fraserinstitute.org/sites/default/files/EffectsofMassImmigration.pdf

Grujić, M., & Šikman, M. (2020). Certain Manifestation Forms and Proving Money Laundering In The Emerging Market. *Acta Economica*, *18*(32), 175–201.

Guest, G., Namey, E., & McKenna, K. (2017). How Many Focus Groups Are Enough? Building an Evidence Base for Nonprobability Sample Sizes. *Field Methods*, *29*(1), 3–22. doi:10.1177/1525822X16639015

Guevara, M. W. (2016, May 9). *ICIJ releases database revealing thousands of secret offshore companies*. International Consortium of Investigative Journalists. Retrieved from https://panamapapers.icij.org/blog/20160509-offshore-database-release.html

Gujarati, D. N., & Porter, D. (2009). *Basic Econometrics*. McGraw-Hill.

Habibullah, M. S., & Din, B., & Abdul Hamid, B. (2016). Good governance and crime rates in Malaysia. *International Journal of Social Economics*, *43*(3), 308–320. doi:10.1108/IJSE-05-2014-0096

Hadi, D. M., Katircioglu, S., & Adaoglu, C. (2019). The vulnerability of tourism firms' stocks to the terrorist incidents. *Current Issues in Tourism*, *23*(9), 1138–1152. doi:10.1080/13683500.2019.1592124

Hall, J. R. (2009). Apocalypse, History, and the Empire of Modernity. In M. Al-Rashed & M. Shterin (Eds.), *Dying for Faith: Religiously Motivated Violence in Contemporary World*. I.B. Tauris. doi:10.5040/9780755625024.ch-001

Hamin, Z., Wan Rosli, W. R., Omar, N., & Pengiran Mahmud, A. A. (2013). Following the Dirty Money : Legal Issues in Legislating against Money Laundering in Malaysia. *International Conference on Governance, Management & Financial Criminology (ICGMF)*, 2–5.

Hammoudeh, S., & Li, H. (2008). Sudden changes in volatility in emerging markets: The case of Gulf Arab stock markets. *International Review of Financial Analysis*, *17*(1), 47–63. doi:10.1016/j.irfa.2005.01.002

Haralambos, M., & Heald, R. M. (2015). *Sociology: Themes and Perspectives*. Oxford University Press.

Hassan, M. K., Ullah, M. H., & Khanam, R. (2017). Shariah governance practices in Bangladesh. In N. Ali (Ed.), Shariah Governance Systems and Practices in a Globalized World. Academic Press.

Hassan, R., Abdullah, N. I., Hassan, A., Ibrahim, U., & Sawari, M. F. M. (2011). A comparative analysis of Shariah governance in Islamic banking institutions across jurisdictions. Kuala Lumpur: ISRA.

Hassan, M. S., Bukhari, S., & Arshed, N. (2020). Competitiveness, governance and globalization: What matters for poverty alleviation? *Environment, Development and Sustainability*, *22*(4), 3491–3518. doi:10.100710668-019-00355-y

Hathorn, S., & Abbott, C. (2015). Intelligence brief: Reducing the Supply of Weapons to Boko Haram. *Open briefing*. Retrieved from https://www.openbriefing.org/publications/intelligence-briefings/reducing-the-supply-of-weapons-to-boko-haram/)

Heintze, E. A. (2016). *Global Violence: Ethical and Political Issues*. Routledge. doi:10.4324/9781315684642

Helmus, T. C. (2009). Why and How Some People Become Terrorists. In P. K. Davis & K. Cragin (Eds.), *Social Science for Counter Terrorism: Putting the Pieces Together*. RAND Corporation.

Hendriyetty, N., & Grewal, B. S. (2017). Macroeconomics of money laundering: Effects and measurements. *Journal of Financial Crime*, *24*(1), 65–81. doi:10.1108/JFC-01-2016-0004

Hennig, C. (2017, October 2). 'Political will' needed to stop Money Laundering in casinos, former investigator says. *CBC News*. Retrieved from https://www.cbc.ca/news/canada /british-columbia/former-director-of-casino-investigations-political-will-1.4317138

He, P. (2010). A typological study on money laundering. *Journal of Money Laundering Control*, *13*(1), 15–32. doi:10.1108/13685201011010182

Hernandez, J. (2019). Money Laundering is a national crisis. What now? *CPA Canada*. Retrieved from https://www.cpacanada.ca/en/news/pivot-magazine/2019-07-03-jose-hernandez-money-laundering

Hetemi, A., Merovci, S., & Gulhan, O. (2018). Consequences of money laundering on economic growth – The Case of Kosovo and its Trade Partners. *Acta Universitatis Danubius Œconomica*, *14*(3), 113–125.

Hossain, M. M. (2012). Financial statements of banks under Islamic *Shariah*: Status of regulatory compliance. *Thoughts on Economics*, *22*(1), 53–67.

Howard, F. (2014). *Failed States and the Origins of Violence: A Comparative Analysis of State Failure as a Root Cause of Terrorism and Political Violence*. Routledge.

Howell, K. E. (2012). *An Introduction to the Philosophy of Methodology*. SAGE Publications.

Hubbard, D. W. (2014). *The Failure of Risk Management: Why It's Broken and How to Fix it*. John Wiley & Sons, Inc.

Hudak, S. (2017, August 22). FinCEN Targets Shell Companies Purchasing Luxury Properties in Seven Major Metropolitan Areas. *The Financial Crimes Enforcement Network*. Retrieved from https://www.fincen.gov/news/news-releases/fincen-targets-shell-companies-purchasing-luxury-properties-seven-major

IAIS. (2004). Anti-Money Laundering and Combating the Financing of Terrorism (Guidance Paper No: 5). International Association of Insurance Supervisors.

Ibrahim, J., & Bala, S. (2018). *Civilian Led-Governance and Security in Nigeria After Boko Haram*. United States Institute for Peace. Retrieved from www.usip.org

Ibrahim, B. A. (2020). Interest-Free Micro-Finance without any Religious Connotation: An Inclusive Global Model. In A. Rafay (Ed.), *Handbook of Research on Theory and Practice of Global Islamic Finance* (pp. 196–215). IGI Global. doi:10.4018/978-1-7998-0218-1.ch011

Ibrahim, P., & Hoffman, A. C. (2017). *A Gift from Darkness: How I Escaped with my Daughter from Boko Haram*. Other Press.

Idika-Kalu, C. (2020). *The Socioeconomic Impact of the Boko Haram Insurgency in the Lake Chad Basin Region*. Intech Open., doi:10.5772/intechopen.89905

IFSB. (2009). *Guiding principles on Shari'ah governance systems for institutions offering Islamic financial services*. Islamic Financial Services Board.

IIROC. (2019, May 30). IIROC and FINTRAC enhance cooperation to protect against Money Laundering. *Newswire*. Retrieved from https://www.newswire.ca/news-releases/iiroc-and-fintrac-enhance-cooperation-to-protect-against-money-laundering-840123760.html

IMF. (2016, March 21). The IMF and the Fight against Money Laundering and the Financing of Terrorism. *International Monetary Fund*. Retrieved from https://www.imf.org/en/About/Factsheets/Sheets/2016/08/01/16/31/Fight-Against-Money-Laundering-the-Financing-of-Terrorism

INCB. (2001). *Globalization and New Technologies : Challenges to Drug Law Enforcement in the Twenty-first Century*. INCB.

Inclan, C., & Tiao, G. C. (1994). Use of cumulative sums of squares for retrospective detection of changes of variance. *Journal of the American Statistical Association*, *89*(427), 913–923.

International Crisis Group. (2020). *Boko Haram: Executive Summary*. International Crisis Group.

INTERPOL. (2020). *Organised Crimes*. International Criminal Police Organisation. Retrieved from ttps://www.interpol.int/en/Crimes/Organized-crime

Investopedia Staff. (2020, September 2). How Does Supply and Demand Affect the Housing Market? *Investopedia*. Retrieved from https://www.investopedia.com/ask/answers/040215/how-does-law-supply-and-demand-affect-housing-market.asp

Irshad, H., Hussain, H., & Saba, I. (2019). Terrorism and Stock Markets: Cross-Country Evidence. *Pakistan Journal of Social Sciences*, *39*(4), 1295–1306.

Irwin, A. S. M., Choo, K.-K. R., & Liu, L. (2012a). An analysis of money laundering and terrorism financing typologies. *Journal of Money Laundering Control*, *15*(1), 85–111. doi:10.1108/13685201211194745

Irwin, A. S. M., Choo, K.-K. R., & Liu, L. (2012b). Modelling of money laundering and terrorism financing typologies. *Journal of Money Laundering Control*, *15*(3), 316–335. doi:10.1108/13685201211238061

Irwin, A. S., & Dawson, C. (2019). Following the cyber money trail: Global challenges when investigating ransomware attacks and how regulation can help. *Journal of Money Laundering Control*, *22*(1), 110–131. doi:10.1108/JMLC-08-2017-0041

Islamic, B. M. B. (2011). *Global Islamic Finance Report (GIFR) (2011)*. BMB.

Iyi, J. (2018). On the Brink? The Nigerian State and the Making of *Boko Haram*. In J. Iyi & H. Strydom (Eds.), *Boko Haram and International Law*. Springer Nature. doi:10.1007/978-3-319-74957-0_1

Jackson, O. A. (2008). The impact of the 9/11 terrorist attacks on the US economy. *Journal of 9/11 Studies, 20*(1), 1-27.

James, C. (2019, May 9). What steps will province take to combat Money Laundering in B.C. *Global News*. Retrieved from https://globalnews.ca/video/5259885/what-steps-will-province-take-to-combat-money-laundering-in-b-c

Javaid, M. E., & Kousar, S. (2018). Impact of Terrorism, Political System and Exchange Rate Fluctuations on Stock Market Volatility. *Iranian Journal of Management Studies*, *11*(3), 519–546.

Jayasekara, S. D. (2020a). Deficient regimes of anti-money laundering and countering the financing of terrorism: Analysis of short term economic implications. *Journal of Money Laundering Control*, *23*(3), 663–675. doi:10.1108/JMLC-02-2020-0015

Jayasekara, S. D. (2020b). (Forthcoming). How effective are the current global standards in combating money laundering and terrorist financing? *Journal of Money Laundering Control*, *ahead-of-print*(ahead-of-print). Advance online publication. doi:10.1108/JMLC-05-2020-0047

Jayraman, T. K., Lee, C., & Ng, C. (2019). The Causal Factors behind Rising Non-performing Assets of India's Commercial Banks: A Panel Study. *Advances in Pacific Basin Business, Economics and Finance*, *7*, 201–212.

Jensen, D. (1997). Prospective assessment of AI technologies for fraud detection: A case study. In *AAAI Workshop on AI Approaches to Fraud Detection and Risk Management* (pp. 34-38). Retrieved from https://www.aaai.org/Library/Workshops/1997/ws97-07-007.php

Jeyanthi, P., Mansurali, A., & Krishnaveni, V. (2020). Significance of fraud analytics in Indian Banking sectors. *Journal of Critical Reviews*, *7*(4), 209–213.

Joffe, H., & Yardley, L. (2004). *Content and thematic analysis. Research methods for clinical and health psychology*. Sage.

Kander, R. (2001). *Türkiye'de Hususi Sigorta Hukuku* [Private Insurance Law in Turkey]. Beta Publications.

Kane, L. D. (2020, February 27). Canada must expose hidden company owners to end 'snow washing,' inquiry hears. *CBC News*. Retrieved from https://www.cbc.ca/news/canada/british-columbia/money-laundering-bc-inquiry-snow-washing-1.5477916

Kannangara, S. N., & Uguccioni, P. (2013). Risk management in crowdsourcing-based business ecosystems. *Technology Innovation Management Review*, *3*(12), 32–38. doi:10.22215/timreview/751

Kassim, A., & Nwankpa, M. (2018). *The Boko Haram Reader: From Nigerian Preachers to the Islamic State*. Oxford University Press. doi:10.1093/oso/9780190908300.001.0001

Katkov, N. (2014). *Anti-Money Laundering: A Brave New World for Financial Institutions*. CELENT.

Kaufmann, D., Kraay, A., & Mastruzzi, M. (2010). *The Worldwide Governance Indicators: Methodology and Analytical Issues* (Draft Policy Research Working Paper). The World Bank.

Kaur, L. (2020). PNB SCAM: Shining Diamond Trader Took Away PNB's Shine. *International Journal of Engineering Development and Research*, *8*(1), 51–55.

Kaya, M. (2010). Suç Gelirlerinin Aklanmasında Bir Araç Olarak Sigortacılık Sektörünün Kullanılması [The Use of Insurance Sector as a Tool in Laundering Proceeds of Crime]. *Sosyal Güvenlik Dünyası Dergisi*, *68*, 1–10.

Kayode-Adedeji, D. (2019, December 29). Man takes girlfriend to 'pastor' for money ritual where she's beheaded – Police. *Premium Times*. Retrieved from https://www.premiumtimesng.com/news/more-news/370259-man-takes-girlfriend-to-pastor-for-money-ritual-where-shes-beheaded-police.html

Keohane, R. O. (2001). Governance in a Partially Globalized World Presidential Address, American Political Science Association 2000. *The American Political Science Review*, *95*(1), 1–13. doi:10.1017/S0003055401000016

Khan, M. (1994). *Accounting issues and concepts for Islamic banking*. Paper presented at the International Conference on Developing Accounting Standards for Islamic Banks, London, UK.

Khan, N., Rafay, A., & Shakeel, A. (2020). Attributes of Internal Audit and Prevention, Detection and Assessment of Fraud in Pakistan. *Lahore Journal of Business*, *9*(1), 33–58. doi:10.35536/ljb.2020.v9.i1.a2

Khanna, A., & Arora, B. (2009). A study to investigate the reasons for bank frauds and the implementation of preventive security controls in the Indian banking industry. *International Journal of Business Science and Applied Management*, *4*(3), 1–21.

Kim, Y.-C. (2003). *The Effective System of Criminal Investigation and Prosecution in Korea* (No. Resource Material Series No. 60).

Kingston, K. G. (2011). Churches and private educational institutions as facilitator of money laundering in Nigeria. *African Journal of Education and Technology*, *1*(1), 30–38.

Kirpekar, U. (2009). *Information Operation in Pursuit of Terrorists*. Master's Thesis Submitted to The Naval Postgraduate School, Monterrey, CA.

Kirti, A., Kumar, P., & Yadav, R. (2011). The face of honour based crimes: Global concerns and solutions. *International Journal of Criminal Justice Sciences*, *6*(1/2), 343.

Kishore, R. (2018, May 26). Reserve Bank of India data shows rise in big-ticket bank frauds. *Hindustan Times*. Retrieved from https://www.hindustantimes.com/business-news/reserve-bank-of-india-data-shows-rise-in-big-ticket-bank-frauds/story-MJio0ibsS1V31reOx1yhdN.html

Koh, J. (2006). *Suppressing Terrorist Financing and Money Laundering*. Springer.

Kolte, A., & Wagh, P. (2019). Analyzing Punjab National Bank Scam. *Journal of Emerging Technologies and Innovative Research*, *6*(6), 585–592.

Korystin, O. Y., Nekrasov, V. A., Krivolapchuk, V. O., & Sviridyuk, N. P. (2019). The Phenomenology of Money Laundering in Ukraine. *Financial and Credit Activity: Problems of Theory and Practice*, *2*(29), 374–382. doi:10.18371/fcaptp.v2i29.171949

Koščo, M. (2017). *Impact of Terrorism on Stock Markets*. Unpublished Dissertation. Charles University. Retrieved from https://dspace.cuni.cz/handle/20.500.11956/91443

KPMG. (2019). *KPMG Global Banking Fraud Survey 2019*. Retrieved from https://home.kpmg/xx/en/home/insights/2019/05/the-multi-faceted-threat-of-fraud-are-banks-up-to-the-challenge-fs.html

Kumar, S., & Liu, J. (2013). Impact of terrorism on international stock markets. *The Journal of Applied Business and Economics*, *14*(4), 42.

Kvale, S. (1996). *Interviews: an introduction to qualitative research interviewing*. Sage.

Kvale, S. (2008). *Doing Interviews Qualitative Research Kit*. SAGE Publications.

Kwok, D. (2016). New developments in Hong Kong's anti-money laundering laws. *Journal of Money Laundering Control*, *19*(3), 291–297. doi:10.1108/JMLC-06-2015-0023

Lee-Shanok, P. (2019, March 21). Criminals hiding billions of dollars in GTA real estate, watchdog claims. *CBC News*. Retrieved from https://www.cbc.ca/news/canada/toronto/anti-corruption-group-claims-criminals-laundering-money-through-toronto-real-estate-1.5065777

Leslie, D. (2020, March 31). FINTRAC revises expectations for reporting entities amid pandemic. *Financial services: Regulation tomorrow. Norton Rose Fulbright.* Retrieved from https://www.regulationtomorrow.com/ca/fintrac-revises-expectations-for-reporting-entities-amid-pandemic/

Levi, M., & Soudijn, M. (2020). Understanding the laundering of organized crime money. *Crime and Justice*, *49*(1), 1–53. doi:10.1086/708047

Lewisch, P. (2018). Corporate criminal liability for foreign bribery: Perspectives from civil law jurisdictions within the European Union. *Law and Financial Markets Review*, *12*(1), 31–38. doi:10.1080/17521440.2018.1435457

Li, H., Zhang, J., & Sarathy, R. (2010). Understanding compliance with internet use policy from the perspective of rational choice theory. *Decision Support Systems*, *48*(4), 635–645. doi:10.1016/j.dss.2009.12.005

Livingstone, D. (2007). *Terrorism and the Illuminati: A Three Thousand Year History*. BookSurge LLC.

Lochead, D., & Dhanraj, T. (2019, July 11). Empty properties: Money Laundering and housing affordability in GTA. *Global News*. Retrieved from https://globalnews.ca/news/5484606/money-laundering-housing-affordability-in-gta/

Lokanan, M. E. (2019). Data mining for statistical analysis of Money Laundering transactions. *Journal of Money Laundering Control*, *22*(4), 753–763. doi:10.1108/JMLC-03-2019-0024

Lone, J. A., Garnås, A., Myklebust, T., Bjørklund, R., Hoff, T., & Bjørkli, C. (2017). Organizational climate and investigation performance in the Norwegian police: A qualitative study. *Journal of Investigative Psychology and Offender Profiling*, *14*(3), 227–245. doi:10.1002/jip.1474

Lowery, C., & Ramachandran, V. (2015, November 9). Unintended Consequences of Anti–Money Laundering Policies for Poor Countries. *Center for Global Development*. Retrieved from https://www.cgdev.org/publication/unintended-consequences-anti-money-laundering-policies-poor-countries

LTSA. (2021). 8 Key Facts about the Landowner Transparency Registry. *Land and Title and Service Authority*. Retrieved from https://ltsa.ca/

Maddock, R. (May 2018). *How Commonwealth Bank got itself into such a mess*. Financial Review. https://www.afr.com/opinion/cbas-ordeal-does-australia-a-service-20180502-h0zizj

Madinger, J. (2012). Money Laundering: A Guide for Criminal Investigators. CRC Press.

Maloney, M., Somerville, T., & Unger, B. (2019, May 31). Combatting Money Laundering in BC Real Estate. *Cullen Commission*. Retrieved from https://cullencommission.ca/files/Combatting_Money_Laundering_Report.pdf

Mamdani, M. (2000). Good Muslim, Bad Muslim: America, Cold War and the Root of Terror. Washington: Oxford.

Mamdani, M. (2004). *Contemporary Political Terror: Its Origins in the Late Cold War*. Ahmadu Bello University.

Man-wai, T. K. (2005). *Visiting Experts Papers: Investigation of Money Laundering and Corruption*. Academic Press.

Marria, V. (2018, November 21). Criminals are Using Your Dream Home to Clean Dirty Money. *Forbes*. Retrieved from https://www.forbes.com/sites/vishalmarria/2018/11/21/criminals-are-filling-your-dream-home-with-dirty-money/?sh=2b8052fd22e3

MASAK. (2020). *Financial Crimes Investigation Board*. Retrieved from https://en.hmb.gov.tr/fcib-presentation

Masciandaro, D., Takats, E., & Unger, B. (2007). *Black Finance: The Economics of Money Laundering*. Edward Elgar Publishing.

Matthew, O. A., Babajide, A. A., Osabohien, R., Adeniji, A., Ewetan, O. O., Adu, O., & Edafe, O. (2020). Challenges of accountability and development in Nigeria. *Journal of Money Laundering Control, 23*(2), 387–402. doi:10.1108/JMLC-10-2019-0086

Maulidi, A. (2020). Storytelling of bureaucratic white-collar crimes in Indonesia: Is it a matter of reciprocal norm? *Journal of Financial Crime, 27*(2), 573–586. doi:10.1108/JFC-07-2019-0087

Maylam, S. (2002). Prosecution for money laundering in the UK. *Journal of Financial Crime, 10*(2), 157–158. doi:10.1108/13590790310808754

McCahill, E. (2019). *ISIS funded Sri Lanka Easter bombings with Bitcoin donations.* Retrieved from https://www.mirror.co.uk/news/world-news/isis-funded-sri-lanka-easter-14982949

McCarthy, B., & Chaudhary, A. (2014). Rational choice theory and crime. Encyclopedia of Crime and Criminal Justice.

McClelland, C. (2019, October 16). Immigrant-fuelled demand is helping to power Canada's housing market *Financial Post*. Retrieved from https://financialpost.com/real-estate/immigrant-fuelled-demand-is-helping-to-power-canadas-housing-market

McDowell, J., & Novis, G. (2001). The Consequences of Money Laundering and Financial Crime. *Economic Perspectives, 6*(2), 6–8. https://www.hsdl.org/?view&did=3549

McEachern, S. (2018). *Searching for Boko Haram: A History of Violence in Central Africa.* Oxford University Press.

Mclaughlin, J. S., & Pavelka, D. (2013). The use of customer due delligence to combat money laundering. *Accountancy Business and Pbulic Interest*, 57-84. Retrieved from http://visar.csustan.edu/aaba/McLaughlinPavelka2013.pdf

Meissner, D. (2019a, April 8). B.C. Money Laundering report finds no federal officers dedicated to case. *The London Free Press*. Retrieved from https://lfpress.com/pmn/news-pmn/canada-news-pmn/b-c-money-laundering-report-finds-no-federal-officers-dedicated-to-case/wcm/94c06dc8-f147-4095-8f04-d3447a9d1086/

Meissner, D. (2019b, January 18). Money Laundering in B.C. estimated at $1B a year — but reports were not shared with province, AG says. *CBC News*. Retrieved from https://www.cbc.ca/news/canada/british-columbia/money-laundering-billions-bc-david-eby-1.4983471

Memdani, L., & Shenoy, G. (2019). Impact of terrorism on stock markets across the world and stock returns: An event study of Taj attack in India. *Journal of Financial Crime, 25*(3), 793–807. doi:10.1108/JFC-09-2018-0093

MengYun, W., Imran, M., Zakaria, M., Linrong, Z., Farooq, M.U., & Muhammad, S.K. (2017). Impact of Terrorism and Political Instability on Equity Premium: Evidence from Pakistan. *Physica A, 492*, 1753–1762.

Merriam, S. B. (2009). *Qualitative research: A guide to design and implementation.* Jossey-Bass.

Merwin, R. (2020, March 14). YES Bank rescue plan: Will SBI and consortium of private lenders be able to bail out the bank. *The Hindu business Line.* Retrieved from https://www.thehindubusinessline.com/money-and-banking/yes-bank-rescue-plan-will-sbi-and-consortium-of-private-lenders-be-able-to-bail-out-the-bank/article31067637.ece

MinhasI. (2012). *Shari'ah governance model (SGM) and its four basic Pillars.* Islamic Finance News Malaysia Published by Red Money Publication. Retrieved from https://ssrn.com/abstract=2153106

Ministry of Finance. (2019). *Increase in detection and reporting of bank frauds due to Government's proactive measures* (Release ID: 1573465). Retrieved from https://pib.gov.in/PressReleaseIframePage.aspx?PRID=1573465

Miralis, N. G. (2018, May 14). How is money laundered through real estate? *Lexology.* Retrieved from https://www.lexology.com/library/detail.aspx?g=4242839e-373c-4525-a853-3ad5cc84a17b

MLCA. (1986). *The Money Laundering Control Act of 1986:Creating a New Federal Offense or Merely Affording Federal Prosecutors an Alternative Means of Punishing Specified Unlawful Activity?* Retrieved from https://scholarship.law.nd.edu/cgi/viewcontent.cgi?article=1014&context=law_faculty_scholarship

Mnasri, A., & Nechi, S. (2016). Impact of Terrorist Attacks on Stock Market Volatility in Emerging Markets. *Emerging Markets Review, 28*, 184–202. doi:10.1016/j.ememar.2016.08.002

Moamil. (2014). Money Laundering and Its Global Modes. A Serious Challenge to Law Enforcement Agencies. Some Observations. *International Journal of Humanities and Social Science Invention, 3*(12), 40–44.

Mohamed, Z. M., & Ahmad, K. (2012). Investigation and prosecution of money laundering cases in Malaysia. *Journal of Money Laundering Control, 15*(4), 421–429. doi:10.1108/13685201211266006

Monroe, B. (2020, June 18). *Regional Report Canada: As gun-shy FINTRAC regains penalty powers, government strengthens Anti-Money Laundering, will enforcement rise?* Association of Certified Financial Crime Specialist. Retrieved from https://www.acfcs.org/regional-report-canada-as-gun-shy-fintrac-regains-penalty-powers-government-strengthens-aml-will-enforcement-rise/

Montes, G. C., & Paschoal, P. C. (2016). Corruption: What are the effects on government effectiveness? Empirical evidence considering developed and developing countries. *Applied Economics Letters, 23*(2), 146–150.

Moranis, H. (2019, May 16). When it comes to Money Laundering in real estate, there are more unknowns than knowns. *Financial Post.* Retrieved from https://financialpost.com/real-estate/when-it-comes-to-money-laundering-in-real-estate-there-are-more-unknowns-than-knowns

Mordor. (2021). Canada Real Estate Services Market - Growth, Trends, Covid-19 Impact, And Forecasts (2021 - 2026). *Mordor Intelligence.* Retrieved from https://www.mordorintelligence.com/industry-reports/canada-real-estate-services-market---growth-trends-and-forecast-2020---2025

Moses, J. (2017). Small Arms and Light Weapons Proliferation in the Early 21st Century: The Nigerian Case. *International Journal of Development and Sustainability, 6*(11), 1638–1652.

Moussa, F. B., & Talbi, M. (2019). Stock Market Reaction to Terrorist Attacks and Political Uncertainty: Empirical Evidence from the Tunisian Stock Exchange. *International Journal of Economics and Financial Issues*, *9*(3), 48–64. doi:10.32479/ijefi.7968

MREA. (2014). *Money Laundering*. Manitoba Real Estate Association Retrieved from https://realestatemanitoba.com/module3/unit12/unit12new_sess1_money_laundering.htm

Muhammed, A. Y., Sulaiman, L. A., Raji, A., & Oluyemi, J. (2018). Materialism or Paradise: A Psycho-Spiritual Inquiry into Why People go to Prayer Mountains in South-West Nigeria. In S. N. Yaovi, P. U. Nwosu, A. G. Alamu, L. E. Odeh, & A. Y. Mohammed (Eds.), *Ori-Oke spirituality and social change in Africa: Contemporary perspectives* (pp. 45–60). Langaa Research & Publishing Common Initiative Group. doi:10.2307/j.ctvh9vtpk.7

Muller, W. H., Kalin, C. H., & Goldsworth, J. G. (2007). *Anti-Money Laundering: International Law and Practice*. Wiley and Sons.

Müsteşarlığı, H. (2020). Sigortacılık ve BES Faaliyet Raporu-2020 [Insurance and BES Annual Report-2020]. Ankara, 2020. Hazine Müsteşarlığı, 2020 Yılı Sigortacılık ve Bireysel Emeklilik Faaliyet Raporu Basın Özeti, Ankara.

Mutahheri, A. M. (1977). *Islam, man and universe*. The Islamic Seminary.

MW. (2019, June 30). China relaxes some foreign-investment restrictions. *Market Watch*. Retrieved from https://www.marketwatch.com/story/china-relaxes-some-foreign-investment-restrictions-2019-06-30

Narayan, S., Le, T. H., & Sriananthakumar, S. (2018). The influence of terrorism risk on stock market integration: Evidence from eight OECD countries. *International Review of Financial Analysis*, *58*, 247–259. doi:10.1016/j.irfa.2018.03.011

Nasir, M. A. (2018). Compatibility of Islamic finance and anti-money laundering laws: A myth or reality? *IIUM Law Journal*, *26*(1), 55–78. doi:10.31436/iiumlj.v26i1.344

Nasir, M. A. (2020). The Relevance of Maqasid al Shari'ah to Anti-Money Laundering and Terrorism Financing. In A. Rafay (Ed.), *Handbook of Research on Theory and Practice of Global Islamic Finance* (pp. 179–194). IGI Global. doi:10.4018/978-1-7998-0218-1.ch010

Nathanson, S. (2010). *Terrorism and the Ethics of War*. Cambridge University Press. doi:10.1017/CBO9780511845215

National Bureau of Statistics. (2020). *Population of Nigeria*. Retrieved from www.nbs.org

News, U. N. (2018). *Child sexual abuse and exploitation: UN event sheds light on the unthinkable*. UN News. Retrieved from https://news.un.org/en/story/2018/10/1022152

Nikkinen, J., Omran, M. M., Sahlström, P., & Äijö, J. (2008). Stock returns and volatility following the September 11 attacks: Evidence from 53 equity markets. *International Review of Financial Analysis*, *17*(1), 27–46. doi:10.1016/j.irfa.2006.12.002

Nikkinen, J., & Vähämaa, S. (2010). Terrorism and stock market sentiment. *Financial Review*, *45*(2), 263–275. doi:10.1111/j.1540-6288.2010.00246.x

Nofianti, L., & Suseno, N. (2014). Factors affecting implementation of good government governance (GGG) and their implications towards performance accountability. *Social and Behavioral Sciences*, *164*, 98–105.

Nomran, N. M., & Haron, R. (2020). Shari'ah Governance for Islamic Banking: Evidence from Diverse Regulatory Environments. In A. Rafay (Ed.), *Growth and Emerging Prospects of International Islamic Banking* (pp. 213–244). IGI Global. doi:10.4018/978-1-7998-1611-9.ch012

Noordin, N. H., & Kassim, S. (2019). Does *Shariah* committee composition influence *Shariah* governance disclosure? *Journal of Islamic Accounting and Business Research*, *10*(2), 158–184. doi:10.1108/JIABR-04-2016-0047

Nowak, M., & Gsell, A. (2018). *Handmade and Deadly Craft Production of Small Arms in Nigeria*. Palgrave Macmillan.

O'Brien, F. (2015). Property sales spike sparks money laundering fears. *BIV*. Retrieved from https://biv.com/article/2015/04/property-sales-spike-sparks-money-laundering-fears

OAS-CICTE. (2015). Technical Assessment-Comparative Analysis of Typologies and Patterns of Money Laundering and Terrorism Financing in Three Free Trade Zones in Latin America. *Inter-American Committee against Terrorism*. Retrieved from https://www.oas.org/en/sms/cicte/documents.asp

Obiora, C. O., & Olugbuo, B. C. (2011). The economic and financial crimes commission and the accountability of corrupt foreign actors in Nigeria. *The Law and Development Review*, *4*(3), 2–26.

OECD. (2007). *Report on Tax Fraud and Money Laundering Vulnerabilities Involving the Real Estate Sector.* Center for Tax Policy and Administration, OECD. Retrieved from http://www.oecd.org/ctp/exchange-of-tax-information/42223621.pdf

OECD. (2014). *Illicit financial flows from developing countries: Measuring OECD responses*. Organisation for Economic Co-operation and Development. Retrieved from https://www.OECD.org/corruption/Illicit_Financial_Flows_from_Developing_Countries.pdf

OECD. (2014). Risk Management and Corporate Governance. *The Organization for Economic Co-operation and Development*. Retrieved from http://www.oecd.org/daf/ca/risk-management-corporate-governance.pdf

OECD. (2019). *Combatting Tax Crimes More Effectively in APEC Economies*. Organisation for Economic Co-operation and Development.

Ogbeche, D. (2016, March 18). Kwara takes over prosecution of prophet alfa who visit cemetery for human heads. *Daily Post*. Retrieved from https://dailypost.ng/2016/03/18/kwara-takes-over-prosecution-of-prophet-alfa-who-visit-cementary-for-human-heads/

Ogbodo, U. K., & Mieseigha, E. G. (2013). The economic implications of money laundering in Nigeria. *International Journal of Academic Research in Accounting. Finance and Management Sciences*, *3*(4), 170–184.

Okoli, A. (2019). *Boko Haram Insurgency and the Necessity for Trans-Territorial Forestland Governance in the Lower Lake Chad Basin*. ACCORD, AJCR 2019/1.

Okolo, B.I., & Akubo, A. (2019). *Boko Haram Insurgency in Nigeria: Implications for National Security and Restorative Justice*. ACCORD, AJCR 2019/2.

Okoye, E. I., Akamobi, N. L., & Akamobi, A. A. (2008). Effectiveness of Nigeria's Financial System for Prevention of Money Laundering. *Journal of Applied Economics and Business*, *1*(1), 93–103.

Okoye, E. I., & Gbegi, D. O. (2013). Forensic accounting: A tool for fraud detection and prevention in the public sector. (A study of selected ministries in Kogi State). *International Journal of Academic Research in Business & Social Sciences*, *3*(3), 1–19.

Okunlola, O. C. (2014). Money Laundering: A Threat to Sustainable Democracy in Nigeria. *Journal of Economics and Sustainable Development*, *5*(2), 85–98.

Olivier, C. (2016, May 12). $31.1-million Point Grey mansion owned by 'student'. *Vancouver Sun*. Retrieved from https://vancouversun.com/business/real-estate/31-1-million-point-grey-mansion-owned-by-student

Olukoya, S. (2019). *How Climate Change is Fueling Insurgency of Nigeria's Militant Boko Haram*. Relief Web. Retrieved from https://reliefweb.int/report/nigeria/how-climate-change-fuelling-insurgency-nigeria-s-militant-boko-haram

Omar, N., Johari, R. J., & Sathye, M. (2015). Malaysian DNFBPs' Perceptions on Awareness, Perceived Impact and Views on the AML/CFT Requirements. *Procedia Economics and Finance*, *31*(15), 595–600. doi:10.1016/S2212-5671(15)01146-6

Owoyemi, M. Y. (2016). The obsession of Nigerians with miracles in the Islamic and Christian religions. In Y. A. Quadri, R. W. Omotoye, & R. I. Adebayo (Eds.), *Religion in contemporary Nigeria* (pp. 297–322). Adonis & Abbey Publishers.

Palmiotto, M. J. (2012). Financial Investigation. In M. L. Birzer & C. Roberson (Eds.), *Introduction to criminal investigation* (pp. 199–207). CRC Press.

Pande, S., & Prakash, V. (2019). Case Study on Scam in Indian Banking industry (NiravModi). *Pramana Research Journal*, *9*(6), 626–630.

Pandey, N. (2019). Infrastructure Development and Financial Services: A Case Study on IL&FS. *International Journal for Research in Engineering Application & Management,* 65-66.

Pang, G. (2018, April 26). Lawyers Must Keep Client Identity Confidential. *Jackpot Lawyer*. Retrieved from https://www.jackpotlawyer.ca/why-solicitor-client-privilege-matters/#:~:text=A%20lawyer%20cannot%20be%20forced,This%20means%20complete%20confidentiality

Pan, S. (2020). Analysis of Frauds in Indian Banking Sector. *International Journal of Trend in Scientific Research and Development*, *4*(3), 70–73.

Park, J. H., Gu, B., Leung, A. C. M., & Konana, P. (2014). An investigation of information sharing and seeking behaviors in online investment communities. *Computers in Human Behavior*, *31*(1), 1–12. doi:10.1016/j.chb.2013.10.002

Paternoster, R., & Simpson, S. (1996). Sanction Threats and Appeals to Morality: Testing a Rational Choice Model of Corporate Crime. *Law & Society Review*, *30*(3), 549–583. doi:10.2307/3054128

Patton, M. Q. (2002). *Qualitative research and evaluation methods*. SAGE publications.

PERC. (2018). Political & Economic Risk Consultancy. Hong Kong: Corrupt Practices Investigation Bureau.

Pereznieto, P., Montes, A., Langston, L., & Routier, S. (2014, September). The costs and economic impact of violence against children. *Child Fund Alliance*, 1-10. Retrieved from https://www.childfund.org/uploadedFiles/public_site/media/Articles/current/2014/ODI%20Report%20%20The%20cost%20and%20economic%20impact%20of%20violence%20against%20children.pdf

Perves, M. M. (2015). Legal and regulatory framework in Islamic banking system: Bangladesh perspective. *European Journal of Business and Management*, *7*(21), 179–188.

Pesaran, M. H., & Shin, Y. (1998). An autoregressive distributed-lag modelling approach to cointegration analysis. *Econometric Society Monographs*, *31*, 371–413. doi:10.1017/CCOL0521633230.011

Petty, B., & Raiborn, C. (2016). Helping Law Enforcement Secure Successful Financial Crime Prosecutions. *Management Accounting Quarterly*, *17*(2), 21–29.

Ping, H. E. (2008). The measures on combating money laundering and terrorism financing in the PRC: From the perspective of financial action task force. *Journal of Money Laundering Control*, *11*(4), 320–330. doi:10.1108/13685200810910394

Planner, S. J. (2019, May 10). Surprise! Money Laundering DID impact Real Estate Market. *Price Tags*. Retrieved from https://pricetags.ca/2019/05/10/surprise-money-laundering-did-impact-real-estate-market/

Pok, W. C., Omar, N., & Sathye, M. (2014). An Evaluation of the Effectiveness of Anti-Money Laundering and Anti-Terrorism Financing Legislation: Perceptions of Bank Compliance Officers in Malaysia. *Australian Accounting Review*, *24*(4), 394–401. doi:10.1111/auar.12054

Poormazahaeri, M., Geravand, Z., & Hematfar, M. (2013). Money laundering and its effect on social and political economy in Iran. *European Online Journal of Natural and Social Sciences: Proceedings*, *2*(3 (s)), 607.

Prakasa, S. U. W. (2019). Garuda Indonesia-Rolls Royce Corruption, Transnational Crime, and Eradication Measures. *Lentera Hukum*, *6*(3), 409–426. doi:10.19184/ejlh.v6i3.14112

Pratt, T. C. (2008). Rational Choice Theory, Crime Control Policy, and Criminological Relevance. *Criminology & Public Policy*, *7*(1), 43–52. doi:10.1111/j.1745-9133.2008.00489.x

PWC. (2014). *Goods Gone Bad: Addressing Money-Laundering Risk in the Trade Finance System*. PWC.

Rafay, A. (2019). *FinTech as a Disruptive Technology for Financial Institutions*. IGI Global. doi:10.4018/978-1-5225-7805-5

Rafay, A. (Ed.). (2020a). *HandBook of Research on Theory and Practice of Global Islamic Finance*. IGI Global. doi:10.4018/978-1-7998-0218-1

Rafay, A. (Ed.). (2020b). *Growth and Emerging Prospects of International Islamic Banking*. IGI Global. doi:10.4018/978-1-7998-1611-9

Rafay, A., & Ajmal, M. M. (2014). Earnings Management through Deferred Taxes Recognized under IAS 12: Evidence from Pakistan. *Lahore Journal of Business*, *3*(1), 1–19. doi:10.35536/ljb.2014.v3.i1.a1

Rafay, A., & Farid, S. (2017). Maqasid-al-Shari'ah vs. Contemporary Islamic Banking and Finance: The Case of Pakistan. *Journal of Islamic Thought and Civilization*, *7*(2), 41–51. doi:10.29145/2017/jitc/72/070203

Rafay, A., & Farid, S. (2018). Competitive Environment in Banking Industry: Evidence from an Emerging Economy. *Business and Economic Review*, *10*(3), 65–84. doi:10.22547/BER/10.3.4

Rafay, A., & Farid, S. (2018). Shariah Supervisory Board Report (SSBR) in Islamic Banks: An experimental study of Investors' perception and behaviour. *International Journal of Islamic and Middle Eastern Finance and Management*, *11*(2), 274–296. doi:10.1108/IMEFM-07-2017-0180

Rafay, A., Franco, G., & Gilani, U. J. (2019). Measuring Competition in Banking Industry: Evidence from Latin American Economies. *Pakistan Business Review*, *21*(1), 154–163.

Rafay, A., Sadiq, R., & Ajmal, M. M. (2017). Uniform Framework for Sukuk-Al-Ijara – A proposed model for all madhahib. *Journal of Islamic Accounting and Business Research*, *8*(4), 420–454. doi:10.1108/JIABR-09-2015-0042

Rafay, A., Sadiq, R., & Mohsan, T. (2016). X-Efficiency in Banking Industry – Evidence from South Asian Economy. *Global Management Journal for Academic & Corporate Studies*, *6*(1), 25–36.

Rahman, A. A. (2008). An Analysis of the Malaysian Anti-Money Laundering Laws and their Impact on Banking Institutions. University of Western Australia.

Rahman, A. A. (2015). Corporate governance and anti-money laundering measures in the banking industry: Malaysian experience. *International Academic Research Journal of Social Science*, *1*(2), 48–52.

RahmanJ. M. (2014). *Cost-Benefit analysis of implementing Shari'ah auditing as a separate discipline in Bangladeshi Islamic banks*. doi:10.2139srn.2538590

Rajan, T. (2019). The Case of Yes Bank: From the Founders' Dream to a Bank in Distress. *Journal of Advance Research in Dynamical & Control Systems*, *11*(11), 674–678. doi:10.5373/JARDCS/V11SP11/20193083

Ramamoorti, S. (2008). The psychology and sociology of fraud: Integrating the behavioural sciences component into fraud and forensic accounting curricula. *Issues in Accounting Education*, *23*(4), 521–533. doi:10.2308/iace.2008.23.4.521

Ramana, S. V., & Krishna, S. G. (2017). A study on impact of fraud in Indian banking sector (With special reference on retail banking products). *International Journal of Academic Research and Development*, *2*(6), 544–547.

RBI. (2020). *Annual Report 2019-2020*. Reserve Bank of India. Retrieved from https://www.rbi.org.in/Scripts/AnnualReportMainDisplay.aspx

RCMP. (2020). *Currency counterfeiting statistics*. Royal Canadian Mounted Police. Retrieved from https://www.rcmp-grc.gc.ca/fsis-ssji/statistics-Statistiques-eng.htm

Reganati, F., & Oliva, M. (2018). Determinants of money laundering: Evidence from Italian regions. *Journal of Money Laundering Control*, *21*(3), 402–413.

Reiter, K. (2018). *Time Limits on Assignments in Law Enforcement*. Sam Houston State University. Retrieved from http://shsu-ir.tdl.org

Religious Literacy Project. (2018). *The Maitatsine Riots*. Cambridge: Harvard Divinity School. Retrieved from https://rlp.hds.harvard.edu/faq/maitatsine-riots

Reuter, P., & Truman, E. M. (2004). The Anti-Money Laundering Regime. In *Chasing Dirty Money: The Fight against Money Laundering* (pp. 45–103). Peterson Institute for International Economics. Retrieved from https://www.piie.com/publications/chapters_preview/381/4iie3705.pdf

Reynolds, C. (2019, May 10). Why criminals look to Canada to launder their money through real estate. *Financial Post*. Retrieved from https://financialpost.com/pmn/business-pmn/why-criminals-look-to-canada-to-launder-their-money-through-real-estate

Rieff, D. (1995). *Slaughterhouse: Bosnia and the Failure of the West*. Simon & Schuster.

Ritchie, H., Hasell, J., Appel, C., & Roser, M. (2020). Terrorism. *Our World in Data*. Retrieved from https://ourworldindata.org/terrorism

Rock, J. L. (2016). *The Funding of Boko Haram and the Nigeria's Action to Stop it.* Master's Thesis Submitted to University of Indiana in Pennsylvania.

Rodrick, D., & Subramanian, A. (2003). The primacy of institutions (and what this does and does not mean). *Finance and Development, International Monetary Fund*, 31-34. Retrieved from https://www.imf.org/external/pubs/ft/fandd/2003/06/pdf/rodrik.pdf

Rose-Ackerman, S., & Palifka, B. J. (2018). Corruption, organized crime, and money laundering. In K. Basu & T. Cordella (Eds.), *Institutions, Governance and the Control of Corruption* (pp. 75–111). Palgrave Macmillan. doi:10.1007/978-3-319-65684-7_4

Ross, A. (2017, May 9). On Our Doorsteps: Money Laundering in Canadian Real Estate. *The Canadian Bar Association.* Retrieved from https://www.cba.org/Sections/Business-Law/Articles/2017/May/On-our-doorsteps

Royal LePage. (2020, July 9). National home prices rise sharply in second quarter as housing supply struggles to keep up with surge in demand. *Newswire.* Retrieved from https://www.newswire.ca/news-releases/royal-lepage-national-home-prices-rise-sharply-in-second-quarter-as-housing-supply-struggles-to-keep-up-with-surge-in-demand-806605598.html

Roy, B., & Chatterjee, S. (2018). Shadow Banking in India in Relation to the IL&FS Crisis. *Journal of Banking and Insurance Law*, *1*(2), 1–6.

RPS. (2020, December). RPS House Price Index - Public Release. *Real Property Solutions.* Retrieved from https://www.rpsrealsolutions.com/house-price-index/house-price-index

Ryder, N. (2012). *Money Laundering-an Endless Cycle? A Comparative Analysis of the Anti-money Laundering Policies in the United States of America, the United Kingdom, Australia and Canada.* Routledge. doi:10.4324/9780203126783

Saleemi, M. W., & Amir-ud-Din, R. (2019). *How does quality of governance influence occurrence of crime? A longitudinal analysis of Asian countries* (MPRA Paper 94142). Retrieved from https://mpra.ub.uni-muenchen.de/94142/

Sambo, U., Sule, B., Deribe, A. U., & Ahmed, A. (2020). The Impact of Small Arms and Light Weapons (SALW) in the Proliferation of Armed Group Conflicts in Northeastern Nigeria: Interrogating the *Boko Haram* Phenomenon. *International Journal of Humanities, Arts and Social Sciences*, *6*(4), 151–161.

Sanusi, Z. M., Sabri, S. S., Isa, Y. M., & Nassir, M. D. M. (2014). *Money Laundering Risk Assessment by Investment Bankers: How good are they?* Academic Press.

Saperstein, L., Sant, G., & Ng, M. (2015). The Failure of Anti-Money Laundering Regulation: Where is the Cost-Benefit Analysis? *Notre Dame Law Review Online, 91*(1), 12. Retrieved from https://scholarship.law.nd.edu/ndlr_online/vol91/iss1/4

Sarkar, A. (2018, March 6). PNB Fraud Case: Axis Bank discloses Rs. 200 *crore* exposures to NiravModi, Gitanjali Gems Accounts. *Bloomberg Quint*. Retrieved from https://www.bloombergquint.com/business/pnb-fraud-case-axis-bank-discloses-rs-200-*crore*-exposure-to-nirav-modi-gitanjali-gems-accounts

Sarwar, G. (1996). Islamic Education: its meaning, problems and prospects. In Issues in Islamic education. The Muslim Education Trust.

SAS. (2020). *Direct Conflict Deaths*. Small Arms Survey. Retrieved from: http://www.smallarmssurvey.org/armed-violence/conflict-av/direct-conflict-deaths.html

Saunders, B., Sim, J., Kingstone, T., Baker, S., Waterfield, J., Bartlam, B., Burroughs, H., & Jinks, C. (2018). Saturation in qualitative research: Exploring its conceptualization and operationalization. *Quality & Quantity*, *52*(4), 1893–1907. doi:10.100711135-017-0574-8 PMID:29937585

Saunders, M., Lewis, P., & Thornhill, A. (2007). *Research methods for business students*. Prentice Hall.

Savona, E. U., & Riccardi, M. (2019). Assessing the risk of money laundering: Research challenges and implications for practitioners. *European Journal on Criminal Policy and Research*, *25*(1), 1–4.

Scanlon, K. (2019). *Effects of Terrorism on the U.S. Stock Market: Evidence from High Frequency Data* (Paper 781). Honors College Capstone Experience/Thesis Projects. Retrieved from https://digitalcommons.wku.edu/stu_hon_theses/781

Schepers, M. (2016). *Effect of terror attacks on the bond and stock market of European countries*. Nijmegen School of Management, Radboud Universit. Retrieved from https://theses.ubn.ru.nl/handle/123456789/2791

Schmit, J. T., & Roth, K. (1990). Cost-effectiveness of risk management practices. *The Journal of Risk and Insurance*, *57*(3), 455–470. doi:10.2307/252842

Schneider, S. (2020a, May 25). Commission of Inquiry into Money Laundering in British Columbia. *Cullen Commission*. Retrieved from https://cullencommission.ca/data/transcripts/Transcript%20May%2025,%202020.pdf

Schneider, S. (2020b, May 26). Transcripts. *Commission of Inquiry into Money Laundering in British Columbia*. Retrieved from cullencommission.ca/data/transcripts/Transcript%20May%20 26,%202020.pdf

Schneider, F. (2008). Money laundering and financial means of organised crime: Some preliminary empirical findings. *Global Business and Economics Review*, *10*(3), 309–330.

Schneider, S. (2004a). Organized crime, money laundering, and the real estate market in Canada. *Journal of Property Research*, *21*(2), 99–118. doi:10.1080/0959991042000328801

Schneider, S. (2004b). Money laundering in Canada: A quantitative analysis of Royal Canadian Mounted Police cases. *Journal of Financial Crime*, *11*(3), 282–291. doi:10.1108/13590790410809220

Schneider, S. (2006). Testing the limits of solicitor-client privilege: Lawyers, money laundering, and suspicious transaction reporting. *Journal of Money Laundering Control*, *9*(1), 27–47. doi:10.1108/13685200610645201

Schoenmaker, D. (1996). *Contagion risk in banking*. LSE Financial Markets Group. Retrieved from https://www.academia.edu/download/61841734/345_contagion_risk_in_banking20200120-107135-1vlz1ta.pdf

Schroeder, W. R. (2001). Money Laundering: A Global Threat and the International Community's Response. *FBI Law Enforcement Bulletin, 70.*

Scilla, A. (2018). *ICIJ releases database revealing thousands of secret offshore companies.* Retrieved from https://www.icij.org/investigations/panama-papers/former-pakistan-pm-sharif-sentenced-to-10-years-over-panama-papers

Scrinko, J. (2018, December 26). Money Laundering in Toronto's Real Estate Market: Analysis & Facts. *Precondo*. Retrieved from https://precondo.ca/toronto-real-estate-money-laundering/

Sekaran, U., & Bougie, R. (2016). *Research methods for business: A skill building approach.* John Wiley & Sons.

Şentürk, Ş. S. (2009). *Sigortacılıkta Kara Para ile Mücadele* [Fight against Black Money in Insurance] (Unpublished Master's Thesis). Marmara University Banking and Insurance Institute, Istanbul.

Sesay, I. (2019). *Beneath the Tamarind Tree: A Story of Courage, Family, and the Lost School Girls of Boko Haram.* Harper Collins.

Shanmugam, B., Nair, M., & Suganthi, R. (2003). Money Laundering in Malaysia. *Journal of Money Laundering Control*, *6*(4), 373–378. doi:10.1108/13685200310809699

Sharma, M. (2018, February 16). State Control Has Opened India's Banks to Fraud. *Bloomberg Quint*. Retrieved from https://www.bloombergquint.com/opinion/state-control-has-opened-india-s-banks-to-fraud

Sharma, M. (2018, October 3). The Roots of India's Shadow-Bank Crisis. *Bloomberg Quint Opinion*. Retrieved from https://www.bloombergquint.com/opinion/india-needs-better-model-for-funding-infrastructure

Sharma, N., & Sharma, D. (2018). Rising Toll of Frauds in Banking: A Threat for the Indian Economy. *Journal of Technology Management for Growing Economies*, *9*(1), 71–88. doi:10.15415/jtmge.2018.91003

Shaw, R., & Young, J. L. (2019, May 9). $5 billion laundered through B.C. real estate, inflating home prices: report. *Vancouver Sun*. Retrieved from https://vancouversun.com/business/real-estate/money-laundering-hikes-b-c-real-estate-prices-report

Shultz, R. H. Jr, & Dew, A. J. (2006). *Insurgents, Terrorists and Militias: The Warriors of Contemporary Combat*. Columbia University Press.

Simon, R. (1994). *What is Globalisation?* The Helen Kellogg Institute for International Studies.

Simser, J. (2013). Money laundering: Emerging threats and trends. *Journal of Money Laundering Control, 16*(1), 41–54. doi:10.1108/13685201311286841

Sittlington, S., & Harvey, J. (2018). Prevention of money laundering and the role of asset recovery. *Crime, Law, and Social Change, 70*(4), 421–441. doi:10.100710611-018-9773-z

Small, C., & Gilling, T. (2010). Blood Money: Bikies, Terrorists and Middle Eastern Gangs. Crows Nest: Allen & Unwin.

Smith, P. (2012). Violence and Terrorism: The Two Constants. *Journal of International Relations Research, 1*(1), 1–6.

Sohrabuddin, S. M., Zoynul Abedin, M., & Afroz, N. (2020). Islamic Financial Inclusion: An Alternative Approach to Reach the Unbanked of Bangladesh. In A. Rafay (Ed.), *Growth and Emerging Prospects of International Islamic Banking* (pp. 155–173). IGI Global.

Sohraby, F., Habibitabur, H., & Masoudzade, M. R. (2016). Money Laundering Crime and Its Situational Prevention in Iranian Law and International Law. *Journal of Politics and Law, 9*(7), 57–63. doi:10.5539/jpl.v9n7p57

Solomon, H. (2015). *Terrorism and Counter-Terrorism in Africa: Fighting Insurgency from AlShabab, Ansar Dine and Boko Haram*. Palgrave Macmillan. doi:10.1057/9781137489890

Start, K. Y. C. Limited. (2019, February 24). Money laundering in real estate. *Start KYC*. Retrieved from https://startkyc.com/en/blog/money-laundering-in-real-estate/

Statistics Canada. (2021). Gross domestic product (GDP) at basic prices, by industry (x 1,000,000). *Statistics Canada*. Retrieved from https://www150.statcan.gc.ca/t1/tbl1/en/tv.action?pid=3610040101

Strader, J. K. (2011). *Understanding White Collar Crime*. LexisNexis.

Strauss, A. L. (1987). *Qualitative analysis for social scientists*. Cambridge University Press. doi:10.1017/CBO9780511557842

Sudhin, S. (2018). The Punjab national bank: Nirav Modi Scam, 2018. *International Journal of Advanced Research and Development, 3*(3), 180–182.

Sule, B., & Gombe, S. Y. (2020). *Overview of the Sources of Finance, Weapons and Logistics of Boko Haram*. (Unpublished)

Sule, B., Ahmed, A., Alhaji, A. U., Yahaya, M. A., & Gambarawa, K. I. (2019). The Challenges of the Fight Against Insurgency in Northeastern Nigeria. *Journal of Techno Social, 11*(1), 7–15. doi:10.30880/jts.2019.11.01.002

Sule, B., Sambo, U., & Tal, M. K. (2018). Islamic Militants and Insurgency in Northeastern Nigeria: A Comparison of the Ideology and Methodology of Maitatsine and *Boko Haram. Journal of Academia, 7*(2), 76–91.

Sule, B., Yahaya, M. A., Rabiu, A. A., Ahmad, M., & Hussaini, K. (2019). Strategies of Combating Insurgency in Northeastern Nigeria: A Non-Traditional Approach. *Journal of American Studies*, *16*(2), 54–75.

Sule, B., Yahaya, M. A., & Sambo, U. (2019). Global Agenda and the Politics of Double Standard: War Against Terrorism or War of Terrorism. *International Journal of Religion and Civilisational Studies*, *2*(2), 172–205.

Sun, K. (2015). *Foreign investment in real estate in Canada: Key issues* (Occasional Paper Series Vol. 2, Issue No. 3). China Institute, University of Alberta. Retrieved from https://era.library.ualberta.ca/items/33a5de89-1e3d-4607-a22b-650f0b807875/view/30cef061 -41e7-41e3-92f6-322bbfe1324f/CIOPS_2_2_2015.pdf

Sutherland, E. H. (1983). *White-collar crime: The uncut version* (Vol. 58). Yale University Press.

Swiss Re. (2013). *World Insurance in 2013: Steering Towards Recovery*. Retrieved from http://media.swissre.com/ documents / sigma3_2014_en.pdf

Talatona, C., & Centre, C. (2014). *28th Task Force of Senior Officials and the 14th Council Of Ministers' Meeting Ccta Talatona Convention Centre Typologies Report on Money Laundering and Terrorist Financing through the Money Remittance and Currency Exchange Sector in the Esaamlg Region*. Academic Press.

Tarter, A. (2017). Importance of cybersecurity. In *Community Policing-A European Perspective*. Springer. doi:10.1007/978-3-319-53396-4_15

Tauringana, V., & Tingbani, I. (2020). Terrorism and global business performance. *International Journal of Finance & Economics*. Retrieved from https://onlinelibrary.wiley.com/doi/full/10.1002/ijfe.2085

Teichmann, F. M. J. (2017). Twelve Methods of Money Laundering. *Journal of Money Laundering Control*, *20*(2), 130–137. doi:10.1108/JMLC-05-2016-0018

Teichmann, F. M. J. (2019). Money laundering and terrorism financing through consulting companies. *Journal of Money Laundering Control*, *22*(1), 32–37. doi:10.1108/JMLC-10-2017-0056

Thacuk, K. L., & Lal, R. (2018). *Terrorist Criminal Enterprises: Financing Terrorism Through Organised Crimes*. Praeger.

Thangam, M., & Bhavin, P. (2019). Banking Frauds in India; A case analysis. *Journal of Emerging Technologies and Innovative Research*, *6*(1), 29–35.

The Baltic Times. (2020, July 16). FCMC fines Signet Bank with EUR 906,600 for breaching AML rules. *The Baltic Times*. Retrieved from https://www.baltictimes.com/fcmc_fines _signet_bank_with_eur_906_600_for_breaching_aml_rules/

The Economic Times. (2018, February). *How did everyone miss the PNB scam? An accountant explains what could have gone wrong*. Retrieved from http://widgets.economictimes.com/industry/banking/finance/banking/how-did-everyone-miss-the-pnb-scam-an-accountant-explains-what-could-have-gone-wrong/articleshow/62928611.cms

Thurston, A. (2018). *Boko Haram: The History of an African Jihadist Movement*. Princeton University Press. doi:10.1515/9781400888481

Transparency International (UK). (2009). *Combating Money Laundering and Recovering Looted Gains : Raising the UK's Game*. Retrieved from https://star.worldbank.org/corruption-cases/sites/corruption-cases/files/documents/arw/Transparency_Intl_UK_Recovering_Looted_Gains_June_2009.pdf

Uche, U. C. (1998). The adoption of a money-laundering law in Nigeria. *Journal of Money Laundering Control*, *1*(3), 220–228. doi:10.1108/eb027144

Ullah, M. H. (2014). Shari'ah compliance in Islamic banking - An empirical study on selected Islamic banks in Bangladesh. *International Journal of Islamic and Middle Eastern Finance and Management*, *7*(2), 182–199. doi:10.1108/IMEFM-06-2012-0051

Ullah, M. H., & Khanam, R. (2018). Whether *Shariah* compliance efficiency a matter for the financial performance: The case of Islami Bank Bangladesh Limited. *Journal of Islamic Accounting and Business Research*, *9*(2), 183–200. doi:10.1108/JIABR-01-2016-0001

Ullah, M. H., Khanam, R., & Tasnim, T. (2018). Comparative compliance status of AAOIFI and IFSB standards: An empirical evidence from Islami Bank Bangladesh Limited. *Journal of Islamic Accounting and Business Research*, *9*(4), 607–628. doi:10.1108/JIABR-11-2014-0040

Undersecretariat of Treasury. (2020). *Insurance and BES Annual Report-2014*.

UNDP. (2019). *Measuring the Economic Impact of Violent Extremism Leading to Terrorism in Africa*. United Nations Development Programme.

UNEP. (2018). *Environmental crimes are on the rise, so are efforts to prevent them*. United Nations Environment Programme. Retrieved from https://www.unenvironment.org/news-and-stories/story/environmental-crimes-are-rise-so-are-efforts-prevent-them

Unger, B. (2013). Can money laundering decrease? *Public Finance Review*, *41*(5), 658–676.

Unger, B., & den Hertog, J. (2012). Water always finds its way: Identifying new forms of money laundering. *Crime, Law, and Social Change*, *57*(3), 287–304. doi:10.100710611-011-9352-z

UNICEF. (2019). *Education: Nigeria*. Abuja: UNICEF. Retrieved from https://www.UNICEF.org/nigeria/education

United Nation. (2009). *Millennium Development Goals Report 2009*. United Nations, Department of Economic and Social Affairs.

United Nations Office on Drugs and Crime. (2011, October). *UNODC estimates that criminals may have laundered US $ 1.6 trillion in 2009*. Retrieved from https://www.unodc.org/

UNODC. (2010). *Money-Laundering and Globalization*. Retrieved from https://www.unodc.org

UNODC. (2011). *World Drug Report 2011*. United Nation Office of Drug and Crime.

UNODC. (2018). *Global Report on Trafficking in Persons 2018*. United Nations Office on Drugs and Crimes.

UNODC. (2019). *Money laundering and globalization*. United Nations Office of Drug and Crime. Retrieved from https://www.unodc.org/unodc/en/money-laundering/globalization.html

UNODC. (2019a). *United Nations Office on Drugs and Crime*. Retrieved from https://www.unodc.org/unodc/en/money-laundering/laundrycycle.html

UNODC. (2019b). *Global Overview of Drug Demand and Supply*. Vienna: United Nations Office on Drugs and Crimes.

UNODC. (2020). *Human trafficking and smuggling of migrants*. United Nations Office on Drugs and Crime. Retrieved from https://www.unodc.org/westandcentralafrica/en/newrosenwebsite/TIPSOM/Human-trafficking-and-smuggling-of-migrants.html

UNSC. (2018). *United Nations Security Council Counter-Terrorism Committee Executive Directorate: Terrorism Finance*. United Nations Security Council.

Upadhyay, D. (2018). Banking Scams in India. *Journal of Banking and Insurance Law*, *1*(2), 7–13.

Urama, N. E., Ekeocha, Q., & Iloh, E. C. (2018). *Nigeria's debt burden: implications for human development* (AfriHeritage Policy Brief No 20). Enugu: African Heritage Institution. Retrieved from https://media.africaportal.org/documents/Nigerias_debt_burden.pdf

US SEC. (2020). *SEC Enforcement Actions; Insider Trading*. U S Securities and Exchange Commission. Retrieved from https://www.sec.gov/spotlight/insidertrading/cases.shtml

USDG. (2019). *Asset Forfeiture Policy Manual*. U.S. Department of Justice, Criminal Division, Money Laundering and Asset Recovery Section. Retrieved from https://www.justice.gov / criminal-afmls/file/839521/download

USDHS. (2009). *Rightwing Extremism: Current Economic and Political Climate Fueling Resurgence in Radicalisation and Recruitment*. United States Department of Homeland Security.

Usluoğlu, Ç. (2002). Dünyada Ve Türkiye'de Kara Paranın Aklanmasının Önlenmesine İlişkin Düzenlemelerin Türk Sigorta Sektörü Açısından Genel Bir Değerlendi [An Overview of Turkish Insurance Sector in terms of the Regulations for the Prevention of Money Laundering in the world and in Turkey]. *Reasürör*. Retrieved from http://tsrsb.org.tr/private/trk/sayi37/ince37.htm

Üstün, O. (2003). Mali Eylem Görev Gücü"nün Yeni Kırk Tavsiye Kararı Neler Getiriyor? [What Do the Financial Action Task Force's New Forty Recommendations Bring?]. *Bankacılar Dergisi, 47*.

Uwaisu, I. (2018). Experts Say Nigeria Must Change its Strategy to Defeat *Boko Haram. AFP Reuters*. Retrieved from https://p.dw.com/p/3ANl8

Vaithilingam, S., & Nair, M. (2007). Factors affecting money laundering: Lesson for developing countries. *Journal of Money Laundering Control*, *10*(3), 352–363.

Verhage, A. (2009). Between the hammer and the anvil? the anti-money laundering-complex and its interactions with the compliance industry. *Crime, Law, and Social Change*, *52*(1), 9–32. doi:10.100710611-008-9174-9

Verver, J. (2017, February 24). Why You Really Need to Pay Attention to Money-Laundering Risks. *Corporate Compliance Insights*. Retrieved from https://www.corporatecomplianceinsights.com/why-you-really-need-to-pay-attention-to-money-laundering-risks/

Vittori, J. (2011). *Terrorists Financing and Resourcing*. Palgrave Macmillan. doi:10.1057/9780230117716

Wakefield, J. (2019, May 21). Is Alberta really Canada's Money Laundering capital? B.C. report met with skepticism, calls for more study. *Edmonton Journal*. Retrieved from https://edmontonjournal.com/news/crime/is-alberta-really-canadas-money-laundering-capital-b-c-report-met-with-skepticism-calls-for-more-study

Walker, A. (2016). *Eat the Heart of the Infidel: The Harrowing of Nigeria and the Rise of Boko Haram*. Hurst and Company.

Walker, J., & Unger, B. (2009). Measuring Global Money Laundering: "The Walker Gravity Model. *Review of Law & Economics*, *5*(2), 821–853. doi:10.2202/1555-5879.1418

Webel, C. P., & Arnaldi, J. A. (2012). The Global War on Terrorism: How Ethical and Effective. *Journal of International Relations Research*, *1*(1), 8–18.

Weilert, A. K. (2016). United Nations Convention against Corruption (UNCAC) – After Ten Years of Being in Force. *Max Planck Yearbook of United Nations Law Online*, *19*(1), 216–240. doi:10.1163/18757413-00190008

Weischedel, B., Matear, S., & Deans, K. (2005). A Qualitative Approach to Investigating Online Strategic Decision Making. *Qualitative Market Research*, *8*(1), 61–76. doi:10.1108/13522750510575444

Wentworth, I. (2018, September 6). What are the Anti-Money Laundering Laws and Regulations? *Delta Net International*. Retrieved from https://www.delta-net.com/compliance/anti-money-laundering/faqs/what-are-the-anti-money-laundering-laws-and-regulations

Whittaker, D. J. (2004). *Terrorists and Terrorism in the Contemporary World*. Routledge. doi:10.4324/9780203003824

Wittig, T. (2011). *Understanding Terrorist Financing*. Palgrave Macmillan. doi:10.1057/9780230316935

Wolf, S. O. (2017). Pakistan and State-Sponsored Terrorism in South Asia. In P. Casaca & S. O. Wolf (Eds.), *Terrorism Revisited: Islamism, Political Violence and State-Sponsorship*. Springer Nature. doi:10.1007/978-3-319-55690-1_5

Wood, G. (2020, January 21). Public B.C. corporate registry would be 'game changer' for Money Laundering. *Western Investor*. Retrieved from https://www.westerninvestor.com/news/british-columbia/public-b-c-corporate-registry-would-be-game-changer-for-money-laundering-1.24057481

World Bank. (2017). *World Bank list of economies.* The World Bank. Retrieved from https://www.worldbank.org/en/search?q=list+of+economies+&currentTab=1

World Bank. (2020). *World Development Indicators*. Retrieved from https://datacatalog.worldbank.org/dataset/world-development-indicators

Worldometer. (2020). *World Population Statistics by Countries*. Retrieved from https://www.Worldometers.info/world-population/nigeria-population/

WSJ. (1997, February 21). Money laundering alert. *Wall Street Journal*. Retrieved from https://www.wsj.com/articles/SB856480045800862500

Yildirim, I. (2019). Emergence of Insurance Technologies (InsurTech): The Turkish Case. In A. Rafay (Ed.), *FinTech as a Disruptive Technology for Financial Institutions* (pp. 42–60). IGI Global. doi:10.4018/978-1-5225-7805-5.ch003

Young. (2017, August 18). Islamic Cleric Caught With Human Parts in Ilorin. *Information Nigeria*. Retrieved from https://www.informationng.com/2017/08/islamic-cleric-caught-human-parts-ilorin.html

Zia, M. A., Abbas, R. Z., & Arshed, N. (2020). *Money laundering and terror financing: Issues and challenges in Pakistan. Journal of Money Laundering and Control*. Early Print.

About the Contributors

Abdul Rafay is a practitioner cum academician. For more than 25 years, Mr. Rafay has been working as a freelance advisor, consultant & trainer to a wide variety of public & private sector national and multinational companies in the areas of Corporate Finance, Financial Policy & Implementation, Auditing & Assurance, Accountancy, Corporate Tax Management, Financial Technology and System Consultancy. He has been providing consultancy to various industries including Textile, Auto Assembling, Footwear, Industrial/Agro Chemicals, Ice Cream/Dairies, Glass/Ceramics, Healthcare, Mining/Natural Resources, Packaging/Paper Sacking, Steel/Pipe Casting, Rice Processing, Brokerage/Co-operative Financing, Software Development, Real Estate, Printing/Publishing, and Construction/Civil Engineering etc. Mr. Rafay is a Fellow member of the Institute of Chartered Accountants of Pakistan. He is also member of various national and international professional bodies including Institute of Internal Auditors (IIA), USA; Association of Certified Fraud Examiners (ACFE), USA. Since 2001, he has been a life time member of Lahore Tax Bar Association. He has served as Co-regional Director (Founding) of Lahore-Islamabad Chapter of Professional Risk Managers International Association (PRMIA), Washington, USA (2011-2013). In 2012, he was nominated as Member: Education & Training Committee (ETCOM) of The Institute of Chartered Accountants of Pakistan (ICAP). He is also a member of ICAP's "Islamic Finance working group" which is closely in liaison with State Bank of Pakistan and other stakeholders for Islamic Finance Accounting and Auditing Standards. He is Alumni of Rausing Executive Development Center (REDC), Lahore University of Management Sciences (LUMS), Pakistan. In 2014, International Finance Corporation (World Bank Group) selected him for Training of Trainers (ToT) for Corporate Governance Action Planning for SMEs. He is also an approved trainer for Institute of Financial Markets of Pakistan (IFMP) established by Securities and Exchange Commission of Pakistan, the corporate regulator. In 2013, his name got included in the list of "Certified Directors" as per Clause (xi) of The Code of Corporate Governance 2012 issued by SECP. Since 1994, Mr. Rafay has also been associated with teaching in some of the top business schools of Pakistan. His specialized subjects of interest include: Strategic Corporate Finance, Financial Derivatives, Investments/Portfolio Analysis, International Financial Reporting Standards, Corporate Restructuring (Mergers & Acquisitions), Financial Statement Analysis & Corporate Taxation. He also served as an instructor in Civil Services Academy, Pakistan to train the CSS Officers selected by Federal Public Service Commission of Pakistan (FPSC). Currently he is a Professor of Finance & Accounting in University of Management & Technology, Pakistan. He has published more than two dozen research papers in SSCI, ESCI and Scopus indexed journals published by reputed global publishers including Emerald, Sage, Taylor & Francis and IGI Global. He contributed multiple chapters in Books edited by International Editors. Since 2019, he edited multiple international books on FinTech, Islamic Finance and financial Crimes published by IGI Global, USA.

* * *

Md. Kausar Alam holds a Ph.D. from Universiti Putra Malaysia (UPM), an AACSB accredited university ranked 159 in World QS Ranking for 2020. His research interest areas are Shariah governance, Institutional theory, Islamic banking, roles, and functions of Shariah supervisory board, corporate governance, institutional theory, legitimacy theory, legitimacy, resource dependence theory, Shariah audit, and Shariah compliance.

Maryam Muhammad Amjad is a graduate in Economics from the University of Management and Technology. She is an active researcher.

Muhammad Awais Anwar holds a Ph.D. from Shandong University, Jinan, China. Currently, he is an Assistant Professor of economics at the University of Education, Pakistan. He has published several research papers.

Noman Arshed holds a Ph.D. in Islamic Banking and Finance from the University of Management & Technology, Pakistan. Currently, he is working as a lecturer at the same University. He is engaged in research related to the field of development economics and Islamic Finance.

Bappaditya Biswas holds a Ph.D. from the University of Calcutta, India. Currently, he is an Assistant Professor in the Department of Commerce, University of Calcutta, India. He has over 12 years of teaching experience has published more than 35 articles in different journals and edited volumes of repute. Dr. Biswas has co-authored 4 books from McGraw Hill, India for Undergraduates students of Commerce.

Normah Omar holds a Ph.D. in Accounting. Currently, she is a professor at the Accounting Research Institute, Universiti Teknologi MARA, Malaysia. She is a passionate researcher and her interest is in Islamic financial criminology.

Sadia Saeed holds a PhD in Management Sciences (Finance). Currently, she is serving as a Lecturer in the Faculty of Management Sciences, National University of Modern Languages (NUML), Pakistan. Dr. Sadia has published numerous research papers and also attended various trainings/workshops conducted under the Faculty Development Programs.

Usman Sambo holds a PhD in Public Administration from the University of Maiduguri, Nigeria. Currently, he is a Senior Lecturer at the Department of Public Administration in Yobe State University Damaturu Nigeria. His research interest includes Corruption and Development Studies. He spent six years as Director of Administration, Federal Medical Centre Nguru, Yobe State Nigeria. He has published more than twenty (20) papers and book chapters both locally and internationally in reputable journals.

Sachin Shah is a CAMS certified Financial Crime Compliance professional associated with one of the Big 4 in India. He has worked with 4 of the top 15 global banks in a career spanning 20 years. He is also a regular writer on the Fincrime matters and has various global publications in his name. Recently his academic paper got featured in the Central Bank of Future Conference, co-hosted by Reserve Bank of San Francisco in USA.

Abhishek Sinha holds a Ph.D. in finance and FRM Certification from GARP, US. Currently, he is an Assistant Professor at IBS Hyderabad, India. He is an expert in the area of Risk Management and Finance. He has more than 16 years of combined experience in the area of teaching and practicing finance.

Babayo Sule holds a PhD in Political Science from Universiti Utara Malaysia. Currently, he is a Lecturer in the Department of Political Science, Faculty of Humanities Management and Social Sciences, Federal University of Kashere Gombe, Gombe State Nigeria. His research interest includes Political Economy, Political Theory, Security Studies, and Islamic Political Thought. He spent over thirteen (13) years as a Lecturer in the Department of Political in Gombe State University and the Federal University of Kashere Gombe where he holds several administrative positions including Faculty Exams Officer and Coordinator Postgraduate Studies. He has published over forty (40) papers and fifteen (15) book chapters and conference proceedings in local and international reputable journals.

Sharifah Nazatul Faiza Syed Mustapha Nazri holds a Ph.D. She is an associate professor in the Faculty of Accountancy UiTM. Her research area is audit assurance & investigation, auditors skepticism, fraud and money laundering.

Mosab I. Tabash holds a Ph.D. in Finance from the University of Delhi, India. Currently is currently working as MBA Director and Risk Management Supervisor at the College of Business, Al Ain University, UAE. His research interests include Islamic banking, monetary policies, financial performance, and investments.

İsmail Yıldırım holds a Ph.D. in Insurance from Erciyes University, Turkey. Currently, he is an Associate Professor at the Department of Insurance and Actuary, Hitit University, Turkey. He has published several international articles and book chapters in the field of insurance. His research interests include insurance business, risk management in insurance sector.

Salwa Zokaflil holds a Ph.D. and is currently working as a research assistant. Her research interest is in forensic accounting, money laundering and terrorism financing.

Sehar Zulfiqar holds a Ph.D. in Human Resource Management from the University of Debrecen, Hungary. Currently, she is an Assistant Professor at the National University of Modern Languages, Pakistan. Her current research interests encompass organizational behavior, knowledge management, and corporate governance. Her work has been presented and published at international conferences and journals.

Gaurav Chopra holds a Master's degree in Global Management from Royal Roads University, Canada. He is a risk analyst and an expert in Anti Money Laundering Compliance. His research interests include Data Analytics, Business development, and project management.

Rohan Prasad Gupta is a Research Scholar in the Department of Commerce, University of Calcutta, India.

Md Farjin Hassan is a master of science student at Putra Business School, Malaysia, and completed a Bachelor of Business Administration at Jagannath University, Dhaka, Bangladesh. His research interests include Islamic bank Shariah Governance, Shariah capital markets and conventional capital markets.

Nihad Hossain is a final year undergraduate student of Universiti Putra Malaysia. He is doing bachelor at School of Business and Economics with a major of Economics. His scientific interests are included Human Resource Management (HRM), Marketing and Economics. He has also expertise on data analysis and comparative resources.

Adebayo Ibrahim holds a PhD. in Islamic Studies from the University of Ilorin, Nigeria. He is currently the Director, Centre for Affiliated Institutions, University of Ilorin and Deputy Chief Imam of the University. He is a Professor of Islamic Studies in the Department of Religions, University of Ilorin. He specializes in Islamic Thought with emphasis on the Islamization of Knowledge and Contemporary issues. He has published more than 120 works in academic outlets at local, national, and international levels. He received a letter of commendation from the Faculty of Arts, University of Ilorin, for submitting the highest number of publications during the 2018 promotion exercise. Adebayo belongs to many professional bodies and was for many years the Kwara/Southwest zonal Coordinator of the International Institute of Islamic Thought (IIIT) Nigeria Office.

Md. Akib Javed is an undergraduate final year student at Universiti Putra Malaysia. He is studying International Business (IB) at the School of Business and Economics. His research interest includes International Finance & Law, Investment Policy, Foreign Direct Investment (FDI) and Management Information System (MIS). He is also a member of the Faculty of Economics and Management Students' Association (FEMSA).

S. G. Sisira Dharmasri Jayasekara has been with the Central Bank of Sri Lanka (CBSL) for more than 15 years and currently holds office as Deputy Director,

Financial Intelligence Unit of CBSL. He is an experienced examiner in conducting supervision of financial institutions. He has have published several articles on risk-based supervision in international and local journals. Mr. Jayasekara is a Fellow of the Institute of Chartered Accountants of Sri Lanka, a Fellow of the Association of Chartered Certified Accountants (UK), and an Associate Member of the Institute of Certified Management Accountants of Sri Lanka. Mr. Jayasekara also holds an MBA from the University of Peradeniya, Sri Lanka, MSc from the University of Birmingham. He has also involved as an assessor in conducting a mutual evaluation under the FATF 2012 methodology.

Tasiu Tijjani Kademi is a Chartered Accountant and is currently a lecturer at Rabiu Musa Kwankwaso College of Advance and Remedial Studies, Nigeria. He is also a part time lecturer at the Institute of Chartered Accountant of Nigeria.

Mark Lokanan holds a Ph.D. in "Accounting for Financial Crimes" from Simon Fraser University, Canada. He also a Master of Science in Forensic Accounting from the University of Portsmouth, UK, a Master of Science in Financial Crimes from the University of San Diego, USA (2004), and a Master of Arts in Sociology from the University of Guelph, Canada. Currently, he is an Associate Professor at Royal Roads University, Canada. He is a certified Microsoft data analyst and a member of the ACFE, CPA, and ACAMS organizations. He has published in the areas of accounting, securities fraud, Anti-money laundering, and regulatory compliance. Before joining academia, he worked for the Ministry of the Attorney General in Ontario as a fraud investigator, managing numerous projects and investigations from inception to completion.

Laila Memdani holds a Ph.D. in economics from Osmani University, India. Currently, she is an Associate Professor at IBS Hyderabad, a constituent of IFHE University. India. She has almost 30 years of teaching experience and she has published papers a number of articles in reputed journals listed indexed in SCOPUS and ABDC.

Fauzia Mubarik holds a PhD in Management Sciences (Finance). Currently, she is an Assistant Professor in the Faculty of Management Sciences, National University of Modern Languages (NUML), Pakistan. She is a member of the National Curriculum Review Committee (NCRC), HEC. Dr. Fauzia has published numerous research papers in the HEC recognized journals and few editorials in The Frontier Post Newspaper and has the honor to attend and present the research papers in the local conferences.

Index

G

H

I

J

L

N

P

R

S

T

U

W

Z

www.ingramcontent.com/pod-product-compliance
Lightning Source LLC
LaVergne TN
LVHW081544300926
849161LV00006B/1511